An Economic History of Regional Industrialization

This book offers a comprehensive study of regional industrialization in Europe and Asia from the early nineteenth century to the present. Using case studies on regional industrialization, the book provides insights into similarities and differences in industrialization processes between European, Eurasian, and Asian countries. Important factors include the transition from traditional to modern industrial production, industrial policy, agglomeration forces, market integration, and the determinants of industrial location over time. The book is an invaluable reference that attempts to bridge the fields of economic history, political history, economic geography, and economics while contributing to the debates on economic divergence between Europe and Asia as well as on the role of economic integration and globalization.

Bas van Leeuwen is Senior Researcher at the International Institute of Social History.

Robin C. M. Philips is PhD Researcher at Utrecht University and the International Institute of Social History.

Erik Buyst is a full professor in economics at the Catholic University of Leuven (KU Leuven), Belgium.

Routledge Explorations in Economic History

Edited by Lars Magnusson

Uppsala University, Sweden

The Western Allies and Soviet Potential in World War II
Economy, Society and Military Power
Martin Kahn

Money, Currency and Crisis
In search of Trust, 2000 BC to AD 2000
Edited by R.J. van der Spek and Bas van Leeuwen

The Development of Modern Industries in Bengal
Re-Industrialisation, 1858–1914
Indrajit Ray

The Economic Development of Europe's Regions
A Quantitative History Since 1900
Edited by Nikolaus Wolf and Joan Ramón Rosés

Family Firms and Merchant Capitalism in Early Modern Europe
The Business, Bankruptcy and Resilience of the Höchstetters of Augsburg
Thomas Max Safley

An Economic History of Famine Resilience
Edited by Jessica Dijkman and Bas van Leeuwen

Modern Advertising and the Market
The US Advertising Industry from the 19th Century to the Present
Zoe Sherman

A Global History of Money
Akinobu Kuroda

An Economic History of Regional Industrialization
Edited by Bas van Leeuwen, Robin C. M. Philips and Erik Buyst

For more information about this series, please visit www.routledge.com/series/SE0347

An Economic History of Regional Industrialization

Edited by Bas van Leeuwen,
Robin C. M. Philips
and Erik Buyst

Routledge
Taylor & Francis Group
LONDON AND NEW YORK

First published 2021
by Routledge
2 Park Square, Milton Park, Abingdon, Oxon OX14 4RN

and by Routledge
605 Third Avenue, New York, NY 10017

First issued in paperback 2022

Routledge is an imprint of the Taylor & Francis Group, an informa business

British Library Cataloguing-in-Publication Data
A catalogue record for this book is available from the British Library

Library of Congress Cataloging-in-Publication Data
A catalog record for this book has been requested

ISBN: 978-0-367-56195-6 (pbk)
ISBN: 978-0-367-19752-0 (hbk)
ISBN: 978-0-367-19753-7 (ebk)

DOI: 10.4324/9780367197537

Typeset in Galliard
by Apex CoVantage, LLC

Contents

Figures

Tables

Contributors

Jean-Pascal Bassino is a professor in economics at the Ecole Normale Supérieure de Lyon, France.

Patrizio Bianchi is a professor in economics at the University of Ferrara, Italy.

Erik Buyst is a full professor in economics at the Catholic University of Leuven (KU Leuven), Belgium.

Péter Földvári is a lecturer and post-doctoral researcher at the Amsterdam School of Economics at the University of Amsterdam, the Netherlands.

Kyoji Fukao is a full professor at the Institute of Economic Research at Hitotsubashi University, Japan.

Leonard Kukić is an assistant professor in the Department of Social Sciences at Universidad Carlos III de Madrid, Spain.

Sandrine Labory is an associate professor at the University of Ferrara, Italy.

Jieli Li is a research assistant at the International Institute of Social History, the Netherlands.

Julio Martinez-Galarraga is an associate professor in the Department of Economic Analysis at the University of Valencia, Spain.

Anna Missiaia is a post-doctoral researcher in the Department of Economic History of Lund University, Sweden.

Stefan Nikolić is a post-doctoral researcher at the Dondena Centre for Research on Social Dynamics and Public Policy at Università Bocconi, Italy.

Robin C. M. Philips is a PhD researcher at the International Institute of Social History and Utrecht University, the Netherlands.

Glenn Rayp is a full professor in international economics at Ghent University, Belgium.

Stijn Ronsse is a former post-doctoral researcher and visiting professor in economics at Ghent University, Belgium.

Tokihiko Settsu is a professor at Musashi University, Japan.

Daniel A. Tirado-Fabregat is a professor of economic history at the University of Valencia, Spain.

Bas van Leeuwen is a post-doctoral researcher at Utrecht University and a senior researcher at the International Institute for Social History, the Netherlands.

Meimei Wang is an assistant professor at the Chinese Academy of Social Sciences in Beijing, China.

Yi Xu is a professor at Guangxi Normal University, China.

Zipeng Zhang is a PhD researcher at Utrecht University, the Netherlands.

Zicheng Zhuang is an assistant-researcher at Guilin University of Electronic Technology, China.

Preface

Industrialization changed the face of the earth by making many products available to the world, creating economic growth, and even changing our world view. Whereas initially this was mainly studied on the national level, in recent decades a wide literature in economic history and economic geography has emerged which argues that this industrialization is largely a regional phenomenon. This shift in unit of analysis has profound implications for how it is analyzed. In this volume, we bring together papers dedicated to the topic of regional industrialization, dealing with the patterns, drivers, theories, and empirics of regional industrialization over the past two centuries. This work is derived from a workshop on the economic geography of long-run industrialization (approx. 1800–2010), organized in Amsterdam on 22–23 March 2018 and funded by the European Research Council (ERC) under the European Union's Horizon 2020 Programme/ERC-StG 637695 – HinDI (The historical dynamics of industrialization in Northwestern Europe and China ca. 1800–2010: a regional interpretation).

Bas van Leeuwen, Robin C. M. Philips, and Erik Buyst

Introduction

1 Global patterns of regional industrialization[1]

Bas van Leeuwen, Robin C. M. Philips, and Erik Buyst

1.1 Background

The Industrial Revolution and its aftermath present one of the most fascinating topics in the field of economic history. Within a century, per capita gross domestic product (GDP) tripled in the Western countries, an increase unprecedented in the centuries before (Maddison Project Database 2018). Like a slick of oil, new manufacturing technologies spread, during the nineteenth and twentieth centuries, first over England, followed by Western Europe and eventually the rest of the world. This growth spurt was, however, uneven and hence created an economic divergence between the rapidly industrializing Western countries and the other parts of the world, some of which even experienced de-industrialization. Although this gap has become smaller in recent decades, convergence has been unequal across the global periphery: whereas China has become the world's leader in industry output, many parts of Africa remain an industrial periphery. In addition, multiple obstacles – such as limitations of factor mobility – remain in place, preventing further convergence. Therefore, the link between industrialization, international welfare, inequality, and, more recently, environmental degradation, has lent urgency to understanding the spread of industrialization in the past two centuries.

For a long time, industrialization has been predominantly studied on the national level. Studies such as the collective work of Broadberry and O'Rourke (2010a, 2010b) and Saito and Shaw-Taylor (forthcoming) have cemented our view on long-run industrialization, explaining which countries were earlier to industrialize and which countries were slower in catching up. Yet, although this line of research has been hugely informative, this aggregated single national measure merely provides a glimpse at the historical process of industrialization. Indeed, since the 1980s, economic historians have increasingly acknowledged that the spread of industries has been a predominant regional phenomenon, with industries clustering in relatively small regions across nation-states (e.g. Wrigley 1961; Pollard 1981; Tilly 1983). These studies note that these industrial regions often shared more similarities with each other than with other regions within their respective nation-state, thus implying that the study of regions offers more compelling evidence for industrial development than the analysis of national differences. Even though this became acknowledged by most historians, the quantification of regional differences has only recently gained increasing attention in economic history (e.g. Kim 1998; Geary and Stark 2002, 2015; Crafts 2005; Combes et al. 2011), with a milestone achieved by the book of Rosés and Wolf (2019) in providing regional GDP for the European Nomenclature of Territorial Units for Statistics (NUTS)-2 regions from 1900 onwards.

Not only the field of economic history but also economists long neglected regional differences in industrialization, as the inclusion of these differences in economic theory violates the paradigm of perfect competition and constant returns to scale. This changed during the 1990s, when a paradigm shift took place in three areas (for a detailed description, see Rayp and Ronsse in Chapter 9 of this volume). The first change occurred by introducing exogenous differences among regions in the availability of factor endowments. This implies that a region will specialize in producing goods in which the abundant factor endowments are dominant. The second occurred by accepting the existence of non-competitive markets, as space implies indivisibilities over locations and the existence of transportation costs. And the third shift occurred by allowing increasing returns to scale as industries benefit from being located in close proximity of one another, a mechanism that is commonly addressed as Marshallian externalities (see, e.g., Marshall 1890; Ellison et al. 2010). Combined, these three factors imply an inverse U-curve of regional concentration of industrial activities over time (see Martinez-Galarraga and Tirado-Fabregat in Chapter 2 of this volume). In new economic geography (e.g. Krugman 1991), increasing returns lead to concentration under a high (and decreasing) transport cost regime, with industries locating near consumer markets and industries with similar input and output linkages (e.g. Vanhove 2018). Yet, once transportation costs decline further, factories start to disperse again, implicating convergence across regions.

Due to these recent lines of research, empirical testing – as had occurred in economic history – gained impetus. Models, including those from Kim (1995), Midelfart-Knarvik et al. (2000) and Davis and Weinstein (2003), allowed measurement of the importance of the different factors explaining the location of industry. Even though empirical issues in applying these models remain (see Rayp and Ronsse in Chapter 9 of this volume), in recent years they have inspired economic historians and economists to test for spatial patterns of industrialization in the long run (e.g. Aiginger and Davies 2004; Fan 2004; Wolf 2007; Betran 2011; Berger et al. 2012; Nikolic 2018; Missiaia 2019). Yet, although these studies have undoubtedly greatly contributed to our understanding of regional industrialization, the lack of comparison and synthesis between these studies has so far largely inhibited the connection between economic theory and historical empirics. In this perspective, it is understandable that Pollard (1994: 58) argued that "location theory as developed by economists, has relatively little to offer to the historian: its objective, in each case, has been to establish the equilibrium position, from which there would be no reason to move, while the historian looks for causes and mechanisms of change".

Therefore, in this volume, we bring together empirical and theoretical studies on regional industrialization in one coherent framework, in order to explain spatial development of industrialization and deindustrialization on the Eurasian continent over the past two centuries. The questions that this book aims to address can be subdivided into three groups: which theories can explain regional industrialization and deindustrialization, the scope of regional industrialization in Europe, and the extent to which this pattern of regional industrialization was similar in Asia. In particular, in this introduction, we briefly outline the general patterns one can derive from such a narrative by first providing an overview of regional industrialization in Britain, followed by continental Europe and Asia, before arriving at a brief conclusion.

1.2 Regional industrialization in England and Wales since the Industrial Revolution

The patterns of industrialization in the first industrializer, England and Wales, from the Industrial Revolution until present have been widely studied. There is a general consensus among economic historians that the starting point of the Industrial Revolution can be placed around the 1760s, with the introduction of the spinning jenny. Yet, the question of whether this constituted a break with the past or was rather a part of a long-run gradual change has been more a topic of debate. On the one hand, scholars have described the Industrial Revolution in England as the "key break in world history" (Clark 2012: 85) and "one of the most celebrated watersheds in human history" (Allen 2011: 357). Consequently, a large number of scholars have sought to explain this break (e.g. Berg and Hudson 1992; Temin 1997), most notably pointing to institutions (North and Weingast 1989), access to land (Pomeranz 2000), or ideology (Mokyr 2010). On the other hand, other scholars argued in favour of a more gradual transition. For instance, the recent evidence presented by Saito and Shaw-Taylor (forthcoming) indicates that the main structural shift from employment in agriculture to industry took place gradually during the sixteenth and, particularly, the seventeenth century in England and Wales, whereas this transition for the earliest industrial followers on the European continent – Belgium, France, and Germany – largely took place during the end of the eighteenth century and the nineteenth century.

A second debate focusses on the reason why the Industrial Revolution first took place in Britain. Following Crafts (2011) and Clark (2012), one might divide these studies in two branches. On the one hand, there is the so-called "idealist" approach in which the arrival of culture, ideology, or social norms opens up existing potential for economic growth (e.g. Mokyr 2010; McCloskey 2010). On the other hand, the so-called "incentive" approach focusses on material incentives necessary for economic growth. Examples consist of favourable institutions (e.g. North and Weingast 1989; Acemoglu and Robinson 2012), human capital necessary to develop new technologies (e.g. Squicciarini and Voigtländer 2015), or rising living standards and consumption levels (e.g. De Vries 2008). In particular, the hypothesis of Allen (2011: 364), which argues that Britain was the first country to experience an Industrial Revolution due to a favourable ratio between high wages and low coal prices . . ., has gained popularity. Whereas the importance of low coal prices has been largely agreed upon in the literature (e.g. Pomeranz 2000; Wrigley 2010; Fernihough and O'Rourke 2014), the importance of high wages has been more debated. Whereas Broadberry and Gupta (2009) and Allen (2019), for example, argue for its importance, others have doubted its relevance for the Industrial Revolution or even its very existence (e.g. Humphries and Weisdorf 2015; Stephenson 2018; Humphries and Schneider 2019).

Whereas the question of why England developed first is hotly debated, the role that geography played in this process is a topic relatively less developed. As pointed out by Horrell and Oxley (2012), initial regional differences were substantial in mid-nineteenth century England and Wales. Indeed, looking at Figure 1.1, by 1851 industry was heavily concentrated in the northwestern part of England, especially the Lancashire textiles cluster, where 46% of the world production of spindles was concentrated despite only covering 0.002% of the land mass in the world (Crafts and Wolf 2014). The reason behind the prominence of this cluster is rather debated; besides the study of Crafts and Wolf (2014), which shows that advantages such as access to water power and coal help to explain its prominence (see also Crafts and Mulatu 2005; Fernihough and O'Rourke 2014), the low-wage character of the region is often argued to have caused industrial growth in the Midlands and North of England (e.g. Mokyr 1976; Pollard 1978; Hunt 1986). This focus on low wages is confirmed by Kelly et al. (2015), who add a large population and a productive agricultural sector to the list of the region's advantages. There are various ways these initial regional advantages turned into agglomeration benefits, e.g. cheaper products due to advantageous factor endowments (Leunig 2003), increasing returns to scale (e.g. Crafts and Wolf 2014), and lower transport cost (Bogart 2014). But no matter what factors are advocated, all studies agree that they are ultimately related to increasing technology and productivity levels (e.g. Nuvolari et al. 2011).

Irrespective of what factors drove initial regional industrialization, Figure 1.1 shows that, at the eve of World War I, the formation of the industrial heartlands in England – with a profound secondary sector share clustering in the Northwest and the West Midlands, specializing in textiles and metal manufacturing – had been complete. This happened at the expense of the Southeast, Southwest, and East – all of which had been notable textile-producing regions in the early modern period (e.g. Hudson 1989).

Yet, regional concentration of industries in Britain did evolve over time. As found in the literature (Crafts and Malutu 2005; Philips et al. 2020), regional industrialization increased until a peak was reached during the Interbellum period, to decline thereafter. These industries had initially clustered, inter alia, due to increasing returns as predicted by the new economic geography literature (e.g. Krugman and Venables 1995). That is, the Northwest and Midlands strengthened their positions as industrial heartlands due to lower costs related to more readily available factor endowments, most notably these region's coal reserves, and external economies of scale. Yet, in turn, these agglomeration benefits in

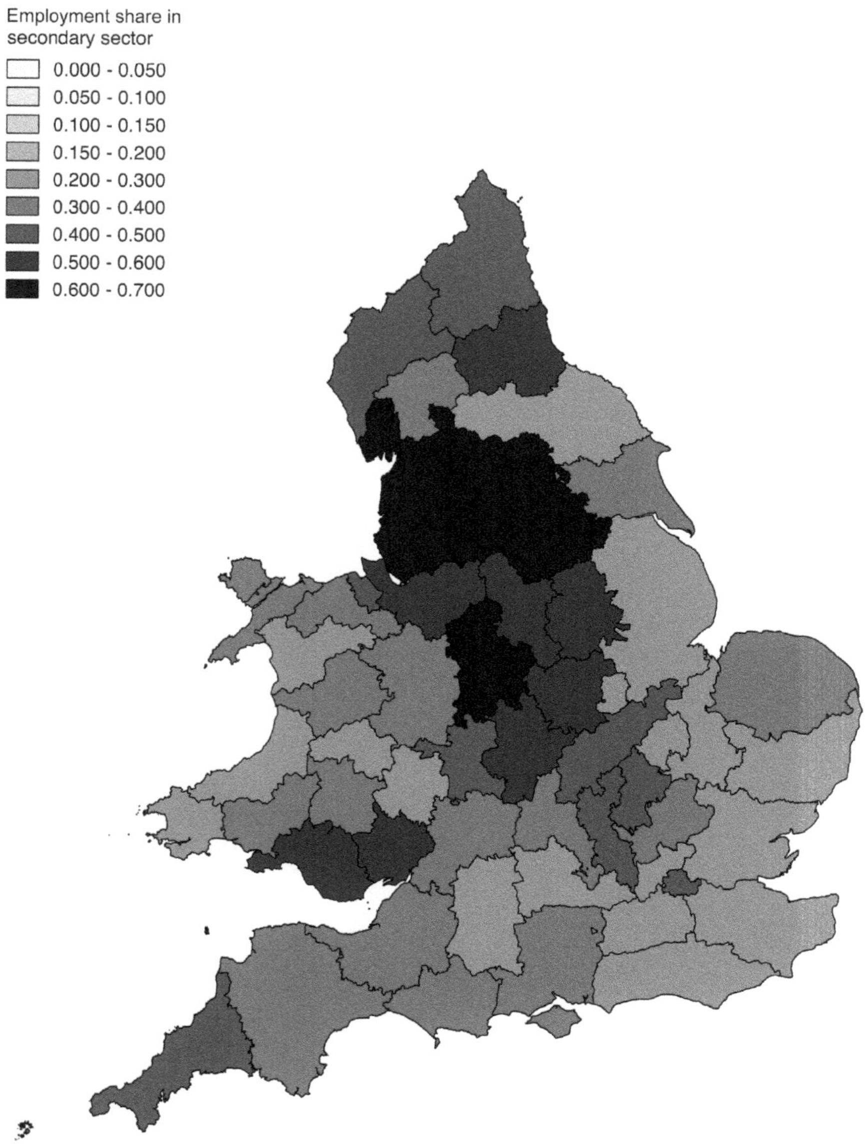

1851

Figure 1.1 The share of the secondary sector in the total labour force in England and Wales, 1851–2001

Source: For 1851, we used Census of the Population 1851, obtained from the Integrated Public Use Microdata Series (IPUMS) and constructed by Schurer and Higgs (2020). For 1911 and 1939, we refer to Philips et al. (2020). For 1971 and 2001, we turned to the United Kingdom Census of Population made available by the Office for National Statistics (2005).

Notes: For constructing estimates for the secondary sector, we followed the latest version of the Primary, Secondary, Tertiary system of occupational coding (PSTi), encapsulating roughly mining, manufacturing, and construction activities.

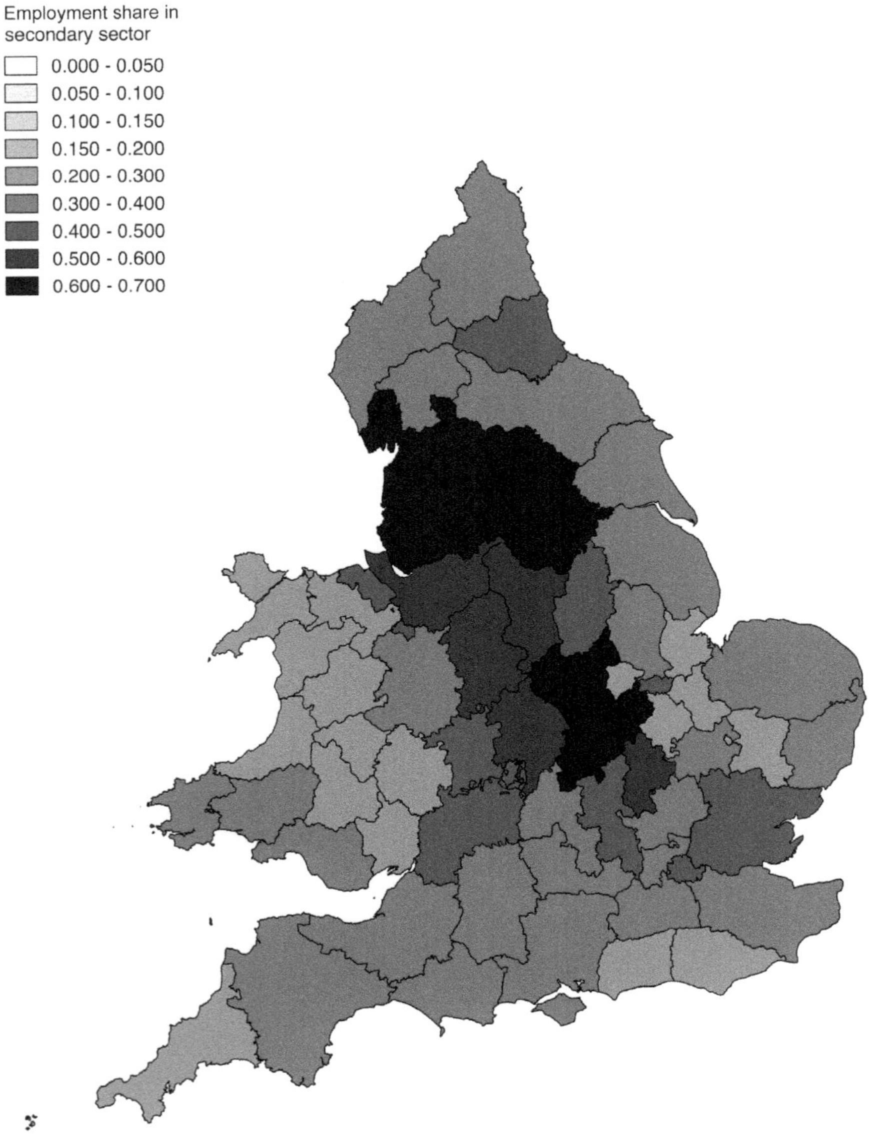

1911

Figure 1.1 (Continued)

combination with favourable market access resulted in higher wages for these regions. Consequentially, when during the Interbellum period transport costs started to decline, the Midlands and North started to fall victim to their own economic success, an evolution which would proceed in the following decennia.

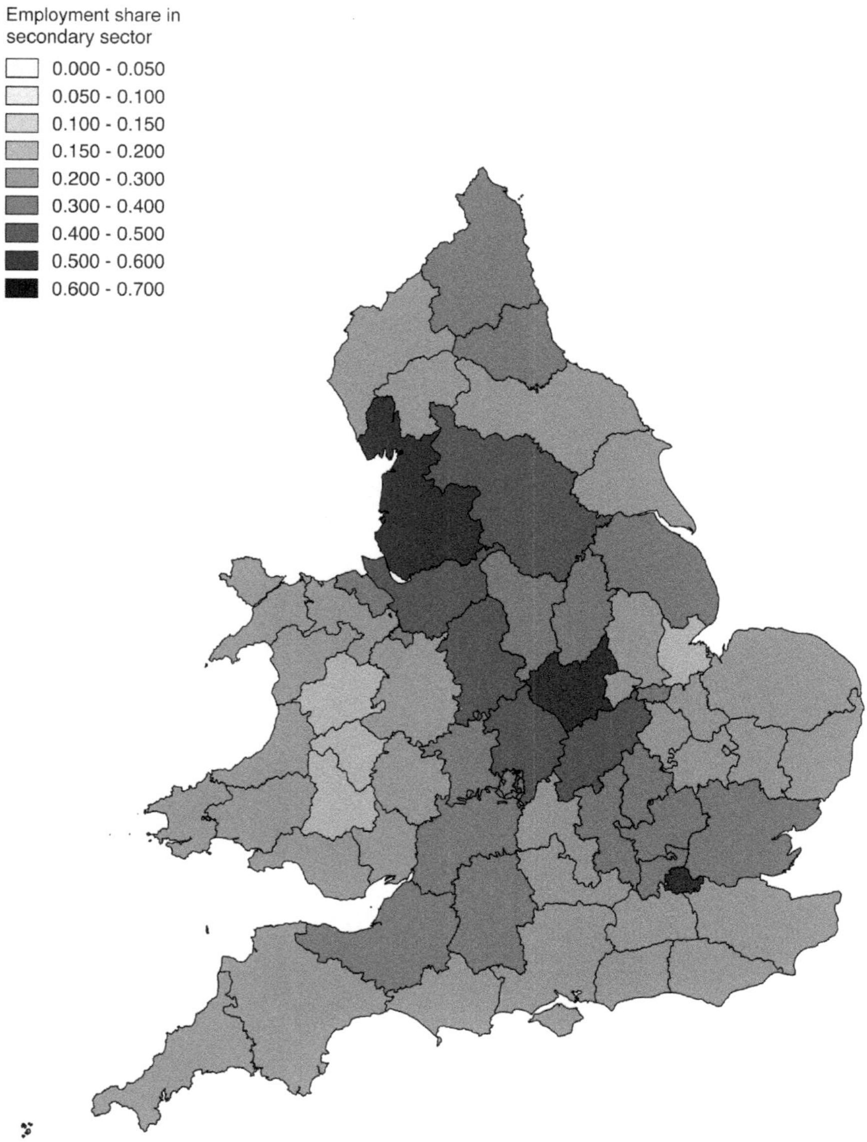

1939

Figure 1.1 (Continued)

The decline of these initial industrial regions after World War II was further strengthened by increasing factor price-equalization (e.g. Stobart 2004) and rapidly declining transport costs. Together with the breakthrough of car transport and the transition to oil, this especially hurt the Northwest, and soon thereafter

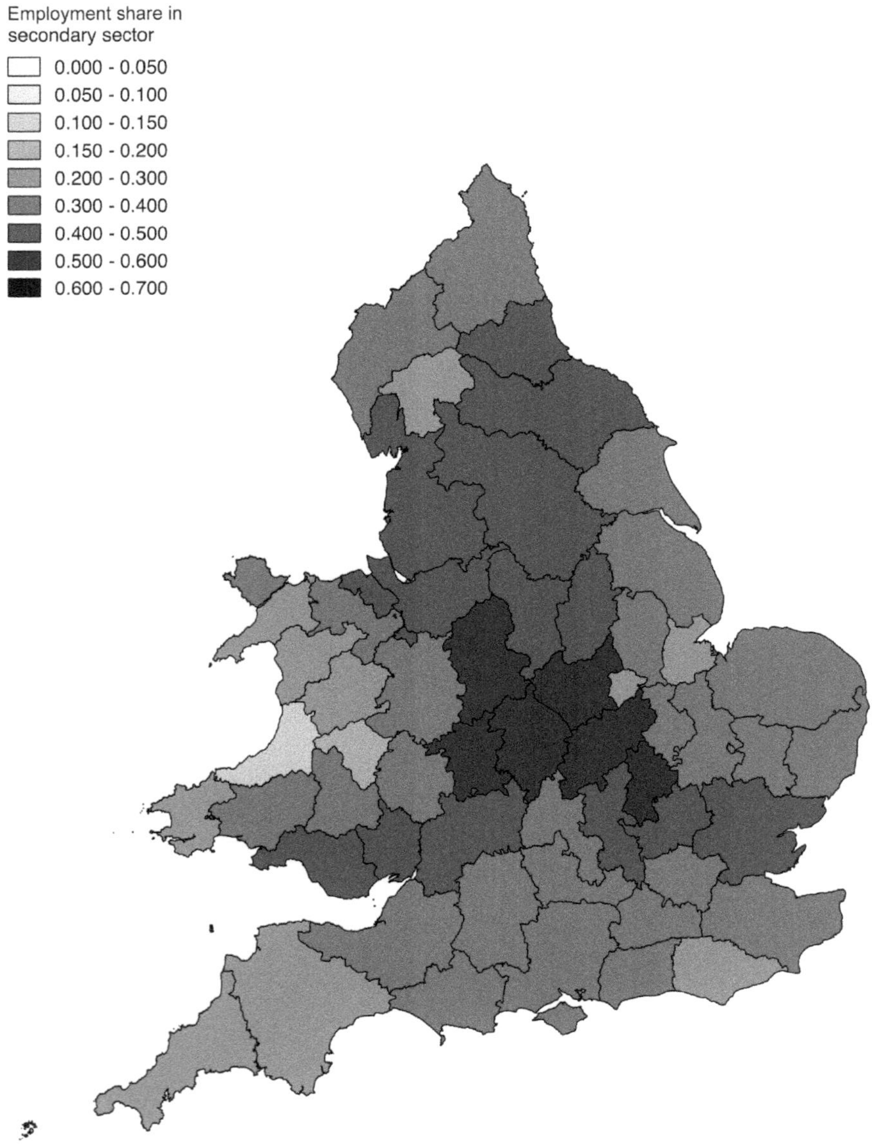

1971

Figure 1.1 (Continued)

the Midlands. Besides increasing intracountry similarities, increasing international competition from other regions in the world in precisely those sectors in which Britain held a comparative advantage, along with the production of textiles and metal goods, put increasing pressure on Britain's exports (Kurth 1979).

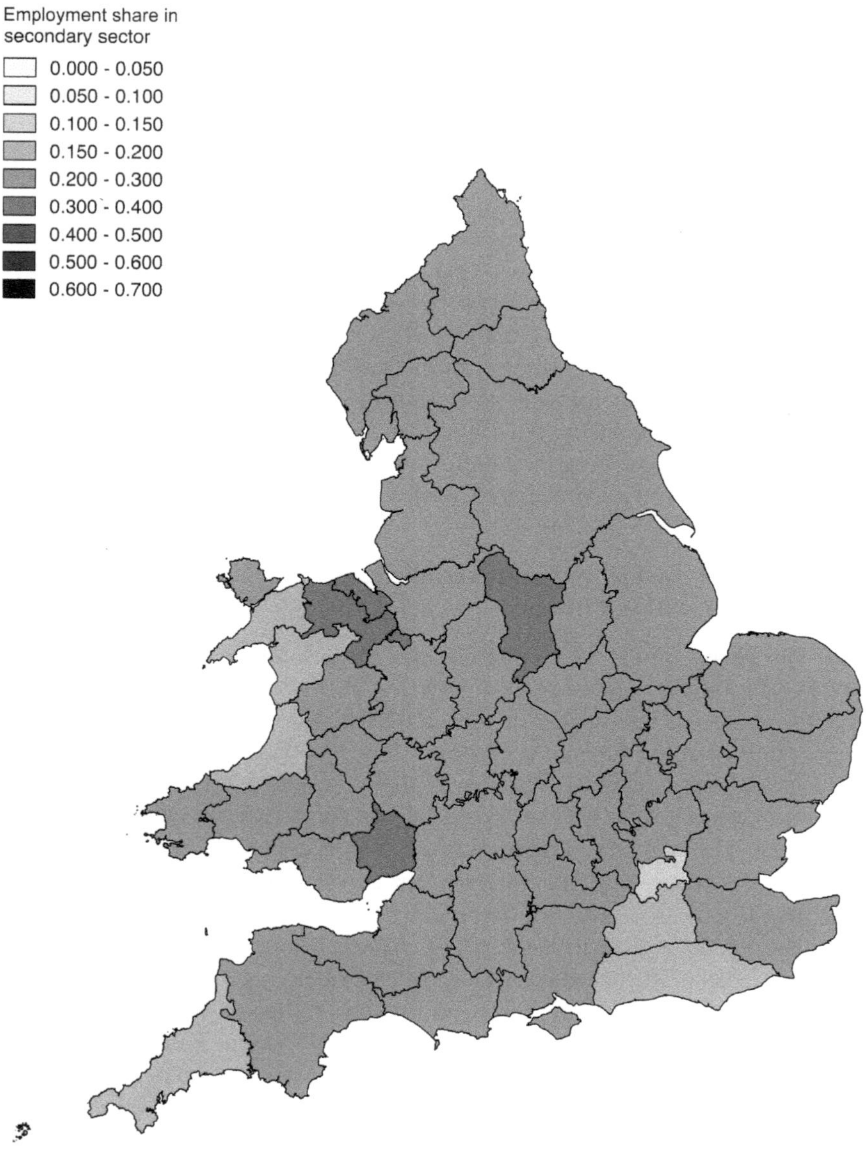

2001

Figure 1.1 (Continued)

The economic decline of the former industrial heartlands in Britain stimulated the need for regional policy. Although the role of industrial policy in Britain during the Industrial Revolution has traditionally been considered limited (e.g. Gerschenkron 1962), other studies considered it not just important (e.g. Bairoch

1993) but also well in existence before the seventeenth century (see Bianchi and Labory in Chapter 11 of this volume). This latter view matches the observation of Stobart (2004) that, from the industrial revolution onwards, the uniqueness of regions declined, which made regional industrial policy less efficient (see also Cox 2020). No matter its arguably declining effectiveness, the attention for regional policy increased since the depression of the 1930s, with a major challenge being the saving of declining industries in the de-industrialized regions in the Midlands and North (Rodrik 2007) and developing alternative routes to economic growth. This occurred mostly via the Regional Selective Assistance (RSA) and its expansions after the 1980s, i.e., supporting companies in exchange for creating employment. Yet, as pointed out by Criscuola et al. (2019), even though this policy improved employment and welfare in poorer regions, it also reduced productivity. In 1975, the national aid policies became supported on a European level with the establishment of the European Regional Development Fund (ERDF). Yet, it was not until the 1980s that a real European policy was created, i.e., with Europe supporting local industries directly rather than offering indirect support via supporting national government policy (Hall 2014).

1.3 How 'regional' was industrialization in continental Europe?

After the British Industrial Revolution, new manufacturing technologies spread slowly from Britain to other parts of Europe. Yet, the receptiveness of these new technologies was highly uneven across countries and regions, for which a wide range of explanations have been proposed. Some studies stress differences in the efficiency of factor endowments. For example, Wrigley (2018) argued that on the continent, coal was relatively expensive compared to firewood and peat, and only when steam engines became more efficient in the middle of the nineteenth century did coal become the more efficient choice of fuel. Other studies argue that British growth during the first Industrial Revolution was invention-based, while the second Industrial Revolution in Western Europe was innovation-based (Amsden 1989). In innovation-based development, open knowledge leading to practical innovation became important (Mokyr 2016). These points (cheap energy and education) are reiterated by Allen (2009), who further argues that a high wage economy combined with low capital costs contributed to Britain's uniqueness, i.e., expensive fuel and lower wages contributed to the slower growth of industries on the continent. Yet other studies point out that differences also existed in terms of policy. Gerschenkron (1962) famously argued that countries away from the industrial frontier in Britain used various measures to compensate for the lack of the previously mentioned fundamentals for growth, i.e., the more "backward" a country is, the bigger the emphasis on producer and capital goods and the stronger government intervention are necessary to catch up with the technological forerunner, Britain. A recent restatement of such a view for Russia was made by Allen (2003).

Although countries have predominantly featured as the standard unit of analysis in studying this spread of industrialization across Europe, economic history studies also looked at this debate from a regional dimension. Indeed, one wonders why the question of which countries in Europe were earlier to catch up with Britain needs to be asked when looking at Figure 1.2, as in 1900, differences in industrialization were higher within than between countries. A seminal work in this tradition has been the study of Wrigley (1961) who, looking from a transnational regional perspective at the European coalfields stretching from north-eastern France through Belgium to the Ruhr area, argued that the cross-country regions were more similar to each other than to the other regions within the same national territory. A similar point was famously made by Pollard (1978). These seminal studies have grown into a rich literature on how "regional" these "industrial revolutions" in Europe were (e.g. Crafts 2005; Combes et al. 2011). Indeed, based on the work of Rosés and Wolf (2019), we find that in 1900 the industrial belt in the North of the United Kingdom comprised of respectively 24.6% of the national labour population in industry (compared to 20.2% of the total population). Likewise, this is 22.5% (compared to 16.9% of the total population) for North Rhine-Westphalia (comprising the Rhine-Ruhr area) in Germany, and 11.7% (compared to 6.8% of the total population) for the Nord-Pas-de-Calais region in France.

By 1900, with the second Industrial Revolution in full swing, we find in Europe the highest values of secondary sector employment shares in the regions of the first Industrial Revolution. For instance, in the Low Countries, we find how the Liège and Hainaut regions remained the industrial forerunners throughout the nineteenth century (see Philips and Buyst, Chapter 3 of this volume). These industrial heartlands of Europe, as can be seen in Figure 1.2, roughly spanned from Northern France across Belgium and West Germany, with a southern border in Switzerland/Northern Italy and a northern border in Northwest Britain. In Southern and Northern Europe, only a limited number of regions came close to catching up with these frontier Western European regions. A case in Spain is the Barcelona and Madrid region (see, e.g., Betran 2011), and in Italy the northern and central regions (see Missiaia, Chapter 5 of this volume). Yet, the further east one goes, the less industrialization occurred, although even in this general pattern substantial regional differences emerged. For instance, despite being spatially proximate and living under the same Austro-Hungarian regime, Slovenia witnessed an almost double industry sector share compared to the rest of former Yugoslavia (see Kukić and Nikolić, Chapter 4 of this volume).

A branch of literature has aimed to explain the within-country spread of the secondary sector with the theoretical drivers of industrialization for a wide range of European countries in the late nineteenth and early twentieth centuries (e.g. Wolf 2007; Betran 2011; Berger et al. 2012; Nikolic 2018; Missiaia 2019; for a detailed overview, see Rayp and Ronsse in Chapter 9 of this volume). In this perspective, the distribution of land, energy, labour, human capital, and physical

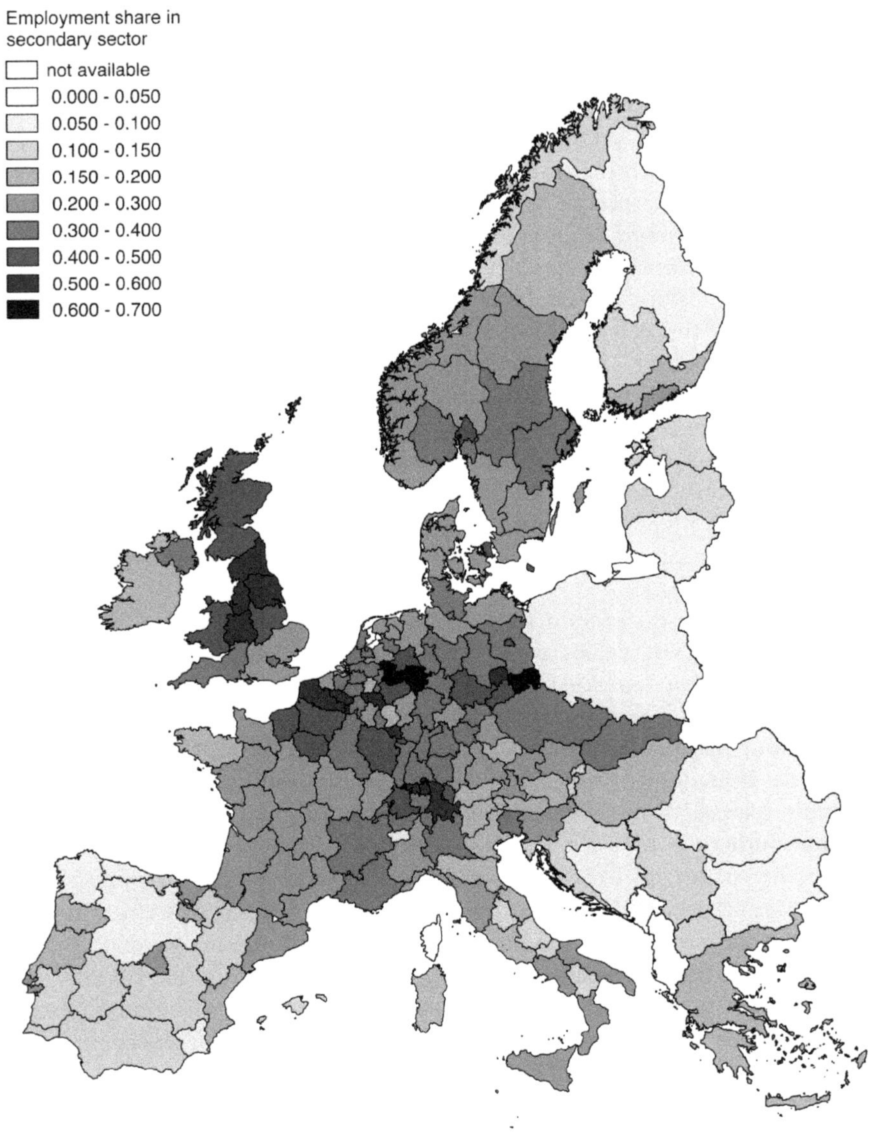

ca. 1900

Figure 1.2 The share of the secondary sector in the total labour force in Europe, 1900–2000

Source: For the estimates on Bosnia-Herzegovina, Croatia, Montenegro, North Macedonia, Serbia, and Slovenia, we refer to Kukić and Nikolić (see Chapter 4 of this volume). For the estimates on Estonia, Bulgaria, Czech Republic, Greece, Hungary, Latvia, Lithuania, Poland, Slovakia, and Romania in 1900, we refer to League of Nations, Economic and Financial Section (1930). For the other countries, we refer to Rosés and Wolf (2019). For the latter countries in 2000, we turned to the International Labour Organization Database, ILOSTAT (2020).

Notes: We define the secondary sector as all employment in mining, manufacturing, and construction sectors.

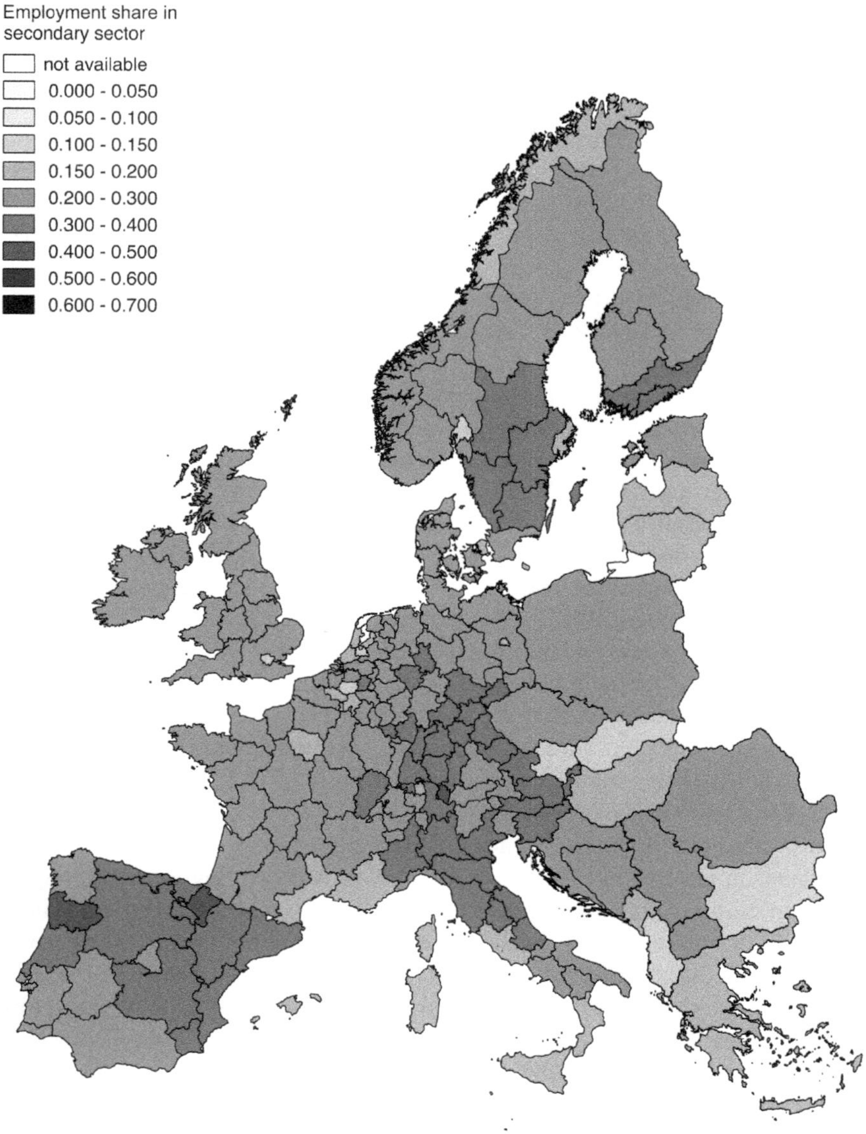

ca. 2000

Figure 1.2 (Continued)

capital are used to proxy a region's available factor endowments, whereas the size of the region's market and access to other domestic and foreign markets impacts a region's potential agglomeration benefits. Looking from a broad European perspective, such a narrative attributes the existence of the aforementioned

Northwestern European industrial heartlands in 1900 to the higher market potential in Western Europe (e.g. Caruana-Galizia 2015), as well as the access to resource-rich coalfields spanning from Germany to France. Notwithstanding changes in transport prices and overseas trade during the nineteenth century, agglomeration benefits locked in the locational advantage of these regions of the first Industrial Revolution. For the other parts of Europe with a more peripheral market position, especially those regions lacking coal reserves, triggering an industrial revolution was more cumbersome. For example, Acemoglu (1998) has pointed out that technical change often was difficult for the periphery, as many innovations have a bias towards particular factor endowments of the core, whereas Nikolić (2018) indicates that regions lagging in industrialization, such as the former Yugoslavia, had to focus on export-led industrialization and importing intermediate goods. Yet, even though these government-driven activities in socialist countries initially were effective (Allen 2003), in the long run they turned out to be less effective in replacing labour by capital (Easterly and Fischer 1994) and, hence, resulted in stagnant labour productivity.

Nonetheless, just like England in the twentieth century, convergence in factor prices and labour productivity, combined with fewer differences in market potential due to declining transportation and transaction costs, caused a decrease in early twentieth century regional specialization on the European mainland (e.g. Marti-Henneberg 2017). For example, Betran (2011) found for Spain (1856–2002) empirical evidence for the existence of such a bell-shaped pattern of regional specialization in industry, with the highest point of the regional specialization curve placed during the Interbellum period and declining regional specialization thereafter. Evidence on shorter time spans suggests similar evolutions for a larger number of European countries (e.g. Wolf 2007; Berger et al. 2012; Missiaia 2019; Nikolic 2018).

This transregional pattern during the twentieth century, where the industrial heartlands in Central and Northwestern Europe declined due to higher wages, led to an economic rehabilitation of the periphery. As a result, many differences across the European regions in the share of the secondary sector had flattened out by 2000 (see Figure 1.2). In Western, Northern, and Southern Europe, this resulted in the fall of many industrial clusters. For instance, in Belgium, this resulted in the economic standstill of the Sambre-Meuse region (see Philips and Buyst, Chapter 3 of this volume). Nonetheless, some regions such as Northern Spain, West Germany, North Italy, and Central Europe have been able to maintain relatively higher levels of secondary sector employment shares. Yet, in Central and Southern Europe, this opened opportunities; compared to 1900, many regions were able to shake off their status of industrial periphery and become forerunners of manufacturing activities in Europe. As such, deindustrialization offered contrasting experiences. Indeed, the first industrializing regions were also the ones to suffer first from deindustrialization, some of which even turning into so-called "rust belts". Conversely, many later industrializing regions were better able to diversify their economies, although these regions – many of which had a past under socialist regimes – were also not free from challenges, as many saw their investments in physical capital depreciate fast during the reforms of the 1990s (Foldvari et al. 2015).

1.4 How similar was regional industrialization in Asia?

Of course, looking only at European cases would not only ignore a substantial and interesting part of global history but also risk creating a European-based development theory on regional industrialization. To avoid this pitfall, we include in this volume case studies of regional industrialization in Asia. This not only makes it possible to test if existing theories on regional industrialization can be globally applied, but also contributes to the debates on the economic divergence between Europe and Asia.

The question of why the Industrial Revolution occurred in Northwestern Europe rather than in Asia especially sprung up in the late 1990s, in the wake of the so-called Great Divergence debate, which resolved around the question as to what degree (parts of) China remained on par with Western Europe until the nineteenth century (e.g. Frank 1998). Among those studies, the California School famously argued how Britain and Holland were able to overtake the Yangzi Delta in China as the wealthiest region in the world due to colonial expansion and more accessible coal reserves (Pomeranz 2000). Since then, other influential explanations such as institutions (e.g. Acemoglu and Robinson 2012), a higher European receptiveness to technology (e.g. Mokyr 2010), and a favourable factor price combination (Allen 2011) have arisen. Despite the new economic geography literature featuring less in this historiographical debate, factors such as the importance of market potential and transport costs nonetheless explain much of the advantage of Northwestern Europe compared to China or Japan. Even though most of the studies arguing in favour of the importance of these factors have dealt with India (e.g. Bogart and Chaudhary 2013), some of these studies have also focussed on China and Japan (e.g. Kingsmill 1898; Bogart 2010).

Even though there are many region-specific factors explaining why some regions rather than others industrialized in Asia, Figure 1.3 reveals that mostly regions with high market potential held the highest shares of secondary sector employment in Asia around 1900. In this perspective, similar to the European case, changes in transport networks and the spatial distribution of economic activity explain to a large extent the location of industry. In particular, the port cities of Tokyo and Osaka in Japan (see Bassino et al., Chapter 8 of this volume) and the (port) cities of Hongkong, Guangzhou, Shanghai, and Beijing in China (see Chapters 6 and 7 of this volume) saw notable industrial clusters arise around 1900 due to benefits of having a large population, thus ensuring a domestic market, and their traditional access to foreign markets. In landlocked Russia, large cities like Moscow and Saint Petersburg with extensive transport networks had notable industries, next to smaller, more traditional industry regions in its periphery, such as in parts of Ukraine and Uzbekistan.

Yet, besides these similar explanations to Europe, in line with Gerschenkron (1962) and Amsden (1989), studies have argued that later industrializers such as

ca. 1900

Figure 1.3 The share of the secondary sector in the total labour force in Asia, 1900–2000

Source: For the estimates on Japan, we refer to Bassino, Fukao, and Settsu (see Chapter 8 of this volume). For the estimates on China, we refer to Xu, van Leeuwen, and Zhuang (see Chapter 7 of this volume). For the estimates on Russia, we refer to Kessler and Markevich (2020).

Notes: We define the secondary sector as all employment in mining, manufacturing, and construction sectors.

in Asia differed in the first phase of their industrialization from early industrializers such as Europe in two ways. First, from a Gerschenkron (1962) point of view, one would expect that later industrializers in Asia relied more upon capital and energy-intensive production compared to their European counterparts (see, e.g., Allen 2003; Foldvari et al. 2015). This view is contradicted by Saito (1996) and Sugihara (2003), for example, who argue that Japan – and more generally, many East Asian countries – followed a more labour-intensive or "industrious" path of industrialization in which population growth and small increases in standards of living accommodated the adoption of labour-intensive technologies. Both views are nuanced by Vries (2019), who argues that, even though Japan during 1868–1937 was indeed characterized by low productivity levels and low wages, nevertheless labour intensity was not a sufficient condition to spur levels of modern economic growth.

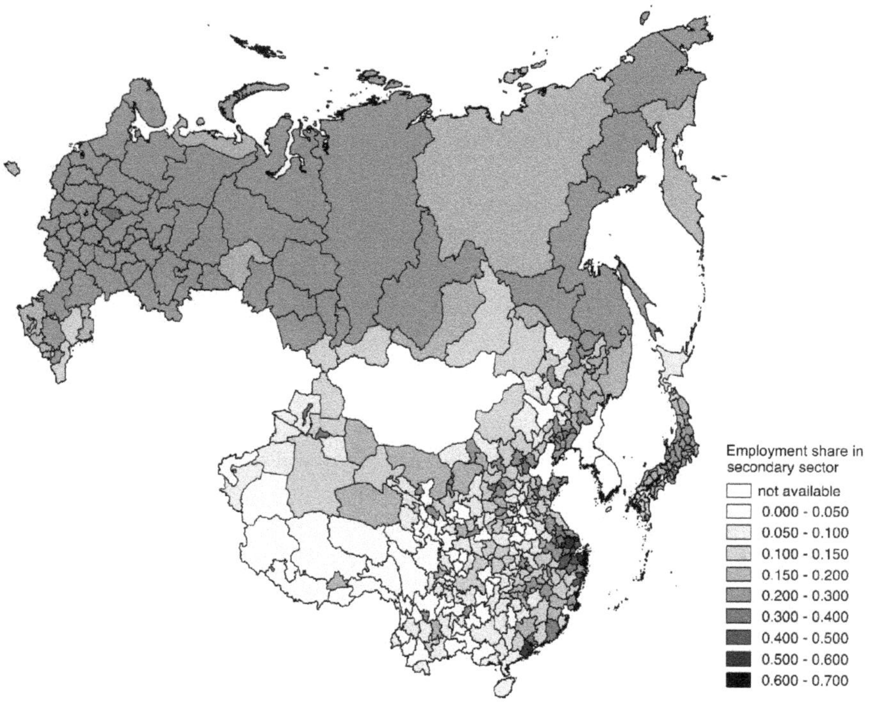

ca. 2000

Figure 1.3 (Continued)

Second, Gerschenkron (1962) and Amsden (1989) argued that in late industrializers, the government took a more active role in the industrialization process, in particular by supplying capital and promoting entrepreneurship. For instance, Macpherson (1995) and Vries (2019) argue that for Japan's industrial takeoff, the state was responsible for creating the necessary physical and institutional infrastructure for modern industry, and the state was the most important contributor to human and physical capital formation (see Bianchi and Labory, in Chapter 11 of this volume). Likewise, whereas the nineteenth-century Chinese state was considered non-interventionist (Vries 2015), growth in the second half of the twentieth century was largely state driven.

Nonetheless, the form this government intervention took was very different between Japan, on the one hand, and China and the USSR on the other hand. In Japan, government policy was mostly indirect, via consultation of companies with the government. In this indirect way, the allocation of resources shifted among sectors based on long-run government development plans. On the contrary, in the USSR (from the 1920s) and China (from the 1950s), policy was directly targeted to increase physical capital accumulation, and also led initially to high growth rates (Foldvari et al. 2015). Some authors have favoured this state-socialist policy as the best choice at the time (Allen 2003), even though it inhibited stagnation or decline in technological innovation. With the reforms in the 1980s (China) and 1990s (USSR), China was, contrary to the USSR, able to both reduce the inefficiency of physical capital and safeguard the physical capital against depreciation by massively investing in education. So it was soon able to expand its production frontier, something the USSR/Russia only managed in the twenty-first century (Van Leeuwen et al. 2015). Yet, the extent to which this government intervention also actively reshaped the economic geography in Asia to a different extent than a less interventionist Europe remains a topic left largely unexplored (for an example of market-related government policy, see van Leeuwen et al., Chapter 10 this volume).

To a large extent, the location of industrial regions in Asia, as well as its drivers, has stayed in force until the present day. Indeed, Xu et al. (Chapter 7 of this volume) and van Leeuwen et al. (Chapter 10 in this volume) show the importance of closeness to markets in China both at the start and end of the twentieth century. Also, studies like Redding and Venables (2004) and Liu and Meissner (2015) have provided evidence that a substantial amount of cross-country differences in GDP per capita today are due to access to domestic and foreign markets. Yet, looking at Figure 1.3 it appears that, just like in Europe, some regional convergence did take place. This suggests, as it did for Europe, that a partial shift took place, away from transport and infrastructure to a more important direct role for government policy. A fundamental difference in government policy with Europe, however, is twofold. First, in Japan, government policy had been indirect in the twentieth century and was reduced in recent decades. Second, whereas China and the United States have arranged policy largely at the regional government level, in Europe it is organized at the level of the nation-state and the European Union (Wei et al. 2010; Cox 2020).

1.5 Conclusion

The following chapters in this volume outline the evolutions in the location of industry in Europe and Asia over the past two centuries. Such a challenge is hard to overcome considering two limitations. On the one hand, theoretically, it is far from easy to model the location of industry, as not only the location of industry but also its determinants change over time. For instance, Rayp and Ronsse (see Chapter 9 in this volume) indicate that the discussion of whether factor endowments or new economic geography forces are more likely to explain the location of industry stems in large part from methodological differences across studies. On the other hand, country-specific effects are also likely to exist. For instance, Bianchi and Labory (see Chapter 11 of this volume) have shown how the relevance and usage of industrial policy was very different between Britain, the first industrializer, and the industrial periphery, be it in Europe, Asia, or elsewhere.

In this introduction, we have provided a brief overview of industrialization and deindustrialization during 1800–2010 on the Eurasian continent. The remainder of this volume offers more detailed evidence on how and why industrialization spread across the regions and over time, bringing forward ten chapters written by twenty-one specialists from different academic disciplines to tackle this topic. In Chapter 2, Martinez-Galarraga and Tirado-Fabregat elaborate on this by showing, using the existing literature, that today's spatial economic inequalities are linked to developments in the past.

In part one, the various chapters critically evaluate how "regional" the industrialization process was in early followers of industrialization (the Netherlands and Belgium, see Philips and Buyst, Chapter 3), late followers (Italy, see Missiaia, Chapter 5), and cases of state-led industrialization (former Yugoslavia, see Kukić and Nikolić, Chapter 4) in Europe. In part two, this volume presents two chapters on China (see Zhang, van Leeuwen, and Li in Chapter 6 and Xu, van Leeuwen, and Zhuang in Chapter 7) and one chapter on Japan (Bassino, Fukao, and Settsu in Chapter 8), in which it is explored, inter alia, to what degree existing theories on industrialization can be globally applied. Finally, in part three, theories on regional industrialization are reviewed in light of the recent literature and the new evidence brought forward in this book. In particular, Chapter 9 (Rayp and Ronsse) critically assesses the econometrics behind measuring the locational determinants of manufacturing, Chapter 10 (van Leeuwen, Földvári, Philips, and Wang) looks at the existence of (co-) agglomeration over time, and Chapter 11 (Bianchi and Labory) discusses the role of industrial policy.

With this overview of regional industrialization in the past two centuries, this volume offers some notable questions for the future. First, the New Economic Geography literature (e.g. Krugman and Venables 1995) predicts that de-industrialization in the core and industrialization in the periphery is likely to continue as trade and transport costs fall. Hence, one wonders to what extent regions will be able to face the challenges of further disintegrated globalized production chains. Second, for the early industrializers such as Europe, do policymakers have to enable agglomeration benefits to increase – or, in the very least, not hinder – existing industry clusters? Similarly, for the global periphery, which has so far focused on competition in low-cost manufacturing sectors, will challenges arise as to diversify their industrial clusters and replicate clusters of the early industrializers? Third, what future challenges for the manufacturing sector are likely to arise, amid the information and communication technology (ICT) revolution, skill-biased technological change, and declining productivity growth? As challenges in a converging world are more likely to rearrange the role of geography and regional disparities rather than abolish them, inter alia, path dependence in technology, institutions, and geography are likely to increase in importance. Hence, we hope that the lessons from the past described in this book might serve as an admittedly incomplete first step towards understanding these future challenges.

Note

1 This research received funding from the European Research Council under the European Union's Horizon 2020 Programme/ERC-StG 637695 – HinDI, as part of the project "The historical dynamics of industrialization in Northwestern Europe and China ca. 1800–2010: a regional interpretation".

References

Acemoglu, D. 1998. "Why do new technologies complement skills? Directed technical change and wage inequality." *Quarterly Journal of Economics* 113(4): 1055–1089.

Acemoglu, D., and J. Robinson. 2012. *Why nations fail: the origins of power, prosperity, and poverty*. New York: Crown Publishers.

Aiginger, K., and S. Davies. 2004. "Industrial specialisation and geographic concentration: two sides of the same coin? Not for the European Union." *Journal of Applied Economics* 7: 231–248.

Allen, R. C. 2003. *Farm to factory: a reinterpretation of the Soviet industrial revolution*. Princeton: Princeton University Press.

Allen, R. C. 2009. *The British industrial revolution in global perspective*. Cambridge and New York: Cambridge University Press.

Allen, R. C. 2011. "Why the industrial revolution was British: commerce, induced invention, and the scientific revolution." *The Economic History Review* 64(2): 357–384.

Allen, R. C. 2019. "Real wages once more: a response to Judy Stephenson." *Economic History Review* 72(2): 738–754.

Amsden, A. 1989. *Asia's next giant: South Korea and late industrialization*. New York: Oxford University Press.

Bairoch, P. 1993. *Economic and world history*. Brighton: Wheatsheaf.

Berg, M., and P. Hudson. 1992. "Rehabilitating the industrial revolution." *Economic History Review* 45(4): 24–50.

Berger, T., K. Enflo, and M. Henning. 2012. "Geographical location and urbanisation of the Swedish manufacturing industry, 1900–1960: evidence from a new database." *Scandinavian Economic History Review* 60(3): 290–308.

Betran, C. 2011. "Regional specialisation and industry location in the long run: Spain in the US mirror (1856–2002)." *Cliometrica* 5(3): 259–290.

Bogart, D. 2010. "A global perspective on railway inefficiency and the rise of state ownership, 1880–1912." *Explorations in Economic History* 47(2): 158–178.

Bogart, D. 2014. "The transport revolution in industrializing Britain." In *The Cambridge economic history of modern Britain*, edited by R. Floud, J. Humphries, and P. Johnson, 368–391. Cambridge: Cambridge University Press.

Bogart, D., and L. Chaudhary. 2013. "Engines of growth: the productivity advance of Indian Railways, 1874–1912." *The Journal of Economic History* 73(2): 339–370.

Broadberry, S., and B. Gupta. 2009. "Lancashire, India, and shifting competitive advantage in cotton textiles, 1700–1850: the neglected role of factor prices." *Economic History Review* 62(2): 279–305.

Broadberry, S., and K. H. O'Rourke, eds. 2010a. *The Cambridge economic history of modern Europe, volume 1: 1700–1870*. New York: Cambridge University Press.

Broadberry, S., and K. H. O'Rourke, eds. 2010b. *The Cambridge economic history of modern Europe, volume 2: 1870 to the present.* New York: Cambridge University Press.

Caruana-Galizia, P. 2015. *Economic development and market potential: European regional income differentials, 1870–1913.* Unpublished Ph.D. thesis, The London School of Economics and Political Science.

Clark, G. 2012. "A review essay on the enlightened economy: an economic history of Britain 1700–1850 by Joel Mokyr." *Journal of Economic Literature* 50(1): 85–95.

Combes, P. P., M. Lafourcade, J. F. Thisse, and J. C. Toutain. 2011. "The rise and fall of spatial inequalities in France: a long-run perspective." *Explorations in Economic History* 48(2): 243–271.

Cox, K. 2020. "Urban and regional development policy: its history and its differences." In *Regional economic development and history*, edited by M. Molema and S. Svensson, 145–163. London and New York: Routledge.

Crafts, N. 2011. "Review article: explaining the first industrial revolution: two views." *European Review of Economic History* 15(1): 153–168.

Crafts, N., and A. Mulatu. 2005. "What explains the location of industry in Britain, 1871–1931?" *Journal of Economic Geography* 5(4): 499–518.

Crafts, N., and N. Wolf. 2014. "The location of the UK cotton textiles industry in 1838: a quantitative analysis." *The Journal of Economic History* 74(4): 1103–1139.

Criscuolo, C., R. Martin, H. Overman, and J. Van Reenen. 2019. "Some causal effects of an industrial policy." *American Economic Review* 109(1): 48–85.

Davis, D., and D. Weinstein. 2003. "Market access, economic geography and comparative advantage: an empirical test." *Journal of International Economics* 59(1): 1–23.

De Vries, J. 2008. *The industrious revolution: consumer behavior and the household economy, 1650 to the present.* Cambridge: Cambridge University Press.

Easterly, W., and S. Fischer. 1994. *The Soviet economic decline: historical and republican data.* Policy, Research Working Paper no. WPS 1284, World Bank, Washington, DC.

Ellison, G., E. L. Glaeser, and W. R. Kerr. 2010. "What causes industry agglomeration? Evidence from coagglomeration patterns." *American Economic Review* 100(3): 1195–1213.

Fan, J. 2004. "Market integration, regional specialization, and the trend in industrial agglomeration – including a discussion on the influence of regional disparity." *Social Sciences in China* 6: 39–54. (范剑勇. 2004. 市场一体化、地区专业化与产业集聚趋势 – 兼谈对地区差距的影响. 中国社会科学2004年06期: 39–54).

Fernihough, A., and K. O'Rourke. 2014. *Coal and the European industrial revolution.* The Institute for International Integration Studies Discussion Paper Series iiisdp439, IIIS.

Foldvari, P., B. van Leeuwen, and D. Didenko. 2015. "Capital formation and economic growth under central planning and transition: a theoretical and empirical analysis, ca. 1920–2008." *Acta Oeconomica* 65(1): 27–50.

Frank, A. G. 1998. *ReORIENT: Global Economy in the Asian Age.* Berkeley: University of California Press.

Geary, F., and T. Stark. 2002. "Examining Ireland's post-Famine economic growth performance." *The Economic Journal* 112: 919–935.

Geary, F., and T. Stark. 2015. "Regional GDP in the UK, 1861–1911: new estimates." *Economic History Review* 68(1): 123–144.

Gerschenkron, A. 1962. *Economic backwardness in historical perspective, a book of essays*. Cambridge: Belknap Press.
Hall, R. 2014. "The development of regional policy in the process of European integration: an overview." In *Regional economic development compared: EU-Europe and the American South*, edited by G. Bischof, 13–33. Innsbruck: Innsbruck University Press.
Horrell, S., and D. Oxley. 2012. "Bringing home the bacon? Regional nutrition, stature, and gender in the industrial revolution." *Economic History Review* 65(4):1354–1379.
Hudson, P. 1989. "The regional perspective." In *regions and industries: a perspective on the industrial revolution in Britain*, edited by P. Hudson, 5–38. Cambridge: Cambridge University Press.
Humphries, J., and B. Schneider. 2019. "Spinning the industrial revolution." *Economic History Review* 72(1): 126–155.
Humphries, J., and J. Weisdorf. 2015. "The wages of women in England, 1260–1850." *Journal of Economic History* 75: 405–447.
Hunt, E. H. 1986. "Industrialization and inequality: regional wages in Britain, 1760–1914." *Journal of Economic History* 46: 935–966.
ILOSTAT (2020). *Labour force survey statistics, yearly indicators, annual employment by sex and economic activity (thousands)*. EMP_TEMP_SEX_ECO_NB_A, Accessed 26 January 2020.
Kelly, M., J. Mokyr, and C. O'Grada. 2015. *Roots of the industrial revolution*. UCD Centre For Economic Research Working Paper Series 2015, WP15/24.
Kessler, G., and A. Markevich. 2020. "Electronic repository of Russian historical statistics, 18th – 21st centuries." https://ristat.org/
Kim, S. 1995. "Expansion of markets and the geographic distribution of economic activities: the trends in US regional manufacturing structure, 1860–1987." *Quarterly Journal of Economics* 110(4): 881–908.
Kim, S. 1998. "Economic integration and convergence: U.S. regions, 1840–1987." *Journal of Economic History* 58(3): 659–683.
Kingsmill, Th. W. 1898. *Inland communications in China*. Shanghai: Kelley & Walsh.
Krugman, P. R. 1991. *Geography and trade*. Cambridge: MIT Press.
Krugman, P. R. and A. J. Venables. 1995. "Globalization and the inequality of nations." *Quarterly Journal of Economics* 110(4): 857–880.
Kurth, J. 1979. "The political consequences of the product cycle: industrial history and political outcomes." *International Organization* 33(1): 1–34.
League of Nations. Economic and Financial Section. 1930. *Statistical year-book of the league of nations 1929*. Geneve: League of Nations, Economic and Financial Section.
Leunig, T. 2003. "A British industrial success: productivity in the Lancashire and New England cotton spinning industries a century ago." *Economic History Review* 56(1): 90–117.
Liu, D., and C. M. Meissner. 2015. "Market potential and the rise of US productivity leadership." *Journal of International Economics* 96(1): 72–87.
Macpherson, W. J. 1995. *The economic development of Japan 1868–1941*. Cambridge: Cambridge University Press.
Maddison Project Database, version 2018. Bolt, J., R. Inklaar, H. de Jong, and J. L. van Zanden. 2018. *Rebasing 'Maddison': new income comparisons and the shape of long-run economic development*. Maddison Project Working Paper no. 10.

Marshall, A. 1890. *Principles of economics*. London: Macmillan.

Martí-Henneberg, J. 2017. "The influence of the railway network on territorial integration in Europe (1870–1950)." *Journal of Transport Geography* 62(C): 160–171.

McCloskey, D. 2010. *Bourgeois dignity: why economics can't explain the modern world*. Chicago: University of Chicago Press.

Midelfart-Knarvik, K. H., H. G. Overman, S. J. Redding, and A. J. Venables. 2000. *The location of European industry*. European Economy Economic Papers 142, European Commission.

Missiaia, A. 2019. "Market versus endowment: explaining early industrial location in Italy (1871–1911)." *Cliometrica* 13(1): 127–161.

Mokyr, J. 1976. "Growing-up and the industrial revolution in Europe." *Explorations in Economic History* 13(4): 371–396.

Mokyr, J. 2010. *The enlightened economy: an economic history of Britain 1700–1850*. New Haven and London: Yale University Press.

Mokyr, J. 2016. *A culture of growth: the origins of the modern economy*. Princeton and Oxford: Princeton University Press.

Nikolić, S. 2018. "Determinants of industrial location: kingdom of Yugoslavia in the interwar period." *European Review of Economic History* 22(1): 101–133.

North, D. C., and B. R. Weingast. 1989. "Constitutions and commitments: the evolution of institution governing public choice in seventeenth-century England." *The Journal of Economic History* 49(4): 803–832.

Nuvolari, A., B. Verspagen, and N. von Tunzelmann. 2011. "The early diffusion of the steam engine in Britain, 1700–1800: a reappraisal." *Cliometrica* 5(3):291–321.

Office for National Statistics. 2005. *1971 and 2001 Census aggregate data*. UK Data Service, Casweb.

Philips, R., M. Calabrese, R. Keenan, and B. van Leeuwen. 2020. *The regional occupational structure in interwar England and wales*. Working Paper version, available upon request.

Pollard, S. 1978. "Labour in Great Britain." In *The Cambridge economic history of Europe*, Part 1, Vol. VII, edited by P. Mathias and M. M. Postan, 97–179. Cambridge: Cambridge University Press.

Pollard, S. 1981. *Peaceful conquest. The industrialization of Europe 1760–1970*. Oxford: Oxford University Press.

Pollard, S. 1994. "Regional and inter-regional economic development in Europe in the eighteenth and nineteenth centuries." In *Debates and controversies in economic history*, 57–94. Eleventh International Economic History Congress, Milan.

Pomeranz, K. 2000. *The great divergence. China, Europe, and the making of the modern world economy*. Princeton and Oxford: Princeton University Press.

Redding, S. and A. J. Venables. 2004. "Economic geography and international inequality." *Journal of International Economics* 62(1): 53–82.

Rodrik, D. 2007. *One economics, many recipes*. Princeton: Princeton University Press.

Rosés, J. R., and N. Wolf, eds. 2019. *The economic development of Europe's regions: a quantitative history since 1900*. London: Routledge.

Saito, O. 1996. "Gender, workload and agricultural progress. Japan's historical experience in perspective." In *Protoindustrialisation. Recherches recentes et Nouvelles perspectives. Melanges en souvenir de Franklin Mendels*, edited by R. Leboutte, 129–151. Geneva: Librairie Droz.

Saito, O. and L. Shaw-Taylor, eds. forthcoming. *Occupational structure and industrialization in a comparative context*. Cambridge: Cambridge University Press.

Schurer, K., and E. Higgs. 2020. *Integrated Census Microdata (I-CeM), 1851–1911.* [data collection1]. UK Data Service.

Squicciarini, M. P., and N. Voigtländer. 2015. "Human capital and industrialization: evidence from the age of enlightenment." *Quarterly Journal of Economics* 130(4): 1825–1883.

Stephenson, J. Z. 2018. "'Real' wages? Contractors, workers, and pay in London building trades, 1650–1800." *Economic History Review* 71: 106–132.

Stobart, J. 2004. *The first industrial region: North-West England, c. 1700–60.* Manchester: Manchester University Press.

Sugihara, K. 2003. "The East Asian path of economic development. A long-term perspective." In *The resurgence of East Asia. 500, 150, and 50 year perspectives*, edited by G. Arrighi, T. Hamashita, and A. Selden, 78–123. London: Routledge.

Temin, P. 1997. "Two views of the British Industrial Revolution." *The Journal of Economic History* 57(1): 63–82.

Tilly, C. 1983. "Early forms of capitalist industry." *Theory and Society* 12(2): 123–142.

Vanhove, N. 2018. *Regional policy: a European approach*, 3rd ed. London and New York: Routledge.

Van Leeuwen, B., D. Didenko, and P. Földvári. 2015. "Inspiration vs. perspiration in economic development of the former Soviet Union and China (ca. 1920–2010)." *Economics of Transition* 23(1): 213–246.

Vries, P. 2015. *State, economy and the great divergence: Great Britain and China, 1680s–1850s.* New York: Bloomsbury Academic.

Vries, P. 2019. *Averting a great divergence: state and economy in Japan, 1868–1937.* New York: Bloomsbury Academic.

Wei, H., M. Bai, and Y. Wang. 2010. *The micro-analysis of regional economy in China: a perspective of firm relocation.* Singapore: World Scientific Publishing.

Wolf, N. 2007. "Endowment vs. market potential: what explains the relocation of industry after polish reunification in 1918?" *Explorations in Economic History* 44(1): 22–42.

Wrigley, E. A. 1961. *Industrial growth and population change; a regional study of the coalfield areas of North-West Europe in the later nineteenth century.* Cambridge: Cambridge University Press.

Wrigley, E. A. 2010. *Energy and the English industrial revolution.* Cambridge: Cambridge University Press.

Wrigley, E. A. 2018. "Reconsidering the industrial revolution: England and wales." *The Journal of Interdisciplinary History* 49: 9–42.

2 Economic geography and economic history

A literature overview

Julio Martinez-Galarraga and Daniel A. Tirado-Fabregat

2.1 Introduction

The spatial inequalities in the distribution of economic activity and income that we see today are the result of a long-term evolution that can be traced back at least to the start of the Industrial Revolution in Great Britain at the end of the eighteenth century. Its gradual spread to more and more countries enabled the various economies that joined the process to follow the path of what Simon Kuznets defined as "modern economic growth" (Kuznets 1966, 1971). This process is characterized by high self-sustained growth in per-capita income, often accompanied by an increase in population and by structural change. The transfer of resources from low-productivity agricultural activities to high-productivity industrial activities – industry being the sector that was gradually adopting technological change – created the conditions for this form of economic growth. However, differences in growth rates brought about an increase in income inequality across countries and, given the self-sustained nature of modern economic growth, these differences in income levels became more pronounced over time.

Sidney Pollard (1981) suggested that industrialization processes were unique and non-repetitive, notable for their marked regional character.[1] A good many examples illustrate the regional nature of these processes: Lancashire in Great Britain, the Sambre and Meuse Valley in Belgium, the Ruhr in Germany, the Genoa-Milan-Turin triangle in northern Italy, and the manufacturing belt in the United States, to name just a few. Furthermore, the industrialization processes that in many cases were set in motion in the nineteenth century coincided with the economic integration of national markets. The reduction in trade costs between different areas of the same country and between countries was due to the elimination of institutional obstacles that hindered the free movement of goods and factors between them and to cheaper haulage costs deriving from technological improvements made during the Industrial Revolution.

Economic geography plays an important role in the analysis of economic development. Space is heterogeneous, which means that the conditions in some areas could initially be more suitable for human settlement and economic activity. Economic history, on the other hand, shows us that the reality can change and that the opportunities initially offered by these conditions may be strengthened or modified over time due to human activity. In each wave of technology there have been changes in the use of raw materials or new sources of energy that have given advantages to some locations over others, thus bringing about changes in the location of economic activity. In addition, new means of transport and new transport networks have appeared over time, making it possible to increase the size of the domestic market and connect markets that were previously far apart. With this changing scenario, it is not only companies that can relocate to more attractive areas. People have also tended to migrate, mainly towards dynamic urban settings, generating increased economic density in certain areas.

The emergence of the new economic geography literature (Krugman 1991; Fujita et al. 1999; Combes et al. 2008) provides an invaluable analytical framework for studying the location of economic activity in the geographical space and its evolution over time. Particularly, one aspect that the new economic geography literature may help to explain is the spatial distribution of manufacturing in the course of the industrialization process. These theoretical models can shed some light on the forces behind the spatial concentration of economic activity in a context characterized by decreasing transport costs and the increasing presence of economies of scale. And to a large extent, this is what has happened in the world economy over roughly the last 200 years. Since the Industrial Revolution, the continuous advance of technology has generated increasing returns to scale in production, and this in turn has brought about considerable reductions in trade costs both within and between countries. While in 1800 the crossing from London to New York by sailing ship took over thirty days (as did postal communications), today these cities are connected by plane in eight hours and online instantly thanks to communication technologies.

New economic geography studies make it possible to analyze the changes that took place in the location of industrial activity over the years as technology advanced and both the internal and external markets became more integrated. In this overview, we therefore aim to show the usefulness of economic geography as a tool to help us better understand economic history and to prove that economic history is just as useful as a laboratory that provides empirical evidence in support of the theoretical predictions that emerge from the new economic geography models. The chapter is organized as follows. First, we introduce the seminal theoretical papers of the new economic geography literature that explain the relationship between economic development, market integration, and the spatial distribution of economic activity (i.e., manufacturing) over time. Second, we look at some of the economic history papers that – through the use of an economic geography framework – have analyzed the historical evolution of manufacturing in different countries, including the United States, the United Kingdom, and some mainland European countries. Finally, the chapter closes with some brief conclusions.

2.2 Industrialization and agglomeration: What does new economic geography have to say?

The new economic geography literature concerns itself with studying the uneven spatial distribution of human activity. In its models, transport costs and increasing returns interact in a framework of monopolistic competition that favours the spatial agglomeration of economic activities and then reinforces it once it is under way. In this context, the gradual market integration of goods and factors plays a key role, as lower transport costs may encourage the spatial concentration of economic activities, which depends on the interaction of two types of forces operating in opposite directions: the *centripetal* or *agglomeration forces* and the *centrifugal* or *dispersion forces*. The model developed by Krugman (1991) describes a cumulative process similar to those envisaged by Hirschman (1958) and by Myrdal (1957), in which the concentration of economic activity resulted from the interaction of two centripetal forces linked to market access. In turn, agglomeration is subject to a snowball effect that results in a continuous strengthening of this spatial concentration once it is set in motion.

Two main effects linked to the factors of production operate in Krugman's (1991) core-periphery model, one related to companies and the other to workers. To study the location decisions of these two elements, it is assumed that one region becomes slightly larger than the other. This increase in the market size of one region leads to an increase in its demand for manufactured goods, so it becomes advisable for companies to be located close to the higher demand in order to save on transport costs. This means that activities with economies of scale become concentrated in locations with good market access (backward linkages). The home market effect then ensures that this increase in market size generates a more than proportional increase in the number of companies in that location, pushing up nominal wages. The presence of more companies means a greater variety of locally produced goods, with consumption benefitting from lower transport costs. A lower local price index and the consequent increase in real wages in the region attract new flows of workers to the big urban industrial centres (forward linkages). These two centripetal forces feed off each other and encourage agglomeration, with proximity to large markets standing out as one of the main mechanisms at work. Market access therefore becomes a key element in new economic geography analyses because it has a positive influence on the location decisions of companies and workers alike and induces factor mobility – of capital in the case of backward linkages and of labour in forward linkages.

In this framework, the result of economic integration is the emergence of a core-periphery geographical pattern. When transport costs are high, trade is so expensive that companies sell their products on the local market. As a result, companies are spatially dispersed and the manufacturing sector is distributed evenly between regions, which have the same nominal wages and price indices. However, when transport costs become low enough, there is a shift to an asymmetric equilibrium characterized by agglomeration. Thus, economic integration gives rise to a geographical concentration of manufacturing resulting from worker mobility, which enables a cumulative causation to appear that strengthens the agglomeration by increasing the market size advantage. The greater demand generated in the core region means that all companies in the manufacturing sector – where increasing returns operate – locate to the same region, and this simultaneously leads to deindustrialization in the periphery. In other words, economic integration generates an abrupt transition from dispersion to agglomeration.

The shift to a core-periphery structure leads to an increase in regional inequalities. Thus, Krugman (1991) provides a theoretical explanation for the substantial and persistent territorial inequalities seen in the real world. In this case, and unlike in international trade theories, regions that initially present similar characteristics end up diverging considerably, as even a small transitory *shock* can give rise to permanent regional imbalances.[2] Finally, Krugman (1991) emphasizes the pecuniary as opposed to the technological externalities. When companies and workers move from one region to another, this unintentionally affects the welfare of all agents. Agglomeration therefore has to be considered a man-made economic factor.

In Krugman's (1991) model, agglomeration lies in the mobility of the labour factor. However, one limitation is that agglomeration is also present in areas characterized by a low spatial mobility of labour, both between and within countries. Later developments in new economic geography studies have provided more detail. Krugman and Venables (1995) and Venables (1996) explained the emergence of big industrial regions in economies characterized by low labour mobility, assuming that the labour factor is immobile. Their studies have the virtue of adding a key element to the analysis that was not present in Krugman's (1991) pioneering study: the existence of intermediate goods. In this case, companies produce differentiated varieties incorporating labour and intermediate goods supplied by other firms. Labour is homogeneous and, as there are no intersectoral mobility costs, workers can be employed in either of the two sectors. The other assumptions are the same as those made by Krugman (1991).

Taking into account the existence of intermediate goods provides a better fit to real patterns and implies that, when they make their decisions, the producers of intermediate goods prefer to locate where the final goods are produced. Likewise, the producers of final goods tend to locate where the suppliers of intermediate goods are. This reciprocal influence captures the Marshallian externality related to the availability of specialized intermediate inputs, which Marshall (1890) considered a fundamental element for the existence of industrial clusters.[3] When firms concentrate in a region, the high demand for intermediate goods attracts producers of these types of goods. In addition, the lower price indices of the regions that produce more varieties lead to a decrease in production costs for firms in the manufacturing sector. As a result, intermediate goods are supplied at a lower price in the core region, and this leads more producers of final goods to move there. Thus, producers have an incentive to locate to the region with the highest number of varieties because they will benefit from lower production costs, and it results in agglomeration.[4]

Thus, Krugman and Venables (1995) and Venables (1996) provide an alternative mechanism to help explain agglomeration when there is no labour mobility: the presence of input-output linkages. If the production of intermediate goods represents a large proportion of industrial output, companies will have an incentive to locate near their suppliers and consumers, and this can favour agglomeration in a given region. If up to this point agglomeration had occurred endogenously because of the size of the local markets and it was caused by consumer/worker mobility, then the presence of input-output linkages in industry lead to the emergence of new forces that play an important role in shaping the spatial pattern of manufacturing and economic activity.

Among these new forces we find not only those that tend to favour agglomeration but also centrifugal or dispersion forces. There is more competition in the core region's manufacturing sector because of the greater number of companies located there as a result of agglomeration (*market-crowding effect*), but there is also a dispersion force linked to the increase in the region's nominal wages and the consequent increase in labour costs. And given that the workforce is immobile, it needs to be taken into account that there is still a substantial demand for manufactured goods in the periphery. Together these factors can lead to the relocation of industry from the core to the periphery, where lower wage costs can offset the lower demand for the company's goods and the lower demand for intermediate goods, and therefore higher costs when acquiring intermediate inputs.

With the inclusion of these new forces in the analysis, the relationship between economic integration and the spatial concentration of manufacturing is no longer monotonic and shows a bell-shaped evolution. While in Krugman's (1991) model the reduction in transport costs led to the emergence of a core-periphery pattern, here the pattern is different. When transport costs are high, a symmetric equilibrium is recorded in which manufacturing is distributed equally between the two regions, without there being any spatial inequality. When transport costs fall, the symmetric equilibrium is broken and a core-periphery structure like that described by Krugman (1991) appears. As a result of the high demand for the manufactured good, agglomeration forces cause the regions to diverge. However, this asymmetric equilibrium is no longer stable when transport costs reach a sufficiently low value because dispersion forces bring the agglomeration process to a halt or even reverse it, resulting in the reindustrialization of the periphery and the simultaneous deindustrialization of the core.

Then, the initial impact of market integration could therefore be the concentration of the manufacturing sector and the strengthening of regional disparities. Nevertheless, greater economic integration leads to a dispersion of manufacturing and a reduction in regional inequalities. The theoretical models suggest that reindustrialization of the periphery may occur when the dispersion forces start to act once transport costs have reached a low enough level. However, market integration must have progressed sufficiently in order for this to happen. The political implications of this are not as alarming as regards the consequences of the market integration process, and the theoretical predictions seem to match more closely the patterns observed in the real world. Indeed, this is in line with a number of empirical studies, including that of Williamson (1965), who suggested that throughout the economic development process, regional inequality exhibited an inverted U-shaped pattern. Therefore, the theoretical predictions of the new economic geography literature fit this evidence better.

2.3 Linking economic geography and economic history: A brief survey of the empirical work to date

Industrialization and market integration over time: A potted history

The brief overview of the new economic geography models showed the importance of industrialization processes when it comes to understanding the distribution of economic activity in the geographical space due to the greater presence of increasing returns to scale in the manufacturing sector. Also important are market size and the reduction in transport costs, so all of these elements need to be included among our main lines of study. These aspects have varied greatly throughout history, not just in recent decades but over a much longer time frame, going back at least two centuries to the beginnings of industrialization – an industrialization that was accompanied by both national and international market integration processes.[5]

The field of economic history has supplied various explanations as to why the Industrial Revolution took off in Great Britain at the end of the eighteenth century. From the viewpoint of economic geography, one aspect that stands out, given the importance of its effect on market size, is the degree of urbanization already reached by the British economy in comparison with other countries. According to data in De Vries (1984), the rate of urbanization in Great Britain in 1800 – considering cities with over 10,000 inhabitants – was 20.3%, a value much higher than in France (8.8%) or Germany (5.5%) at that time.[6] And while there were many reasons for the Industrial Revolution, there were also many consequences. Industrialization meant the appearance of new technologies, many of them involving steam power. The textile sector, metallurgy, and steam stood out in the early decades of the nineteenth century as the most dynamic sectors of industry into which technological change was being introduced. Indeed, it was in these sectors that the transition from artisanal to factory production took place, thus increasing the scale of production. And it was in these early urban agglomerations that factories were often located, where growing returns to scale became more important and where greater market size and greater economic density were reached.

Technology not only allowed industrial output to be increased; it also had an effect on transport costs. The arrival of the railways and the spread of the rail network from the mid-nineteenth century were fundamental in boosting domestic market integration in many countries over the rest of the century. The greater distances covered by paved roads, the development of coastal shipping, and the construction of river and canal systems also encouraged the integration of national markets. However, rugged terrain and poor roads posed a major challenge because overland transport was still expensive. Unit transport costs decreased after the 1840s with the construction of the rail networks, thus encouraging intracountry and interregional trade.[7] Besides, the implementation of liberal policies and institutional reforms brought about the elimination of other internal barriers.[8] As a result, the integration of the national markets was well under way or close to completion by the end of the nineteenth century or the turn of the twentieth century. In addition, the second half of the nineteenth century saw the gradual substitution of sailing ships with steam-powered navigation, which led to a considerable reduction in ocean transport costs (Mohammed and Williamson 2004) and voyage times, establishing communication with large areas of the world in the process. Finally, added to all this was the decrease in the costs of exchanging information due to the arrival of the telegraph and the telephone.

As regards all these aspects, it should be pointed out that market integration has normally been measured by comparing the differences in prices between markets, i.e., studying the rate by which these differences became smaller as suggested by the "law of one price" and the speed of the return to equilibrium after a shock. Various methods have been used in the field of economic history to study the degree and evolution of market integration. These range from analyzing standard deviation to cointegration analysis normally applied to cereal prices. Whatever the methodology, most research shows that the economic integration processes in European countries were reaching completion in the nineteenth century, mainly after the Napoleonic Wars (Federico and Persson 2010; Federico 2010; Chilosi et al. 2013). A high degree of integration could already be seen early in the century, for example in Great Britain (Shiue and Keller 2007; Jacks 2011), in France in the first half of the century (Erjnaes and Persson 2000), and in Italy before 1880 (Federico 2007). In other cases market integration arrived later, as in Germany, Austria-Hungary, and Spain (Uebele 2013). The nineteenth century is also seen as a key moment for the integration of international markets, mainly those of the Atlantic economy. Although the last quarter of the century, from 1870 onwards, has been considered a time of great importance in some cases (Harley 1988; O'Rourke 1997), other investigations point to the advances made before that date, in the first half of the century (Jacks 2005; Federico and Persson 2007; Uebele 2013) or even before (Sharp and Weisdorf 2013).

Partly due to this decrease in trade costs from at least the beginning of the nineteenth century until World War I, i.e., during the first globalization, there was a substantial reduction in the cost of moving goods between countries, and of moving people, capital, and information. These years also saw the arrival of a second wave of technologies and new energy sources such as electric power, which triggered a technological advance in various sectors (e.g., iron and steel, chemicals, and automotive). In these technologically more advanced sectors, production took place in increasingly bigger plants and factories. The introduction of mass production and assembly lines thus strengthened the existence of increasing returns to scale in a context of sharply falling transport costs.

At this time there was also a push towards greater economic liberalization that resulted in lower tariffs (O'Rourke 2000). However, this reduction in tariffs was not maintained over time due to the fact that every country in Europe was following different trade policies – including, for example, protectionist policies to help nascent industry or to support local producers against the invasion of cereals from the New World in the closing decades of the century. It was also at this time and in this context, in the opening decades of the twentieth century, that the United States overtook Great Britain as the principal industrial and economic power in the world.

Although the spread of new technologies continued between World War I and World War II, it took place in the context of a disintegrating world economy. During the globalization backlash of the interwar years, tariffs were increased, more international capital controls were introduced, and the fall in trade costs was halted. In other words, the advance of both internal and external market integration stopped. Nevertheless, once World War II was over, the reconstruction planned under the 1944 Bretton Woods Agreement promoted – among other things – trade liberalization through the introduction of the General Agreement on Tariffs and Trade (GATT) and laid the basis upon which greater integration of the world economy was achieved in the decades that followed (O'Rourke 2002; Federico and Persson 2007). Along with tariff reductions and the appearance of the first regional trade agreements between groups of countries, transport costs again fell. This came about due to the continuing decrease in shipping costs and the widespread use of containers. It was also helped by advances made in land transport, which involved road improvements, more motorways, and the widespread use of haulage trucks. Finally, it should be mentioned that air transport was also progressing. All these improvements meant not only lower transport costs but also, and just as important, less time needed to transport goods both within and between countries (Hummels 2001).

Over recent years the increasingly globalized world economy has undergone notable changes, many in connection with advances in information and communication technologies (ICTs), which have revolutionized the technology and altered the organization of industry and its relative importance in the production structure of societies. The most advanced economies have experienced a process of tertiarization and their production structure today generally sees around two-thirds of the active population employed in the services sector. The sidelining of traditional industry in western economies is in part connected to a delocalization process set in motion by companies that affects certain stages of production activity, which have been transferred to countries on the periphery in search of lower labour costs. The result of this is that an increasing number of areas of the planet, especially in southeastern Asia, have undergone recent industrialization processes that have enabled – and are enabling – them to fully participate in modern economic growth, as European economies did as far back as two centuries ago but this time in the context of a more integrated world economy.

Industrial location, economic geography, and economic history

Various historical studies have undertaken long-term analyses of the geographical distribution of manufacturing using the new economic geography framework. Most have examined either industrialization as a whole or one or more of its stages, which from the nineteenth century took place accompanied by a rapid decrease in transport costs, integration of the national economies, and integration of the international markets (globalization). In this section, we present some of the studies that have sought to analyze the geographical distribution of industry over time and its determinants. The review is necessarily incomplete and limited to regional analyses, partly due to lack of space and partly due to the fact that there have been a great many investigations into the subject in recent years.

One study that has aimed to provide a comprehensive picture of the relationship between globalization and history over the last two centuries is that by Crafts and Venables (2003). The starting point for these authors is the economic geography model developed by Krugman and Venables (1995) based on economies of scale and linkage effects. They go on to explain the main changes affecting the location of industry on an international scale since the beginning of the nineteenth century. To do this, they divide the period into three stages. The first of these is characterized by an increased concentration of industry worldwide. In the years of the Industrial Revolution, industrialization in Great Britain and Western Europe was accompanied by the deindustrialization of other areas that had been prominent as product manufacturers, mainly India and China. The second stage, which they situate during the first globalization between the mid-nineteenth century and World War I, saw the dispersion of industry mainly towards the United States, which became the main industrial and economic power in the world.[9] Dispersion continues in the third and final stage, which covers from the mid-twentieth century until the present. In this case, economic integration, trade openness, and wage differentials would explain the current industrial progress of Southeast Asia. Thus, over the course of the three stages we see – broadly speaking – a reproduction of the non-monotonic relationship between market integration and the location of industry predicted in Krugman and Venables (1995) and Venables (1996).

Most research from an economic geography perspective has focused on analyzing individual countries. One of the economies that has received the most attention is the United States. Since colonial times and its independence in 1776, the United States has had to make an enormous effort to achieve integration of its vast internal market, which spread remarkably quickly from coast to coast.[10] In these special circumstances of frontier expansion, Kim and Margo (2004) put forward a historical view of US industry from the perspective of economic geography as evolving over the long term in line with the gradual integration of the domestic market. Broadly speaking, they review the main historical stages, noting that in colonial times the differences in industrial structures in the US economy (still limited to the East Coast) were small. However, from the early decades of the nineteenth century these industrial structures began to diverge, especially with the industrialization of the Northeast. These differences within the United States intensified notably during the postbellum period in the second half of the nineteenth century, with the formation of the manufacturing belt. Nevertheless, in the course of the twentieth century and especially after World War II, there was convergence in regional production structures. In other words, the initial increase in the spatial concentration of industry was followed by a dispersion that continued throughout the twentieth century.

Other investigations have studied these matters in detail, checking the relevance of explanations based on comparative advantage (Heckscher-Ohlin) and increasing returns (new economic geography) for US industry. Kim's (1995) pioneering work examined long-term trends in the location of manufacturing in the United States. First it showed that, despite a slight dip in the second half of the nineteenth century, the long-term dynamics followed a bell-shaped curve for the spatial concentration of industry during the long industrialization process, which peaked in the 1920s.[11] Nevertheless, Crafts and Klein (2017) used a wide range of indicators to perform a detailed analysis of the long-term evolution of industry location in the United States since 1880. This led them to question the long-term picture drawn by Kim (1995) of an inverted U-shape depicting geographical concentration and to support the idea of a steady decline since the start of the twentieth century.

Kim's (1995) next step was to identify its determinants. The results showed that, along interregional differences in resource endowments, economies of scale had a significant impact on spatial distribution of US industry, which meant evidence in support of the new economic geography. Adopting an alternative approach based on Midelfart-Knarvik et al. (2000), Klein and Crafts (2012) focused on the period between 1880 and 1920. For these authors, the emergence and consolidation of the US manufacturing belt over these years was particularly linked to the interaction of the forces underlined by the new economic geography. Of the six interactions considered, only one of the three involving Heckscher-Ohlin (HO) factor endowments was significant – that relating agricultural employment to industries that made extensive use of agricultural inputs – and even then, only prior to 1900. The interactions that captured the skill level of the workforce and coal abundance were not statistically significant. However, all three new economic geography interactions involving market potential showed a significant impact as determinants of industrial location. The interaction with economies of scale (Krugman 1991) appeared as a decisive factor throughout the period and was gradually joined by the intensity of sales to industry and the intensity of use of intermediate input (Krugman and Venables 1995; Venables 1996), the combined effect of which in 1920 was greater than that of all the other variables.

As a pioneer of industry and the birthplace of the Industrial Revolution, Great Britain has also received a great deal of attention. Crafts and Mulatu (2005, 2006) focused on the location of industry there between 1871 and 1931, a period marked by a sharp fall in transport costs, by estimating an equation based on Midelfart-Knarvik et al. (2000). The coefficients of the interactions linked to factor endowments corroborated the importance of Heckscher-Ohlin elements when explaining the location pattern of British industry in this period, the determinants being the traditional variables of factor endowments (agriculture, human capital, and coal abundance). However, these forces were accentuated by the new economic geography forces, as the interaction between market potential and economies of scale (Krugman 1991) was also a significant variable, whereas the linkage effects were not significant. However, the scale effects weakened over time and had ceased to be significant by the observation for 1931.

Crafts and Wolf (2014) analyzed the distribution of the cotton textile industry in Great Britain in 1838, which after the early years of the Industrial Revolution had become massively concentrated in the county of Lancashire. Among the reasons for this spatial concentration, in this case at a sector level, the authors included fundamental geographical aspects linked to climate and orography along with aspects of comparative advantage and economic geography, while also taking into account the importance of path dependence. They concluded that a combination of various aspects together influenced the location of the British cotton textile industry, leading to it becoming established mainly in Lancashire. It was important to have a location with waterpower available that featured rugged terrain and proximity to ports. Another contributing factor was the availability of cheap coal, plus the greater potential of the Lancashire market along the lines suggested by the new economic geography. Finally, the legacy of history was also important, in that the region had a textile tradition and a reputation for inventiveness, and there was also the existence of sunk costs, e.g., investments in hydraulic energy, which paved the way for the steam engines that would follow.[12]

For mainland Europe, Combes et al. (2011) provided a long-term perspective of the location of industrial activity in France at the territorial level of *départements* (NUTS3). They showed that the decrease in transport costs from the mid-nineteenth century led to a bell-shaped evolution in the spatial distribution of activity in the manufacturing and services sectors. This underwent greater concentration between 1860 and 1930 before dispersing between 1930 and 2000. They also found evidence of an agglomeration effect in the French economy during the same period. The intensification of economic density led to an increase in labour productivity in both manufacturing and services. During the period 1860–1930, this agglomeration effect was linked to market potential, while between 1930 and 2000 it was explained by the differences in educational attainment recorded by the *départements*. The parameters estimated in the study suggested that the doubling of employment density in a French *département* would result in labour productivity gains of around 5%. The results of this long-term analysis are in line with those in the pioneering studies by Ciccone and Hall (1996) and Ciccone (2002) for the United States and the European Union respectively.

However, it is not only the countries that led industrialization in Europe that have received attention. A'Hearn and Venables (2012) studied the long-term picture in Italy from the viewpoint of economic geography. Since the beginning of industrialization at the end of the nineteenth century, Italian industry has tended to concentrate in the north of the country, and this is one of the reasons behind the traditional North–South divide. The authors began by considering the three determining factors of industrial location: natural advantages (e.g., water supply, mineral deposits, climate, and orography), access to the domestic market, and access to the foreign market. They concluded that each of these factors was important – sequentially over time – in each of the three historical stages into which they divided their long-term analysis. And in all of these, the North always benefitted most.

Hence at the time of unification, when industry was a minority sector and still traditional and the domestic market was not fully integrated, the North had an advantage in its endowment of water. This favoured higher production in agriculture that resulted in greater population density, i.e., greater market size. During the second stage, which began in the final decades of the nineteenth century, progress was made in the integration of the domestic market. Meanwhile, the advance of the Italian economy had come about in a relatively closed environment since 1878, and in such a context a key factor for industry location in Italy was access to this domestic market. Because the market was bigger in the North, this was the area that attracted and concentrated industry, mainly textiles, shipbuilding and – in the twentieth century and still under the protectionist umbrella – engineering activities (steel and mechanical). It was at this time that the Genoa-Milan-Turin industrial triangle was consolidated. After the 1950s with the opening of the Italian economy to the exterior and the process of European integration, the potential of the external market, as interpreted by these authors, began to play a predominant role in determining industrial location. And once again, the North benefitted more than the South due to its proximity to the rich markets of central and northern Europe.

Daniele et al. (2018) further analyzed this issue, focusing on the period from 1871 to 2011 at the provincial level. First, they showed that, in line with the new economic geography model predictions, the geographical concentration of manufacturing in Italy followed an inverted U-curve over time, steadily increasing until 1961 and decreasing thereafter. They then showed that both total market potential and domestic market potential were key elements in modulating the regional distribution of industry from at least the 1910s.[13] For the previous period from 1871 to 1911, Basile and Ciccarelli (2018) found a positive market potential effect as an explanatory element for the concentration of manufacturing, although they did point out that comparative advantage also played an important role as regards both water abundance and a wider pool of human capital (literacy). Missiaia (see Chapter 5 of this volume) also found that these factor endowments had an important impact, and added the interaction between domestic market potential and economies of scale.

Another set of articles has analyzed the evolution and determinants of the economic geography of Spain from the very beginning of its industrialization process. Following the line of analysis proposed by Davis and Weinstein (1999, 2003), Rosés (2003) identified the existence of a "home market effect" around the mid-nineteenth century. He concluded that during the rise of Catalonia as a centre of industrial production, two types of basic explanatory elements came together: factor endowments, in connection with the availability of human capital, and home market size, which resulted in advantages for the location of manufacturing around Barcelona. Tirado et al. (2002) focused on the second half of the century and carried out an analysis of the explanatory factors of spatial concentration of Spanish industry in line with Kim (1995). They identified economies of scale and market size as determinants of Spanish industrial geography in 1856. Besides, at the end of the century, factor endowments (in this case the accumulation of human capital) also contributed to explaining industrial location, while at the same time new economic geography elements (economies of scale and market access) increased their explanatory power with the advance of the economic integration process.

Taken together, these studies suggest that agglomeration forces were already present in Spain by the second half of the nineteenth century and that they grew stronger as time passed, maintaining much of their impact into the interwar years. Adopting the approach developed by Midelfart-Knarvik et al. (2000, 2002), Martinez-Galarraga (2012) confirmed the previous findings for the period 1856–1929. As the domestic market became integrated and industrialization continued, new economic geography forces grew to be the main explicative factor of Spain's industrial landscape, determining that industries with increasing returns tended to concentrate in provinces with better access to demand up to the 1930s. In a somewhat similar line of analysis, Martinez-Galarraga et al. (2008) provided evidence of the existence of an "agglomeration effect" linking the spatial density of economic activity and interregional differences in industrial labour productivity for the period 1860–1999. In line with Ciccone and Hall (1996) and Ciccone (2002), the study showed that the estimated elasticity of employment density with respect to labour productivity – which is how the agglomeration effect has been defined – was already playing a key role from the mid-nineteenth century, i.e., during the early stages of industrialization.[14] However, its evolution presents a progressive decline over time and, in the final period they consider (1985–1999), the agglomeration effect is no longer significant.[15]

2.4 Conclusions

The world is a very unequal place. One of the key questions traditionally posed in economic history concerns how we arrived at this situation, marked by huge differences in per capita income between countries. Why are rich countries rich? Why are poor countries poor, and why do they stay poor? The usual answer to these questions, though complex and taking into account multiple causes and explanations, has looked for the origins of this inequality in the beginnings of industrialization in the nineteenth century. Industrialization, with its increasing returns and economies of scale, does not take place at the same rate and at the same time in every country, and neither does it in all the regions of the same country.

In this respect, we have shown in the course of this chapter how the new economic geography literature makes it possible to identify a number of elements that are essential for understanding this reality. This line of research provides an economic foundation for the existence of a relationship between the economic development processes and the advance of production sectors characterized by the presence of economies of scale (i.e., manufacturing), market integration, and the genesis of an unequal distribution of economic activity across the territory. The new economic geography literature thus considers that the inequality that today characterizes the most developed economies has its roots in the early stages of their economic development processes, brought about almost 200 years ago by the technological change typical of the first and second Industrial Revolutions and the integration of the national and international markets.

All this has shown how studying the industrialization processes from a historical perspective using an economic geography framework is essential in order to verify the hypotheses deriving from this type of modelling and to understand some of the explanatory elements of territorial inequality thus generated. In other words, in the course of these pages we have aimed to show how the connection between economic history and economic geography contributes not only to a better understanding of the geography of the historical industrialization processes, but also to the identification of the elements that explain the current unequal economic geography of the world. We should learn from the lessons of history.

Notes

1 Unlike the assumption made by "... *Gerschenkron, Kuznets, and others, that countries within their political boundaries are the only units within which it is worthwhile to consider the process of industrialisation*" (Pollard 1981: vii).

2 By assuming that regions are symmetric, the new economic geography does not take primary geographical elements into account, and therefore the theory does not establish which region will become the industrialized core and which the periphery.

3 Along this externality, Marshall (1890) noted a further two: informational spillovers and the formation of a skilled labour market.

4 Unlike new trade theory, the new economic geography literature can explain the mechanisms whereby sizeable differences can be generated in regions' productive structures and income levels, even when these regions present similar factor endowments. What makes the new economic geography models attractive is the fact that the cost parameters and level of demand are endogenous and vary between locations as they depend on location decisions taken by all the agents. This distinguishes these models from those of international trade with imperfect competition, in which the location of the factors of production is given and fixed (exogenous). Combes et al. (2008: 47).

5 A recent full survey of the "gains of market integration" seen from the viewpoint of trade theory can be found in Donaldson (2015).

6 In a recent work, Allen (2009) stressed the importance of the spread of international trade throughout the eighteenth century in connection with the increase in size of British towns and cities. In addition, in the port cities in which the new activities linked to trade (transport, finance, insurance . . .) were concentrated, there was an increase in wage levels. Thus, by overcoming the Malthusian trap, Great Britain became an economy with large urban agglomerations (i.e., a large market size) and high wages.

7 Transport costs, a key element in the evolution of agglomeration in new economic geography models, have experienced sizeable changes since the application of macro-inventions like steam power to transportation. A recent survey from an economic history viewpoint can be found in Bogart (2019).
8 A paradigmatic example would be the Zollverein customs union in Germany in the 1830s (Ploeckl 2015).
9 The way the United States overtook Great Britain at the start of the twentieth century is difficult to explain using the neoclassical models, which predict catch-up but not overtaking. In this respect, Crafts and Venables (2003) nevertheless point to the importance of migrations and tariff policies.
10 An abundant literature has analyzed the integration of the domestic market in the United States, focusing especially on improvements stemming from the construction of the railways, from Fogel's (1964) pioneering work up to more recent contributions such as Donaldson and Hornbeck (2016).
11 Together with the United States, another case study that stands out for the quality of its historical regional data is Japan. In the early nineteenth century, manufacturing activities were scattered across the territory. While the spatial concentration of manufacturing activities in the largest cities (e.g., Tokyo, Nagoya, Osaka) came about at the turn of the twentieth century, it took longer to spread to other regions. Thus, the Japanese experience also shows a bell-shaped evolution in the concentration of manufacturing over time, as explained in Chapter 8 in this volume.
12 See also Ronsse and Rayp (2016) for the case of Belgium in the first half of the twentieth century. Other investigations have explored cases in Eastern Europe in the context of the border changes that came about after World War I. The reunification of Poland, which until then had been partitioned between Austria-Hungary, Prussia, and Russia, and the creation of Yugoslavia through the unification of former Austro-Hungarian territories and the Kingdom of Serbia with Montenegro, called for the integration of new domestic markets. In the context of this shock, the cases of both Poland (Wolf 2007) and Yugoslavia (Nikolic 2018) in the interwar years are particularly suitable for testing the theoretical predictions of the new economic geography literature.
13 They measured market potential using distances as the crow flies. A more detailed study of transport costs from an economic history perspective, i.e., taking into account the transport network, the various means of transport, and their different freight, can be found in Crafts (2005) and Martinez-Galarraga (2014).
14 This hypothesis is confirmed by Díez-Minguela et al. (2016), who, following an alternative empirical strategy based on a Barro-style empirical analysis (Brülhart and Sbergami 2009), stress the importance of agglomeration economies in the manufacturing sector between 1870 and 1930.
15 Other studies have focused on the existence of backward linkages in Spain's industry over time verifying the wage equation (Paluzie et al. 2009b; Tirado et al. 2013), and have also tested the existence of the forward linkage, i.e., the relationship between market potential and migrations (Pons et al. 2007; Paluzie et al. 2009a).

References

A'Hearn, B., and A. J. Venables. 2012. "Regional disparities: internal geography and external trade." In *Oxford handbook of the Italian economy, 1861–1911*, edited by G. Toniolo, 599–630. Oxford: Oxford University Press.

Allen, R. C. 2009. *The British industrial revolution in global perspective*. Cambridge: Cambridge University Press.

Basile, R., and C. Ciccarelli. 2018. "The location of the Italian manufacturing industry, 1871–1911: a sectoral analysis." *Journal of Economic Geography* 18(3): 627–661.
Bogart, D. 2019. "Clio on speed: a survey of economic history research on transport." In *Handbook of cliometrics*, edited by C. Diebolt and M. Haupert, 1–26. Heidelberg, Springer.
Brülhart, M., and F. Sbergami. 2009. "Agglomeration and growth: cross-country evidence." *Journal of Urban Economics* 65(1): 48–63.
Chilosi, D., T. E. Murphy, R. Studer, and A. Coskun Tunçer. 2013. "Europe's many integrations: geography and grain markets, 1620–1913." *Explorations in Economic History* 50(1): 46–68.
Ciccone, A. 2002. "Agglomeration effects in Europe." *European Economic Review* 46(2): 213–227.
Ciccone, A., and R. E. Hall. 1996. "Productivity and the density of economic activity." *American Economic Review* 86(1): 54–70.
Combes, P. P., M. Lafourcade, J. F. Thisse, and J. C. Toutain. 2011. "The rise and fall of spatial inequalities in France: a long-run perspective." *Explorations in Economic History* 48(2): 243–271.
Combes, P. P., T. Mayer, and J. F. Thisse. 2008. *Economic geography. The integration of regions and nations.* Princeton: Princeton University Press.
Crafts, N. 2005. "Market potential in British regions, 1871–1931." *Regional Studies* 39(9): 1159–1166.
Crafts, N., and A. Klein. 2017. *A long-run perspective on the spatial concentration of manufacturing industries in the United States.* CEPR Discussion Papers 12257.
Crafts, N., and A. Mulatu. 2005. "What explains the location of industry in Britain, 1871–1931?" *Journal of Economic Geography* 5(4): 499–518.
Crafts, N., and A. Mulatu. 2006. "How did the location of industry respond to falling transport costs in Britain before World War I?" *Journal of Economic History* 66(3): 575–607.
Crafts, N., and A. J. Venables. 2003. "Globalization in history: a geographical perspective." In *Globalization in historical perspective*, edited by M. D. Bordo, A. M. Taylor, and J. G. Williamson, x–y. Chicago: The University of Chicago Press.
Crafts, N., and N. Wolf. 2014. "The location of the UK cotton textiles industry in 1838: a quantative analysis." *Journal of Economic History* 74(4): 1103–1139.
Daniele, V., P. Malanima, and N. Ostuni. 2018. "Geography, market potential and industrialization in Italy 1871–2001." *Papers in Regional Science* 97(3): 639–662.
Davis, D. R., and D. E. Weinstein. 1999. "Economic geography and regional production structure: an empirical investigation." *European Economic Review* 43(2): 379–407.
Davis, D. R., and D. E. Weinstein. 2003. "Market access, economic geography and comparative advantage: an empirical test." *Journal of International Economics* 59(1), 1–23.
De Vries, J. 1984. *European urbanization 1500–1800.* London: Metheun.
Díez-Minguela, A., J. Martinez-Galarraga, and D. A. Tirado. 2016. "Why did Spanish regions not converge before the Civil War? Agglomeration economies and (regional) growth revisited." *Revista de Historia Económica/Journal of Iberian and Latin American Economic History* 34(3): 417–448.
Donaldson, D. 2015. "The gains from market integration." *Annual Review of Economics* 7: 619–647.

Donaldson, D., and R. Hornbeck. 2016. "Railroads and American economic growth: a 'market access' approach." *Quarterly Journal of Economics* 131(2): 799–858.

Erjnaes, M., and K. G. Persson. 2000. "Market integration and transport costs in France 1825–1903: a threshold error correction approach to the law of one price." *Explorations in Economic History* 37(2): 149–173.

Federico, G. 2007. "Market integration and market efficiency: the case of the 19th century Italy." *Explorations in Economic History* 44(2): 293–316.

Federico, G. 2010. "When did European markets integrate?" *European Review of Economic History* 15(1): 93–126.

Federico, G., and K. G. Persson. 2007. "Market integration and convergence in the world wheat market, 1800–2000." In *The new comparative economic history: essays in honor of Jeffrey G. Williamson*, edited by T. Hatton, K. H. O'Rourke, and A. M. Taylor, 87–114. Cambridge: MIT Press.

Federico, G., and K. G. Persson. 2010. *Market integration and convergence in the world wheat market, 1800–2000.* University of Copenhagen, Department of Economics Discussion Paper 06–10.

Fogel, R. W. 1964. *Railroads and American economic growth: essays in econometric history.* Baltimore: Johns Hopkins University Press.

Fujita, M., P. Krugman, and A. J. Venables. 1999. *The spatial economy: cities, regions, and international trade.* Cambridge: The MIT Press.

Harley, K. 1988. "Ocean freight rates and productivity, 1740–1913: the primacy of mechanical invention reaffirmed." *Journal of Economic History* 48(4): 851–876.

Hirschman, A. O. 1958. *The strategy of economic development.* New Haven: Yale University Press.

Hummels, D. 2001. *Time as a trade barrier.* GTAP Working Papers, 1152.

Jacks, D. S. 2005. "Intra- and international commodity market integration in the Atlantic economy, 1800–1913." *Explorations in Economic History* 42(3): 381–413.

Jacks, D. S. 2011. "Foreign wars, domestic markets: England, 1793–1815." *European Review of Economic History* 15(2): 277–311.

Kim, S. 1995. "Expansion of markets and the geographic distribution of economic activities: the trends in U.S. regional manufacturing structure, 1860–1987." *Quarterly Journal of Economics* 110(4): 881–908.

Kim, S., and R. A. Margo. 2004. "Historical perspectives on U.S. economic geography." In *Handbook of regional and urban economics*, Vol. 4, edited by J. V. Henderson and J. F. Thisse, 2981–3019. Amsterdam: Elsevier.

Klein, A., and N. Crafts. 2012. "Making sense of the manufacturing belt: determinants of U.S. industrial location, 1880–1920." *Journal of Economic Geography* 12(4): 775–807.

Krugman, P. 1991. "Increasing returns and economic geography." *Journal of Political Economy* 99(3): 483–499.

Krugman, P., and A. J. Venables. 1995. "Globalization and the inequality of nations." *Quarterly Journal of Economics* 110(4): 857–880.

Kuznets, S. 1966. *Modern economic growth: rate, structure, and spread.* New Haven: Yale University Press.

Kuznets, S. 1971. *Economic growth of nations: total output and production structure.* Cambridge: Harvard University Press.

Marshall, A. 1890. *Principles of economics.* London: Macmillan.

Martinez-Galarraga, J. 2012. "The determinants of industrial location in Spain, 1856–1929." *Explorations in Economic History* 49(2): 255–275.

Martinez-Galarraga, J. 2014. *Market potential estimates in history: a survey of methods and an application to Spain, 1867–1930.* EHES Working Papers in Economic History No. 51.

Martinez-Galarraga, J., E. Paluzie, J. Pons, and D. A. Tirado. 2008. "Agglomeration and labour productivity in Spain over the long term." *Cliometrica* 2(3): 195–212.

Midelfart-Knarvik, K. H., H. Overman, S. Redding, and A. J. Venables. 2002. "The location of European industry." In *European economy. European integration and the functioning of product markets*, edited by European Commission, 213–269. Brussels: Directorate-General for Economic and Financial Affairs.

Midelfart-Knarvik, K. H., H. Overman, and A. J. Venables. 2000. *Comparative advantage and economic geography: estimating the location of production in the EU.* CEPR Discussion Papers 2618.

Mohammed, D. and J. G. Williamson. 2004. "Freight rates and productivity gains in British tramp shipping 1869–1950." *Explorations in Economic History* 41(2): 172–203.

Myrdal, G. 1957. *Economic theory and under-developed regions.* London: Methuen & Co.

Nikolic, S. 2018. "Determinants of industrial location: kingdom of Yugoslavia in the interwar period." *European Review of Economic History* 22(1): 101–133.

O'Rourke, K. H. 1997. "The European grain inversion, 1870–1913." *Journal of Economic History* 57(4): 775–801.

O'Rourke, K. H. 2000. "Tariffs and growth in the late 19th century." *Economic Journal* 110(463): 456–483.

O'Rourke, K. H. 2002. "Europe and the causes of globalization, 1790 to 2000. In *From europeanization of the globe to the globalization of Europe*, edited by H. Kierzkowski, 64–86. London: Palgrave.

Paluzie, E., J. Pons, J. Silvestre, and D. A. Tirado. 2009a. "Migrants and market potential in Spain over the twentieth century: a test of the new economic geography." *Spanish Economic Review* 11(4): 243–265.

Paluzie, E., J. Pons, and D. A. Tirado. 2009b. "A test of the market potential equation in Spain." *Applied Economics* 41(12): 1487–1493.

Ploeckl, F. 2015. "The Zollverein and the sequence of a customs union." *Australian Economic History Review* 5(3): 277–300.

Pollard, S. 1981. *Peaceful conquest: the industrialization of Europe, 1760–1970.* Oxford: Oxford University Press.

Pons, J., E. Paluzie, J. Silvestre, and D. A. Tirado. 2007. "Testing the new economic geography: migrations and industrial agglomerations in Spain." *Journal of Regional Science* 47(2): 289–313.

Ronsse, S., and G. Rayp. 2016. "What determined the location of industry in Belgium, 1896–1961?" *Journal of Interdisciplinary History* 46(3): 393–419.

Rosés, J. R. 2003. "Why isn't the whole of Spain industrialized? New economic geography and early industrialization, 1797–1910." *Journal of Economic History* 63(4): 995–1022.

Sharp, P., and J. Weisdorf. 2013. "Globalization revisited: market integration and the wheat trade between North America and Britain from the eighteenth century." *Explorations in Economic History* 50(1): 88–98.

Shiue, C. H., and W. Keller. 2007. "Markets in China and Europe on the eve of the industrial revolution." *American Economic Review* 97(4): 1189–1216.

Tirado, D. A., E. Paluzie, and J. Pons. 2002. "Economic integration and industrial location: the case of Spain before World War I." *Journal of Economic Geography* 2(3): 343–363.

Tirado, D. A., J. Pons, E. Paluzie, and J. Martinez-Galarraga. 2013. "Trade policy and wage gradients: evidence from a protectionist turn." *Cliometrica* 7(3), 295–318.
Uebele, M. 2013. "What drives commodity market integration? Evidence from the 1800s." *CESifo Economic Studies* 59(2): 412–442.
Venables, A. J. 1996. "Equilibrium locations of vertically linked industries." *International Economic Review* 37(2): 341–359.
Williamson, J. G. 1965. "Regional inequality and the process of national development: a description of the patterns." *Economic Development and Cultural Change* 13(4, Part II): 84.
Wolf, N. 2007. "Endowment vs. market potential: what explains the relocation of industry after polish reunification in 1918?" *Explorations in Economic History* 44(1): 22–42.

Part I

Regional industrialization in Europe

3 Regional industrialization in Belgium and the Netherlands[1]

Robin C. M. Philips and Erik Buyst

3.1 Introduction

In 1815, the Congress of Vienna combined the Netherlands and Belgium into one state named the United Kingdom of the Netherlands. Both constituent areas had quite a different backstory, however, which eventually contributed to the Belgian secession in 1830. The Netherlands inherited an advanced economy from the Dutch Golden Age of the seventeenth century: in per capita income, it had only been surpassed by Britain. Belgium, on the contrary, recovered only slowly from the dislocations of the wars of Louis XIV. At the beginning of the nineteenth century, gross domestic product per capita in Belgium was about one-third lower than that of its northern neighbour. Nevertheless, it was Belgium that became the second industrializer after Britain, while the Netherlands fell behind its southern neighbour for the rest of the nineteenth century (Mokyr 1976). To a certain extent, the publications in the Low Countries over the last decades reflect the relative importance of the Industrial Revolution in both countries; whereas the industry sector in Belgium has been the subject of many monographs (e.g. Olyslager 1947; De Brabander 1983, 1984; Pluymers 1992; Wautelet 1995), publications in the Netherlands are somewhat less abundant (e.g. De Jonge 1968; Jansen 1999; De Jong 1999).

If we compare the employment structure of Belgium and the Netherlands (see Figure 3.1), we immediately notice that industrial activities continued to take a relatively larger share in the economy of Belgium than that of the Netherlands throughout the 1820–2010 period, although the Netherlands overtook Belgium in absolute employment numbers during the 1990s. Instead, the labour structure in the Netherlands focused more on commerce, a tradition they had held since the early modern period, and on agriculture, most prominently dairy (De Jong and Van Zanden 2014: 95–96). In contrast, the Belgian labour structure started out with a significant larger industry sector in 1820 due to its strong focus on mining and textiles production. Nonetheless, both the Netherlands and Belgium experienced increasing employment in industry during the nineteenth century, continuing in the first half of the twentieth century,

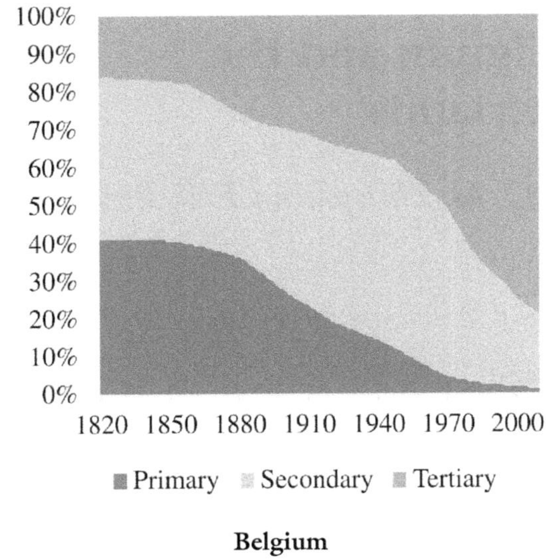

Figure 3.1 Employment in Belgium and the Netherlands, by sector (1820–2010)

Source: For Belgium, we used the censuses of Population of 1846–1991, supplemented with the labour structure in 1819 as estimated by Buyst (forthcoming) and the statistics of the RSZ and RSVZ for 2000 and 2010. For the Netherlands, we used the Centraal Bureau voor Statistiek (CBS) statistics (2001) and the LISA dataset.

a period in which the Netherlands saw the rapid expansion of its industry base. An absolute peak was reached in the 1950s for Belgium and in the 1960s for the Netherlands, followed by a deindustrialization process that continues even today.

Although these national patterns of industrialization have been thoroughly studied, this is far less the case for the regional dimension (e.g. De Brabander 1983, 1984). Yet, starting in the 1980s, scholars started stressing that the rate and timing of industrialization not only differed between countries, but even more across regions within the same country. For instance, O'Brien (1986: 297) argued that "industrialization [. . .] was a regional and not a national process", and Sidney Pollard (1981: VII) noted that "this [industrialization] process is essentially one of regions". Subsequently, since the late 1990s, spatial patterns have increasingly come to the forefront in studies on industrialization (e.g. Kim 1995; Crafts and Mulatu 2005; Missiaia 2019). Notwithstanding this change in the international research agenda, a systematic account of the location of industry throughout the nineteenth and twentieth centuries has been lacking for the Low Countries. Nonetheless, anecdotal evidence about the relevance of these regional processes exists. In Belgium, the social and political alienation between the northern Dutch-speaking

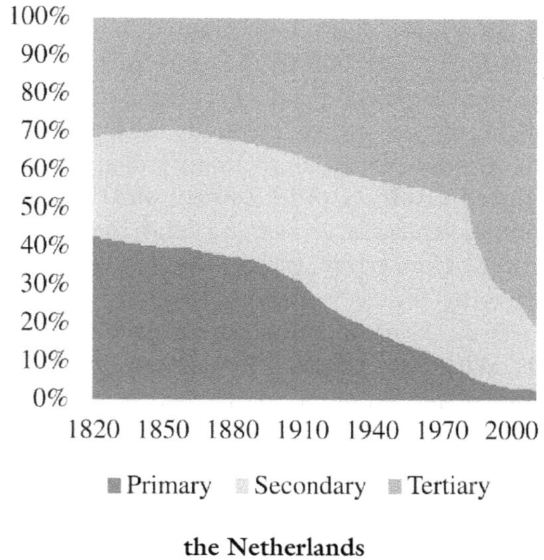

Figure 3.1 (Continued)

and southern French-speaking populations poses an important friction in the country. Similarly, in the Netherlands, the view that the Dutch western regions, or *Randstad*, benefit disproportionally from political attention is a popular and longstanding belief.

Therefore, in this chapter, we explore the regional dimension behind the industrialization process in both countries. For a long time, such an exploration was hindered by the absence of a standardized dataset. Therefore, we draw upon a recently constructed dataset by Philips (2020), which allows us to reconstruct the location of industrial activities on the provincial or NUTS-2 level (Nomenclature of Territorial Units for Statistics) for the 1820–1850 period and the municipal or LAU (Local Administrative Units) level for the 1850–2010 period. We do not exclusively look at the manufacturing sectors, defined as sectors 10–33 in the ISIC (International Standard Industrial Classification of All Economic Activities) classification, but – due to the frequently stressed importance of coal and other natural resources in the early industrialization process (e.g. Allen 2009; Wrigley 2010) – also at the mining and quarrying sectors (sectors 05–09 in the ISIC classification). In section 3.2, we briefly present the aggregate trends in industrialization in both countries. In sections 3.3–3.5, we shed light on the regional dimension of these trends in industrial development in the Low Countries, in which we differentiate across three time periods. Finally, we end with a brief conclusion in section 3.6.

3.2 Aggregate patterns of industrial development

In 1820, based on Figure 3.2, both countries started with a significantly different industry mix before the start of the Industrial Revolution. The Netherlands inherited from its seventeenth-century Golden Age an advanced and highly diversified economy with a broad industry mix, oriented towards its trade facilities to import commodities from abroad and export processed products (Van Zanden and Van Riel 2004). Most notably, shipbuilding, tobacco processing, and foodstuffs such as sugar and grain benefitted. Conversely, the production of textiles and wearing apparel dominated the industry mix in Belgium, depending heavily on small-scale linen sweatshops and domestic-grown flax production (Vandenbroeke 1979). With the Industrial Revolution, mining of coal and iron ore grew exponentially in Belgium, providing the inputs for the production of basic metals and finished goods, such as mechanic pumps and steam engines.

During the nineteenth and early twentieth centuries, although both countries embarked on a path of technological progress and labour productivity increased, the more "traditional" sectors continued to dominate the industry mix. So did the production of foodstuffs in the Netherlands, and the production of coal and metal goods in Belgium, remain the largest sectors. After the mid-twentieth century, the "traditional" textiles and metal industries were hit by a process of automation and delocalization, first to other regions within Europe and later to other regions in the world. Belgium was hit the hardest by the deindustrialization process, with its larger manufacturing base and its focus on mining and textiles production. Simultaneously, a rise of new manufacturing activities occurred, with increasing production in electrical equipment, rubber, and plastics. Whereas Belgium specialized relatively more in the production of motor vehicles, pharmaceuticals, and chemicals, the Netherlands specialized in the production of computers, machinery, and other equipment. In this process, the Netherlands proved more able to attract these new manufacturing sectors compared to Belgium, in part due to the growth of several large Dutch multinationals, as well as a strong government-led policy of industrial expansion during the 1950s and 1960s (Atzema and Wever 1994).

Yet, when looking at the distribution of industrial activities on the macro-regional level (NUTS-1 level) in Table 3.1, we find that this evidence already highlights substantial differences across regions. In Belgium, the balance shifted from the northern Flemish side to the southern Walloon side during the 1820–1930 period. After 1930, due to the closure of the coal mines and a relocation of many metal factories out of Wallonia, we see the balance shifting back to its northern half, although the entire country suffered heavily from deindustrialization. In the Netherlands, we notice a more stable pattern, in which the

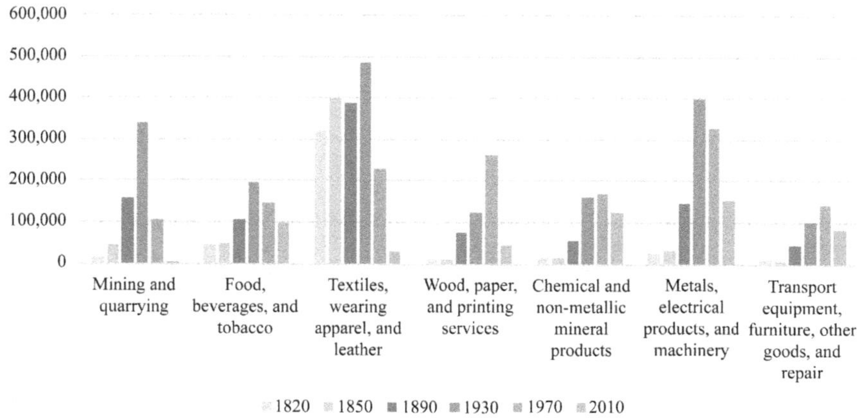

Belgium

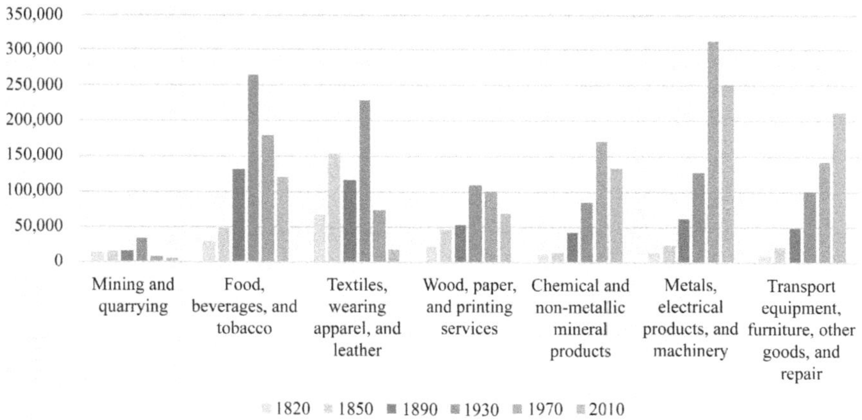

the Netherlands

Figure 3.2 Employment in Belgium and the Netherlands, by mining and manufacturing sectors

Source: See Philips (2020)

western regions – the most urbanized, prosperous part of the country since the early modern times (e.g. De Vries 1974) – encompassed the Dutch industrial heartland. However, a reversal of fortune took place among the more peripheral regions, with the northern regions losing ground during the nineteenth century

Table 3.1 Employment in the mining and manufacturing sectors in Belgium and the Netherlands, over macro-regions (NUTS1)

	1820	*1850*	*1890*	*1930*	*1970*	*2010*
Flanders	326,764	324,083	357,986	718,287	790,328	336,415
Brussels-Capital*	10,177	29,501	110,474	287,749	230,100	84,567
Wallonia	112,496	214,482	515,794	803,052	363,079	120,525
Belgium total	**449,437**	**568,066**	**984,254**	**1,809,088**	**1,383,507**	**541,507**
Northern Netherlands	31,041	65,961	37,759	118,589	99,936	93,585
Eastern Netherlands	32,608	57,585	90,922	185,350	193,552	184,491
Southern Netherlands	29,484	58,922	101,434	188,228	284,231	254,130
Western Netherlands	80,066	148,762	242,867	457,958	408,199	278,206
The Netherlands total	**173,199**	**331,230**	**472,982**	**950,125**	**985,918**	**810,412**

Source: See Philips (2020)

Note: *As the industry census of 1820 only reported the location of industry on the NUTS-2 region of Brabant (which is subdivided over the NUTS-1 regions of Flanders, Wallonia, and the Brussels-Capital region), we used the 1850 distribution of the employment in the Brabant province over the three NUTS-1 regions (32.69% for Flanders, 53.51% for Brussels-Capital and 13.80% for Wallonia) to subdivide the 1820 employment number of Brabant.

and, only afterwards, a similar pattern of relative decline unfolding in the eastern part of the country.

In order to study these regional patterns in greater detail, we differentiate in the next three sections across three time periods: the Industrial Revolution (1820–1870), a phase of industrial maturity (1870–1960), and the post-industrial phase (1960–2010).

3.3 The Industrial Revolution (ca. 1820–1870)

In 1820, Belgium had already taken a substantial lead over the Netherlands in terms of industrialization (see Table 3.1). Likewise, in terms of steam engines, Belgium counted 313 steam engines in the mining and manufacturing sectors in 1820, whereas merely thirteen steam engines had been installed in the Netherlands. Following the studies of Mokyr (1974, 1976), many scholars used the comparison of early industrializing Belgium and the "industrial retardation" in the Netherlands (Griffiths 1979) to investigate the causes of the Industrial Revolution (e.g. Bos 1979; Lintsen and Steenaard 1991). However, based on Figure 3.3, one might wonder whether this juxtaposition is correct. Both in employment as in number of steam engines, the Belgian lead in 1820

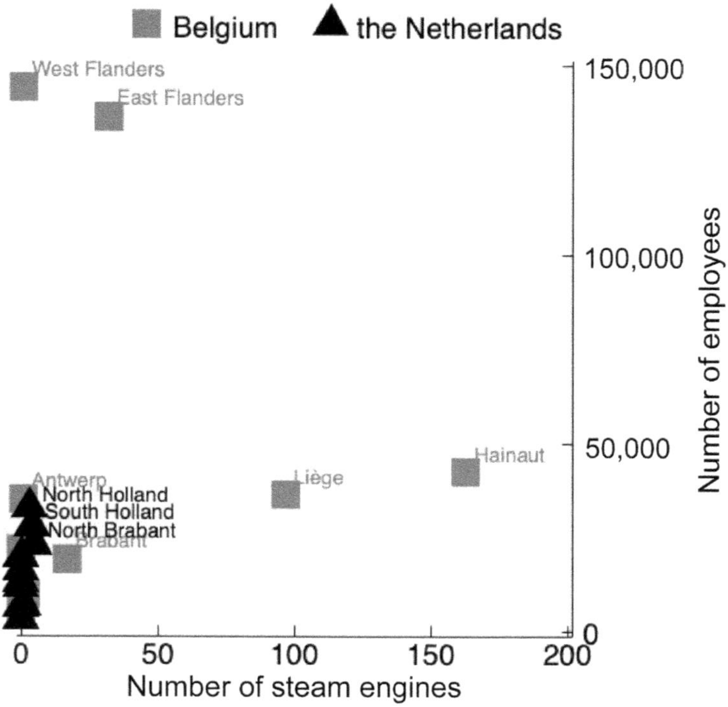

1820

Figure 3.3 Employment and steam engines in Belgium and the Netherlands, 1820–1850

Source: For 1820 employment numbers, we used Brugmans (1956). For 1850 employment numbers, we turned for Belgium to the 1846 industry census and for the Netherlands to the 1859 report of the Nederlandsche Maatschappij ter bevordering van Nijverheid. For the number of steam engines in Belgium, we turned to Van Neck (1979) for 1820 and the 1846 industry census. For the number of steam engines in the Netherlands, we turned to Steenaard (1989) and various surveys of the Dutch ministry of manufacturing in 1851.

had a significant regional component. It was not Belgium in its totality where mechanization had taken place by 1820, rather only in a much smaller geographical area – the Hainaut and Liège provinces. In this limited geographical area – not surprisingly, the coal-producing regions – almost 80% of all steam engines in the Low Countries had been installed by 1820, thus not only far surpassing all Dutch provinces but the other provinces in Belgium as well. By 1850, a catching-up process had started in terms of steam engines, with the Belgian provinces of East Flanders and Brabant and the Dutch provinces of North Holland and South Holland catching up with the Hainaut and Liège provinces.

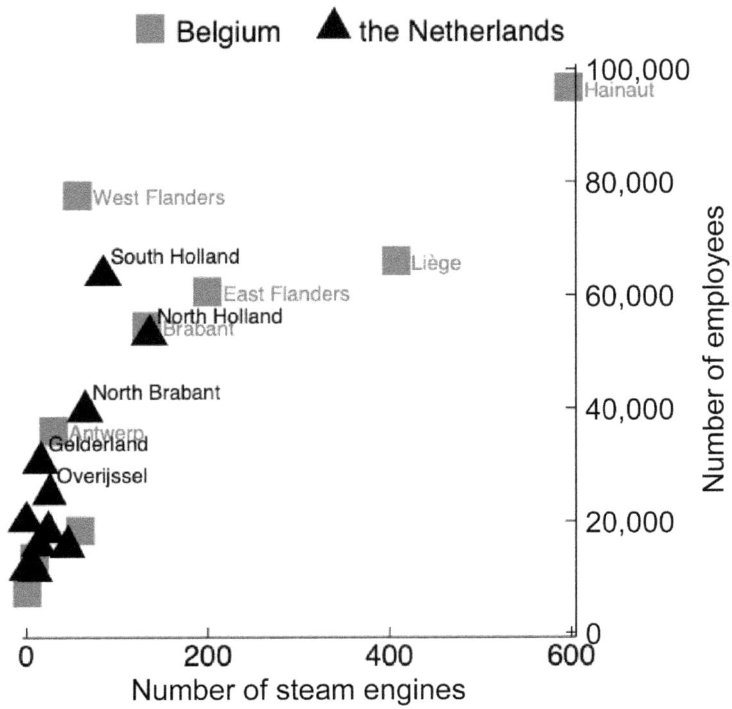

1850

Figure 3.3 (Continued)

Notwithstanding that by 1820 the Industrial Revolution had already taken off in the Liège and Hainaut provinces, based on Figure 3.4 it appears that this did not fundamentally challenge the preindustrial geographical distribution of employment in industry (yet). In absolute employment numbers, 45% of the employment in industry in the Low Countries was located in the Belgian East and West Flanders provinces, where the widespread textiles industry dominated the picture. Next to these two Belgian provinces, the other Belgian and Dutch regions were relatively on par at the beginning of the nineteenth century in terms of employment numbers in industry. Here, the more populated North Holland, South Holland, Utrecht, Antwerp, and Liège regions were the forerunners, although the gap with the other regions remained relatively small.

At the beginning of the nineteenth century, East and West Flanders were dominated by employment in the age-old rural linen industry. Its value added per worker, however, is considered small compared to that of factory

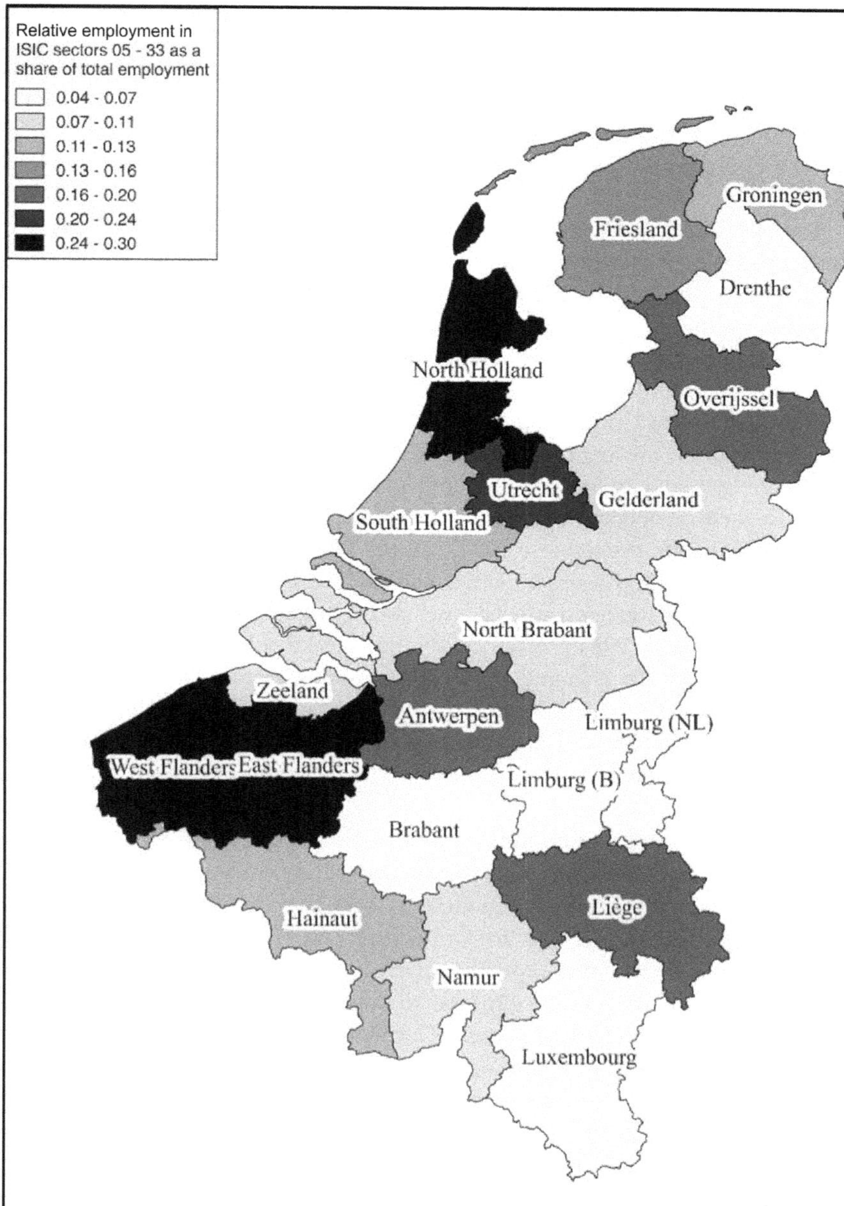

Figure 3.4 Employment in mining and manufacturing sectors in Belgium and the Netherlands in 1819, as a percentage of the labour force

Source: Brugmans (1956). For a methodological note, we refer to Philips (2020).

production, and therefore the importance of the rural linen industry is frequently overlooked in Belgian historiography.[2] Additionally, East Flanders developed considerable factory production in cotton textiles. Most notably, Lieven Bauwens smuggled machinery out of England in the 1790s to set up the first mechanized cotton spinning mill in Ghent. Soon, other entrepreneurs followed his example of starting a business in cotton and linen production, and the city counted approximately 10,000 factory workers by 1812 (Périer 1885).

However, most modern factory production in 1820 could be found in the Liège and Hainaut provinces. The English emigrant technician William Cockerill started the production of the first modern water-driven carding and woollen spinning machines in Verviers (Lebrun 1948). The net creation of jobs should not be exaggerated; often, this new factory labour simply replaced homeworkers in the surrounding countryside (Servais 1982). However, it was William's youngest son, John Cockerill, who added a spectacular dimension to the industrial revolution in this region. He quickly diversified output by starting the production of hydraulic presses, pumps, and steam engines in Seraing, building the first blast furnace operating on coke in continental Europe, and exploiting coal and iron ore mines (Veraghtert 1981). In the Hainaut province, a major centre of metallurgy emerged around Charleroi in the 1820s. At this occasion the latest British techniques were introduced, such as the puddling process and coke furnaces (Lebrun et al. 1981). Additionally, the breakthrough of cokes over charcoal as fuel drastically changed the localization of the iron industry. While the abundance of wood and the presence of iron ore had for centuries lured the iron industry to the provinces of Luxembourg and Namur, after the introduction of coke furnaces the coal-producing provinces of Hainaut and Liège became the new places to be.

In the Netherlands, most industrial activities in 1820 were located in the province of North Holland, where industry relied heavily on the inheritance of the seventeenth century Dutch Golden Age. In particular, Amsterdam and its trade facilities were crucial for importing raw materials and intermediate products from abroad and exporting thereafter the finished products: Baltic grain imports for the Dutch gin (the so-called *jenever*) distilleries and beer breweries, Dutch overseas colonies for tobacco processing and sugar refining activities (Van Zanden and Van Riel 2004). Parallel to the development of these industries there occurred a growth in shipbuilding and supporting industries. Meanwhile, the relatively high living standards in the western cities drove the rise of retail-oriented industries – for example, notable production in bread, glass, and domestic iron appliances in Utrecht. Furthermore, we find several regional clusters in the west, such as paper milling in the Zaan area (Davids 2006), textile industry in Haarlem, and ship construction in Den Helder.

Meanwhile, the more peripheral part of the Netherlands was characterized by a great deal of specialization, in part based on sales to the urbanized, western part of the country. In the east of the country, we find a concentration of textiles production in the Twente and Achterhoek countryside, for which Holland and neighbouring Germany acted as the local suppliers of flax and functioned as their main consumer markets (Hendrickx 1993). In the Dutch north, we find substantial employment in peat extraction and processing of agricultural products such as butter and cheese. Although the former is largely associated with the heydays of the Dutch Republic, consumption of this energy source rose during the nineteenth century for the brick, tile, and bakery product factories as well as for household consumption (Gerding 1995).

By 1850, we encounter substantial changes in the location of industry compared to 1819, partly attributable to the economic policies of Willem I during the United Kingdom of the Netherlands (1815–1830) and the subsequent split between both countries. Willem's reforms targeted economic integration in his kingdom by stimulating the already-existent industry in the south with the establishment of a new bank, the General Dutch Company for the Promotion of Public Industry (Algemeen Nederlandsche Maatschappij ter Begunstiging van de Volksvlijt), and trade in the northern part with the establishment of the Netherlands Trading Society (Nederlandsche Handelmaatschappij), a de facto successor of the Dutch East India Company. Although these institutions succeeded in accelerating growth in the southern Belgian regions (see Figures 3.4 and 3.5), they have been argued to hinder the development of a Dutch industry sector (Van Zanden 1996: 84).

The breakup between both countries was most felt in the largest industry sector of both countries, the production of textiles. For instance, the Netherlands Trading Society initially bought almost exclusively textiles from Ghent for sale in Indonesia. After the split of Belgium and the Netherlands in 1830, the Society turned to Dutch textile producers, benefitting the new textiles centres in Overijssel and Gelderland and the old textiles cities of Tilburg, Haarlem, Leiden, and Amsterdam. Moreover, with the Indonesian cultivation system in place, the supply of colonial commodities soared to the benefit of sugar refining, tobacco processing, and coffee branding activities in the Netherlands. Similarly, ship construction flourished along the Holland coastline, putting increasingly more pressure on the smaller shipyards in Zeeland, Friesland, and Groningen (Jansen 1999).

On the losing side, we find the rural linen industry in the Belgian provinces of East and West Flanders. First, these regions suffered from the growing popularity of cotton cloth and from the quick mechanization of British flax spinning after the 1820s (Vandenbroeke 1979; Hendrickx 1993). A deep crisis followed during the years 1845–1847, when the potato blight and harvest failures caused a famine (Rapport 1846). Yet, Figure 3.5 does not fully reflect this decline in employment, as unemployed people often mentioned their previous occupation to the census officials – in which case, Figure 3.5 could potentially even show an overvaluation of employment in manufacturing. Meanwhile, the export-oriented Ghent factory

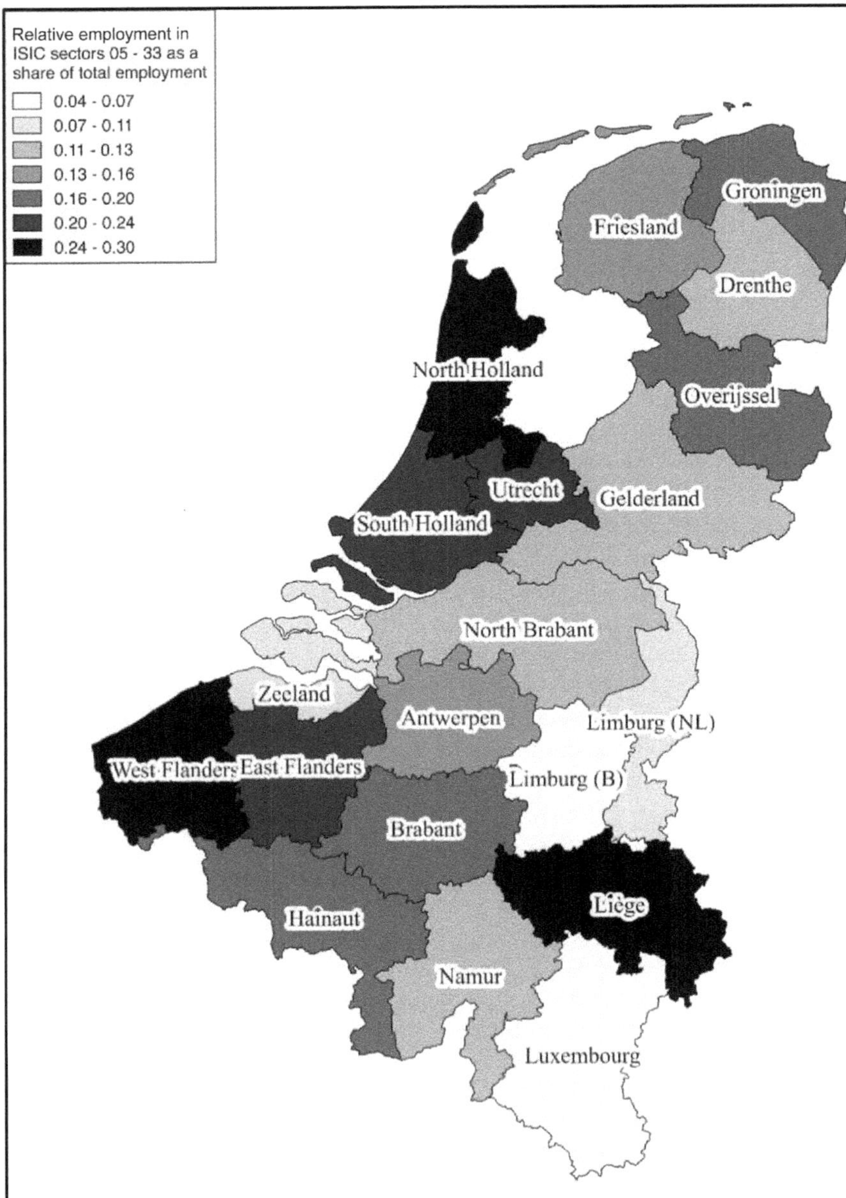

Figure 3.5 Employment in mining and manufacturing sectors in Belgium and the Netherlands in 1846/1859, as a percentage of the labour force (province level)

Source: For Belgium, we used the 1846 census of industry; for the Netherlands, we used the 1859 report of the Nederlandsche Maatschappij ter bevordering van Nijverheid. For a methodological note, we refer to Philips (2020).

cotton industry took a blow when access to the Dutch East Indies was closed in 1830, causing some of the Ghent textile barons to migrate to the Netherlands (Mokyr 1976).

In contrast, the Hainaut and Liège provinces, and to a lesser degree the adjacent Namur and Luxembourg provinces, grew rapidly in Belgium. The railway boom, which started in the mid-1830s, gave coal mining and metal processing another boost. In Liège, the construction of locomotives and other railway equipment soared. Benefitting from cheap inputs, many other energy-intensive sectors arose alongside the Belgian coal belt. So did the glass working industry flourish, with the establishment of the Val Saint Lambert factory in Seraing in 1826 and Petrus Regout's glass grinding company in Maastricht in 1834, which eventually culminated in his conglomerate of nails, pottery, and guns.

As direct followers in terms of the steam engine installation, we find the South Holland and Brabant provinces (see Figure 3.3). In these regions, more retail-oriented industries arose, benefitting from the proximity to large consumer markets such as the cities of Rotterdam and Brussels, with the opening of the first starch factory in Gouda in 1819 and the sugar refinery in Tienen in 1836. Meanwhile, the peripheral provinces of Dutch Zeeland and Belgian Limburg lost ground. The Northern Netherlands faced a relative standstill as well, with many smaller, low-productive handicraft producers able to withstand increasing competition during the first half of the nineteenth century (De Jonge 1968). One illustrative example is the northern peat extraction sites that benefitted from increasing domestic demand, as a result of a temporal vacuum created by the installation of an excise in 1830 on imported coal from Germany and Belgium (Van Zanden and Van Riel 2004) and the nearly-emptied peat bogs in the Dutch south (Gerding 1995).

3.4 Phase of industrial maturity (ca. 1870–1960)

As follows from the previous section, the early industrial development resulted in 1850 in a relatively equal distribution of manufacturing activities across both countries (see Figure 3.6). In most of these municipalities, the production of textiles and leather was by far the largest manufacturing sector. Nonetheless, high employment numbers are found in East and West Flanders, where many families still participated in domestic textiles activities, just as in the regional clusters surrounding the cities of Liège, Charleroi, Groningen, Tilburg, and Eindhoven. Other examples of regional specialization include mining and quarrying in the Belgian south, peat cutting in the Dutch north, and food-producing clusters in Holland and Brabant. By 1890 (see Figure 3.7), we find that clustering has been taken to another level. By this time, mechanization extended from the pioneering industrializing sectors such as mining and textiles, to newly mechanized industries such as metallurgy and more retail-oriented industries. Furthermore, in Figure 3.7, we find that Belgium focused more on

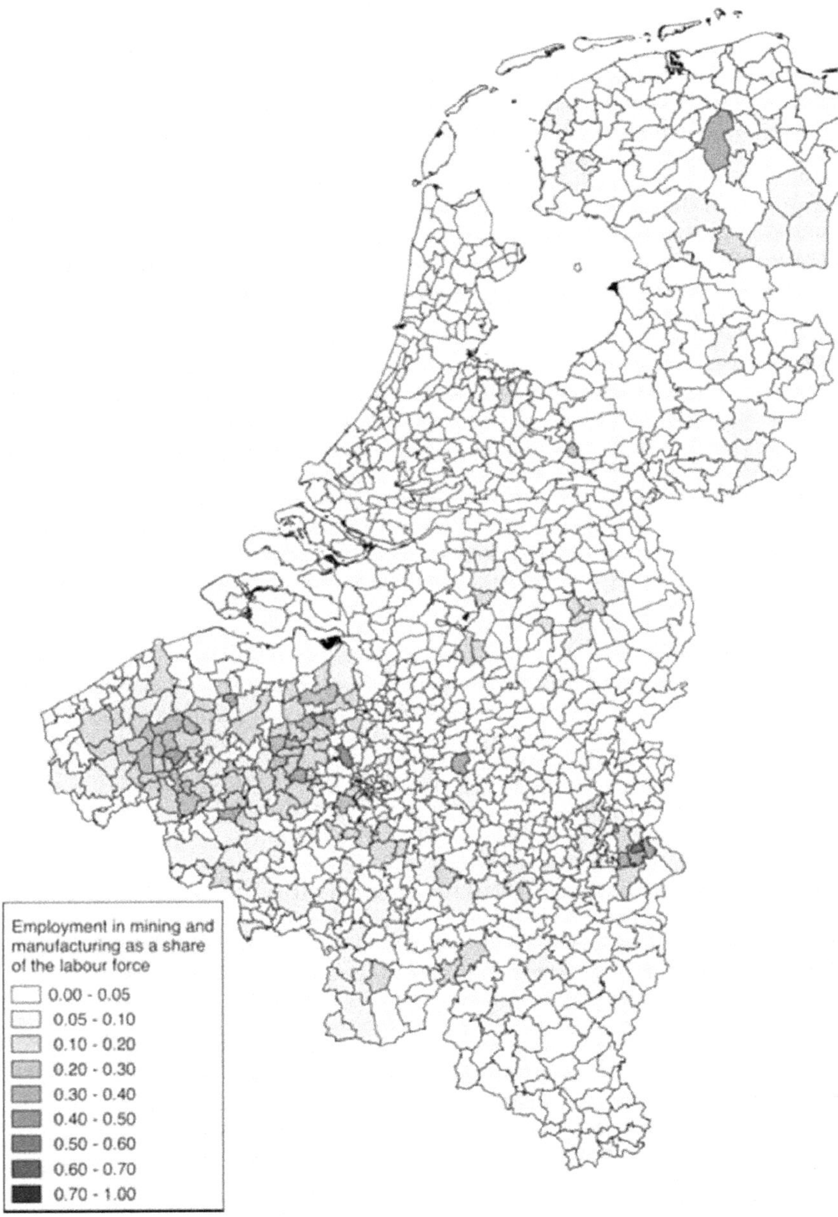

Figure 3.6 Employment in mining and manufacturing sectors in Belgium and the Netherlands in 1846/1859, as a percentage of the labour force (municipality level)

Source: For Belgium, we used the 1846 census of industry; for the Netherlands, we used the 1859 report of the Nederlandsche Maatschappij ter bevordering van Nijverheid. For a methodological note, we refer to Philips (2020).

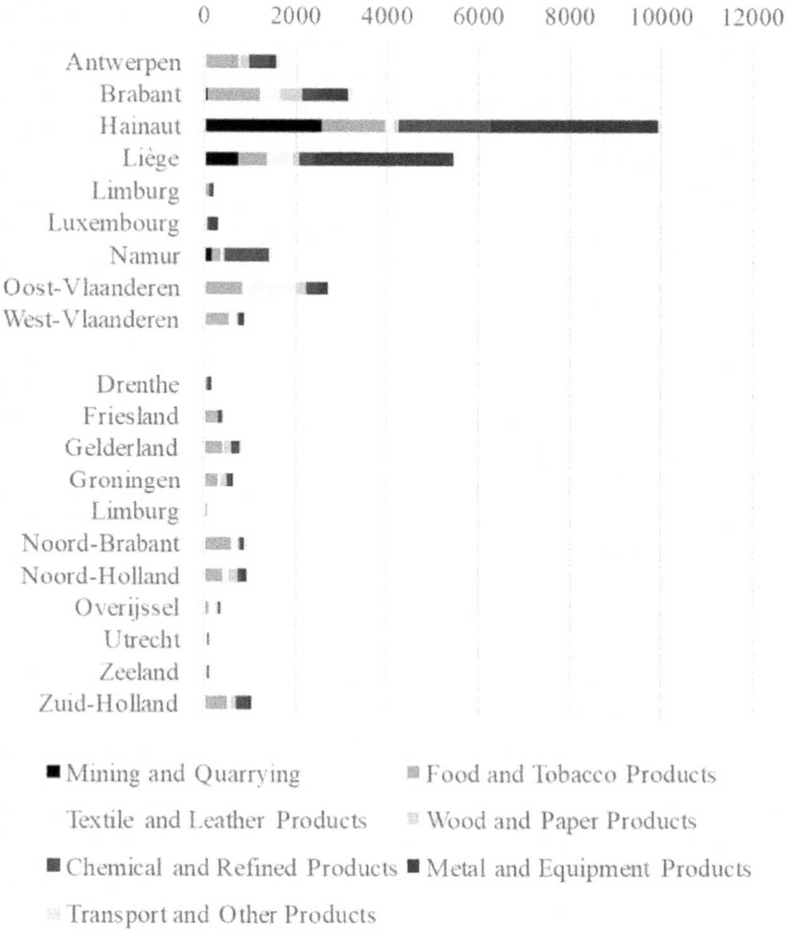

Figure 3.7 Steam engines in mining and manufacturing sectors in Belgium and the Netherlands in 1896

Source: For Belgium, we used the 1896 census of industry; for the Netherlands, we used the dataset of Philips (2019). For a methodological note, we refer to Philips (2020).

heavy, energy-intensive industries such as metallurgy and chemicals, whereas the Netherlands relied more on light industries including foodstuffs, beverages, and tobacco production.

Although the railway boom had already taken off in the Low Countries during the 1830s, railway construction would peak during the 1860s and 1870s. Additionally, from the second half of the 1870s, a transition took place from iron to steel production, after which the output of steam engines, locomotives, and other railway equipment soared, most notably in the Hainaut-Liège region. The other decisive location factor for metallurgy, water, benefitted this region as well. By 1890, a fully connected industrial axis or *Sillon Industriel* was formed alongside the Sambre and Meuse rivers. In the Netherlands, changes in the metallurgy sector had a smaller impact on its economic geography, although clusters arose around the IJssel River, which had direct access to coal from the Ruhr area (Smit and van Straalen 2007) and the outskirts of Amsterdam alongside the Amstel River (Van Zanden 1987).

The economic geography in the Netherlands changed considerably more by the scaling-up of another sector during the 1870s to 1890s: food processing. A well-documented example is the production of butter, for which the consumer revolution in domestic and international markets during the second half of the nineteenth century stimulated the demand for inferior but large quantities of butter (Jansen 1999). Local producers in North Brabant jumped into this market because they had access via the Maas River not only to the port of Rotterdam, but to the English and German markets as well. Soon, two local merchants – Van der Bergh and Jurgens in Oss – became the largest traders in butter in the world (Atzema and Wever 1994). Eventually, both developed artificial butter, which circumvented costly and hard-to-get dairy inputs, and set up business together in Rotterdam, establishing the Unilever company in 1929. Similar clusters arose for sugar refining in North and South Holland, tobacco production in South Holland and North Brabant, spirits and alcoholic beverages in South Holland, and potato starch in Groningen.

What happened to the metal-processing and food-producing sectors was the reverse of what the textiles- and leather-producing sectors endured. In East and West Flanders, the unequal battle between hand and mechanized textiles production finally came to a close. First, rural flax spinning vanished from the economic scene in the 1850s and 1860s – a sector that had employed about 150,000 workers in the region in 1843 (Moniteur Belge 1846). In the 1870s, the same happened with rural flax weaving, causing many workers in West and East Flanders to return to agriculture or take up a part-time job in lace production, shoemaking, and other sweatshop activities (Verhaegen 1961). However, just as in Figures 3.5–3.6, this is not entirely reflected in Figure 3.8, as many of the unemployed stated their former or part-time occupation in the 1896 census.[3] In contrast, mechanized textiles production flourished in other parts of Flanders, although these activities were located in other sub-regions than the former linen heartland. Thus, the traditional centres of Tielt, Torhout, and Geraardsbergen went into decline, whereas mechanized production flourished in the cities of Ghent, Aalst, and Sint-Niklaas.

In the Netherlands, we find a similar pattern of flourishing and declining industrial clusters. Here, textiles clusters emerged in the east and south of the country – Tilburg, Enschede, Helmond, Hengelo, and Almelo – where the concentration of industries went hand in hand with the formation of new urbanized centres. In contrast, many smaller manufacturing firms continued to coexist in the Dutch northern provinces throughout the 1850–1870 period. However, when the

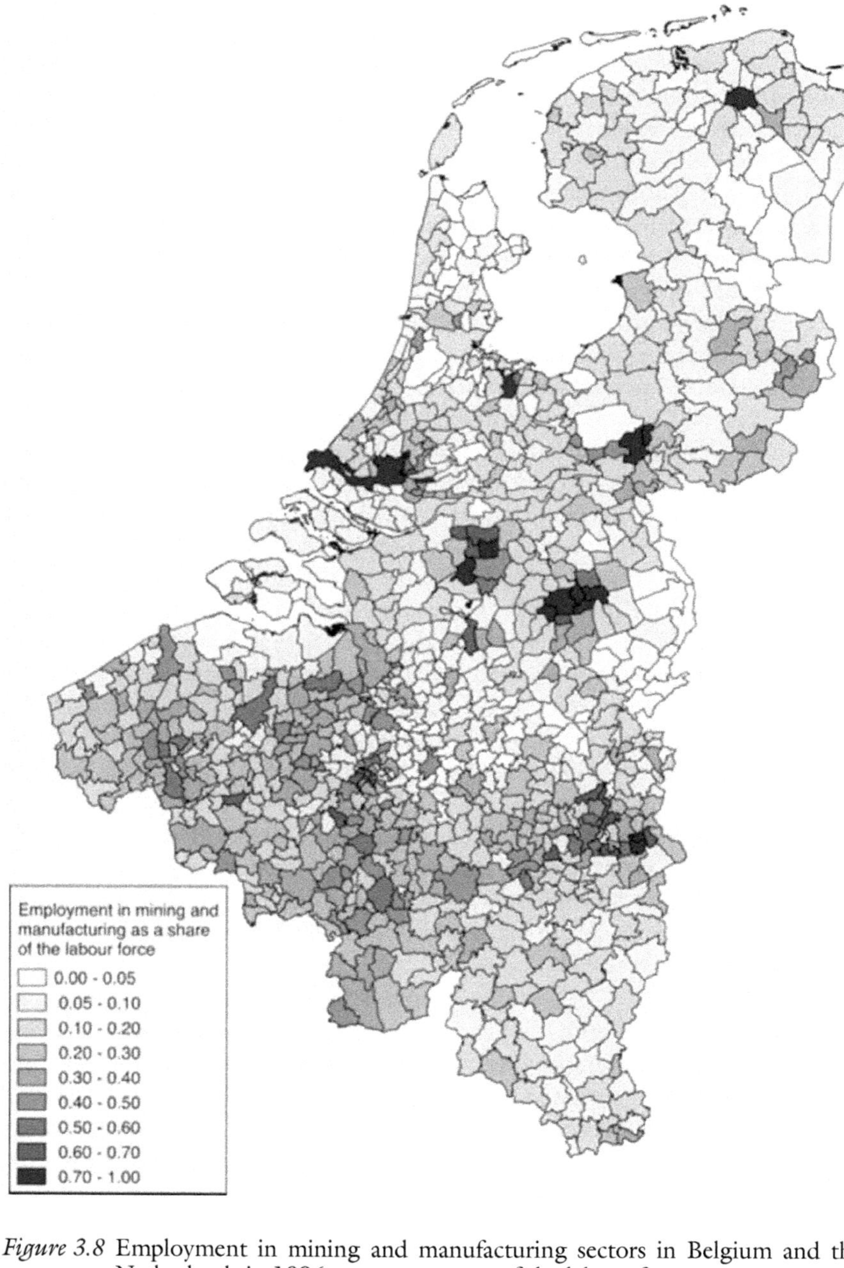

Figure 3.8 Employment in mining and manufacturing sectors in Belgium and the Netherlands in 1896, as a percentage of the labour force

Source: For Belgium, we used the 1896 census of industry; for the Netherlands, we used the dataset of Philips (2019). For a methodological note, we refer to Philips (2020).

Dutch mechanization process accelerated during the 1870–1910 period and an agricultural crisis took place during the 1880s (De Jonge 1968), many of these northern industry workers were inevitably driven out of their traditional jobs. Soon, it became clear that the northern peripheral provinces did not participate in industrialization and the formation of new urban centres, in contrast to the Dutch eastern and southern periphery (Atzema and Wever 1994). For the inhabitants of these regions, one of the escape routes from poverty was migration to the Dutch west. Another one was to look for the few job opportunities available in the industrial sectors of the region, such as the few peat fields which remained profitable (most notably in Drenthe, where peat extraction even increased during the second half of the nineteenth century),[4] or in the sectors dependable upon agricultural inputs such as the dairy factories in Friesland or straw paperboard and potato starch factories in Groningen.

An exogenous shock to the industry sector occurred with World War I and its aftermath, which impacted both countries in a very different way. Although the main battles happened outside its manufacturing belts, Belgian machinery and equipment fell prey to German policies of dismantlement, plunder, and deliberate destruction. On the other hand, Dutch neutrality during the war stimulated import substitution policies to replace former imports from belligerents such as Belgium and Germany. In the 1920s and 1930s, the economies of Belgium and the Netherlands drifted even further apart. Although reconstruction proceeded swiftly after the Armistice, Belgian industry missed opportunities to modernize its industrial infrastructure, with the steel sector not adopting American mass production techniques and machine building factories continuing to focus on old steam technology rather than electrical engineering (Geerkens 2004). Consequently, rising protectionism hit Belgium particularly hard. The nationalization of railway networks in many countries led to dwindling exports of locomotives and rolling stock (Maizels 1963). For Dutch industrial companies, on the contrary, the fall in international trade during the 1920s and 1930s offered an opportunity to grow, in part thanks to continuing import substitution and decreasing foreign competition (De Jong 1999).

In 1930 (see Figure 3.9), we thus arrive at a new economic geography of the industry sector in both countries. Over the long nineteenth century and the interwar period, regional specialization caused regions with human capital, large consumer markets, and export facilities to become more appealing for firms (Ronsse and Rayp 2016; Philips et al. 2017). The ports of Amsterdam, Rotterdam, Antwerp, and Zeebrugge and their surroundings benefitted strongly from these changing location factors. Growth for the port of Rotterdam was most spectacular when the construction of the Nieuwe Waterweg in 1872 enabled direct access from the harbour to the sea, thereby becoming an important chain between the Ruhr area and its export regions (Loyen et al. 2003). Most of these gateways quickly broadened their manufacturing base beyond the traditional port-related industries, such as ship construction,

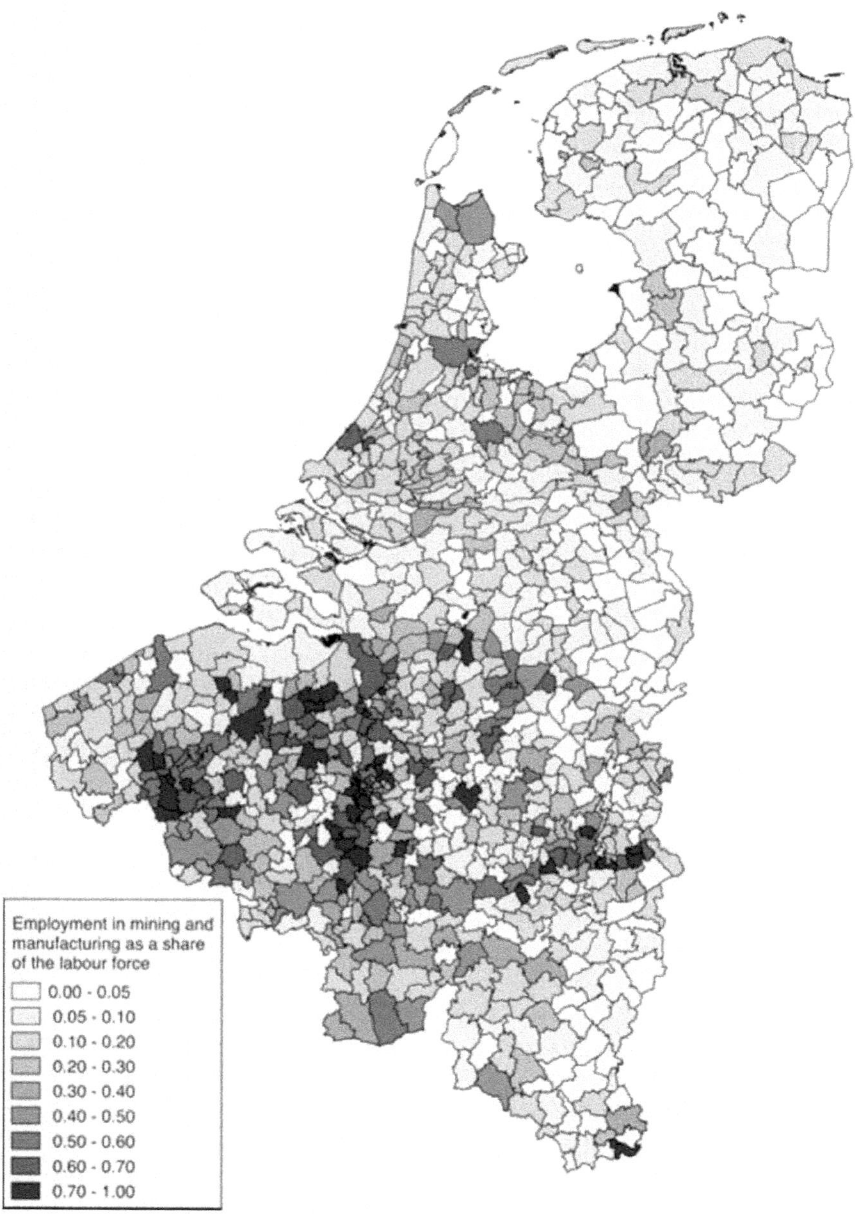

Figure 3.9 Employment in mining and manufacturing sectors in Belgium and the Netherlands in 1930/1937, as a percentage of the labour force

Source: For Belgium, we used the 1937 census of industry; for the Netherlands, we used the 1930 census of companies. For a methodological note, we refer to Philips (2020).

to newly-emerging industries such as coke smelting, chemical products, and the production of domestic appliances such as telephone equipment, photographic paper, and cars. Most exemplary in this perspective was the rise of a small light bulb company that would evolve into a key player for the domestic appliance products market: Philips. Lastly, the discovery of coal deposits in the late 1890s pulled Belgian and Dutch Limburg out of their peripheral status (Gales 1996).

3.5 Post-industrial phase (ca. 1960–2010)

Similar to World War I, World War II hit both countries in an unequal fashion, but the Netherlands suffered relatively more than its southern neighbour thanks to the earlier liberation of Belgium and its swift incorporation in the allied war machine. For example, the loss in capital stock in 1945 relative to the pre-war numbers was estimated in Belgium to be 5%, whereas in the Netherlands it was 27% (Griffiths and Van Zanden 1989: 186).

Nevertheless, both countries recovered quickly; the Netherlands, for instance, by 1948 saw its capital stock already surpassing the capital stock of 1938 (De Jong 1999: 332). The coal mining sector in the Hainaut, Liège, Dutch Limburg, and Belgian Limburg provinces initially even benefitted from the aftermath of the war, as they were specialized in products that served the reconstruction of Europe, such as coal, cement, and glass (Baudhuin 1958). Both countries benefitted from the Marshall plan, although its effect on economic growth has been considered fairly modest. Most aid in the Netherlands went to the restoration of financial and price stability (Clerx 1986), whereas in Belgium it was used for investments in traditional sectors such as metallurgy and mining, at the expense of higher innovating industry branches (Cassiers 1993). The early economic unification of (Western) Europe had a more beneficial effect on both countries, with the establishment of the Benelux customs union in 1944, the European Coal and Steel Community in 1951, and the European Economic Community in 1957.

Turning to the results of 1970 in Figure 3.10, we find that the rising importance of oil caused an even larger shock to the industrial geography of both countries. The breakthrough of oil as the major energy source in the mid-1950s resulted in two contrasting outcomes. On the one hand, the major trade hubs and their surroundings benefitted strongly from the invasion of cheap oil, as ports became a favoured location for oil refineries and petrochemical plants. In Antwerp, the expansion in car assembly, chemicals, metal processing, ship construction, food products, and the production of consumer durables more than covered the loss of employment in more traditional activities (Van der Wee 1997). In Rotterdam, not only a significant part of the city centre had suffered by the Luftwaffe in 1940, but so did the harbour infrastructure. During reconstruction, the harbour territory was significantly extended with the Europoort and the Maasvlakte, thanks to which

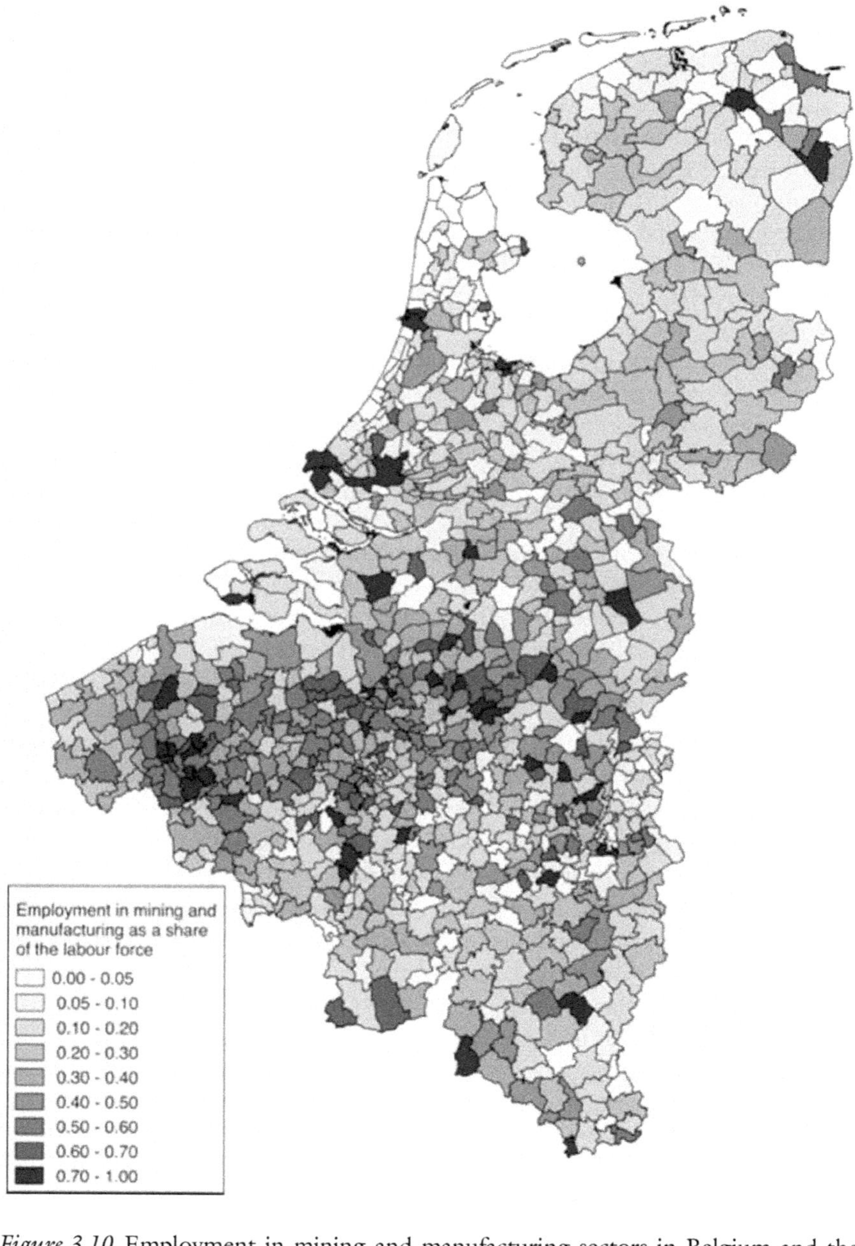

Figure 3.10 Employment in mining and manufacturing sectors in Belgium and the Netherlands in 1970/1978, as a percentage of the labour force

Source: For Belgium, we used the 1970 census of industry; for the Netherlands, we used the 1978 census of companies. For a methodological note, we refer to Philips (2020).

Rotterdam had become the largest harbour in the world by 1962 – a position they were able to maintain until Shanghai took it over in 2005. As a result of agglomeration, the industrial heartland in Belgium had moved by 1970 to the triangle between the major cities of Ghent, Antwerp, and Brussels, with smaller clusters around the cities of Kortrijk and Liège. In the Netherlands, a similar pattern of agglomeration unfolded, with the development of an industrial heartland in the North Holland, South Holland, Utrecht, and North Brabant provinces.

Yet, the shift to oil dealt a blow to the Hainaut and Liège regions, where suddenly dozens of coal pits had to be closed down. To cope with these and other structural problems, the Belgian government launched in 1959 the so-called expansion laws, the Belgian variant of regional policy. These reforms launched various tax incentives, subsidies, and the development of well-equipped industrial sites, in order to lure foreign investments to areas facing structural difficulties. But it was to little avail for the mining provinces; the high wages in coal mining had pushed up labour costs in other sectors too, decreasing the attractiveness of these regions for foreign investors. After the collapse of mining, it proved very difficult to reduce wages due to labour market rigidities. Competitiveness problems and adverse labour relations often deterred potential investors, which triggered a long deindustrialization process (Brion and Moreau 1998). In Belgian and Dutch Limburg, employment in the mining sectors faced a similar but smaller shock compared to Hainaut and Liège, due to the construction of more recent infrastructure, a lower wage rate, and a broader industry mix.

By 2010 (see Figure 3.11), we arrive at a relatively equal distribution of manufacturing activities, not in the least due to the much lower level of employment in manufacturing. The oil shocks of the 1970s, global market integration, and the continuous widening and deepening of European integration provided a strong incentive for domestic and multinational companies to move industrial activities to other countries in the European and global periphery. Additionally, technological improvements and productivity increases implicated decreasing employment numbers, especially for the sectors with high unit labour costs.

This disappearance of industry jobs occurred very unequally across regions. For most regions, deindustrialization highlighted a beneficial trajectory in which a shift took place from a manufacturing-centred economy to a higher productive service-based economy. In this setting, the loss of industrial employment was more than compensated by the creation of new service-based jobs. Such a pattern unfolded in most of the Antwerp, North Holland, South Holland, and the Flemish and Walloon Brabant provinces (after the subdivision between Flemish-Brabant and Walloon-Brabant in 1995), due to the relatively easy access to export facilities and their location in the centre of Western Europe. For the more peripheral regions, efforts for safeguarding existing employment or attracting new (foreign) investments appeared to be a greater challenge. In Figure 3.11,

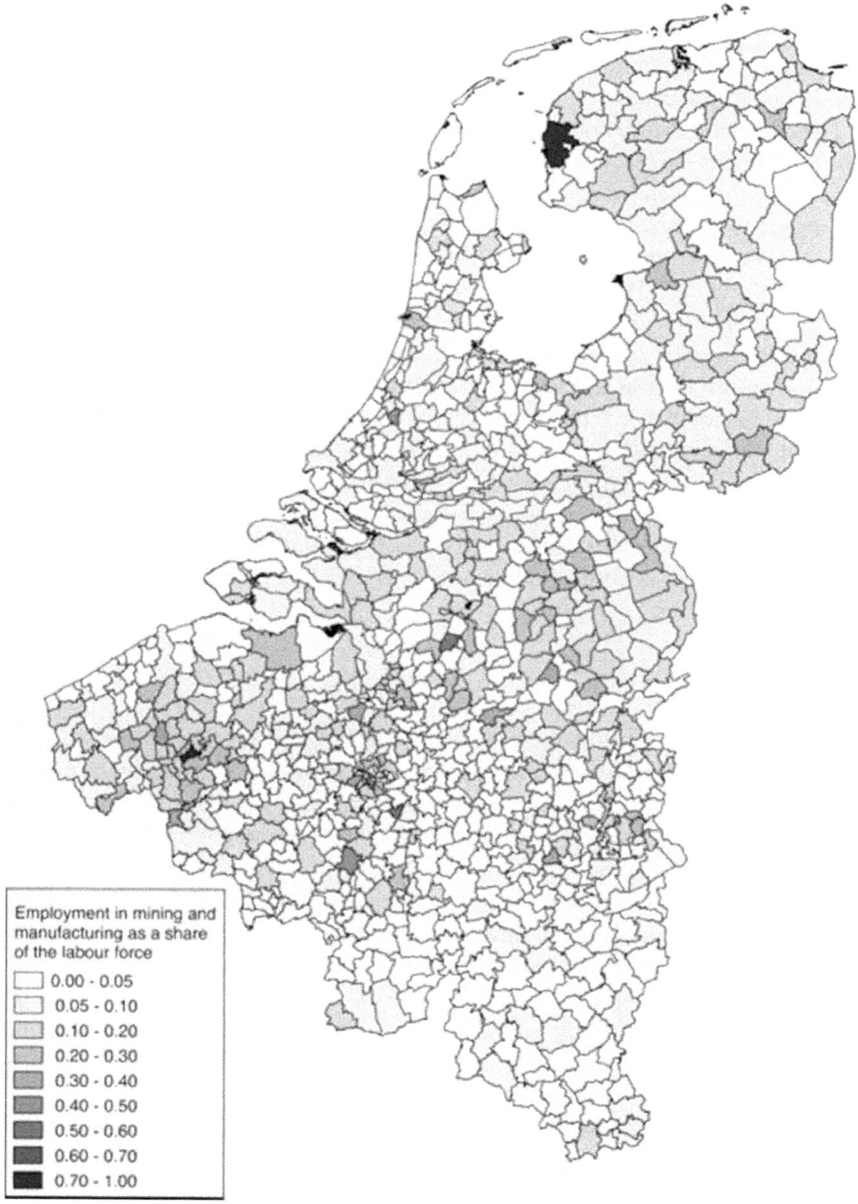

Figure 3.11 Employment in mining and manufacturing sectors in Belgium and the Netherlands in 2010, as a percentage of the labour force

Source: For Belgium, we used the RSZ and RSVZ statistics of 2010; for the Netherlands, we used the 2010 LISA dataset. For a methodological note, we refer to Philips (2020).

the success of the North Brabant province comes to the forefront, with the city of Eindhoven becoming a cluster for high technology, whereas the province was able to attract various large multinational companies in chemicals, transport, food processing, and equipment products. A similar pattern emerged for West Flanders and Belgian Limburg.

However, the victims of deindustrialization include the Dutch northern and eastern regions and the Belgian southern regions, where industrial activities nearly faded away. In hindsight, the reversals of fortune in Hainaut, Namur, Luxembourg, and Liège stand out especially, as they belong to the top four regions in Europe where relative gross domestic product per capita levels have dropped the most during the 1900–2010 period (Rosés and Wolf 2019). In these regions, the steel industry had to go through a painful process of downsizing as a result of growing international competition (Buyst 1997; Nagels 2002). This process was even more hurtful due to the so-called "waffle iron politics", according to which government funds had to be distributed equally across the Belgian northern and southern half. As a result, the political parties linked to the powerful miners' unions obtained ever more subsidies from the government to cover for the mounting losses in dwindling industries, leading to a misallocation of investments to existing activities in an attempt to safeguard employment in the Hainaut and Liège regions, instead of devising a future-oriented restructuring economic policy.

3.6 Conclusion

Like most parts of Europe, the regions in Belgium and the Netherlands experienced a process of industrialization and rapid economic growth during the nineteenth and twentieth centuries. In this chapter, we reviewed the trends in the location of industry in these two small Western European countries, in order to shed a new light on the literature of the Industrial Revolution and subsequent periods of industrialization in both countries. For this, we have drawn upon a new dataset on employment numbers, derived from the 1820–2010 Belgian and Dutch population and industry censuses. During this period, both countries revealed very divergent spatial patterns of industrialization, depending on the regional-varying capacity to maintain old industrial activities while attracting newly emerging industries during the different phases of (de)industrialization and technological advancements.

On the eve of the Industrial Revolution and when both countries were united in the United Kingdom of the Netherlands (1815–1830), we find an unequal regional distribution of industrial activities in both countries. Whereas many historical studies have used the example of Belgium as an early industrializer and the Netherlands as suffering from "industrial retardation" (Griffiths 1979) based on both larger labour and capital numbers in the former country (e.g. Mokyr 1974; Mokyr 1976; Lintsen and Steenaard 1991; Mokyr 2000), the higher employment in industry in Belgium could mostly be attributed to the widespread textiles activities in East and West Flanders, and the steam engines to the coal mining sector in the Hainaut and Liège regions. During the 1820–1850 period, we find that the industry sector in the Dutch southern and eastern provinces benefitted the most from the Belgian and Dutch breakup, at the expense of the mechanizing textiles sector in the Belgian northwest.

Looking at lower geographical levels and sectoral evolutions, we find that in most regions textiles manufacturing composed by far the largest industry sector in both countries in 1850, although soon a pattern of diffusion started, with regional specialization and cluster formation as a consequence. Most notably, we find new factories in metals and machinery in the Belgian south next to the Sambre-Meuse coal belt arising in 1850–1890. During the breakthrough of the second phase of industrialization and the mechanization of retail-oriented and capital-intensive sectors, industry started concentrating near centres of consumer markets and export facilities, benefitting disproportionally the Brabant and Antwerp regions in Belgium and the Holland and Utrecht regions in the Netherlands. In contrast, the Belgian deep south and Dutch north pauperized. During the post-industrial phase, a process of relative decline emerged in the Dutch northeastern and Belgian southern provinces, shaping to a large extent the current economic geography of industry in both countries.

Notes

1 The research leading to these results received funding from the European Research Council under the European Union's Horizon 2020 Programme / ERC-StG 637695 – HinDI, as part of the project "The historical dynamics of industrialization in Northwestern Europe and China ca. 1800–2010: a regional interpretation". The authors would like to thank the Historical Database of Local and Cadastral Statistics LOKSTAT-POPPKAD (Quetelet Center, Ghent University), specifically Sven Vrielinck and Eric Vanhaute, for providing data. Furthermore, we would like to thank Bas van Leeuwen, Ron Boschma, and Jan Luiten van Zanden for suggestions.

2 For instance, De Brabander (1983) estimated that in 1846, only 32,000 full-time workers in textiles were active in the West Flanders province. Instead, an official count of 1843 – when the heydays of the linen sector were already over – registered about 150,000 linen workers in West Flanders, and 62% of them considered the linen industry as their main occupation (Moniteur Belge 1846).

3 So did 25,547 women in West-Flanders and 18,016 women in East Flanders state lace production (*kantklosters)* as their occupation in the census of industry of 1896, although this occupation was most likely a part-time job for these women.

4 The measurement of employment in peat extraction is heavily complicated, due to the high seasonal variation and the annual variation related to the exhaustion of peat fields. Nonetheless, taking the Drenthe province as an example, our results indicate an increase of 1,447 to 5,542 full-time equivalent employees during 1820–1890, whereas Gerding (1995) estimated an increase of 2,380 to 8,680 employees (expressed in number of people involved in peat extraction) for the 1825–1900 period.

5 The following codes provide the dates when the lists of steam engines were sent by the provincial governments and their inventory number, all to be found in the National Archive of the Netherlands, in the archives of the Ministerie van Nationale Nijverheid. For Drenthe: Nationale Nijverheid, 07/03/1851, number 66. For Friesland: Nationale Nijverheid, 24/03/1851, number 122. For Gelderland: Nationale Nijverheid, 31/03/1851, number 95. For Groningen: Nationale Nijverheid, 24/03/1851, number 123. For Limburg: Nationale Nijverheid, 22/08/1851, number 130. For Noord-Brabant: Nationale Nijverheid, 15/04/1851, number 67. For Noord-Holland: Nationale Nijverheid, 16/04/1851, number 75. For Overijssel: Nationale Nijverheid, 05/04/1851, number 103. For Utrecht: Nationale Nijverheid, 08/03/1851, number 102. For Zeeland: Nationale Nijverheid, 17/04/1851, number 63. For Zuid-Holland: Nationale Nijverheid, 25/03/1851, number 60.

References

Primary Sources

CBS, or *Centraal Bureau voor Statistiek*, statistics. 2001. *Tweehonderd jaar statistiek in tijdreeksen 1800–1999*. Heerlen: Centraal Bureau voor de Statistiek.

Census of companies, or *bedrijfstelling*, of the Netherlands. Editions of 1930 and 1978.

Census of industry, or *recensement d'industrie*, of Belgium. Editions of 1846, 1896, 1937 and 1970.

Census of population, or *recensement de la population*, of Belgium. Editions of 1846, 1856, 1866, 1880, 1890, 1900, 1910, 1920, 1930, 1947, 1960, 1970, 1981 and 1991.

LISA dataset. 2010. *LISA: het werkgelegenheidsregister van Nederland*. Enschede: Stichting LISA.

National archive of the Netherlands, or the *nationaal archief*, various surveys of the Dutch ministry of manufacturing in 1851.[5]

RSVZ, or *Rijksinstituut voor de Sociale Verzekeringen der Zelfstandigen*, statistics. 2001. *Aangeslotenen per provincie en gemeente: gegevens op 31 december 2000*. Brussel: Rijksinstituut voor de Sociale Verzekeringen der Zelfstandigen.

RSVZ, or *Rijksinstituut voor de Sociale Verzekeringen der Zelfstandigen*, statistics. 2011. *Aangeslotenen per provincie en gemeente: gegevens op 31 december 2010*. Brussel: Rijksinstituut voor de Sociale Verzekeringen der Zelfstandigen.

RSZ, or *Rijksdienst voor Sociale Zekerheid*. 2001. *Werknemers onderworpen aan de sociale zekerheid naar plaats van tewerkstelling: gegevens op 31 december 2000*. Brussel: Rijksdienst voor Sociale Zekerheid.

RSZ, or *Rijksdienst voor Sociale Zekerheid*, statistics. 2011. *Werknemers onderworpen aan de sociale zekerheid naar plaats van tewerkstelling: gegevens op 31 december 2010*. Brussel: Rijksdienst voor Sociale Zekerheid.

Secondary Literature

Allen, R. C. 2009. *The British industrial revolution in global perspective*. Cambridge: Cambridge University Press.

Atzema, O. A. L. C., and E. Wever. 1994. *De Nederlandse industrie: Ontwikkeling, spreiding en uitdaging*. Assen: Van Gorcum.

Baudhuin, F. 1958. *Histoire économique de la Belgique 1945–1956*. Brussels: Bruylant.

Bos, R. W. J. M. 1979. "Factorprijzen, technologie en marktstructuur: De groei van de Nederlandse volkshuishouding, 1815–1914." *AAG Bijdragen* 22: 109–137.

Brion, R., and J. L. Moreau 1998. *La Société générale de Belgique, 1822–1997*. Antwerp: Mercatorfonds.

Brugmans, I. J. 1956. *Statistieken van de Nederlandse nijverheid uit de eerste helft der 19de eeuw*'s. Gravenhage: Martinus Nijhoff.

Buyst, E. 1997. "The decline and rise of a small open economy: the case of Belgium (1974–1990)." In *The economic development of Belgium since 1870*, edited by H. Van der Wee and J. Blomme, 67–76. Cheltenham-Lyme: Elgar.

Buyst, E. 2018. "The causes of growth during Belgium's industrial revolution." *Journal of Interdisciplinary History* 49(1): 71–92.

Buyst, E. forthcoming. "Changes in the occupational structure of Belgium: new estimates for the 1846–1910 period." In *Occupational structure and industrialisation in a comparative context*, edited by O. Saito, and L. Shaw-Taylor. Cambridge: Cambridge University Press.

Cassiers, I. 1993. "Du miracle belge à la croissance lente: l'impact du plan Marshall et de l'Union Européenne des paiements." *Bulletin de l'Institut de Recherches Economiques et Sociales* 166: 1–20.

Clerx, J. M. M. J. 1986. *Nederland en de liberalisatie van het handels- en betalingsverkeer, 1945–1958*. Groningen: Wolters Noordhoff.

Crafts, N., and A. Mulatu. 2005. "How did the location of industry respond to falling transport costs in Britain before World War I?" *Journal of Economic History* 66(3): 575–607.

Davids, C. A. 2006. "The transformation of an old industrial districts: firms, family and mutuality in the Zaanstreek. *Enterprise and Society* 7(3): 550–580.

De Belder, J., E. Vanhaute and S. Vrielinck. 1992. Naar een kwantitatieve databank van de Belgische Gemeenten, 19de en 20ste eeuw. Verslag van een proefproject. *Belgisch Tijdschrift voor Nieuwste Geschiedenis* 3(4): 355–414.

De Brabander, G. L. 1983. *Regionale structuur en werkgelegenheid: Een economische en geografische studie over de Belgische lange-termijn-ontwikkeling*. Brussels: Koninklijke academie voor wetenschappen, letteren en schone kunsten van België.

De Brabander, G. L. 1984. *De regionaal-sectoriële verdeling van de economische activiteit in België (1846–1979): Een kritische studie van het bronnenmateriaal*. Brussels: Uitgeverij Nauwelaerts.

De Jong, H. J. 1999. *De Nederlandse industrie, 1913–1965. Een vergelijkende analyse op basis van de productiestatistieken*. Amsterdam: NEHA.

De Jong, H. J., and J. L. van Zanden. 2014. "Debates on industrialization and economic growth in the Netherlands." *The Low Countries Journal of Social and Economic History* 11(2): 85–109.

De Jonge, J. A. 1968. *De industrialisatie in Nederland tussen 1850 en 1914*. Amsterdam: Scheltema & Holkema NV.

De Vries, J. 1974. *The Dutch rural economy in the Golden Age, 1500–1700*. London: Yale University Press.

Gales, B. P. A. 1996. *Delfstoffenwinning in Nederland in de twinstige eeuw*. Eindhoven: Stichting Historie der Techniek.

Geerkens, E. 2004. *La rationalisation de l'industrie belge de l'entre-deux-guerres*. Brussels: Académie royale de Belgique.

Gerding, M. A. W. 1995. *Vier eeuwen turfwinning, de verveningen in Groningen, Friesland, Drenthe en Overijssel tussen 1550 en 1950.* Wageningen: AAG Bijdragen.

Griffiths, R. T. 1979. *Industrial retardation in the Netherlands 1830–1850.* Den Haag: Martinus Nijhoff.

Griffiths, R. T., and J. L. van Zanden. 1989. *Economische geschiedenis van Nederland in de 20e eeuw. Van een veelzijdige volkshuishouding met een omvangrijk koloniaal bezit naar een 'klein land' binnen Europa.* Utrecht: Het Spectrum.

Hendrickx, F. M. M. 1993. "From weavers to workers: demographic implications of an economic transformation in Twente (the Netherlands) in the nineteenth century." *Continuity and Change* 8(2): 321–355.

Jansen, M. 1999. *De industriële ontwikkeling in Nederland, 1800–1850.* Amsterdam: Nederlands Economisch Historisch Archief.

Kim, S. 1995. "Expansion of markets and the geographic distribution of economic activities: the trends in US regional manufacturing structure, 1860–1987." *Quarterly Journal of Economics* 110(4): 881–908.

Lebrun, P. 1948. *L'industrie de la laine à Verviers pendant le XVIIIe siècle et le début du XIXe siècle. Contribution à l'étude des origines de la révolution industrielle.* Liège: Faculté de Philosophie et Lettres.

Lebrun, P., M. Bruwier, J. Dhondt, and G. Hansotte. 1981. *Essai sur la révolution industrielle en Belgique, 1770–1847. Histoire quantitative et développement de la Belgique (II-1).* Brussels: Académie Royale de Belgique.

Lintsen, H. W., and R. Steenaard. 1991. "Steam and polders. Belgium and the Netherlands, 1790–1850." *Yearbook for History of Science, Medicine, Technology and Mathematics* 3: 121–147.

Loyen, R., E. Buyst, and G. Devos, eds. 2003. *Struggling for leadership: Antwerp-Rotterdam port competition between 1870–2000.* Heidelberg: Physica-Verlag.

Maizels, A. 1963. *Industrial growth and world trade.* Cambridge: Cambridge University Press.

Missiaia, A. 2019. "Market versus endowment: explaining early industrial location in Italy (1871–1911)." *Cliometrica* 13(1): 127–161.

Mokyr, J. 1974. "The industrial revolution in the low countries in the first half of the 19th century: a comparative case study." *Journal of Economic History* 34(2): 365–391.

Mokyr, J. 1976. *Industrialization in the low countries, 1795–1850.* New Haven: Yale University Press.

Mokyr, J. 2000. "The industrial revolution and the Netherlands: why did it not happen?" *Economist* 148(4): 503–520.

Moniteur Belge: journal official. 1846. Brussels: Ministère de l'Intérieur.

Nagels, J. 2002. "La situation économique de la Flandre et le rurales flamand." *Cahiers économiques de Bruxelles* 45: 95–136.

Nederlandsche Maatschappij ter bevordering van Nijverheid. 1859. *Staat van de Nederlandsche fabrieken volgens de verslagen der gemeenten, die aan het Ministerie van Binnenlandsche Zaken worden gezonden.* Haarlem: De Erven Loosjes.

O'Brien, P. K. 1986. "Do we have a typology for the study of European industrialization in the XIXth century?" *Journal of European Economic History* 15(2): 291–333.

Olyslager, P. M. 1947. *De localiseering der Belgische nijverheid.* Antwerpen: Standaard Boekhandel.

Périer, O. 1885. *Lieven Bauwens en de opkomst der katoennijverheid in Vlaanderen.* Ghent: Hoste.

Philips, R. C. M. 2019. "Construction of a census of companies for the Netherlands in 1896." *TSEG/Low Countries Journal of Social and Economic History* 16(1): 87–108.

Philips, R. C. M. 2020. *Continuity or change? The evolution in the location of industry in the Netherlands and Belgium (1820–2010).* Utrecht, Ph.D. manuscript submitted at Utrecht University.

Philips, R. C. M., P. Foldvari, and B. van Leeuwen. 2017. *Drivers of industrialisation: intersectoral evidence from the low countries in the nineteenth century.* MPRA Working Papers 83304, 1–25.

Pluymers, B. 1992. *De Belgische industriële productie 1811–1846, reconstructie van een databank van de fysieke productie en de toegevoegde waarde.* Leuven: Centrum voor Economische Studiën.

Pollard, S. 1981. *Peaceful conquest. The industrialization of Europe 1760–1970.* Oxford: Oxford University Press.

Rapport sur l'état de l'administration dans la Flandre Occidentale. 1846. Bruges: De Plancke.

Ronsse, S., and G. Rayp. 2016. "What determined the location of industry in Belgium, 1896–1961?" *Journal of Interdisciplinary History* 46(3): 393–419.

Rosés, J. R., and N. Wolf. 2019. *The economic development of Europe's regions: a quantitative history since 1900.* London: Routledge.

Servais, P. 1982. "Industries rurales et structures agraires: le cas de l'Entre-Vesdre-et-Meuse aux 18e et 19e siècles." *Revue Belge d'Histoire Contemporaine* 12: 179–206.

Smit, J., and B. van Straalen. 2007. *IJzergieterijen langs de Oude Ijssel (1689 – heden).* Utrecht: Stichting Gelders Erfgoed.

Steenaard, R. 1989. *Stoom en stoomwezen, 1824–1850.* Rotterdam, Ph.D. manuscript submitted at Erasmus Universiteit van Rotterdam.

Vandenbroeke, C. 1979. "Sociale en conjuncturele facetten van de linnennijverheid in Vlaanderen (late 14de-midden 19de eeuw)." *Handelingen der Maatschappij voor Geschiedenis en Oudheidkunde te Gent* 23: 117–174.

Van der Meer, A., and O. Boonstra. 2011. *Repertorium van Nederlandse gemeenten 1812–2011.* Den Haag: DANS.

Van der Wee, H. 1997. "The economic challenge facing Belgium in the 19th and 20th centuries." In *The economic development of Belgium since 1870*, edited by H. Van der Wee and J. Blomme, 52–66. Elgar: Cheltenham-Lyme.

Van Neck, A. 1979. *Les débuts de la machine à vapeur dans l'industrie Belge 1800–1850.* Bruxelles: Palais des Académies.

Van Zanden, J. L. 1987. *De industrialisatie in Amsterdam 1825–1914.* Bergen: Octavo.

Van Zanden, J. L. 1996. "Industrialization in the Netherlands." In *The industrial revolution in national context: Europe and the USA*, edited by M. Teich and R. Porter, 78–94. Cambridge: Cambridge University Press.

Van Zanden, J. L., and A. Van Riel. 2004. *The strictures of inheritance. The Dutch economy in the nineteenth century.* Princeton: Princeton University Press.

Veraghtert, K. 1981. "Ambacht en nijverheid in de Zuidelijke Nederlanden, 1790–1844." In *Algemene Geschiedenis der Nederlanden: deel 10, Nieuwste Tijd,*

1770-heden, edited by H. F. J. M. Van Den Eerenbeemdt, 253–360. Haarlem: Fibula-Van Dishoek.

Verhaegen, B. 1961. *Contribution à l'histoire économique des Flandres*. Leuven: Nauwelaerts.

Wautelet, J.-M. 1995. *Structures industrielles et reproduction élargie du capital en Belgique (1850–1914)*. Louvain-la-Neuve: Louvain-la-Neuve Academia.

Wrigley, E. A. 2010. *Energy and the English industrial revolution*. Cambridge: Cambridge University Press.

4 Regional industrialization in Yugoslavia

Leonard Kukić and Stefan Nikolić

4.1 Introduction

How did industry spread at the southeastern periphery of Europe? The consensus view is that deindustrialization, in place since the 1990s, was preceded by rapid industrialization from 1945 and a lack of considerable development before that (Gerschenkron 1962; Lampe and Jackson 1982; Teichova 1985; Kopsidis and Ivanov 2017). This consensus is, however, based on a country-level approach that ignores potentially large within-country differences. Recent empirical evidence shows that industry was highly unevenly distributed in interwar Yugoslavia, with the northwest of the country being the most industrially advanced (Nikolić 2017). In the postwar period, under the new socialist regime, the northwest of the country remained the most industrially advanced part (Kukić 2017).

From its creation in 1918 until its breakup in 1991, Yugoslavia was the most populous country in southeastern Europe (matched only by Romania). Yugoslavia – which translates to "South Slavia" – brought together all South Slavic peoples (except Bulgarians) into one country. For many centuries, South Slavic peoples had lived under imperial rule. After long struggles for independence, Serbia and Montenegro gained internationally recognized independence from the Ottoman Empire in the late nineteenth century. In the aftermath of World War I, the Kingdoms of Serbia and Montenegro joined several former Austro-Hungarian territories to form Yugoslavia. Bringing together peoples and territories that spent centuries under various imperial powers led to pronounced social, cultural, and economic diversity. These territories also differed in terms of institutions and geography. This heterogeneity makes Yugoslavia an interesting case in which to study regional industrialization.

In this chapter, we use a new dataset on industrial employment and recent empirical findings to explore regional industrialization of Yugoslavia in the long term.[1] We explore regional industrialization using a new dataset based on social insurance statistics. This dataset provides industrial employment figures across three dimensions – industrial branches, regions, and time. To ensure comparability over time, we base the industrial dimension on the International Standard Industrial Classification of All Economic Activities (ISIC, revision 4). From the present day point of view, we find it most sensible to trace long-term

Figure 4.1 Political map of post-World War II Yugoslavia

Source: Own illustration based on Kukić (2019).

industrial development in the area according to Yugoslav successor states – Bosnia-Herzegovina, Croatia, Former Yugoslav Republic of Macedonia (recently renamed North Macedonia, and for ease of reference, henceforth Macedonia), Montenegro, Serbia, and Slovenia (hereafter we refer to these geographical units as "regions" (see Figure 4.1). For these regions, we cover benchmark years spanning both interwar and socialist Yugoslavia, as well as the Yugoslav successor states. We explain the long-term pattern of regional industrialization that follows from our data by considering the role of comparative advantage, new economic geography forces, path dependence, and institutional and policy-related factors.

We arrive at several conclusions on the history of industrialization in Yugoslavia. First, the pace of industrialization was highly uneven among its regions. Neither capitalist nor socialist modes of production were able to ensure a more egalitarian pace of industrialization. Second, various forces drove regional industrialization patterns at various periods. No single theory can explain regional industrialization patterns over the long term. Finally, industrialization in Yugoslavia was characterized by a more direct state involvement than in Western Europe.

4.2 Exploring regional industrialization

There are two main types of data sources that can be used to study regional industrialization of Yugoslavia in the long term: population censuses and social insurance statistics. These sources differ in terms of the type of data they record, their coverage, and their granularity. Population censuses record data on occupations covering the whole economy and are useful to compute occupational shares across the main sectors of the economy: agriculture, industry, and services. The main drawback to using population censuses for our purpose relates to the interwar period; only the census of 1931 reported occupational statistics (the 1921 census did not), the census did not differentiate between industry and crafts, and spatially disaggregated data that would allow us to make comparisons with the postwar period at the regional level are only available at the sectoral level. On the other hand, insurance statistics record employment data, on the number of people actually employed in industrial companies, and crucially provide a breakdown of employment by regions and branches of industry. We exploit the granularity of insurance statistics to calculate the share of industrial employment in the working population (Table 4.1), regional distribution of industrial employment (Tables 4.2 and 4.3), and Krugman's specialization index (Table 4.4) for seven benchmark years during Yugoslavia's existence (1932, 1939, 1953, 1961, 1971, 1981, 1989). We also extend our time-series in Table 4.1 in order to comment on the process of deindustrialization in Yugoslav successor states later in the text.

How did Yugoslav industry develop over time and across space? Employment statistics show that industry accounted for an increasing share of the total economy over time, as the share of industrial workers in the total workforce grew from 4% in 1932 to 23% in 1981 and further to 26% in 1989.[2]

There were important organizational differences over time. From being mostly privately owned during the interwar period, the industry became completely

Table 4.1 Share of industrial employment in total working population (in percent), 1932–2017

	BH	*CRO*	*MK*	*MNE*	*SER*	*SLO*	*YUG*
1932	4	5	1	1	4	8	4
1939	5	6	4	2	5	11	6
1953	7	9	5	4	6	16	8
1961	14	16	10	10	10	25	13
1971	16	18	15	15	15	31	17
1981	22	24	20	19	20	36	23
1989	27	25	26	23	24	39	26
2000	21	21	25	17	22	31	23
2010	19	17	21	10	18	25	19
2017	18	17	20	6	18	26	19

Notes and sources: ***Industrial employment*** – 1932 and 1939: Own calculation using Središnji ured za osiguranje radnika (1932–1941) supplemented with Kraljevina Jugoslavija (1932–1941) for the mining sector; 1953–1989 from Savezni zavod za statistiku (1953, 1962, 1972, 1982, 1991). ***Working population*** – for 1932 and 1939 own estimates for 1931, calculated using Kraljevina Jugoslavija (1940); 1953–1981 from Savezni zavod za statistiku (1953, 1962, 1972, 1982, 1991); and for 1989, World Bank estimates for 1990/1991 are used (https://data.worldbank.org/indicator/SL.TLF.TOTL.IN) and Republički zavod za statistiku (2000: 48). Data for 2000, 2010, and 2017 are ILO modelled estimates of employment by sector (https://ilostat.ilo.org/data/).

Table 4.2 Regional distribution of industrial employment (in percent), 1932–1989

	BH	*CRO*	*MK*	*MNE*	*SER*	*SLO*	*YUG*
1932	14	30	2	1	35	19	100
1939	14	27	4	1	37	17	100
1953	15	28	5	1	33	19	100
1961	16	27	5	1	34	17	100
1971	14	24	6	2	37	17	100
1981	16	22	7	2	37	16	100
1989	17	21	8	2	38	14	100

Source: Own calculations based on sources reported for Table 4.1.

Table 4.3 Regional distribution of industrial employment (population weighted; in percent), 1932–1989

	BH	*CRO*	*MK*	*MNE*	*SER*	*SLO*	*YUG*
1932	15	19	3	7	17	39	100
1939	14	18	5	8	19	37	100
1953	15	20	10	7	13	36	100
1961	15	20	10	9	13	33	100
1971	13	18	12	11	14	32	100
1981	14	18	14	11	14	30	100
1989	15	17	15	12	15	26	100

Source: Own calculations based on sources reported for Table 4.1.

Table 4.4 Krugman's specialization index, 1932–1989

	BH	*CRO*	*MK*	*MNE*	*SER*	*SLO*	*Regional average*
1932	0.81	0.24	0.83	0.90	0.47	0.31	0.59
1939	0.81	0.32	1.13	0.74	0.39	0.36	0.62
1953	0.92	0.35	0.75	0.78	0.52	0.39	0.62
1961	0.71	0.32	0.58	0.77	0.37	0.31	0.51
1971	0.53	0.33	0.54	0.55	0.29	0.26	0.42
1981	0.35	0.18	0.36	0.38	0.18	0.15	0.27
1989	0.32	0.19	0.35	0.39	0.18	0.13	0.26

Source: Own calculations based on sources reported for Table 4.1.

publicly owned during the socialist period (Horvat 1971). During the interwar period, state ownership was mainly limited to large-scale industry (Ministarstvo trgovine i industrije 1941). With the communists taking hold of power in 1945, all industrial enterprises, no matter their size, were nationalized. Only small-scale crafts, petty trade, and agriculture were privately owned.

There was also a strong compositional change in industrial employment over time (see Appendix, Tables A4.2–A4.5). Light industry, including food and textiles, was much more important during the interwar period. During the socialist period, heavy industry – including capital goods, chemicals, and metal processing – became much more important. The socialist planners put a strong emphasis on heavy industries as a device to spearhead the industrialization process. Nevertheless, the role of heavy industry in Yugoslavia was of lesser importance than in the other socialist economies (Horvat 1971). Light industries were of comparatively higher importance in Yugoslavia.

Table 4.1 also shows that there was considerable and persistent regional variation in industrialization. Throughout Yugoslavia's existence, the northwest was the most industrialized part of the country. Slovenia was a clear leader and surpassed the national average of 1981 already twenty years earlier. Croatia was able to perform above the national average until 1981. Interestingly, Bosnia-Herzegovina improved its relative position over time, overtaking Serbia by 1953. Montenegro remained the least industrially developed region throughout.

After the dissolution of Yugoslavia, there has been a clear trend of deindustrialization in all Yugoslav successor states. Deindustrialization was especially pronounced during the 1990s and 2000s and has slowed down in the current decade. Little has changed, however, in terms of international comparisons of industrialization. Slovenia has remained a leader and Montenegro a laggard to the present day. Like the situation in 1989, other Yugoslav successor states remain close to the Yugoslav average.

How was industry distributed across Yugoslav regions? As Table 4.2 shows, the highest share of industrial employment was captured by the two most populous regions – Serbia and Croatia. To account for large regional differences in population, Table 4.3 provides population weighted shares of regional industrial employment. Accounting for population, Slovenia and Croatia once again emerge as the most industrially developed regions, jointly capturing around 60% of industrial employment at the start and around 40% at the end of the period. Macedonia recorded a notable improvement in the period after World War II, first overtaking Montenegro and by 1989 even rising to the level of Bosnia-Herzegovina and Serbia.

How specialized were regions when compared to the rest of the country? Table 4.4 provides the values of Krugman's specialization index (Krugman 1991a) for six regions as well as the sample average for selected benchmark years from 1932 to 1989. Krugman's specialization index compares a region's industrial employment structure with the rest of the country's average and is defined in the range from zero to two. The index will take the value of zero if a region's industrial employment structure is identical to the rest of Yugoslavia, and the value of two if a region's industrial employment structure has no resemblance to the rest of Yugoslavia.

In the interwar period, Bosnia-Herzegovina, Macedonia, and Montenegro had relatively high levels of specialization in accordance with their narrow industrial base. On the other hand, Croatia and Slovenia had relatively low levels of specialization, which reflects their wide industrial base. As regions broadened their industrial base over time, industrial specialization decreased. This is largely the result of the less developed regions developing heavy industries, which were initially nonexistent. Regional specialization of Yugoslavia therefore followed a bell-shaped pattern – increasing in the 1930s and decreasing since the 1960s. This bell-shaped curve confirms the theoretical predictions of new economic geography and is in line with, for example, the empirical findings for the United States (Kim 1998).

4.3 Explaining regional industrialization

Interwar Yugoslavia, 1918–1939

Industrialization advanced in Yugoslavia during the interwar period. Occupational statistics show that the share of industry and crafts in total working population increased between 1921 and 1931 (Kraljevina Jugoslavija 1940: VII). Industrial employment data based on social insurance statistics suggest that industrial development continued between 1932 and 1939 as industrial employment relative to working population increased on both the national and regional level (Table 4.1). In the 1930s, all regions managed to increase their level of industrial development in similar proportion, and as a result the regional distribution of industry changed only marginally (Table 4.2 and Table 4.3).

There were, however, changes in regional specialization. As Table 4.4 shows, specialization increased in Slovenia, Croatia, and Macedonia, decreased in Serbia and Montenegro, and remained unchanged in Bosnia-Herzegovina. On average, regional specialization increased. In 1932, Montenegro was the most specialized region, mainly specializing in food and beverages. By the end of the interwar period, Montenegro managed to decrease its specialization by developing other industries, most notably the metal processing industry. Despite increasing specialization in the 1930s, Croatia and Slovenia remained the least specialized regions, which reflected their wide industrial base.

What can explain these regional patterns of industrial development in interwar Yugoslavia? Recent empirical studies in economic history (Rosés 2003; Crafts and Mulatu 2005, 2006; Wolf 2007; Klein and Crafts 2012; Martinez-Galarraga 2012; Crafts and Wolf 2014; Nikolić 2018; Missiaia 2019) have explained patterns of regional industrialization by considering the role of comparative advantage, new economic geography forces, and path dependence.[3] In the remainder of this section, we provide a discussion on the importance of these factors for regional industrial development in interwar Yugoslavia.

Around 45% of the factories in existence in 1938 were created before Yugoslavia was formed, and Slovenia and Croatia accounted for more than a half of these inherited factories (Ministarstvo trgovine i industrije 1941). This suggests that regional differences in industrial development were already high at the start of the interwar period. Path dependent industrial development is evident, as Slovenia and Croatia remained the most industrialized regions at the end of the interwar period. Sunk costs are one reason why these regional differences persisted throughout the interwar period. High sunk costs in buildings and equipment prevented the relocation of capital-intensive industries from the more developed to the less developed regions (Nikolić 2018).

Natural resources and unskilled labour were necessary inputs for a large part of the Yugoslav industry. Coal was the main energy source (Demokratska Federativna Jugoslavija 1945). Slovenia, Bosnia-Herzegovina, and Serbia were the most abundant regions in terms of coal deposits and mines (Petaković 2011), and accounted for the largest share of employment in coal mining. The application of electricity for industrial purposes was negligible and hydroelectric potential was severely underutilized (Kukoleča 1941: 354). Mineral resources and forests provided the basis for extractive and wood industry. Agricultural inputs and unskilled labour allowed for the development of food and beverage, textile, and tobacco industries. These industries remained dominant in Macedonia and Montenegro. In Serbia, the share of textiles, but also metal processing, increased at the expense of food and beverages. In Slovenia, the share of textiles increased as well (Središnji ured za osiguranje radnika 1932–1941).

Human capital was a highly demanded yet scarce production factor in interwar Yugoslavia. The available human capital was extremely unevenly distributed across the country. For example, in Slovenia, literacy rates were 95%, while in Macedonia they were around 30% (calculated based on Kraljevina Jugoslavija 1938). Moreover, interregional mobility was very low – as much as 94% of people born in Yugoslav territories were living in their region of birth during the interwar period (Kirk 1946: 143). Scarce and unevenly distributed human capital, coupled with low interregional mobility, made comparative advantage in human capital key for the development of skill-intensive industries in the northwest.

Markets played a big role in the regional industrial development of interwar Yugoslavia. According to new economic geography theory, in the presence of intermediate goods and "intermediate levels" of transport costs, industry tends to develop in areas with large market potential in order to minimize on transport costs (Krugman 1991a, 1991b; Krugman and Venables 1995; Venables 1996). The creation of Yugoslavia profoundly changed market potential in the region (Nikolić 2018). Border changes created a new market of approximately twelve million people (Kraljevina Jugoslavija 1932). Becoming part of Yugoslavia considerably increased the size of the domestic market for Serbia, Montenegro, and Macedonia, while the opposite was true for the former Austro-Hungarian regions. Border changes, however, opened the opportunity for Slovenia and Croatia to secure a larger share of the domestic market, as these regions went from being among the least developed parts of Austria-Hungary to being the most developed in Yugoslavia. Moreover, the extension of the Serbian tariff law to the whole of Yugoslavia in 1925 meant that industries in other parts of Yugoslavia were now more protected than before (Šimunčić 1974).

Despite protective tariffs, foreign markets played a vital role in regional industrial development. A large part of interwar industry developed based on exporting raw materials and intermediate goods to Germany, Austria, Italy, and Czechoslovakia. These relationships intensified after the signing of bilateral trade agreements in the 1930s (Drabek 1986). Slovenia and Croatia profited from their proximity to Yugoslavia's main trading partners through high foreign market potential (Nikolić 2018). Throughout the interwar period, Yugoslav industry remained largely dependent on imports of machinery and intermediate goods (Teichova 1985: 253; Drabek 1986: 474). Accordingly, tariffs on these imports were kept relatively low. Utilizing their old business connections, former Austro-Hungarian regions made more use of this industrial policy than other parts of Yugoslavia (Šimunčić 1974).

In sum, all regions managed to increase their level of industrial development during the interwar period, and the regional distribution of industry changed marginally. Factor endowments, markets, and path dependence help explain why some regions were more industrialized than others. Regions with a more developed industry – Croatia and Slovenia – had a comparative advantage in human capital, higher market potential, and inherited more industry from the past.

Socialist Yugoslavia, 1945–1989

If World War II was a war of destruction in Western Europe, in Eastern Europe it was a war of annihilation. The destruction of physical capital was unprecedented, while the destruction of human capital was apocalyptic. Approximately 7% of Yugoslavia's population died during the war (Kočović 1985). In addition to this immense loss of lives, the authorities expelled minority Germans and Italians after 1945. Moreover, many bourgeois Yugoslavs left the country that came under communist rule. Like elsewhere in Europe, the war induced a shortage of working-age men, who traditionally constitute the backbone of the industrial workforce. Furthermore, the Holocaust and the deportation of minority Germans and Italians bequeathed industrial assets to the remaining Yugoslavs, but without the necessary skills to manage and operate them.

The first task of the new state in the aftermath of World War II was to repair war damages. This task was rapidly completed: Yugoslavia attained its prewar output level already in 1947 (Horvat 1971). The second task was to organize the state on socialist principles. All relevant human and physical assets were centralized based on these aims. Agriculture, industry, and the financial system were nationalized, except for petty trade and small-scale agriculture (Horvat 1971). Industrialization was pursued through forced savings, primarily derived from the agricultural sector. Consumption was squeezed, and the heavy hand of the government channelled capital to heavy industries and infrastructure.

Horvat (1971) reports that the industrialization policy during the socialist period was characterized by an economic discussion dominated by two themes: (1) planning for fast growth and (2) the search for authentic socialism. Concerning theme (1), Table 4.1 reveals that industrial employment as a share of working population increased rapidly during the socialist period, albeit from a low level. In just eight years, from 1953 to 1961, industrial employment share increased by five percentage points, which is equivalent to the total 1939 industrial employment share. In relative terms, the industrial employment share increased the most in Montenegro – one of the least developed republics – where it more than doubled during this short period of time, from 4% to 10%. In absolute terms, Slovenia achieved the largest increase in industrial employment share. It increased by 9 percentage points, from 16% to 25%.

Concerning theme (2), the search for authentic socialism yielded the greatest decentralization and democratization drive among the former socialist countries. The search for a unique form of socialism was largely a consequence of the conflict between Tito and Stalin in 1948, and the desire of the Yugoslav leadership to distance themselves from the Soviet Union. The Yugoslav leadership made two institutional changes that were of critical importance. First, economic and political power was devolved from the federal centre to the constituent republics of Yugoslavia. Second, economic power was devolved from central planners to work councils of labour-managed firms. Central planning was abandoned, and self-management became the guiding ideological principle of firm management, as well as of social and political life. Yugoslavia embarked on a unique experiment, earning the nickname, as Bergson (1968: 655) put it, of the "venturesome" country.

Due to these institutional changes, Yugoslavia symbolized to many a viable market socialist system. The viability of the system seemed corroborated by the extremely rapid industrial growth during the 1950s, but also during the overall socialist period in general. Of importance are the labour-managed firms, which attracted great international interest. Ward (1958), Vanek (1970) and Meade (1972) argue that labour-managed firms maximized income per worker, unlike their capitalist, profit-maximizing counterparts.[4] Labour-managed firms were maximizing income through capital accumulation (Sapir 1980; Kukić 2018). Capital accumulation caused income generation, and therefore led to a larger income for the members of labour-managed firms. Rapid capital accumulation also led to a rapid expansion of firms and industries, and thus to an expansion of industrial employment.

The rapid capital accumulation in socialist economies was supported by the soft-budget constraint (Kornai 1980). This type of constraint had important implications concerning efficiency and the incentive to accumulate capital. Kornai (1980) argues that, in order to assure the fulfilment of output targets, socialist firms were ultimately allowed to use more resources than initially planned. Firms could disregard costs because they were bailed out by the state if they ran into problems.

Both Bateman et al. (1988) and Kukić (2017) argue that labour-managed firms influenced the patterns of regional industrialization. Kukić (2017) argues that the capital intensity bias was particularly salient in the poor regions for two reasons. First, regional development policy consisted of capital aid. This effectively decreased the cost of capital in the poor regions, stimulating further capital accumulation. Second, the poor regions received more subsidies enhancing capital accumulation than the rich regions did.

Due to capital aid and subsidies, the poor regions strongly converged towards the capital-to-labour ratios of the rich regions (Kukić 2017). The less developed regions also strongly converged towards the human capital intensities of the richer regions (Kukić 2017). The federal aid undoubtedly stimulated human capital accumulation. The less developed regions received capital transfers earmarked for the expansion of public goods, including school systems. In general, all socialist states engaged in a massive expansion of their educational systems and in a society-wide campaign to increase the educational attainment levels of their citizens. Some consider the rapid increase of human capital a rare lasting achievement of socialist systems. Regional development in Yugoslavia also demonstrates that socialist systems were able to decrease educational inequality.

To the extent that capital and labour are complementary factors of production, this convergence in factor intensities is also indicated by Table 4.2 and Table 4.3. They both show that the less developed regions (Bosnia-Herzegovina, Macedonia, Montenegro, and Serbia) strongly increased their share in total industrial employment over time, whether weighted or unweighted by population. Commensurately, the more developed regions (Slovenia and Croatia) experienced a strong decrease in the total industrial employment share.

Despite the strong regional convergence in industrial employment shares, however, Yugoslav regions did not converge in terms of labour productivity and incomes. Kukić (2017) finds that regional efficiency levels have strongly diverged during the socialist period, causing income divergence. Efficiency levels diverged because the capital accumulation in the poor regions stood at odds with the relative abundance of labour (Kukić 2017). By extension, the poor regions were developing along lines of comparative disadvantage, in a twist to the predictions of the Heckscher-Ohlin model.

It seems unlikely that labour-managed firms can explain the sharp slowdown and eventual stagnation of the economy during the 1980s. Broadberry and Klein (2011) argue that socialist economies could not adapt to the requirements of flexible production technology during the 1980s. Their explanation, however, holds little relevance for Yugoslavia. The slowdown of Yugoslavia's economy was very sharp, while the process of technology adoption tends to be drawn out. It seems instead that external shocks caused the stagnation of Yugoslavia during the 1980s. In particular, the 1979 oil shock is of critical importance. It was a major supply-side shock to Yugoslavia, given that Yugoslavia was using two to three times more energy per unit of output than an average Organisation for Economic Co-operation and Development (OECD) country did (Dyker 1990).

The increase in oil prices had a further debilitating impact on the economy across the regions. Increasing oil prices led to an increase in interest rates in creditor nations to curb inflation. Hence, global interest rates increased Yugoslavia's debt servicing costs, eventually causing a debt crisis which was met by major austerity measures. This led to a collapse of aggregate demand, which did not recover during the second half of the 1980s (Dyker 1990). Yugoslavia thus experienced a combination of negative demand and supply-side shocks during the 1980s. These caused the stagnation of the economy during the 1980s and contributed towards the collapse of the country itself.

After the dissolution of Yugoslavia in 1991

The fall of socialism in Eastern Europe in 1989 is one of the key junctures in recent world history. A decades-long bifurcation of the world into two economic blocks ended. While some claimed that the world had reached the "end of the history", the fall of socialism signified in former Yugoslavia yet another one of various twentieth-century upheavals. While it brought prosperity to some, it brought poverty and long-term unemployment to others. While some experienced democracy and national liberation, others experienced authoritarianism and extreme nationalism. The country became the site of the greatest violent struggle in Europe after World War II.

The rapid deindustrialization that characterized the successor states of Yugoslavia during the 1990s and 2000s was determined by two factors. First, the transition to a market economy, with the liberalization of markets, the removal of import restrictions, and the hardening of budget constraints, exposed the inefficiency of many industrial firms, leading to their downsizing and bankruptcy. Moreover, the development path of socialist Yugoslavia was skewed towards industries, with a relatively low share of services in output. The output mix of Yugoslavia did not correspond to consumer preferences because of restricted consumer choice. The restructuring towards services with the liberalization of the economy was thus inevitable.

The second factor that stimulated deindustrialization was the implosion of the common market and the dissolution of the country. Although difficult to quantify, the direct effects of the dissolution of the country were undoubtedly large. The implosion of Yugoslavia had further indirect effects, which are possibly even greater. The Yugoslav wars of the 1990s retarded the rule of law and institutional development of the successor states and postponed their entry into the large single market of the European Union (EU). One of the side effects of these developments was that the new states were largely unattractive to Western direct investments that otherwise modernized and rejuvenated the industries of the other former socialist states in Central Europe (Klein et al. 2017). As of 2019, only Croatia and Slovenia are part of the EU, with the other states lacking a clear prospect of joining it in the foreseeable future.

The successor states of Yugoslavia have thus made a full circle in their historical development over the past 100 years. Croatia and Slovenia are again part of the European core (EU now, Habsburg Empire before), while the other states are remaining at its periphery, just like at the time of the Ottoman Empire before World War I. Nevertheless, all of them have experienced rapid industrialization in the meantime and are now struggling with the challenges of modern postindustrialized societies.

4.4 Conclusion

In its reasonably short but highly tumultuous history, Yugoslavia's pace of industrialization was very uneven. In the second half of the nineteenth century, Slovenia and Croatia started systematic industrializing (Schulze 2000, 2007), while the other regions experienced some stirrings of modern industrial growth (Vučo 1974a, 1974b; Lampe 1996). Following World War I and the creation of Yugoslavia, the internationally depressed interwar period was not conducive to industrialization. Despite this negative global environment, Yugoslav regions further industrialized during the interwar period. After World War II and the establishment of the socialist regime, Yugoslavia experienced super-charged industrialization. With the re-establishment of capitalism and the disintegration of the country during the early 1990s, Yugoslav successor states started deindustrializing, mirroring the deindustrialization processes that began in Western countries during the 1980s.

In this chapter, we argue that no single force can explain the dynamics of regional industrialization in Yugoslavia. Different forces drove regional industrialization patterns at different periods. During the interwar period, factor endowments, markets, and path dependence help explain why some regions were more industrialized than others. Regions with a more developed industry had a comparative advantage in human capital, had higher market potential, and inherited more industry from the past. High sunk costs in buildings and equipment ensured path-dependent industrial development, as such costs prevented the relocation of capital-intensive industries from the richer to the poorer regions. Both domestic and foreign market potential mattered as well. Croatia and Slovenia were closer to Western Europe and continued using their old (Austro-Hungarian) business connections to secure foreign markets for their products. Moreover, Croatia and Slovenia were able to secure a larger share of the domestic market, as they had an initial lead in industry. Finally, comparative advantage also mattered. The poorer regions were able to utilize their unskilled labour to develop industries that used low-skilled labour intensively, while the richer regions were able to utilize their higher levels of human capital to develop industries that used human capital intensively.

During the socialist period, regional industrialization patterns were driven by a combination of institutional and policy-related factors. In particular, the labour-managed firms were of critical importance. The unique institutional setting of socialist Yugoslavia makes comparative advantage and new economic geography models less relevant for explaining the patterns of regional industrialization during socialism. First, these models assume that firms maximize profits, while Yugoslav labour-managed firms maximized income. Second, firms were not freely established. Local municipalities decided whether to allow an establishment of a firm within its administrative boundaries. As such, political factors, rather than market factors, often determined the exact location of firms (Horvat 1971). However, this does not mean that new economic geography models cannot help us explain the patterns of industrialization during socialism. If political factors drove the location of firms, it might well be that the location of firms was a source of inefficiency. Moreover, path dependence continued to matter, as poorer regions did not manage to converge towards the industrial structures and ultimately income levels of the richer regions. Finally, given path dependence, larger issues of increasing returns and externalities might be related to this regional income divergence in Yugoslavia (Romer 1986; Lucas 1988).

Notes

1 The Kingdom of Serbs, Croats and Slovenes, established in December 1918, officially changed its name to Kingdom of Yugoslavia in 1929. Throughout the chapter, we use the conventional term "Yugoslavia".

2 According to occupational statistics (Table A4.1), which use a broader definition of the secondary sector, the share of industry in the total economy grew from 12% in 1931 to 29% in 1981.

3 For a quantitative treatment of the determinants of industrial location in interwar Yugoslavia, see Nikolić (2018).

4 Many studies have tried to assess whether labour-managed firms behaved according to theory. In a direct test that relies on a sample of industrial firms, Prašnikar et al. (1994) find that labour-managed firms behaved somewhere between the level implied by theory and the level implied by profit-maximizing firms.

References

Bateman, D. A., M. Nishimizu, and J. M. Page Jr. 1988. "Regional productivity differentials and development policy in Yugoslavia." *Journal of Comparative Economics* 12(1): 24–42.

Bergson, A. 1968. "Market socialism revisited." *Journal of Political Economy* 75(5): 655–673.

Broadberry, S. N., and A. Klein. 2011. "When and why did Eastern European economies begin to fail? Lessons from a Czechoslovak/UK productivity comparison, 1921–1991." *Explorations in Economic History* 48(1): 37–52.

Crafts, N., and A. Mulatu. 2005. "What explains the location of industry in Britain, 1871–1931?" *Journal of Economic Geography* 5(4): 499–518.

Crafts, N., and A. Mulatu. 2006. "How did the location of industry respond to falling transport costs in Britain before World War I?" *The Journal of Economic History* 66(3): 575–607.

Crafts, N., and N. Wolf. 2014. "The location of the UK cotton textiles industry in 1838: a quantitative analysis." *The Journal of Economic History* 74(4): 1103–1139.

Demokratska Federativna Jugoslavija. 1945. *Industrijska statistika: Rezultati industrijskog popisa iz 1939. godine: III Utrošeno gorivo* [Industrial statistics: results of the industrial census from the year 1939: Fuel consumed]. Beograd: Državni statistički ured.

Drabek, Z. 1986. "Foreign trade performance and policy." In *The economic history of Eastern Europe, 1919–1975: economic structure and performance between the two wars*, Vol. 1, edited by M. Kaser and E. Radice, 379–466. Oxford: Oxford University Press.

Dyker, D. 1990. *Yugoslavia: socialism, development and debt.* London: Routledge.

Gerschenkron, A. 1962. *Economic backwardness in historical perspective: a book of essays*. Cambridge: Harvard University Press.

Horvat, B. 1971. "Yugoslav economic policy in the post-war period: problems, ideas, institutional developments." *American Economic Review: Supplement, Surveys of National Economic Policy Issues and Policy Research* 61(3): 71–169.

Kim, S. 1998. "Economic integration and convergence: US regions, 1840–1987." *The Journal of Economic History* 58(3): 659–683.

Kirk, D. 1946. *Europe's population in the interwar years*. Princeton: Princeton University Press.

Klein, A., and N. Crafts. 2012. "Making sense of the manufacturing belt: determinants of US industrial location, 1880–1920." *Journal of Economic Geography* 12(4): 775–807.

Klein, A., M.-S. Schulze, and T. Vonyo. 2017. "How peripheral was the periphery? industrialization in East Central Europe since 1870." In *The spread of modern industry to the periphery since 1871*, edited by K. H. O'Rourke and J. G. Williamson, 63–90. Oxford: Oxford University Press.

Kočović, B. 1985. *Žrtve Drugog Svetskog Rata u Jugoslaviji* [Victims of World War II in Yugoslavia]. London: Veritas Foundation Press.

Kopsidis, M., and M. Ivanov. 2017. "Industrialization and de-industrialization in Southeast Europe, 1870–2010." In *The spread of modern industry to the periphery since 1871*, edited by K. H. O'Rourke and J. G. Williamson, 91–114. Oxford: Oxford University Press.

Kornai, J. 1980. *Economics of shortage*. Amsterdam: North Holland Press.

Kraljevina Jugoslavija. 1932–1941. *Statistički godišnjak, 1929–1940 (knjige I-X)* [Statistical yearbook, 1929–1940 (books I-X)]. Beograd: Opšta državna statistika.

Kraljevina Jugoslavija. 1940. *Definitivni rezultati popisa stanovništva, 1931 (Knjiga IV)* [Definitive results of the population census, 1931 (book IV)]. Beograd: Opšta državna statistika.

Krugman, P. 1991a. *Geography and trade*. Cambridge: MIT press.

Krugman, P. 1991b. "Increasing returns and economic geography." *The Journal of Political Economy* 99(3): 483–499.

Krugman, P., and A. J. Venables. 1995. "Globalization and the inequality of nations." *Quarterly Journal of Economics* 110(4): 857–880.

Kukić, L. 2017. *Regional development under socialism: evidence from Yugoslavia*. Economic History Working Papers, 267/2017, LSE.

Kukić, L. 2018. "Socialist growth revisited: insights from Yugoslavia." *European Review of Economic History* 22(4): 403–429.

Kukić, L. 2019. *The last Yugoslavs: ethnic diversity, national identity, and civil war*. Mimeo. UC3M.

Kukoleča, S. 1941. *Industrija Jugoslavije, 1918–1938* [Industry of Yugoslavia, 1918–1938]. Beograd: Balkanska štampa.

Lampe, J. R. 1996. *Yugoslavia as history, twice there was a country*. Cambridge: Cambridge University Press.

Lampe, J. R., and M. R. Jackson. 1982. *Balkan economic history, 1550–1950: from imperial borderlands to developing nations*. Bloomington: Indiana University Press.

Lucas, R. E. 1988. "On the mechanics of economic development." *Journal of Monetary Economics* 22(1): 3–42.

Martinez-Galarraga, J. 2012. "The determinants of industrial location in Spain, 1856–1929." *Explorations in Economic History* 49(2): 255–275.

Meade, J. E. 1972. "The theory of labour-managed firms and of profit sharing." *Economic Journal* 82(326): 402–428.

Ministarstvo trgovine i industrije. 1941. *Statistika industrije Kraljevine Jugoslavije, sa adresarom industriskih preduzeća* [Industrial statistics of the Kingdom of Yugoslavia, with an address book of industrial firms]. Beograd: Ministarstvo trgovine i industrije.

Missiaia, A. 2019. "Market versus endowment: explaining early industrial location in Italy (1871–1911)." *Cliometrica* 13(1): 127–161.

Nikolić, S. 2017. *New economic history of Yugoslavia, 1919–1939: industrial location, market integration, and financial crises.* Ph.D. Thesis, University of York.

Nikolić, S. 2018. "Determinants of industrial location: Kingdom of Yugoslavia in the interwar period." *European Review of Economic History* 22(1): 101–133.

Petaković, J. 2011. "Prilog proučavanju industrijske konjunkture u Kraljevini Jugoslaviji – proizvodnja uglja od 1920. do 1938. godine [A contribution to the study of industrial situation in the Kingdom of Yugoslavia – coal production 1920–1938]." *Tokovi Istorije* 39(2): 42–61.

Prašnikar, J., J. Švejnar, D. Mihaljek, and V. Prašnikar. 1994. "Behavior of participatory firms in Yugoslavia: lessons for transforming economies." *Review of Economics and Statistics* 76(4): 728–741.

Republički Zavod za Statistiku. 2000. *Statistički godišnjak Srbije* [Statistical yearbook of Serbia]. Beograd: Republički zavod za statistiku.

Romer, P. 1986. "Increasing returns and long-run growth." *Journal of Political Economy* 94(5): 1002–1037.

Rosés, J. R. 2003. "Why isn't the whole of Spain industrialized? New economic geography and early industrialization, 1797–1910." *The Journal of Economic History* 63(4): 995–1022.

Sapir, A. 1980. "Economic growth and factor substitution: what happened to the Yugoslav miracle?" *Economic Journal* 90(385): 294–313.

Savezni zavod za statistiku. 1953, 1961, 1971, 1981. *Popis Stanovništva SFR Jugoslavije* [Population census of Yugoslavia]. Beograd: Savezni zavod za statistiku.

Savezni zavod za statistiku. 1953, 1962, 1972, 1982, 1991. *Statistički Godišnjak SFR Jugoslavije* [Statistical yearbook of Yugoslavia]. Beograd: Savezni zavod za statistiku.

Schulze, M.-S. 2000. "Patterns of growth and stagnation in the late nineteenth Century Habsburg economy." *European Review of Economic History* 4(3): 311–340.

Schulze, M.-S. 2007. "Origins of catch-up failure: comparative productivity growth in the Habsburg Empire, 1870–1910." *European Review of Economic History* 11(2): 189–218.

Šimunčić, Z. 1974. "Osnovne karakteristike industrijskog razvitka na području Hrvatske u međuratnom razdoblju [Basic characteristics of industrial development in the territory of Croatia in the interwar period]." *Acta Historico-oeconomica Iugoslaviae* 1(1): 61–78.

Središnji ured za osiguranje radnika. 1932–1941. *Radnička zaštita: službeni list središnjeg ureda za osiguranje radnika u Zagrebu* [Protection of workers: official journal of the Central Office for the Insurance of Workers in Zagreb]. Zagreb: Središnji ured za osiguranje radnika.

Teichova, A. 1985. “Industry.” In *The economic history of Eastern Europe, 1919–1975: Economic structure and performance between the two wars*, Vol. I, edited by M. C. Kaser and E. A. Radice, 222–322. Oxford: Oxford University Press.

Vanek, J. 1970. *The general theory of labor-managed market economies*. Ithaca: Cornell University Press.

Venables, A. J. 1996. “Equilibrium locations of vertically linked industries.” *International Economic Review* 37(2): 341–359.

Vučo, N. 1974a. “Industrijska revolucija u Jugoslavenskim zemljama (Teme za diskusiju)” [Industrial revolution in Yugoslav lands (Discussion Topics)]. *Acta Historico-oeconomica Iugoslaviae* 1(1): 9–15.

Vučo, N. 1974b. “Pogled na industrijsku revoluciju u Srbiji u XIX Veku [A look at the industrial revolution in Serbia in the XIX century].” *Acta Historico-oeconomica Iugoslaviae* 1(1): 79–98.

Ward, B. 1958. “The firm in Illyria: market syndicalism.” *American Economic Review* 48(4): 566–589.

Wolf, N. 2007. “Endowments vs. market potential: what explains the relocation of industry after the polish reunification in 1918?” *Explorations in Economic History* 44(1): 22–42.

World Bank. n.d. “Labour force, total.” https://data.worldbank.org/indicator/SL.TLF.TOTL.IN, Accessed 22 February 2018.

Appendix 4.1

Working population by major occupational sector, 1931–1989

Table A4.1.1 Occupational distribution of working population by major sector, 1931–1981

	BH	*CRO*	*MK*	*MNE*	*SER*	*SLO*	*YUG*
1931							
Agriculture	90	83	85	93	84	69	84
Industry	7	12	11	5	11	24	12
Services	3	5	5	3	4	7	4
Total economy	100	100	100	100	100	100	100
1953							
Agriculture	68	63	68	67	71	50	67
Industry	11	14	10	8	11	24	13
Services	21	23	22	25	18	26	21
Total economy	100	100	100	100	100	100	100
1961							
Agriculture	64	54	62	58	65	40	60
Industry	17	22	16	14	16	34	19
Services	20	24	22	28	19	27	21
Total economy	100	100	100	100	100	100	100
1971							
Agriculture	52	42	49	45	54	27	48
Industry	22	27	23	19	21	41	24
Services	26	32	29	35	25	32	28
Total economy	100	100	100	100	100	100	100
1981							
Agriculture	28	24	35	18	39	15	31
Industry	30	31	27	27	25	43	29
Services	42	45	38	55	36	42	40
Total economy	100	100	100	100	100	100	100

Source: Kraljevina Jugoslavija (1940) and Savezni zavod za statistiku (1953, 1961, 1971, and 1981).

Notes: Country abbreviations: BH – Bosnia-Herzegovina, CRO – Croatia, MK – North Macedonia, MNE – Montenegro, SER – Serbia, SLO – Slovenia, YUG – Yugoslavia. Agriculture includes agriculture, forestry, and fishing; Industry includes mining, industry, and crafts; Services include trade, credit, transport, public services, free professions, and army; the "other" category is excluded.

Table A4.1.2 Industrial employment, by region and ISIC division, 1932

ISIC Section/Division	*BH*	*CRO*	*MK*	*MNE*	*SER*	*SLO*	*YUG*
B Mining and quarrying							
5 Mining of coal and lignite	7,424	5,899	0	0	8,719	6,697	28,739
7 Mining of metal ores	566	216	0	0	3,029	573	4,384
8 Other mining and quarrying	1,329	7,999	314	84	9,164	3,979	22,869
C Manufacturing							
10 Manufacture of food products, and 11 Manufacture of beverages	3,368	10,675	909	351	17,484	3,685	36,472
12 Manufacture of tobacco products	1,804	2,109	1,830	**552**	3,101	857	10,253
13 Manufacture of textiles	1,061	10,892	297	43	10,596	9,272	32,161
15 Manufacture of leather and related products, and 22 Manufacture of rubber and plastics products	1,239	6,228	990	37	8,372	4,921	21,788
16 Manufacture of wood and of products of wood and cork except furniture; manufacture of articles of straw and plaiting materials	16,638	19,963	423	268	8,336	10,190	55,819
17 Manufacture of paper and paper products, and 18 Printing and sreproduction of recorded media	383	3,426	116	35	4,675	2,953	11,588
20 Manufacture of chemicals and chemical products	2,835	3,282	77	35	1,916	1,690	9,835
24 Manufacture of basic metals, and 28 Manufacture of machinery and equipment n.e.c.	2,140	7,210	602	110	14,667	6,410	31,138
29 Manufacture of motor vehicles, trailers, and semi-trailers	467	1,582	67	250	3,261	284	5,911
D Electricity, gas, steam, and air conditioning supply							
35 Electricity, gas, steam, and air conditioning supply	442	2,509	97	47	2,765	668	6,529
Sum	39,697	81,990	5,724	1,812	96,085	52,179	277,486

Notes: We used the International Standard Industrial Classification of All Economic Activities (ISIC, revision 4) to classify industrial employment data (for data sources, see notes to Table 4.1). Tables A4.2–A4.5 provide industrial employment data by regions and ISIC divisions for 1932, 1953, 1971, and 1989.

Table A4.1.3 Industrial employment, by region and ISIC division, 1953

ISIC Section/Division	*BH*	*CRO*	*MK*	*MNE*	*SER*	*SLO*	*YUG*
B Mining and quarrying							
5 Mining of coal and lignite	22,000	15,800	100	100	19,700	12,400	70,100
6 Extraction of crude petroleum and natural gas	700	3,500	0	0	500	900	5,700
7 Mining of metal ores	2,400	5,900	8,900	1,100	38,000	11,400	67,700
8 Other mining and quarrying	6,200	17,500	3,600	700	23,500	8,900	60,400
C Manufacturing							
10 Manufacture of food products, and 11 Manufacture of beverages	1,800	15,700	1,100	500	18,500	2,900	40,500
12 Manufacture of tobacco products	2,200	1,400	3,200	200	2,600	600	10,200
13 Manufacture of textiles	3,300	23,200	3,600	0	23,700	21,000	74,800
15 Manufacture of leather and related products	900	7,600	900	0	3,600	5,200	18,200
16 Manufacture of wood and of products of wood and cork except furniture; manufacture of articles of straw and plaiting materials	39,400	34,300	2,900	2,300	14,100	15,900	108,900
17 Manufacture of paper and paper products	700	2,700	0	0	1,000	3,200	7,600
18 Printing and reproduction of recorded media	900	3,400	400	100	6,100	1,300	12,200
20 Manufacture of chemicals and chemical products	2,300	6,500	300	100	3,500	2,500	15,100
22 Manufacture of rubber and plastics products	0	200	0	0	900	600	1,800
24 Manufacture of basic metals	4,900	17,500	1,200	200	30,800	19,600	74,300
30 Manufacture of other transport equipment	0	1,000	0	0	1,800	0	2,800
D Electricity, gas, steam, and air conditioning supply							
35 Electricity, gas, steam, and air conditioning supply	2,000	9,200	900	600	8,100	6,900	27,700
Sum	89,700	165,400	27,100	5,900	196,400	113,300	598,000

Notes: We used the International Standard Industrial Classification of All Economic Activities (ISIC, revision 4) to classify industrial employment data (for data sources, see notes to Table 4.1). Tables A4.2–A4.5 provide industrial employment data by regions and ISIC divisions for 1932, 1953, 1971, and 1989.

Table A4.1.4 Industrial employment, by region and ISIC division, 1971

ISIC Section/Division	*BH*	*CRO*	*MK*	*MNE*	*SER*	*SLO*	*YUG*
B Mining and quarrying							
5 Mining of coal and lignite	27,600	4,000	0	400	21,400	10,400	63,800
6 Extraction of crude petroleum and natural gas	1,800	10,800	0	0	4,100	700	17,400
7 Mining of metal ores	24,900	12,800	13,600	5,600	34,000	21,000	111,900
8 Other mining and quarrying	11,100	27,100	11,100	1,500	47,700	14,500	113,000
9 Mining support service activities	1,000	1,600	900	300	1,300	0	5,100
C Manufacturing							
10 Manufacture of food products, and 11 Manufacture of beverages	7,800	39,400	7,800	1,100	56,300	11,500	123,900
12 Manufacture of tobacco products	2,900	2,100	5,800	300	4,000	700	15,800
13 Manufacture of textiles	24,200	58,600	21,000	4,400	88,900	41,000	238,100
15 Manufacture of leather and related products	5,000	13,300	3,800	800	15,700	11,200	49,800
16 Manufacture of wood and of products of wood and cork except furniture; manufacture of articles of straw and plaiting materials	36,200	33,300	7,700	3,700	26,800	27,500	135,200
17 Manufacture of paper and paper products	8,700	6,200	900	1,400	6,400	6,600	30,200
18 Printing and reproduction of recorded media	3,600	13,400	2,600	600	24,500	6,600	51,300
20 Manufacture of chemicals and chemical products	8,600	27,200	5,000	500	34,100	12,300	87,700
22 Manufacture of rubber and plastics products	300	7,600	0	100	7,900	2,700	18,600
24 Manufacture of basic metals	37,200	55,700	7,200	2,200	136,900	59,300	298,500
30 Manufacture of other transport equipment	0	21,000	0	500	3,200	200	24,900
D Electricity, gas, steam, and air conditioning supply							
35 Electricity, gas, steam, and air conditioning supply	16,100	31,500	6,200	3,300	51,300	30,500	138,900
Sum	217,000	365,600	93,600	26,700	564,500	256,700	1,524,100

Notes: We used the International Standard Industrial Classification of All Economic Activities (ISIC, revision 4) to classify industrial employment data (for data sources, see notes to Table 4.1). Tables A4.2–A4.5 provide industrial employment data by regions and ISIC divisions for 1932, 1953, 1971, and 1989.

Table A4.1.5 Industrial employment, by region and ISIC division, 1989

ISIC Section/ Division	*BH*	*CRO*	*MK*	*MNE*	*SER*	*SLO*	*YUG*
			B Mining and quarrying				
5 Mining of coal and lignite	30,525	1,826	368	2,167	26,077	9,993	70,956
6 Extraction of crude petroleum and natural gas	437	2,510	0	0	2,145	0	5,092
7 Mining of metal ores	39,836	14,637	20,073	9,899	50,591	16,689	151,725
8 Other mining and quarrying	20,676	36,019	17,886	1,775	67,915	19,220	163,491
			C Manufacturing				
10 Manufacture of food products	22,378	51,088	13,274	2,806	98,577	18,704	206,827
11 Manufacture of beverages	3,122	9,305	3,373	721	16,581	4,235	37,337
12 Manufacture of tobacco products	2,468	3,494	7,895	382	3,947	771	18,957
13 Manufacture of textiles	16,014	30,683	23,129	4,776	52,344	19,413	146,359
14 Manufacture of wearing apparel	59,114	61,832	41,232	4,428	121,679	36,828	325,113
15 Manufacture of leather and related products	30,327	38,598	10,836	3,554	47,252	16,002	146,569
16 Manufacture of wood and of products of wood and cork except furniture; manufacture of articles of straw and plaiting materials	61,675	49,974	9,126	5,524	45,915	32,594	204,808
17 Manufacture of paper and paper products	9,726	9,804	2,103	1,437	14,398	10,434	47,902
18 Printing and reproduction of recorded media	5,032	12,044	2,660	694	19,978	6,392	46,800
19 Manufacture of coke and refined petroleum products	1,046	4,904	1,478	0	3,963	1,302	12,693

(*Continued*)

Table A4.1.5 (Continued)

ISIC Section/ Division	*BH*	*CRO*	*MK*	*MNE*	*SER*	*SLO*	*YUG*
20 Manufacture of chemicals and chemical products	21,168	36,857	12,912	1,655	61,544	21,876	15,6012
22 Manufacture of rubber and plastics products	1,924	7,920	284	437	1,9847	4,614	35,026
24 Manufacture of basic metals	53,338	55,030	1,0911	3,619	114,149	36,631	273,678
27 Manufacture of electrical equipment	21,346	36,645	11,594	3,585	67,398	52,083	192,669
28 Manufacture of machinery and equipment n.e.c.	25,782	39,013	3,295	2,356	69,912	27,715	168,073
29 Manufacture of motor vehicles, trailers, and semi-trailers	25,202	16,893	9,869	0	80,331	23,670	155,965
30 Manufacture of other transport equipment	0	21,032	0	1,083	6,549	552	29,216
D Electricity, gas, steam, and air conditioning supply							
35 Electricity, gas, steam, and air conditioning supply	17,441	20,113	9,682	3,542	28,556	8,090	87,424
Sum	468,577	560,221	211,980	54,440	1,019,648	367,808	2,682,692

Notes: We used the International Standard Industrial Classification of All Economic Activities (ISIC, revision 4) to classify industrial employment data (for data sources, see notes to Table 4.1). Tables A4.2–A4.5 provide industrial employment data by regions and ISIC divisions for 1932, 1953, 1971, and 1989.

5 Regional industrialization in Italy[1]

Anna Missiaia

5.1 Introduction

At the time of its Unification in 1861, Italy was characterized by profound regional disparities showing how its regions differed in their social and economic indicators. Scattered quantitative evidence suggests that these disparities originated well before the political unification. The Southern regions presented levels of GDP per capita around 20% lower than the Northwestern regions (Felice 2019). But the South lagged much further behind in literacy rates, school enrolment, and land productivity and in its levels of industrialization (Cafagna 1989; Zamagni 1990; Felice 2015). In the first decades after the Unification, although some of these indicators – such as literacy – improved in the South, fundamental measures of economic performance such as GDP per capita and value added in industry drifted further apart (Felice 2019; Ciccarelli and Fenoaltea 2009, 2014).

From the 1880s onwards, Italy experienced its first industrialization in the modern sense, and by World War I all the major modern industrial sectors were represented (Zamagni 1990). It is in this period that industrialization in the three regions of the Northwest of the country – Piedmont, Lombardy, and Liguria – began to forge ahead, forming the so-called Industrial Triangle and making the location of industries a fundamental element in understanding the general North–South divide. During the Fascist era (1922–1943), the central government did little to revert the trend of divergence. On the contrary, a focus on the existing industrial centres led to the consolidation of the Industrial Triangle. This, along with the restrictions to emigration and the autarkical policies that pushed the South to specialize in agriculture, allowed the North–South divide to reach its historical peak in the 1930s. The war effort during World War II continued to favour the heavy industry largely located in the Northwest (Iuzzolino et al. 2013). Only after World War II did the Italian regions begin to converge, mainly through heavy state intervention (Felice and Lepore 2017). But the state-led industrialization of the South that proceeded over the 1950s and 1960s was not self-sustaining, and the tendency came to a close with the end of the Economic Miracle. From the 1970s on, the North–South gap remained stable. At the same time, through the development of industrial activity in the Northeast and Centre, the so-called Third Italy emerged. Unlike the experience of the Industrial

Triangle, the Third Italy industrialized through small and medium-sized firms organized in industrial districts (Felice 2007).

To explain how economic activity locates, economic geography provides two competing theories: one is the Heckscher-Ohlin theory (H-O), which predicts that economic activity locates according to the endowment of factors in a given location. Most commonly, this endowment consists in natural resources (raw materials or energy sources) or human capital. The other is the new economic geography (NEG) theory that focuses on market access as the main explanatory factor in the location of economic activity. This chapter analyzes the different phases of regional industrialization through both of these theories. We claim that the location of industries across the Italian regions was influenced in different historical periods by different elements. The patterns that developed during the first modern industrialization starting in the 1880s were largely driven by endowment forces and by access to domestic markets. During the Fascist period and World War II, the existing dualism between the Northwest and the rest of the country was consolidated by investing in existing industrial areas, leaving space for a path-dependency explanation. The Economic Miracle of the 1950s and 1960s temporarily reversed the trend with the state-led industrialization in the South, but from the 1970s onwards, new economic georgraphy forces fostered the development of export-oriented industrial districts in the Northeast and Centre. The relative dynamism of the North and Centre appears in sharp contrast with the immobility of the South, which has not been able to reverse its fortunes as the Third Italy did.

This chapter is organized as follows. Section 5.2 provides some historical background on the economic and industrial development of the Italian states before the Unification of 1861. Section 5.3 discusses the evolution of regional performances from 1861 to the outbreak of World War I. Section 5.4 looks at the interwar period. Section 5.5 considers the period from the postwar Economic Miracle to the end of the twentieth century. Section 5.6 concludes and suggests topics for further research.

5.2 The North–South divide before 1861

Italy is a relatively new national state. The political unification of the country dates back to 1861. Before 1861, the Italian peninsula was divided into several small states, some independent and some under the influence of foreign powers, most notably Austria-Hungary and France.

The economic and social conditions of the pre-unitary states were far from uniform, but a common trait was that they were all rather agricultural and their commercial activity was mostly based on agricultural products (Romani 1976). The Kingdom of Sardinia included the regions of Piedmont, Liguria, and Sardinia. The first two were the most economically advanced of the whole peninsula, with a fairly modern agricultural sector boosted by investments in irrigation and the introduction of composts in farming. Some wool and cotton production was based in Piedmont, using raw materials partly imported from the South (Romani

1976). Sardinia was much less developed than the rest of the kingdom, with latifundia-based agriculture and livestock production as its main activities. Lombardy and Venetia were both under Habsburg administration. In spite of this, their level of economic development differed profoundly. Lombardy had very intensive agriculture, including a large silk production. It was also one of the first Italian regions to develop machine manufacture, notably steel production, and had a commercial sector that was developed enough to connect its production to other markets. Venetia was less economically advanced than Lombardy. Its economic decline had started in the eighteenth century with the end of the Republic of Venice. Its commercial sector was not as strong as Lombardy's and its agricultural sector was less productive.

Moving to central Italy, Tuscany was at the time ruled by members of the Habsburg dynasty. The commercial policy implemented in Tuscany had greatly favoured a free market and the state did not provide incentives for the creation of an industrial sector. Most of the exports consisted of raw materials such as iron and marble. The Papal states had a quite heterogeneous agriculture with more intensive agriculture in the northern parts, such as Emilia, and latifundia in Latium and Umbria. There was almost no manufacturing in any of the Papal states, while a large part of the population of Rome lived on activities connected with pilgrimages to the Vatican (Zamagni 1990).

The South was united in one state, the Kingdom of the Two Sicilies. Its economy was based mostly on agriculture. The ownership of land was very much concentrated in the hands of the aristocratic class. Most of the land was farmed as latifundium and produced wheat, together with some high value-added agricultural products. Because wheat requires manpower only for short periods over the year, a large part of the workforce was often unemployed. The low level of technological innovation in farming and the inefficient use of the labour force made it impossible for the Southern regions to enlarge the internal market for either agricultural goods or consumer goods, as the labour force was too poor to consume above the level of subsistence. The infrastructure built in the Kingdom of the Two Sicilies before 1861 was weak and built mostly with foreign capital. Moreover, nearly all manufacturing had been established by foreign entrepreneurs, with almost no participation by the local upper or ruling class (Zamagni 1990).

Quantitative research on the pre-unitary period is in very short supply. Table 5.1 summarizes the main economic and social indicators for the Italian regions at the time of Unification. Column 1 shows the population estimates for the pre-unitary states, among which the Kingdom of the Two Sicilies was the most populous. Columns 2 and 3 show two basic measures of agricultural performance: the value of agricultural production per capita and the land productivity. The latter figures show Piedmont and Lombardy leading with 169 lire and 238 lire respectively, while the Kingdom of the two Sicilies stands at 81. The railways and roads densities reported in Columns 4 and 5 show a marked lead in the North: the Northwestern regions had the most developed system of transportation, with Piedmont leading in terms of the railways built before 1861. Columns 6–8

Table 5.1 Indicators at the time of Unification

	(1)	(2)	(3)	(4)	(5)	(6)	(7)	(8)	(9)	(10)	(11)
	Population	*Agricultural production*	*Agricultural productivity*	*Railway density*	*Roads density*	*Letters*	*Literacy*	*Elementary school attendance*	*Import*	*Export*	*Cotton spindles*
	1861 Millions	*1861 Lire p.c.*	*1861 Lire per hectare*	*1859 Km/100 sqKm*	*1863 Km/100 sqKm*	*1862 p.c.*	*1862 %*	*1862 %*	*1858 Lire p.c.*	*1858 Lire p.c.*	*1857 p.c.*
Piedmont	2.8	143	169	2.784	54	6.1	45.80%	93%	84.17	60.28	0.055
Liguria	0.8										
Sardinia	0.6	80	23	–	5	–	10.30%	29%	30.00	33.33	–
Lombardy	3.3	132	238	1.326	114	5.3	46.30%	90%	26.06	38.48	0.037
Veneto	2.3	117	128				25%	–	39.13	26.09	0.013
Parma-Modena	0.9	219	174	–	36	2.7	22%	36%	48.89	36.67	–
Papal States	3.2	83	68	0.260			20%	25–35%	22.50	19.69	0.009
Tuscany	1.9	127	117	1.243	60	3.1	26%	32%	41.58	23.68	0.002
Kingdom of the Two Sicilies	9.2	95	81	0.120	17	1.6	13%	18%	13.91	15.11	0.008
Italy	25	114	104	0.750	37	–	25%	43%	32.80	28.12	0.018

Source: Our elaborations from Zamagni (2007).

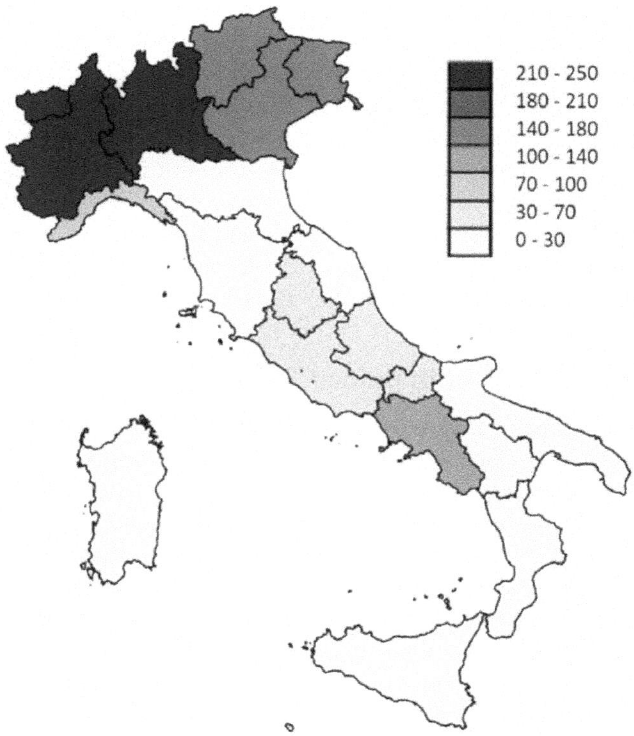

Figure 5.1 Hydropower availability in the Italian regions, 2001 (litres per 1,000 ha).
Source: SVIMEZ (2011).

confirm the well-known gap in human capital and school provision, which went on to be one of the main obstacles to economic development in the South after 1861 as well. Columns 9–10 show the levels of imports and exports per capita, with the Kingdom of the Two Sicilies having the lowest level. In terms of industrial activity, Table 5.1 shows the number of cotton spindles in each state. The quantity of textile manufacturing in Piedmont and Lombardy stands out, with all the other pre-unitary states lagging behind.

The available evidence allows only a qualitative study of the determinants of industrial location before 1871. As Table 5.1 shows, the Kingdom of Sardinia and Lombardy fulfilled most of the preconditions that would later make them the industrial core of Italy. Before the 1880s, most of the modern industrial areas were in the textile sector established during the nineteenth century in the North-western regions. Cafagna (1989) suggests that their activity was set in motion by the natural conditions which favoured silk production in the North, such as a suitable workforce and the availability of hydropower. These hypotheses cannot be formally tested, but Figure 5.1 gives a sense of the gap in the availability of hydropower in favour of the Northern regions. Along with the evidence collected by Ciccarelli and Weisdorf (2018) on the pre-unitary literacy rates, the hypothesis that both water availability and human capital determined the location of the textile industries in the first half of the nineteenth century appears well grounded.

A further development of the study of industries in the pre-unification period will require joint work by scholars specializing in each of the pre-unitary states, using both official statistics such as censuses and more ad-hoc sources such as parish and poor relief records.[2] In the next section, we move on to discuss the regional patterns of industrialization after 1861.

5.3 Economic dualism in unified Italy

Overall, there is a general agreement on the main trends of industrialization in the first decades after Unification until the outbreak of World War I. The progress of the industrial sector was quite modest in the first two decades after Unification; most of the advances were made in the textile industry, silk production being mostly concentrated in Lombardy and cotton production in Piedmont. The other sectors were less dynamic. The iron and steel industry and the engineering industries were still far behind their foreign counterparts, and most of the industrial supplies for these sectors were imported. Before 1880, some small steps forward were taken in the food and chemical industries, but in the two decades after Unification the Italian economy remained predominantly agricultural, with the exception of some initial industrial activity in the Northwestern regions (Cafagna 1989). The first industrial takeoff started in the 1880s, and by 1911 all the industrial sectors in the modern Italian economy were to some extent represented (Zamagni 1990).

In the long-term evolution of the Italian economy, regional differences from both the present and the historical perspectives are arguably the most striking feature. It is in the 1880s that the Italian regions further polarized in terms of GDP per capita and diverged even more sharply in the level of their industrial production.

During the first decades after Unification, the greatest economic gap was between the Northwestern regions (Piedmont, Lombardy, and Liguria) and the rest of the country. Figure 5.2 shows the evolution of GDP per capita between 1871 and 1911 using today's borders.[3] In 1871, the North–South pattern in GDP per capita was present but relatively limited.[4] Some forty years later, on the eve of World War I, the Industrial Triangle stood out.

Measures of human capital are often used as explanatory variables for development at both national and subnational levels. We have claimed in Section 5.2 that human capital, along with water endowment, was a possible determinant of the location of the silk industries in the North before Unification. The role of human capital has also been extensively studied in connection with the first industrialization of unified Italy. Several authors have conducted research on literacy and

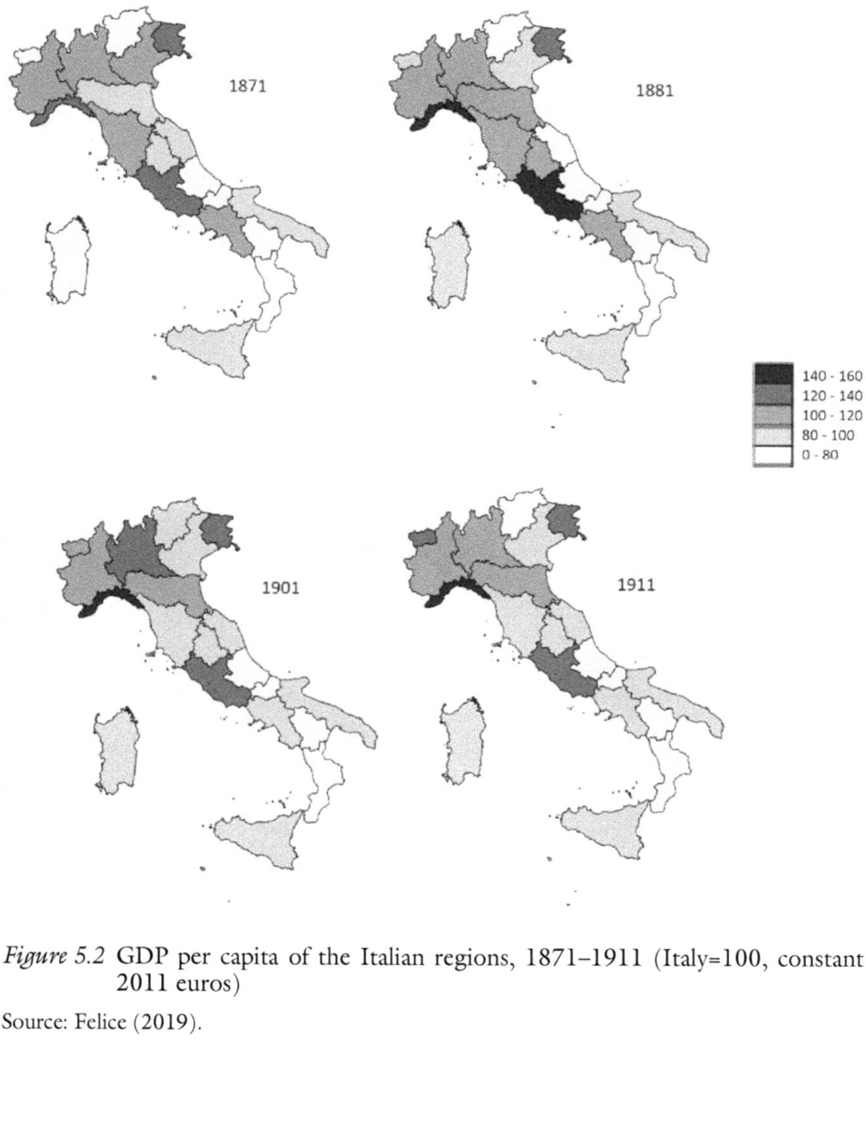

Figure 5.2 GDP per capita of the Italian regions, 1871–1911 (Italy=100, constant 2011 euros)

Source: Felice (2019).

in general on the formation of human capital. The first to touch this topic for Italy was Zamagni (1973), who provides both literacy rates at regional level and estimates of the public expenditure on education. In the first decades after Unification, literacy was one of the social indicators showing the widest regional disparity. A'Hearn et al. (2011) provide an overview of the education performance of unified Italy, reported for benchmark years (see Figure 5.3). In 1871, we note that literacy rates in the Northwestern regions were well above 40%, while in the Southern regions they could be as low as 10%; the Northeastern and Central regions ranged in the middle. These figures clearly confirm the picture that

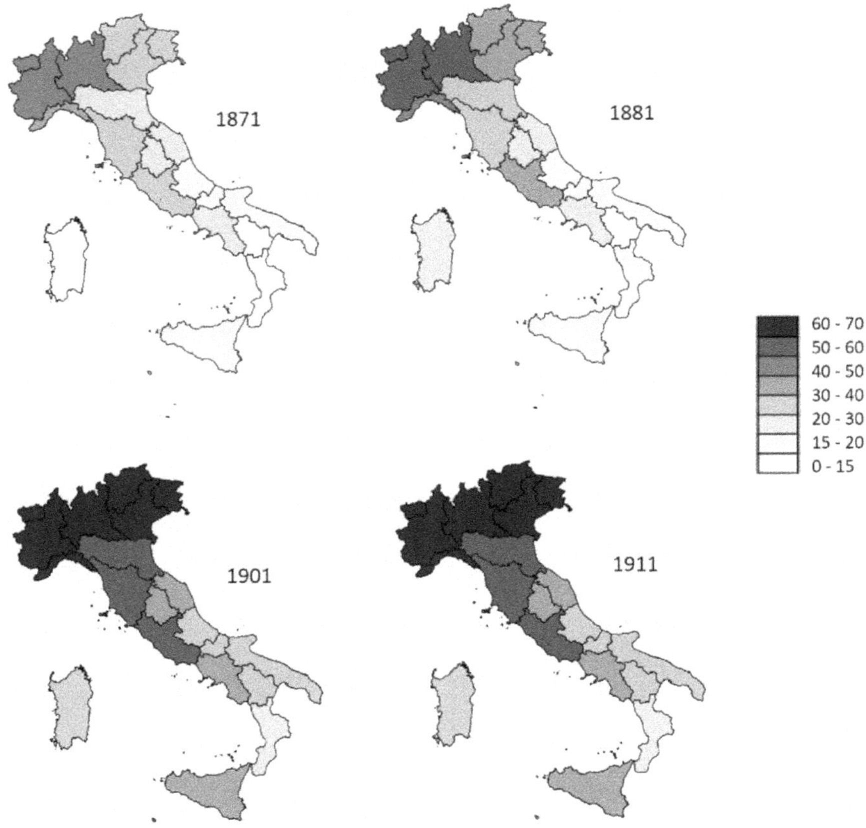

Figure 5.3 Literacy rates in the Italian regions, 1871–1911
Source: A'Hearn et al. (2011).

emerges from Table 5.1 – the Southern regions lagged behind Northern regions, in particular behind the regions forming the Industrial Triangle.

Industrialization represents historically the main driver of GDP performance. Figure 5.4 shows the share of industrial employment in the NUTS-2 regions between 1871 and 1911.[5] We may note that the polarization in terms of GDP per capita in the Northwest during the first decades after 1861 was very closely mirrored in the industrialization of this part of the country. In the later decades, the Northeast and part of the Centre caught up with the Northwest, consolidating the North–South gap.

Fenoaltea (2011) notes that most of the regional divergence started in the 1880s. To understand how the North–South gap developed, it is helpful to discuss the spatial distribution of the industrial activity. In 1871, the regions were fairly similar to each other in their industrial structures; almost all the sectors were

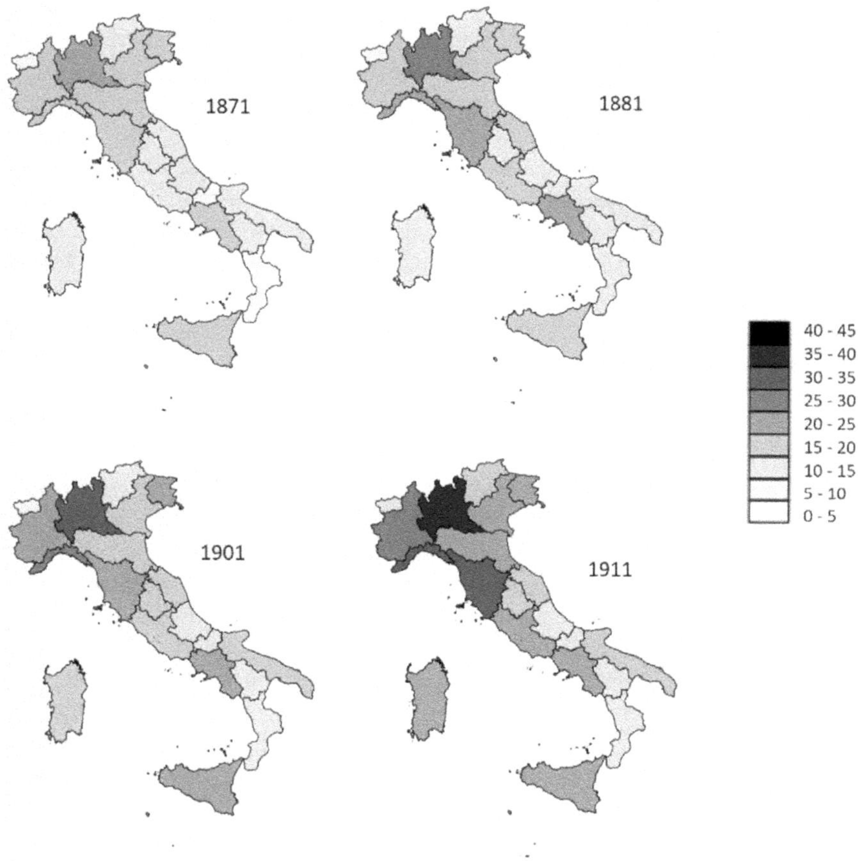

Figure 5.4 Industrial employment in the Italian regions, 1871–1911 (as a share of total employment)

Source: SVIMEZ (2011).

represented in each of the regions. This initial similarity was due to the political divisions before 1861 and to the high transport costs that impeded specialization in any region. The sector showing the highest concentration was mining, based in Sardinia, Sicily, and Tuscany. In the broader manufacturing sector in 1871, only textile production was already concentrated in the Northwest; and only in Lombardy, Piedmont, and Liguria combined was there more than 60% of the total production (Fenoaltea 2006). Within the Industrial Triangle, the industrial structure of Liguria, Piedmont, and Lombardy evolved differently during the first decades of the industrial takeoff. Thanks to its ports, where coal could easily be imported, Liguria specialized quite early in engineering and iron and steel production. Piedmont and Lombardy were more specialized in manufacturing, with almost all types being overrepresented compared to the national average in 1911. Tuscany and Campania were in this period around the average in manufacturing, but the relative quotas decrease further south, and a region often specialized significantly in only one type of manufacturing (Fenoaltea 2011).

Why was the North better able to face the challenges of modern economic growth than the South in the first decades after Unification? Historiography has offered several explanations for what is often referred to as the "Questione Meridionale", the Southern Question. Nitti (1900) claims that the first Italian tax system redistributed wealth from South to North; De Viti de Marco (1930) was the first to assert that the South was transformed in a colonial market for northern industrial goods; Salvemini (1955) believes that the delay of the South was due to inequalities in the ownership of land which should have led a land reform. The first works focusing on the issue from an historical rather than political perspective began to be published after World War II. Sereni (1947) was one of the first scholars to propose a "colonial explanation" for the failure of the Southern regions to keep pace, claiming that the industrialization of the North had occurred through exploitation of the South. In this view, the tariffs passed in 1887 subsidized the industrial sector of the North while lowering the surplus of the consumers in the South. Moreover, investments in infrastructure were targeted to strengthen the factories of the Industrial Triangle, allowing the North to exploit the market of the South. For Romeo (1969), the marked inequality among southern farmers slowed down their consumption and the use of taxation to build infrastructure in the Northwest redistributed the surplus from South to North. This view has, however, been strongly opposed by many scholars since the 1980s. According to Cafagna (1989), there is no evidence of the South providing raw materials, labour, or capital to the Northern industrial sector, nor of its serving as an internal market for industrial goods. Moreover, the two economies, at the time of the first industrialization, appear not to have been complementary.

The role of agriculture has also been analyzed. The protectionist tariff of 1887 has often been pointed out as an element which not only boosted the industrialization of the North, but also trapped the South in its subsistence agriculture. This hypothesis was, however, dismissed by Federico and Tena (1998) in their work on protectionist policies in Italy. Cafagna (1989) focuses on the agricultural roots of the North–South divide, with the North having a more intensive type of farming and the South with extensive farming relying on latifundia. One of the classical works on the role of agriculture in regional disparities is by Federico (2007), in which he rejects the view that the gap in productivity was caused by institutional arrangements but instead points to the lower investment in innovation and the lower level of human capital.

Another conclusion attributes the origin of Italy's economic dualism to cultural differences between the North and the South. The cultural features of the South were seen by some scholars as less conducive to trust and economic development. In the 1950s, Banfield (1958) used the term "amoral familism" to describe the inability of southern Italians to cooperate beyond the boundaries of their families. The deficit of social capital as an explanation for the Italian case was first proposed by Putnam et al. (1993). Felice (2012) tests the role of both social and human capital as an explanatory variable for long-term regional inequality between Italian regions; the result is that, in contrast to the findings by Putnam et al. (1993), human capital outdoes social capital in explanatory power except in recent decades, suggesting that the backwardness of Southern regions is hard to explain by a single variable.

The institutional view was proposed by Felice and Vasta (2015), who distinguished two types of modernization: active and passive. Active modernization occurs when the whole of society is involved in creating a national market, building infrastructure and developing its human capital; passive modernization takes place without an organic strategy and is imposed from the outside through, for example, state intervention. In this case, the ruling elites establish extractive institutions. The claim regarding Italy was that the North was able to modernize actively as other industrialized countries could, while the South remained trapped in passive modernization. The responsibility for this does not lie in the behaviour of the entire Southern population, as a cultural approach would suggest, but in that of its ruling elites.

Others have pointed to the physical geography of Italy as the primary cause of the backwardness of the South. For instance, Fenoaltea (2006) gives a possible explanation for the regional patterns of industrialization in Italy before World War I based on the comparative geographical advantages of the North – in particular, its energy endowment from water – but he does not translate it into a formal model. Daniele and Malanima (2007) discuss the role of the physical distance of the Southern regions to the centre of Europe and claim that the position of the South constituted a natural disadvantage for its industrialization.

Although numerous qualitative and quantitative studies of the determinants of the North–South divide have been produced in the past few decades, empirical works that explicitly model industrial location are relatively recent. In a classical contribution on regional industrialization in the EU, Midelfart-Knarvik et al. (2000) provided one of the most influential empirical studies of the determinants of industrial location, capable of integrating many of the different aspects that have been proposed as determinants of regional imbalance in the case of Italy. They set up a theoretical framework for modelling industrial location that has found fruitful applications to historical cases also.[6] Their methodology tests both H-O and NEG theories as explanatory variables for the share of industrial employment in a given sector at the regional level, through the inclusion of interactions between industrial and regional characteristics of both the H-O and the NEG types. The use of interactions allows us through certain characteristics of the sectors to test the ability of regions to attract industries, and the channels through which industries are attracted. These regional characteristics include market potential, access to energy, labour abundance, and the availability of skilled labour. Industry characteristics include measures of energy, labour and skill intensity, intermediate input use, mean plant size, and sales to industry. Other controls are size controls for regional population and sector employment. Missiaia (2019) uses the model by Midelfart-Knarvik et al. (2000) for the Italian case in the period 1871–1911. The model is estimated on sixteen regions and twelve manufacturing sectors and uses industrial employment as a dependent variable. It proposes the following as endowment interactions: (1) share of agricultural employment in the region interacted with share of agricultural inputs on the total production in each sector; (2) literacy rates at the regional level interacted with the share of white collar workers in each sector; (3) deposits per capita at the regional level interacted with horsepower per worker (as a proxy for capital intensity); and (4) waterpower production at the regional level interacted with horsepower per unit of production (as proxy for energy intensity). The market interactions are all based on estimates from Missiaia (2016) of market potential, interacted with (1) shares of sales to domestic industry as a proxy for forward linkages; (2) share of intermediates on production as a proxy for backward linkages; and (3) mean number of workers per plant as proxy for economies of scale. The main result is that during the first industrialization of Italy, endowments – and in particular, energy (measured as waterpower production) and human capital – were central in the location decisions.

The role of waterpower as driver of industrial location has already been discussed by several scholars such as Cafagna (1999), who considers it one of the main determinants of the North–South gap along with human and social capital. Fenoaltea (2011) also pointed to the availability of waterpower as an important driver of industrial location. The role of human capital has also been widely discussed by scholars such as Zamagni (1978) and more recently A'Hearn et al. (2011), Felice (2012), and Felice and Vasta (2015). As regards market interactions, only the domestic market potential (see Figure 5.5) had a positive and significant effect through economies of scale. When the model is tested, including the access to international markets (Figure 5.6), the results on the NEG-interaction are not confirmed. By comparing Figures 5.5 and 5.6, we note indeed how these two measures of market access differ, with the domestic one showing a much more classic North–South pattern. This difference is due to the shipping and railway costs of the time: shipping rates per kilometre were far cheaper than railway rates and Southern regions typically had their main economic centres located on the coast line, making them potentially more suited for long-distance trade. At the same time, the core of the domestic market was located in the Industrial Triangle, favouring the most industrialized regions in accessing the internal Italian market. So why was the access to international markets insufficient to attract industries around the large port cities of the South? According to Missiaia (2019), the level of Italian integration in the international markets, at least for nonagricultural products, was not sufficient at this time to shape the industrial geography of the country. Moreover, the obstacle represented by the lack of endowments was a determinant in the location choices.

Other scholars have studied the early location of industry in Italy using a variety of alternative approaches. Cappelli (2017) explains the growth of industrial value added for provinces using human and social capital. Social capital in this case is measured through engagement in charities, mutual aid, and crime incidence. The result is that human capital is indeed stronger than social capital in determining

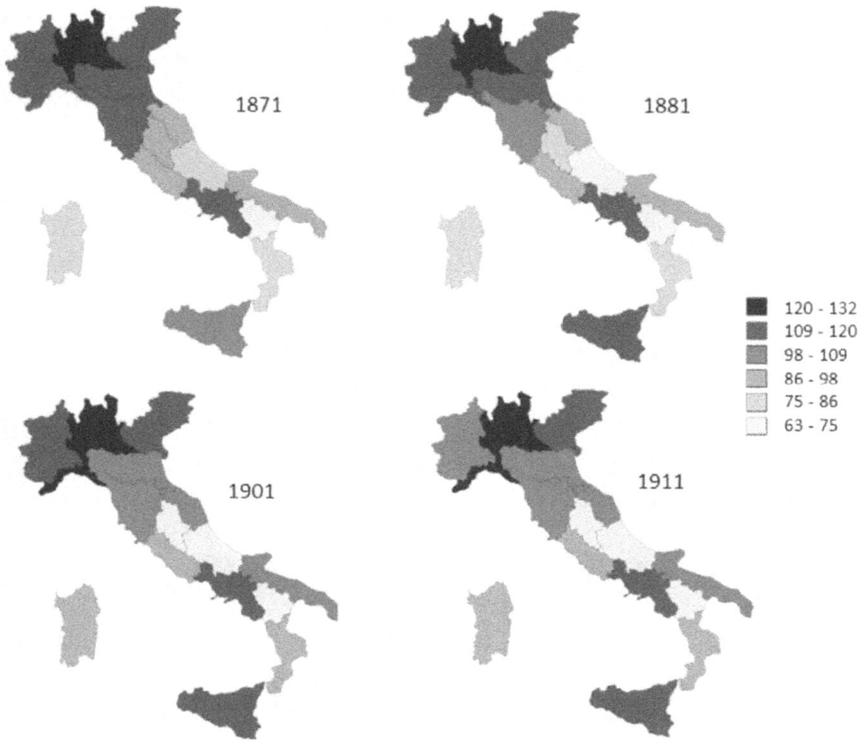

Figure 5.5 Domestic market potential (1871–1911, Italy=100)
Source: Missiaia (2019).

output growth. Unlike that of Missiaia (2019), this study does not include market access as a regressor, but does include waterpower and hydroelectric power, with a nonsignificant result. Nuvolari and Vasta (2017) also use provincial industrial production as a dependent variable, finding that patents and technical education increased industrial production. Here, domestic market potential from Missiaia (2016) is used as regressor but only at the regional and not the provincial level. Ciccarelli and Fachin (2017) explain industrial productivity between 1871 and 1911 by human and social capital, political participation, and the building of infrastructure. The absence of dynamic spillover effects, measured as the growth rate of industrial value added in neighbouring provinces, is seen as evidence that market access was not a driving force behind the first industrialization of Italy. But once again, the paper does not provide a market access measure to account for provincial GDP and transport costs.

Finally, the work by Basile and Ciccarelli (2018) looks at the location of industrial output at provincial level between 1871 and 1911. The authors use both

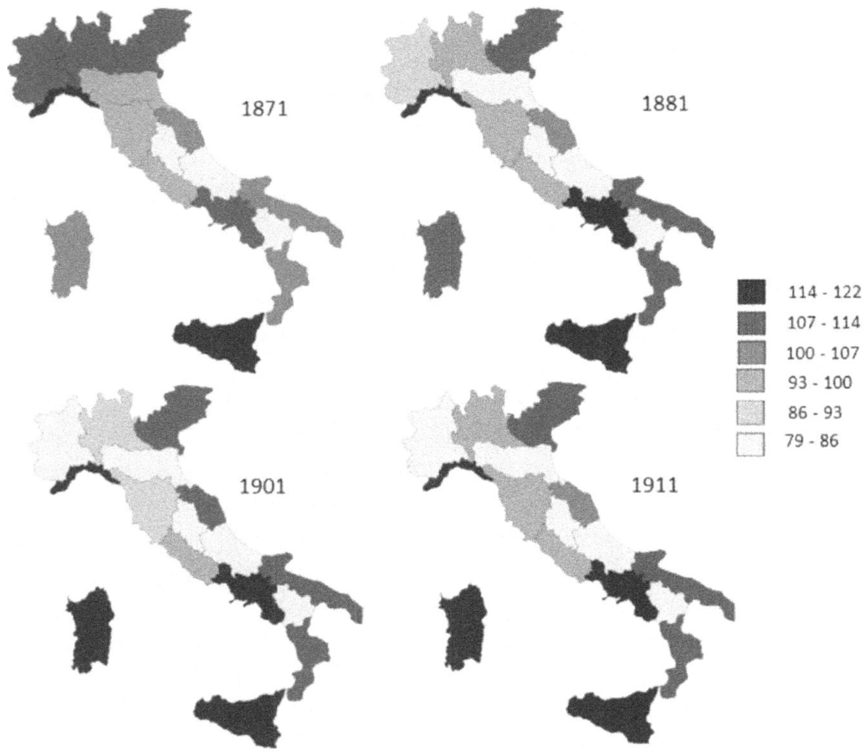

Figure 5.6 Total market potential (1871–1911, Italy=100)
Source: Missiaia (2019).

endowment and market variables such as literacy, market potential, and water-power production and account for each manufacturing sector separately. The authors find that capital-intensive production was driven by domestic market potential and that literacy also was an important driver. The effect of energy gives mixed results once the other controls are included in the model. The variety of approaches used makes it hard to fully compare different empirical results, but the general understanding is that in this period both endowment forces and domestic market access had a role, while international market access did not.

5.4 The fascist regime and the peak of regional polarization

After World War I and during the interwar period, the Italian industrial sector experienced a shift from light to heavy industry. At the end of the conflict, engineering and metal making resumed their expansion until the 1929 crisis, which temporarily slowed down industrial growth. After the crisis, the role of the State in the economy increased; in 1933, the Fascist government set up the Institute for Industrial Reconstruction (IRI), a public entity that controlled almost half of the Italian stock companies, disproportionately in heavy industry (Felice 2015). In terms of regional patterns, the interwar period represented one of increase of GDP per capita differentials. By 1938, the North–South gap was consolidated, with the South appearing more homogeneous (Figure 5.7).

Literacy rates, depicted in Figure 5.8, continued the upward trend across the country, with the South still visibly lagging behind but narrowing the disparity of the regions.

During the interwar years, and especially during the Fascist period, Italy experienced an increase of state intervention in the economy. The Fascist industrial policies crystallized the pre-existing structure, reinforcing the existing industrial agglomerations and leaving little space to regions outside the Industrial Triangle. This policy was dictated by strategic reasons with a view to a possible war effort. Other factors that undermined the possibility of attracting industrial activity to the South were the autarkic policies that required the least industrial regions to specialize further in agricultural productions (the so-called Battle of Wheat). Restrictions on emigration, both domestic and international, put further pressure on the regions of the South which experienced a decline in their standard of living compared to the North (Iuzzolino et al. 2013). Figure 5.9 shows the distribution of industrial workers in this period, with the North leading in all years.

Scholars have rarely approached the study of industrial location through quantitative testing for periods after 1911. This is probably because of the perception of great path dependence in the location of industries in the later periods, along with much stronger State intervention that could undermine the validity of economic geography models. One exception is the work by Daniele et al. (2016) who, following Harris (1954), test the effect of market access, measured as market potential (both domestic and international), on the total of manufacturing employment for the Italian provinces in the long term. These authors also employ geographical controls such as urbanization, latitude, and literacy rates. The econometric analysis, focused on the benchmark years from 1911, points to a strong role for both domestic and international market potential. It should be noted, however, that straight line distances, rather than transport costs, are used in the analysis; that the dependent variable is not disaggregated by sector, neglecting intra-sectoral variation; and that most endowment forces are neglected.

A'Hearn and Venables (2013) also look at the long term but do not use a formal econometric model and rely on descriptive statistics to build their argument. The view here is that different endowment or market forces prevailed in different sub-periods in determining the industrial geography of the country. In their view, natural advantages – water availability in particular – determined the industrial location in the period 1861–1890 while market potential, even in its domestic formulation, was not yet a determinant because of the low degree of internal market integration. Again, in comparison to the work by Missiaia (2019), the lack of accounting for transport costs may have affected the results. Moreover,

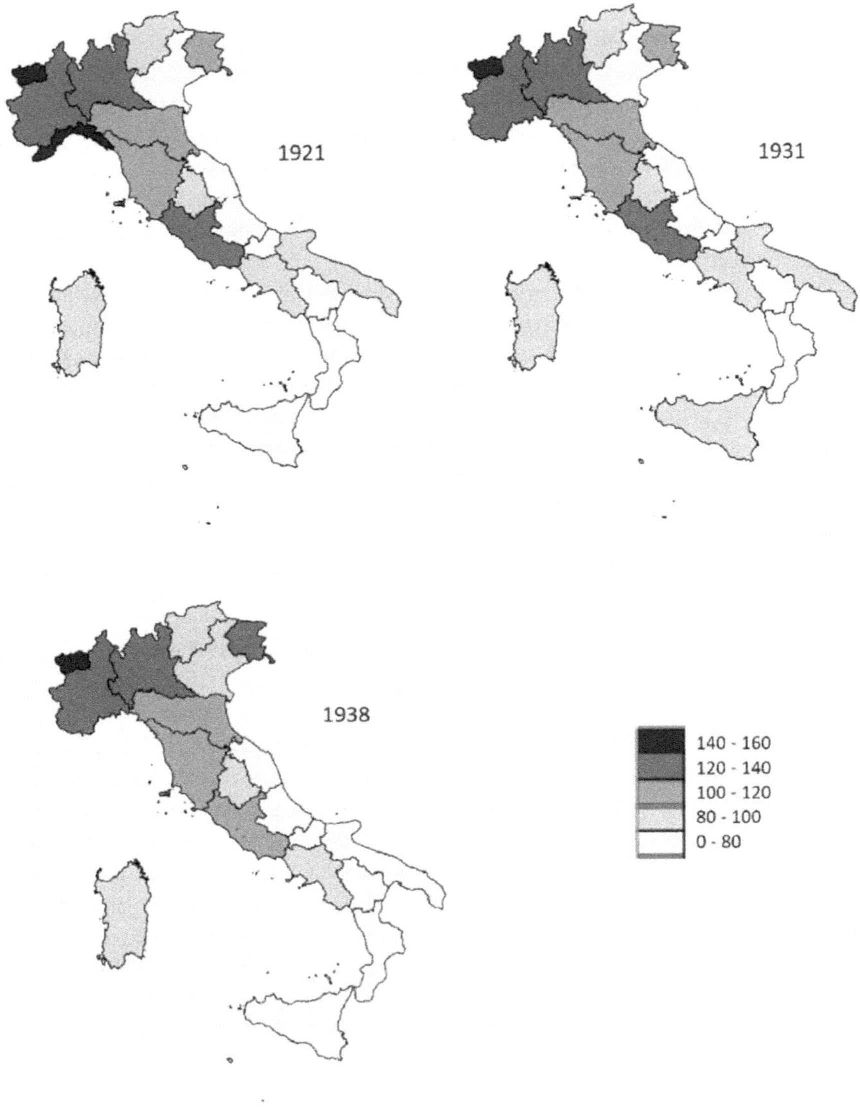

Figure 5.7 GDP per capita of the Italian regions, 1921–1938 (Italy=100, constant 2011 euros)

Source: Felice (2019).

the effect of human capital availability is not discussed in detail, making the analysis only a question of first-nature geography. For the period 1890–1950, domestic market access is suggested as the main driver of industrial location due to the increasing integration of the Italian markets and the relative closure

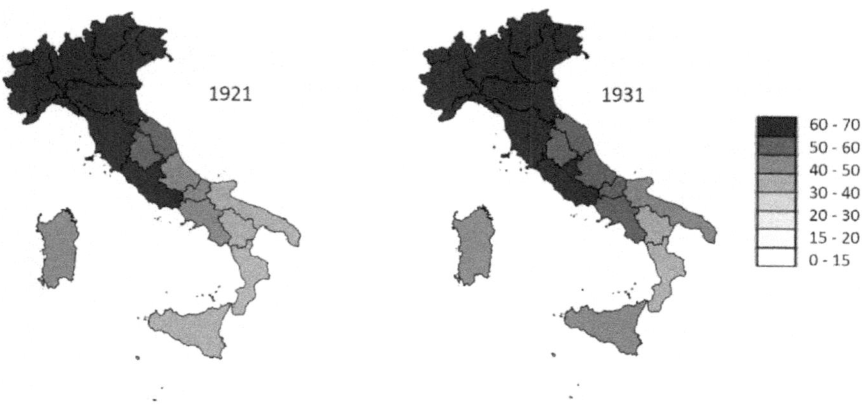

Figure 5.8 Literacy rates in the Italian regions, 1921–1931
Source: A'Hearn et al. (2011).

to international trading. It should be noted that the periodization chosen by the authors is not ideal in that it merges very different periods of Italian history: the years of the first industrialization were in many respects different from the 1920s and 1930s, when a large share of the economy was in public hands. Moreover, the authors point out that the increased role of the internal market does not necessarily preclude the strength of the endowment forces in favouring the Northern industrial sector.

5.5 A short-lived convergence: The Economic Miracle and the return of regional polarization

After World War II, the role of the State was also prominent in turning the country into one of the world's fastest-growing economies. The period of spectacular growth driven by industrial development during the 1960s is often referred to as the country's Economic Miracle. The Italian economy closed the gap between itself and the most advanced economies, but the kind of growth rates experienced in the 1960s came to an end. This was due to both external factors, such as the oil shocks and the change in the international monetary system, and internal factors such as the worsening of the national public finances and high inflation. If the country consistently experienced a rate of GDP growth above the average from 1950 to 1992, the rate in the period from 1992 to today was below the average for all years, certifying the slow economic and industrial decline of the country (Felice and Vecchi 2015).

The years between 1951 and 1973 represent a period of convergence in terms of GDP per capita (Figure 5.10). As regards literacy, the South had almost completed the process during the Miracle, leaving aside a few percentage points.

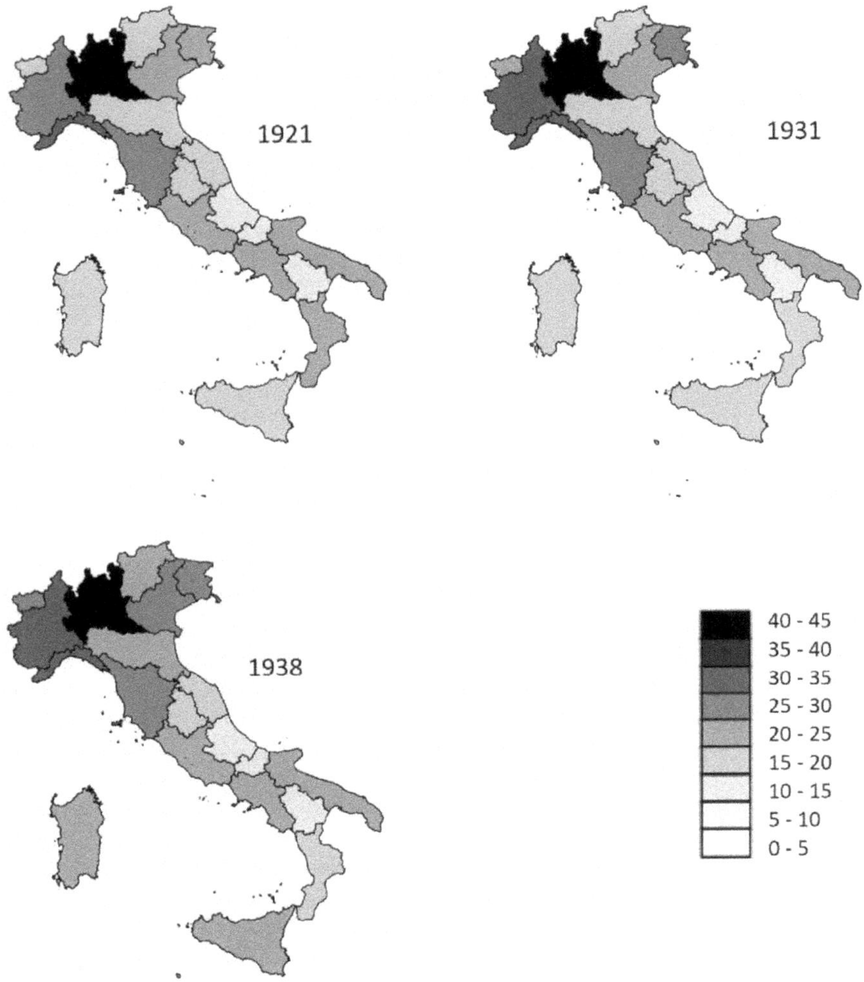

Figure 5.9 Share of industrial employment in the Italian regions, 1921–1938

Source: SVIMEZ (2011).

Looking at Figure 5.11 on the share of industrial employment, we note that after World War II the Industrial Triangle was clearly recognizable. In 1971 the effect of the Economic Miracle is clearly recognizable in the South, while in the following years we note how the industrial employment levels decline. In 1991, the Northeast and Centre finally joined the Northwest as the richest areas, a position that was fully consolidated by 2001.

In regard to industrial development, a public programme to implement regional policies in the South, the Cassa per il Mezzogiorno, was taking effect; by

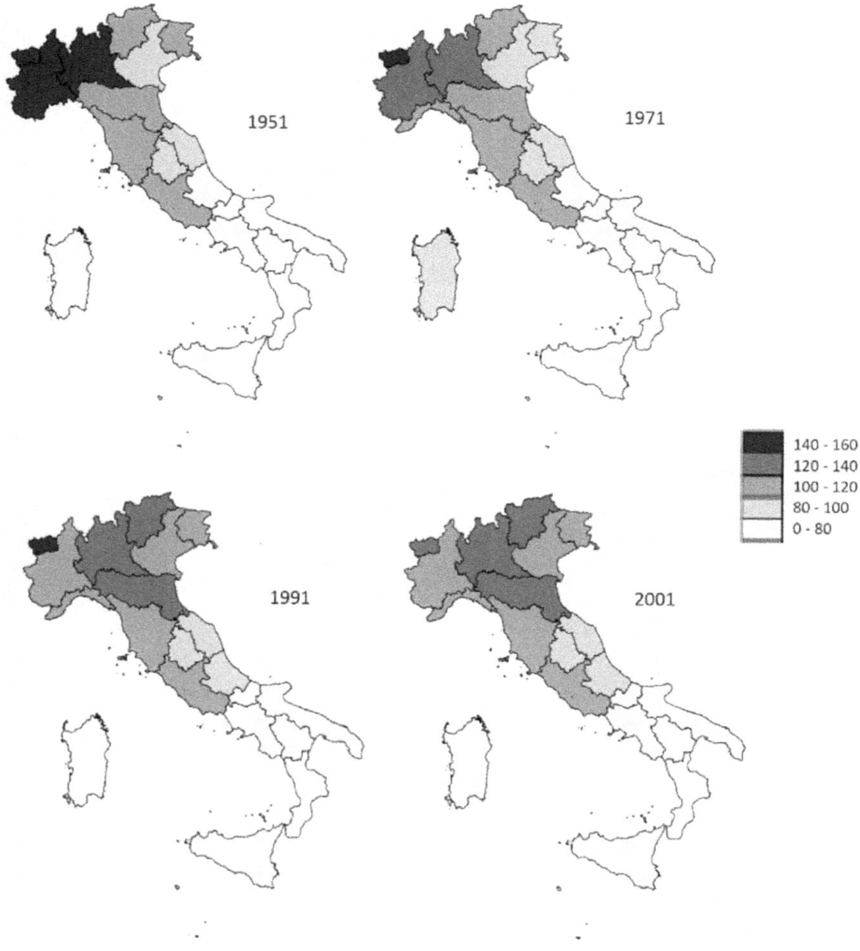

Figure 5.10 GDP per capita of the Italian regions, 1951–2001 (Italy=100, constant 2011 euros)

Source: Felice (2019).

1971, the investment rate in the South was about 37% while remaining at about 21% in the rest of the country (Iuzzolino et al. 2013). However, this period of industrial expansion proved transient, and the convergence process ended in the 1970s. This was due to a number of factors, both internal and external. It is suggested that the oil shocks of the 1970s hit the Southern regions more severely because their industrial sector used energy more intensively (Iuzzolino et al. 2013). At the time, the Third Italy was taking off through export-led light industry, which benefitted from the depreciation of the Lira, while the heavy

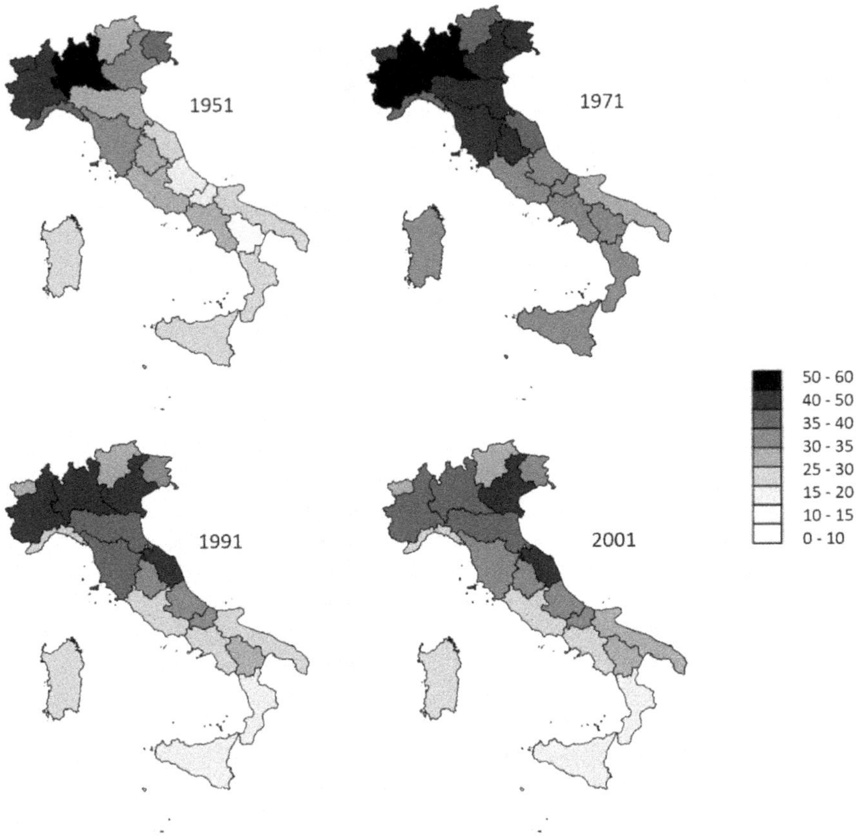

Figure 5.11 Industrial employment in the Italian regions, 1951–2001

Source: SVIMEZ (2011).

industry in the South was penalized in being oriented much more towards the domestic sector. The end of the industrial subsidies revealed that the industrial growth experienced by the South had not been self-sustaining. The subsequent loss of convergence was intimately connected with the inability of the central State to support the South when the nation's finances became unreliable, and with the incapacity of the South to undertake what Felice and Vasta (2015) call "active industrialization". The period immediately following the end of World War II had also been a time when regional disparities consolidated, as the European Recovery Plan was once again aiming to reconstruct the economy in areas that had already industrialized before the conflict. For this period, there are few empirical works on the industrial location of regional industries.

According to A'Hearn and Venables (2013), international market access was the main determinant in the second half of the twentieth century after the domination of domestic markets in the interwar period and endowments in the era of early industrialization. This transformation was driven by the spectacular development of the highway network, which expanded from 479 km in 1950 to 3,913 km in 1973, thanks to a ten-year plan promoted by the State (Felice 2015). The expansion of the transportation network during the Economic Miracle was much better balanced as regards existing industrial areas. This, along with the numerous State-financed industrial initiatives, led to the convergence period that ended in 1971. But after the end of massive public intervention, access to international markets favoured the export-oriented small and medium-sized firms of the Third Italy, again leaving the South behind.

5.6 Concluding remarks and suggestions for future research

The regional dimension of Italy's industrial development is a fundamental one. Italy approached its first industrialization shortly after its political unification, and many of the preconditions for industrialization were unevenly distributed well before 1861. In this chapter, we provided an overview of the economic condition of the pre-unitary states, admittedly limited by almost nonexistent quantitative sources. We went on to review the general economic conditions of Italy as a unified country and to survey the main hypotheses proposed in the literature on the origins of the North–South gap. We then discussed the recent body of empirical literature, formally testing one or more of these hypotheses.

We believe that conceiving both endowment and market forces, along with path dependency, as possible determinants of industrial location for the Italian case is fruitful. By combining the findings of different studies, we come to the following conclusions. First, in spite of the moderate gap in GDP levels at the time of Unification, the preconditions for industrialization in the Italian regions in terms of endowment differed greatly long before 1861. These differences translated into an uneven pattern of industrialization located mainly in the Northwest in the period 1871–1911. International market access, which was higher in the South, did not determine location choices, unlike domestic market access and endowment, which were better in the North. In the interwar period, no market or endowment force was able to gainsay the effect of industrial geography, and the regional disparities further increased. Sustained state intervention during the Economic Miracle was able to start a period of convergence between the North and the South. When the economy as a whole slowed down in the 1970s and 1980s, and further declined during the Second Globalization period, the previous level of public investment could not be maintained, leaving market forces to dominate again and allowing the rise of the Third Italy.

Notes

1 This chapter was written thanks to the financial support of the Handelsbanken Jan Wallanders and Tom Hedelius and Tore Browaldhs Foundations for the project

"Regional backlash in a globalizing world: trade, regional inequality and the rise of protectionism in Italy (1870–1914)" (ID: P19-0239).

2 A pioneering effort is Zucca Micheletto (2013) on the employment structure of 1802 Turin. Further empirical analysis will be carried on by other scholars within the E.N.C.H.O.S. network, which aims to expand the work of the Cambridge Population Group to other European countries.

3 Today's borders are used by Felice (2019) to show the long-term evolution of regional GDP. This approach leads to the inclusion of two regions that until 1918 did not belong to Italy: Trentino-Alto Adige and Friuli Venezia Giulia. Although it is interesting to study their trajectory, we disregard them in the overall discussion of patterns for the first decades in Italy.

4 The use of the terms North and South in this context aims at giving a stylized picture of the economic disparities that would later develop; it is well known that both the North and the South of Italy were quite heterogeneous: for instance, the northeastern region of Venetia, at first among the poorest, became one of the richest.

5 As we see in the next section, industrial employment, rather than value added, is often used to study the location of industrial sectors. This is because value added measures both the presence of industrial sectors in regions and their productivity, making it harder to study location patterns alone (Missiaia 2019).

6 See Crafts and Mulatu (2006) for Britain, Wolf (2007) for Poland, Martínez-Galarraga (2012) for Spain, Klein and Crafts (2012) for the United States, and Nikolić (2017) on the Kingdom of Yugoslavia.

References

A'Hearn, B., C. Auria, and G. Vecchi. 2011. "Reddito." In *In ricchezza e in povertà*, edited by G. Vecchi, 209–234. Bologna: Il Mulino.

A'Hearn, B., and A. J. Venables. 2013. "Internal geography and external rade: regional disparities in Italy, 1861–2011." In *Oxford handbook of the Italian economy, 1861–2011*, edited by G. Toniolo, 599–630. Oxford: Oxford University Press.

Banfield, E. C. 1958. *The moral basis of a backward society*. Chicago: Free Press.

Basile, R., and C. Ciccarelli. 2018. "The location of the Italian manufacturing industry, 1871–1911: a sectoral analysis." *Journal of Economic Geography* 18(3): 627–661.

Cafagna, L. 1989. *Dualismo e sviluppo nella storia d'Italia*. Padova: Marsilio.

Cafagna, L. 1999. "Contro tre pregiudizi." In *Storia economica d'Italia. Interpretazioni*, Vol. 1, edited by P. Ciocca and G. Toniolo, 297–325. Roma: Laterza.

Cappelli, G. 2017. "The missing link? trust, cooperative norms, and industrial growth in Italy." *The Journal of Interdisciplinary History* 47(3): 333–358.

Ciccarelli, C. 2014. *La produzione industriale delle regioni d'Italia, 1861–1913: Una ricostruzione quantitativa. 2. Le Industrie Estrattivo-Manifatturiere*. Roma: Banca d'Italia.

Ciccarelli, C., and S. Fachin. 2017. "Regional growth with spatial dependence: a case study on arly Italian industrialization." *Papers in Regional Science* 96(4): 675–695.

Ciccarelli, C., and S. Fenoaltea. 2009. *La produzione industriale delle regioni d'Italia, 1861–1913: Una ricostruzione quantitativa*. Roma: Banca d'Italia.

Ciccarelli, C., and J. Weisdorf. 2018. "Pioneering into the past: regional literacy developments in Italy before Italy." *European Review of Economic History* 23(3): 329–364.

Crafts, N., and A. Mulatu. 2006. "How did the location of industry respond to falling transport costs in Britain before World War I?" *Journal of Economic History* 66(3): 575–607.

Daniele, V., and P. Malanima. 2007. "Il prodotto delle regioni Italiane e il divario Nord-Sud in Italia, 1861–2004." *Rivista Di Politica Economica* 47: 267–315.

Daniele, V., P. Malanima, and N. Ostuni. 2016. "Geography, market potential and industrialization in Italy 1871–2001." *Papers in Regional Science* 97(3): 639–662.

De Viti De Marco, A. 1930. *Un trentennio Di lotte politiche, 1894–1922*. Roma: Collezione Meridionale Editrici.

Federico, G. 2007. "Ma l'agricoltura meridionale era davvero arretrata?" *Rivista Di Politica Economica* 97(2): 317–340.

Federico, G., and A. Tena. 1998. "Was Italy a protectionist country?" *European Review of Economic History* 2(1): 73–97.

Felice, E. 2007. *Divari regionali e intervento pubblico: Per una rilettura dello sviluppo in Italia*. Bologna: Il Mulino.

Felice, E. 2012. "Regional convergence in Italy, 1891–2001: testing human and social capital." *Cliometrica* 6(3): 267–306.

Felice, E. 2015. *Ascesa e Declino*. Bologna: Il Mulino.

Felice, E. 2019. "The roots of a dual equilibrium: GDP, productivity and structural change in the Italian regions in the long-run (1871–2011)." *European Review of Economic History* 23(4): 499–528.

Felice, E., and M. Vasta. 2015. "Passive modernization? The new human development index and its components in Italy's regions (1871–2007)." *European Review of Economic History* 19(1): 44–66.

Felice, E., and G. Vecchi. 2015. "Italy's growth and decline, 1861–2011." *Journal of Interdisciplinary History* 45(4): 507–548.

Fenoaltea, S. 2006. *L'economia italiana dall'Unità alla Grande Guerra*. Laterza, Bari: Collezione Storica.

Fenoaltea, S. 2011. *The reinterpretation of Italian economic history: from unification to the great war*. Cambridge: Cambridge University Press.

Harris, Ch. D. 1954. "The market as a factor in the localization of industry in the United States." *Annals of the Association of American Geographers* 44(4): 315–348.

Iuzzolino, G., G. Pellegrini, and G. Viesti. 2013. "Convergence among Italian regions, 1861–2011." In *The Oxford handbook of the Italian economy since unification*, edited by G. Toniolo, 571–598. Oxford: Oxford University Press.

Klein, A., and N. Crafts. 2012. "Making sense of the manufacturing belt: determinants of U.S. industrial location, 1880–1920." *Journal of Economic Geography* 12(4): 775–807.

Martínez-Galarraga, J. 2012. "The determinants of industrial location in Spain, 1856–1929." *Explorations in Economic History* 49(2): 255–275.

Midelfart-Knarvik, H., H. G. Overman, S. J. Redding, and A. J. Venables. 2000. *The location of European industry*. European Economy Economic Papers 142, European Commission.

Missiaia, A. 2016. "Where do we go from here? Market access and regional development in Italy (1871–1911)." *European Review of Economic History* 20(2): 215–241.

Missiaia, A. 2019. "Market versus endowment: explaining early industrial location in Italy (1871–1911)." *Cliometrica* 13(1): 127–161.

Nikolić, S. 2017. "Determinants of industrial location: Kingdom of Yugoslavia in the interwar period." *European Review of Economic History* 22(1): 101–133.

Nitti, F. S. 1900. *Nord e Sud: Prime linee di una inchiesta sulla ripartizione territoriale delle entrate e delle spese dello stato in Italia.* Torino: Roux e Viarengo.

Nuvolari, A., and M. Vasta. 2017. "The geography of innovation in Italy, 1861–1913: evidence from patent data." *European Review of Economic History* 21(3): 326–356.

Putnam, R. D., R. Leonardi, and R. Y. Nanetti. 1993. *Making democracy work: civic traditions in modern Italy.* Princeton: Princeton University Press.

Romani, M. 1976. *Storia economica d'Italia nel secolo XIX: 1815–1914.* Milano: Giuffrè.

Romeo, R. 1969. *Risorgimento e capitalismo.* Bari: Laterza.

Salvemini, G. 1955. *Scritti sulla questione meridionale: 1896–1955.* Torino: Einaudi.

Sereni, E. 1947. *Il capitalismo nelle Campagne, 1860–1900.* Torino: Einaudi.

SVIMEZ. 2011. *150 anni di statistiche Italiane: Nord e Sud. 1861–2011.* Bologna: Il Mulino.

Wolf, N. 2007. "Endowments vs. market potential: what explains the relocation of industry after the polish reunification in 1918?" *Explorations in Economic History* 44(1): 22–42.

Zamagni, V. 1973. "Istruzione e sviluppo economico. Il caso italiano. 1861–1913." In *L'economia Italiana (1861–1940)*, edited by G. Toniolo, 137–178. Bari: Laterza.

Zamagni, V. 1978. *Industrializzazione e squilibri regionali in Italia: Bilancio dell'età Giolittiana.* Bologna: Il Mulino.

Zamagni, V. 1990. *Dalla periferia al centro: La seconda rinascita economica dell'Italia (1861–1990).* Bologna: Il Mulino.

Zamagni, V. 2007. *Introduzione alla storia economica d'Italia.* Bologna: Il Mulino.

Zucca Micheletto, B. 2013. "Reconsidering women's labor force participation rates in eighteenth-century Turin." *Feminist Economics* 19(4): 200–223.

Part II

Regional industrialization in Asia

6 Regional industrialization in China

The basic metals sector[1]

Zipeng Zhang, Bas van Leeuwen, and Jieli Li

6.1 Introduction

In this chapter we report our estimates of the basic metal sector, i.e., the smelting of ferrous (iron and steel) and nonferrous (metals other than iron and steel, such as copper, lead, zinc, and tin) metals. The importance of studying the basic metal industry is based on two factors. First, metal smelting is one of the few industrial sectors for which data exist that allows calculating regional output for the nineteenth century in China. Second, even though the metal smelting sector is small, its indirect value as input for other manufacturing sectors is large. Indeed, the better availability, higher quality, and lower price of metals aided in the development of, initially, ships and agricultural tools, and later of boilers, railways, steam engines and, subsequently, a wide variety of machine tools supporting economic development.

This rise in importance, albeit with setbacks, of metal smelting over the past 150 years has been far from uniformly spread across China.[2] Being mostly located in the western regions in the late nineteenth and early twentieth centuries, over the past decades it has slowly moved towards the northeast and the east. In this chapter, we will discuss the development (expressed in number of workers) of ferrous and nonferrous metals production on a regional level between 1850 and 2000, as well as offer a tentative explanation of the resulting geographic patterns. To do so, we start with a brief overview of the literature. In Section 6.3, we deal with the sources and data, which become more fragmentary when going back in time. Section 6.4 brings the changes over time in the regional smelting industry, while Section 6.5 concludes.

6.2 Literature

The importance of metal smelting has certainly generated some academic interest in the metal industry in China. This interest often resulted in studies in which metal smelting was viewed as a sign of modernization. Hartwell (1962, 1966, 1967) concluded that the Chinese iron industry reached its heyday in the Song Dynasty (960–1279) and was superior to all the other dynasties and possibly even to the first half of the twentieth century. He suggested that a Song-Dynasty farmer relied on iron manufacture more than "his counterpart in the early years of the twentieth century" (Hartwell 1962: 157). According to Hartwell (1962: 155), China was able to produce 75,000–150,000 tons of iron annually as early as 1078, whereas in 1930–1934 "in China south of the Great Wall" only 140,000 tons of pig iron were produced per annum.

Hartwell's pioneering studies are marked as having "an extensive influence in both Chinese and global history" (Wright 2007). Not only did they lead to a number of studies refining our view on the metal industry (e.g. Liu 1993; Wang 2005), they were also used to support the traditional view of long-term economic stagnation or decline in post-Song China within the Great Divergence debate (e.g. McNeill 1982). Within this debate, the stagnationist view on metal production was consequently challenged by those scholars who claim that the peak of pre-modern Chinese economy occurred in the Ming Dynasty (1368–1644) or the Qing Dynasty (1644–1911) (see e.g. Pomeranz 2000; Huang 1989). Yet irrespective of these debates, in general it was believed that the traditional Chinese iron industry benefitted from several "very early innovations" and its technology did not fall behind the West until the age of the Industrial Revolution (Wagner 2008). In addition, most scholars agree that pre-modern growth is dwarfed by subsequent post-1950 growth in New China.

Indeed, metal smelting in China had already existed over the centuries but the early modernization only started during the Self-Strengthening Movement (1860–1895). Being viewed as the start of China's early industrialization, the Self-Strengthening Movement was regarded as a period in which China was "managed to develop new structures to handle foreign relations and collect custom dues, to build modern ships and weapons, and to start teaching international law and the rudiments of modern science" (Spence 1991: 216). Even though the smelting industry was thus important, its development nonetheless got somewhat distorted by imports as, notwithstanding the Chinese market already being opened after the First Opium War (1839–1842), there still occurred a significant boom of metal imports. This was caused by a growing demand for metals for making new weapons and building modern infrastructure and ships. For instance, in the years between 1868 and 1895, China's imports of steel rose more than threefold, and pig iron even circa 27-fold (Yang and Hou 1931: 22). Such a flood of imported iron was devastating to China's traditional native iron industry (Zhang 2014: 70). This pushed the Chinese government in the 1880s and 1890s to establish a number of modern mechanical mines for copper, lead, iron, silver, and gold to support the arms industry, to reduce the expense on imports, and to increase the fiscal income (Xia 1992: 269–274).

This decline of traditional metal smelting was enhanced by warfare, especially the civil wars in the second half of the nineteenth century. For the early twentieth century, Chang (1967: 69) suggested a small decline of relative importance between 1917 and 1933 of ferrous metals,[3] implying a continuation from an earlier downward trend argued by Hartwell (1962). Yet, other studies arrived at a different conclusion. In a recent quantitative study, Xu et al. (2017) show that during the years between 1850 and 1933, the total value of ferrous metals first dropped to its lowest point in 1887, then had a more than 2.6-fold rise up to 1911, and later another twofold growth up to 1933. Hence, the downward trend from late Qing Dynasty was reversed in 1887. The same research also shows that in this period for the metallurgical industry as a whole, there was continuous growth from 1850 to 1911 which was mainly caused by the boom of gold. Yet, whereas total value of both ferrous and nonferrous metals went up until 1911, the total value of this industry in 1933 was still circa 22% lower than 1911.

The importance of the metal smelting sector for economic, political, and military developments was also recognized by the Chinese government during the Great Leap Forward (1958–1961) aimed at rapidly industrializing China. During this period, steel production was particularly considered as one of the main indicators of modernization, and pig iron production rose from circa 7.5 million tons to 18.5 million tons (Hsia 1961). Although subsequently a collapse occurred, it was followed by fierce growth up to the present. Indeed, China's crude steel production accounted for only 2.8% of the global total in 1967 (International Iron and Steel Institute 1978: 3). As of today, this share has risen to almost 50% (The World Steel Association 2017: 2). Similarly, nonferrous metals also play a significant role in economic activities. As pointed out by the European Commission (2018), nonferrous metals are indispensable due to their "unique thermal, electrical, and isolating characteristics coupled with endless recyclability and low weight", and hence essential for many products. This importance was even more pronounced before the twentieth century. Indeed, even though present-day scholars put a lot of emphasis on iron, from a historical perspective, nonferrous metals were valued higher by the authorities in traditional China.[4] For instance, in the Qing Dynasty, iron was considered a less important and cheap metal until the late nineteenth century, while nonferrous metals were not just crucial for national defence (e.g., copper and lead, respectively, as materials of firearms and bullets) but more importantly were fundamental for minting (e.g., copper, lead, zinc, and tin), not to mention the precious metals (i.e., gold and silver).

6.3 Sources and data

New China: 1982, 1990, and 2000

Before turning to the data, we first need to define metal smelting. For 1982 and 1990, we can use the Chinese Occupational Classification code 721 (Metal smelting workers). For 2000, we use the Chinese Occupational Classification code 62 (Metal smelting and rolling workers) (Minnesota Population Center 2019). To remove the rolling workers, we use the 1990 population census to calculate for each prefecture the ratio between metal smelting (code 721) and metal rolling and machine operators (code 722). This ratio is used to remove the rolling workers for each prefecture in 2000, thus leaving us with smelters, who make up 60.5% of all smelters and rollers.

Republic of China: 1933

Compared to the post-1949 era, regional industrial data for 1933, especially for administrative units below province, are either far less directly available or even absent in the sources. This forces us to apply an eclectic approach by summing up both direct data as well as proxy estimates to construct the datasets. For the Republic of China (1912–1949) period, we follow Wang Jinyu (1948, 2004) and select 1933 as the benchmark.[5] This choice is based on the availability of sources. Descriptions of sources and data of this benchmark are given in Appendix 6.2.

The Qing Dynasty: 1850

In general, our 1850 data are based on the central government archives of Qing China, especially memorials to the throne, which are accessed from the First Historical Archives of China in Beijing, the Institute of History and Philology (Academia Sinica) in Taipei, and the Palace Museum in Taipei. The archives stored in Taipei share the same origin with those documents in Beijing. Indeed, the collections of Academia Sinica and the Palace Museum were shipped from Beijing to Taiwan in 1949 when the Nationalist Party of China (Kuomintang) was losing the civil war on the Chinese mainland. These reports to the emperor, in certain cases, provide information about factory, product, region, tax, revenue, expenditure, and sometimes output and labour. These reports were essentially products of the fiscal management system of the Qing Dynasty (Appendix 6.3).

We have to stress that the current 1850 estimates are partially based on the reworking of existing studies. The production in tons are re-estimated based on Xu and Zhang (2015), whose results were based on various sources – including memorials to the throne, government books, local gazetteers and surveys – but were presented on a provincial level. The improvement in detail level from province to prefecture still required extensive extra work, as the provincial administrative units in the Qing Dynasty were less than thirty, while the contemporary prefectures were more than 300. The resulting physical outputs were divided by output per worker to obtain the number of employees (see Appendix 6.3 and 6.4).

Creating constant boundaries: 1850–2000

In order to compare regional development in smelting over time, we need to convert our dataset in constant boundaries. Our current data are in principle on county level in contemporary boundaries. Yet, there are three problems. First, given the errors in the data, we consider it preferable to only report the prefectural data, i.e., about 300 regions, instead of on county level which consists of circa 2000 regions. Second, needless to say, boundaries changed strongly between 1850 and the present. To make them comparable over time, we converted all prefectures of 1850, 1933, 1982, and 1990 into 2000 constant boundary prefectures. In order to do so, some prefectures had to be taken together, resulting in circa. 200 geographical regions instead of the currently existing circa 300 prefectures. For 1982–2000, we relied on the Integrated Public Use Microdata Series (IPUMS) constant boundaries (Minnesota Population Center 2019). For 1933 and 1850, we allocated the regions with data to the 1982–2000 constant boundary regions. The remaining regions were set at zero smelters.

6.4 Regional development in metal smelting

Our estimates show that in 1850 there were 127,909 smelters in China, declining to 79,972 in 1933 with obvious rises in 1982 (374,800) and 2000 (1,129,595). But also the geographic distribution varied widely over time. The results are reported in Figure 6.1a-e. Here, we follow the concept of the Greater Administrative Region (GAR),[6] and view mainland China as six regions, i.e., East (Anhui, Fujian, Jiangsu, Jiangxi, Shandong, Shanghai, Zhejiang), North (Beijing, Hebei, Inner Mongolia, Shanxi, Tianjin), Northeast (Heilongjiang, Jilin, Liaoning), Northwest (Gansu, Ningxia, Qinghai, Shaanxi, Xinjiang), South Central (Guangdong, Guangxi, Hainan, Henan, Hubei, Hunan), and Southwest (Chongqing, Guizhou, Sichuan, Tibet, Yunnan).[7]

In general, we witness a move from the West (Northwest and Southwest regions) in 1850 to the Southwest and South Central regions in 1933. Between 1933 and 1982 we see a further shift towards the Southeast, the North, and the

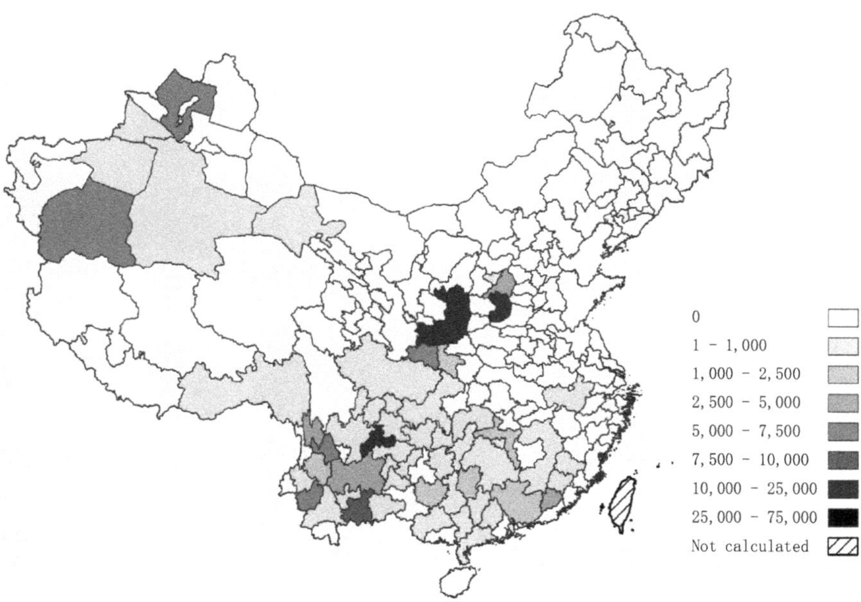

Figure 6.1a Smelting workers in 1850

Source: Appendix 6.5.

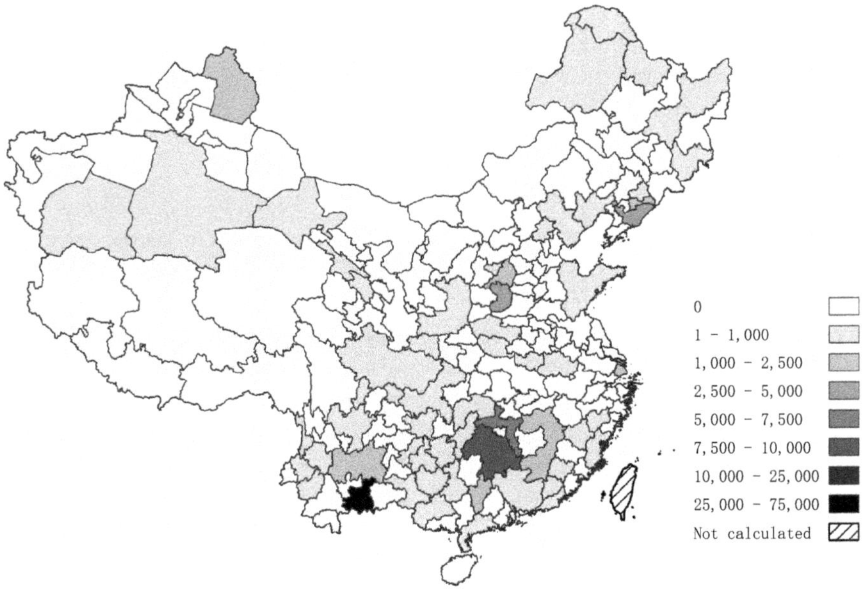

Figure 6.1b Smelting workers in 1933

Source: Appendix 6.5.

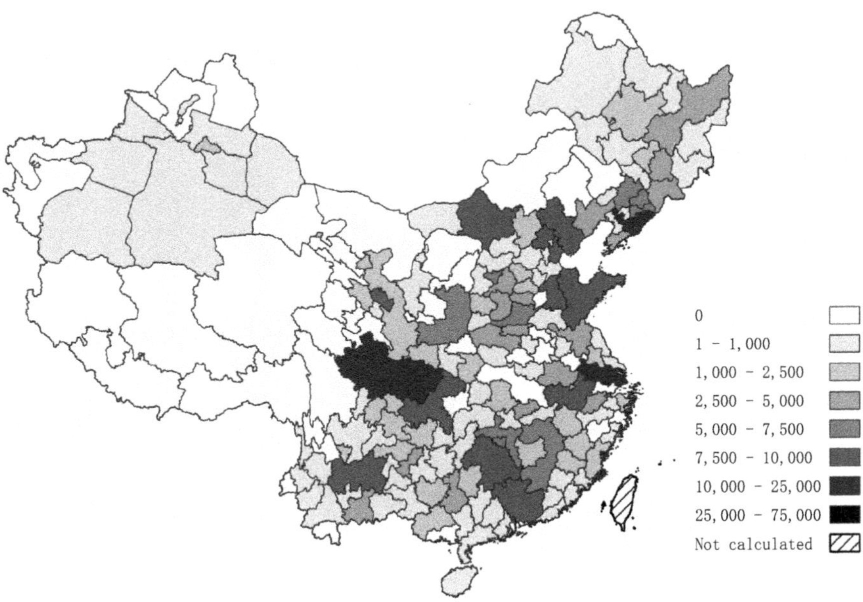

Figure 6.1c Smelting workers in 1982

Source: Appendix 6.5.

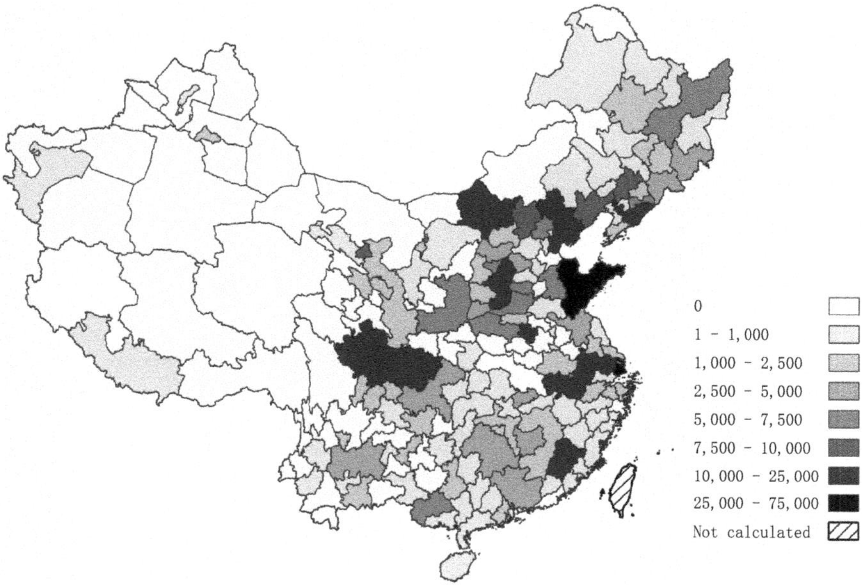

Figure 6.1d Smelting workers in 1990

Source: Appendix 6.5.

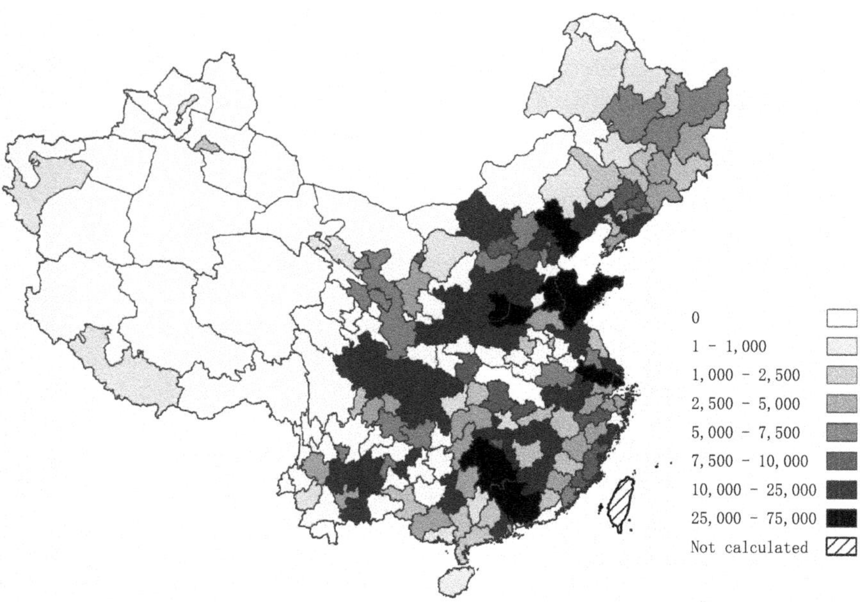

Figure 6.1e Smelting workers in 2000

Source: Appendix 6.5.

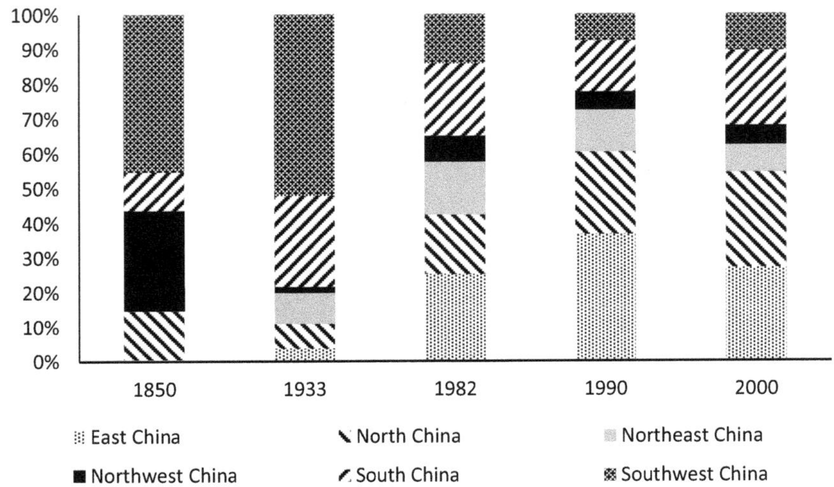

Figure 6.2 Distribution of no. workers in smelting (ferrous and nonferrous) by great region, 1850–2000

Source: This text.

Northwest. This results in a quite even balance of the smelting industry across all regions in China. This equalization continued up to 1990, after which we see a tentative revival of the West and the South Central regions of the country (see Figure 6.2).

This overall geographic shift may be attributed to various reasons – first, the role of factor endowments. Many of these factories were located in the regions with the most iron or other metal deposits. For instance, for iron, according to Figure 6.3, Sichuan province (from the Southwest), Liaoning province (from the Northeast) and Hebei province (from the North), together made up 56% of China's iron ore reserves. Some other provinces, including Shanxi, Shandong, Hubei, Inner Mongolia, and Anhui, were also among the deposit-rich regions. In fact, these eight provinces together had more than 82% of national total iron deposits. From the perspective of physical output, they produced more than 62% of China's pig iron in 1990, and circa 67% in 1984. (National Bureau of Statistics of China 1985: 169; State Statistics Bureau, People's Republic of China 1991: 436).

In the pre-1949 period, iron was smelted in fewer provinces and industrial concentration was even higher. In 1933, four provinces – Liaoning, Shanxi, Sichuan, and Hubei – had more than 85% of China's iron-smelting workers and produced circa 95% of domestic pig iron. Yet in 1850, Shanxi and Sichuan in total had one-third of China's iron-smelting workers and circa 68%of the national total output of pig iron, whereas the other eight deposit-poor provinces, whose iron ore reserves accounted less than 10% of national total, had one-third of total output

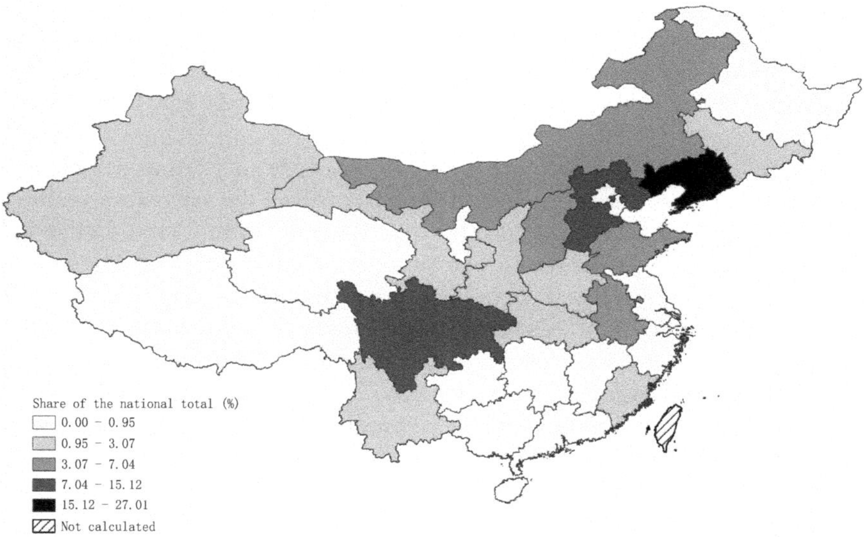

Figure 6.3 Provincial distribution of iron ore reserves in mainland China, 2011

Source: Calculated based on National Bureau of Statistics of China (2012: 410).

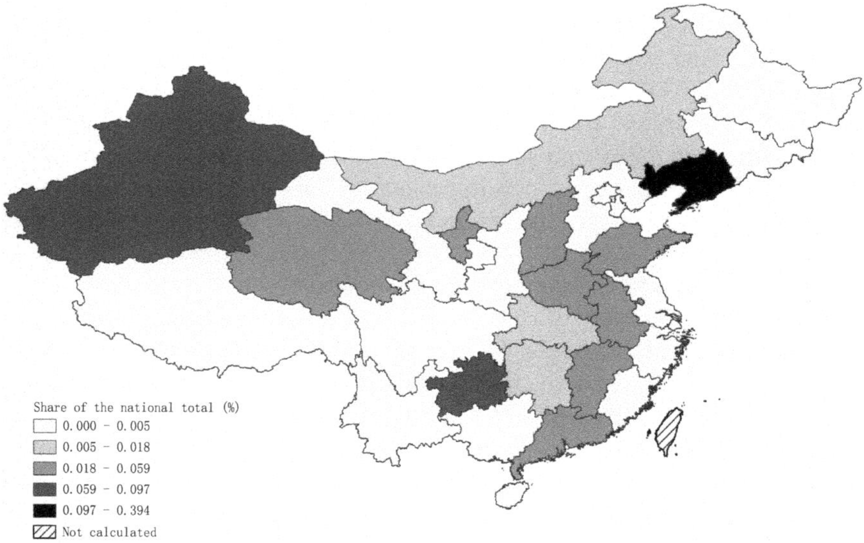

Figure 6.4 Provincial distribution of reserves of major nonferrous metals in mainland China, 2011

Source: Calculated with the totals of copper, lead, zinc, bauxite ore, magnesite ore, and pyrite ore; based on National Bureau of Statistics of China (2012: 411).

of pig iron and two-thirds of smelting workers. In the mid-nineteenth century, the iron smelting business was essentially absent in Liaoning, Hebei, Hubei, and Inner Mongolia. Consequently, as shown in Appendix 6.4, in 1850 the Southwest (Sichuan, together with neighbouring Yunnan and Guizhou provinces) was dominating smelting due to the weight of nonferrous metals, e.g., copper, lead, and zinc.

The shift towards resource-rich provinces over the following century can partly be attributed to modern technology that enabled the exploration and use of more ore deposits. Yet, as argued by Yuan Weipeng (2007), even though for the Chinese industry before the Second Sino-Japanese War (1937–1945), natural resources – especially mineral deposit and water resources – were the preconditions of industrial location, political motivation was an important factor for the late Qing and the Republican period as well. Essentially, those rich mineral deposits in the Northeast were not really excavated during most of the Qing Dynasty due to political reasons.[8] From New China onwards, due to the growing demand and technical improvement, other rich iron reserves located in the North and the Northeast gradually became used as well.

Indeed, as pointed out by various scholars (e.g, Tong et al. 2019: 148), in the first three decades of New China, the development of the iron and steel industry was essentially resource oriented. For instance, among the eight major projects related to the iron and steel industry, which were finished with assistance of the Soviet Union between 1953 and 1957, seven were in the North and the Northeast regions.[9] Later, during the Third Front Movement[10] starting in 1964, many more smelting enterprises were built in the western hinterland, whereas the iron-rich Sichuan province had Panzhihua, the biggest steel plant in Western China, which grew to have more than 300,000 employees in 1993 (Chen 2003: 253–255). Nevertheless, some other scholars (Yu and Chu 1982: 289–290) have argued that the planning and the establishment of new steel plants circa. 1956–1975 were inefficient due to policy reasons, e.g., during the Third Front Movement some new factories were built in mountainous areas for better security during wartime, and hence were inaccessible to both materials and market.

The earlier discussion suggests a correlation between the presence of raw materials and the number of smelters. But besides raw materials, other factor endowments also played a role. Human and physical capital endowment were more abundant in the Eastern and South Central region. As can be seen in Figures 6.5 and 6.6, the Eastern and South Central regions dominated in human and physical capital already in the early phases of New China, a lead they would expand in the post-1978 reform period. Besides factor endowments, the East is argued to also have a better product mix, and better managerial capabilities (Jefferson 1990).

A third reason for these expansions from the Southwest to the North and the East is a process of drawing near the centres of railways and waterways for ease of transport (see Figure 6.7; also see Chapter 10 in this volume). This way, relatively good transportation to the raw materials is ensured while, at the same

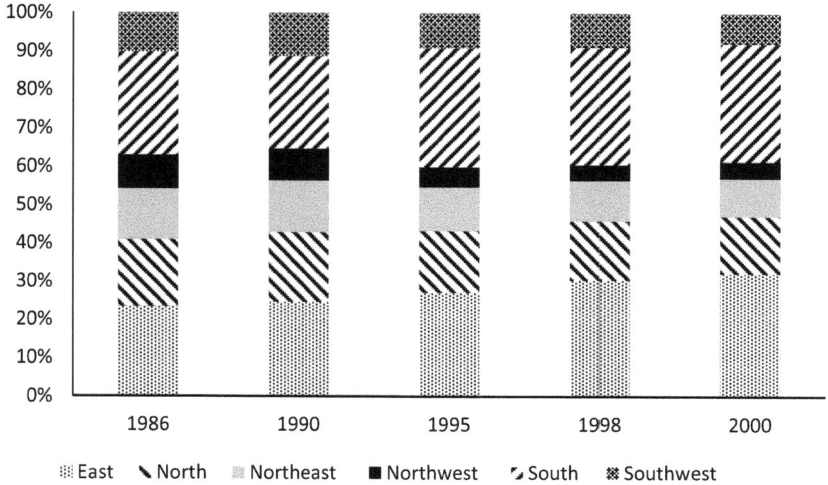

Figure 6.5 Distribution of human capital stock (calculated using the income-based method) in China, by great region, 1986–2000

Source: Calculated based on van Leeuwen et al. (2017).

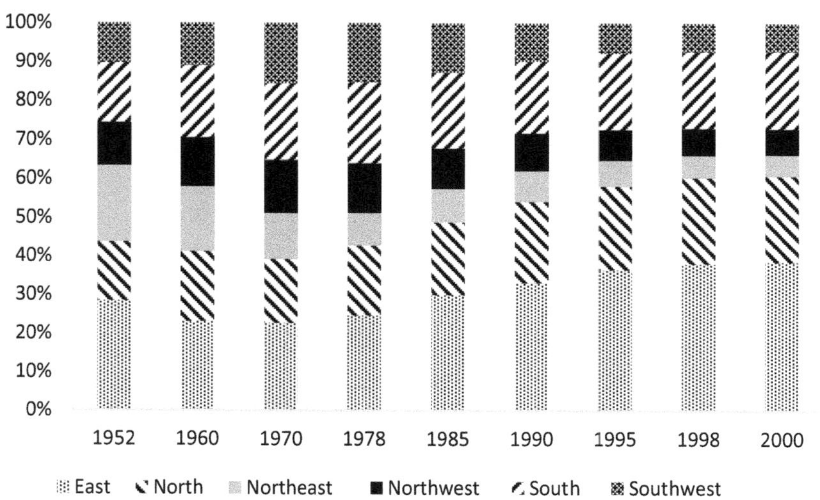

Figure 6.6 Distribution of physical capital stock in China, by great region, 1952–2000

Source: Calculated based on Zhang et al. (2004).

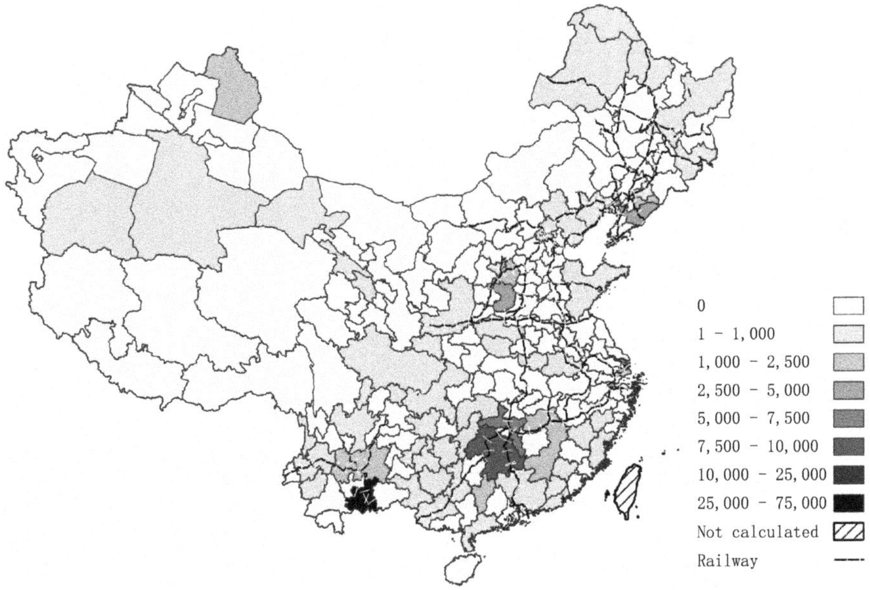

Figure 6.7a Smelting workers and railways in 1933

Source: Appendix 6.5.

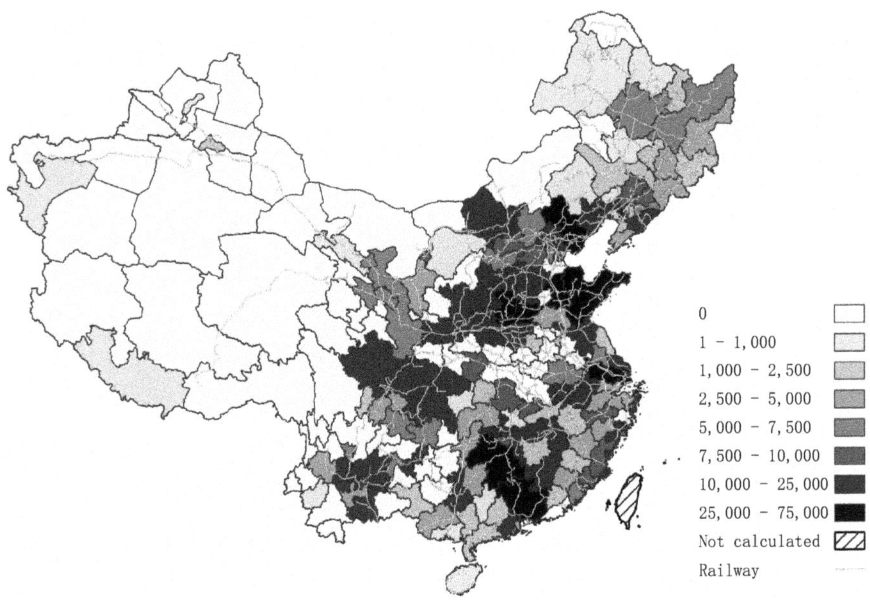

Figure 6.7b Smelting workers and railways in 2000

Source: Appendix 6.5.

time, factories are located closer to their market (of intermediate products). This corroborates the finding by Yuan Weipeng (2007: 171) that the size of markets and the availability of transportation were the most important factors for the rise of the modern factories in the second half of the nineteenth century and the early twentieth century. Transportation also played an important role in the post-1980 period and gradually led to a concentration of industry in the coastal region, especially for the iron and steel industry, as the supply of domestically produced iron ore could not satisfy the demand of the fast-growing Chinese iron and steel industry. Hence, a massive import of iron ore was necessary, while at the same time, the coastal region was also an expanding market of metals (Tong et al. 2019: 148) and offered good opportunities to export metal products. Baoshan Iron and Steel Company, which was established in 1978 in Shanghai, is an example. As shown in Figure 6.3, iron ore deposits are essentially absent in Shanghai, and this city, although it has been a world-class port since the early twentieth century, is far away from the main Chinese iron ore deposits. Thus, the choice of Baoshan Company's location was initially criticized in the public and academic opinions (see, e.g., Yu and Chu 1982: 290). Yet, this port-based steel plant now is viewed as a flagship of this industry and its location is considered as the most efficient solution in the history of China's iron and steel industry, being close to the market as well as having access to sufficient imports (Wang 2015: 42; Xu and Han 2006: 42).

In fact, in a report of the National Economic and Trade Commission (2001), it was clearly stated that the Chinese metallurgical industry at the end of the twentieth century was in a stage of switching from resource-oriented to resource-and-market-oriented. Indeed, in Chapter 7 of this volume, Xu et al. show that the East Coast was dominated by machinery manufacturing, which uses products from the smelting industry. Likewise, in Chapter 10 of this volume, van Leeuwen et al. show that, during the New China period, contrary to most other sectors, the average distance of iron casting firms to railway lines and primary roads declined, while that to waterways remained the same or increased. This implies that a switch to road transport occurred in this sector only to a limited extent, and it remains located close to railway lines. This lack of a move towards road transport can have various reasons. Yet as is argued in Chapter 10 of this volume, in a more coordinated economy such as China it is sometimes, depending on economic sector, more efficient to transport bulk goods via railroads (than road transport in a more liberal market economy).

6.5 Conclusion

In this chapter, we attempt for the first time to provide regional (on the level of prefecture) trends in the Chinese metal smelting industry between 1850 and the present. We do so for five benchmark years – 1850, 1933, 1982, 1990, and 2000. The choice of these years is mainly data driven. For 1850, we face a traditional statistical system in which we had to rely mainly (but not only) on memorials to the throne. For 1933, the statistical system had partly modernized but we still had to rely on a mix of traditional and modern statistics for both the local and national levels. For 1982, 1990, and 2000, we can make use of the modern population censuses.

The resulting database shows a move from the Southwest and the Northwest to the Eastern and the Northern parts of China between 1850 and 2000. Even though not the topic of this chapter, we might tentatively attribute it to four factors. First, Eastern China also had ore reserves but was, in addition, richer in human and physical capital, thus making it more attractive as a place to locate a metal smelting factory.[11] Second, Eastern China had a denser railway network, which was necessary for the transport of raw materials. Third, Eastern China had more abundant machinery and casting industries, which were the buyers of the products of the smelting industry. And fourth, it had better access to international import and export markets.

Notes

1 This research received funding from the European Research Council under the European Union's Horizon 2020 Programme / ERC-StG 637695–HinDI, as part of the project "The historical dynamics of industrialization in Northwestern Europe and China ca. 1800–2010: a regional interpretation".
2 In this chapter, due to the availability of sources, we only account mainland China, whereas Taiwan Province would be included in future revisions.
3 Chang (1967) placed pig iron and iron ore together with steel in the calculation of ferrous metals.
4 Most researchers on the metallurgical history of the Qing period study copper, especially the one from Yunnan. (See, e.g., Ma 2017; Yan 1948). After that, lead and zinc also received some scholarly attention (Chen 2018; Ma 2013, 2018; Wen 2007).
5 Wang Jinyu used the name "Wang Fusun" in his early years, e.g., the publication in 1948, and changed into "Wang Jinyu".
6 This was an administrative level between the central government and provinces which existed in the period 1949–1954. Although it was a temporary institution, it still has influences in contemporary China. (Chen 2004: 396; Fan 2011).
7 In the original GAR system, officially Inner Mongolia and Tibet were under direct administration of the central government, and Jiangxi was in the South Central Region. Yet, customarily Inner Mongolia was in the North, Tibet was in the Southwest, and Jiangxi was in the East. (Chen 2004: 395–396; Fan 2011). For these provinces, here we choose to follow the custom.
8 In short, the Manchu rulers viewed the Northeast as their origin and native land, thus they chose to forbid massive migrations from inland China to the Northeast as well as developing industry and farming there. This national policy was changed only after the mid-nineteenth century.
9 These seven projects were the establishments of three steel plants in Inner Mongolia, Heilongjiang, and Hebei, and two iron factories in Jilin, and the expansions of two steel plants in Liaoning, respectively.
10 At that time, China was under nuclear threat of both the Soviet Union and the United States, and hence was building many new factories in the inland, especially the Southwest and the Northwest, to keep sufficient industrial capacity if the coastal region was destroyed in the potential war(s).

11 As eastern China had more industrial outputs in general and smelting was a relatively small sector in industry, smelting was unlikely to attract capital or skills. For instance, in 1978, the Northeast and the East regions together accounted circa 67% of China's total industrial output, of which 8.7% was from the metallurgical industry (National Bureau of Statistics of China 1985: 142–145).

References

1934. "*Hunan Changning Shuikoushan qian xin kuangju ershi'er nian chanliang biao* [The yield table of Shuikoushan in 1933]." *Kuangye zhoubbo* (307): 1061–1062.

1935. "*Gansu zhi jinkuang chanliang ji shijia* [Production and the market price of gold in Gansu]." *Kuangye zhoubbo* (319): 103.

An, C. 1941. "*Sichuan tufa zhigang* [Native steelmaking in Sichuan]." *Jingjibu kuangye yanjiusuo gangtie huibao* (1): 127–130.

Cao, S., and Q. Jiang. 2010. "*Shicang yetieye zhong suojian Qingdai Zhe nan xiangcun gongye yu shichang* [Southern Zhejiang rural industry and markets during the Qing dynasty: evidence derived from the iron smelting industry in Shicang village]." *Zhongyang yanjiuyuan lishi yuyan yanjiusuo jikan* 81(4): 833–888.

Chang, J. K. 1967. "Industrial development of mainland China 1912–1949." *The Journal of Economic History* 27(1): 56–81.

Chen, C., ed. 2004. *Tuqing liushi nian* [Sixty years with map]. Beijing: Zhongguo ditu chubanshe.

Chen, D. 2003. *Sanxian jianshe beizhan shiqi de xibu kaifa* [The Third Front: the western development during the war-preparation period]. Beijing: Zhonggong zhongyang dangxiao chubanshe.

Chen, F. 2000. "*Qingdai qianqi zouxiao zhidu yu zhengce yanbian* [Regulations on the submission of expense accounts to the Court and their evolution during the first half of the Qing]." *Lishi yanjiu* (02): 63–74.

Chen, H. 2018. *Zinc for coin and brass: bureaucrats, merchants, artisans, and mining laborers in Qing China, ca. 1680s–1830s*. Leiden: Brill.

European Commission. 2018. "Non-ferrous metals." https://ec.europa.eu/growth/sectors/raw-materials/industries/metals/non-ferrous_en, Accessed 7 July 2018.

Fan, B.1985. "*Shanxi jincheng ganguo lian tie diaocha baogao* [Investigation report of crucible iron making in Jincheng, Shanxi]." In *Kejishi wenji ·di 13 ji · jinshushi zhuanji* [Essays on the history of technology], Vol. 13, edited by Institute for History of Natural Sciences, Chinese Academy of Sciences, 143–149. Shanghai: Shanghai kexue jishu chubanshe.

Fan, X. 2011. *Zhongguo daxingzhengqu yanjiu 1949–1954* [A study of China's Great Administrative Region, 1949–1954]. Shanghai: Dongfang chuban zhongxin.

Guangxi Mining Bureau. 1935. "*Guangxi Fu-He-Zhong ge xikuang lianchang zuijin sannian chunti chanliang* [The output of antimony regulus in Fu-He-Zhong of Guangxi in the recent three years]." *Kuangye zhoubbo* (362): 796–797.

Guangxi Provincial Bureau of Statistics, ed. 1934. *Guangxi nianjian di 1 hui* [Guangxi Yearbook, Issue 1]. Nanning: Guangxi Provincial Bureau of Statistics.

Guangxi Provincial Bureau of Statistics, ed. 1999[1936]. *Guangxi nianjian di 2 hui·Zhonghua Minguo ershisi nian* [Guangxi Yearbook, Issue 2]. Taipei: Wenhai chubanshe.

Hartwell, R. 1962. "A revolution in the Chinese iron and coal industries during the Northern Sung, 960–1126 AD." *The Journal of Asian Studies* 21(02): 153–162.

Hartwell, R. 1966. "Markets, technology, and the structure of enterprise in the development of the eleventh-century Chinese iron and steel industry." *The Journal of Economic History* 26(01): 29–58.

Hartwell, R. 1967. "A cycle of economic change in imperial China: coal and iron in Northeast China, 750–1350." *Journal of the Economic and Social History of the Orient* 10(1): 102–159.

Hou, D., ed. 1932. *Zhongguo kuangye jiyao·Minguo shiba nian zhi ershi nian·di si ci* [General statement on the mining industry of China, Issue 4]. Beijing: The Geological Survey of China, Ministry of Industry.

Hou, D., ed. 1935. *Zhongguo kuangye jiyao·Minguo ershiyi nian zhi ershisan nian·di wu ci* [General statement on the mining industry of China, Issue 5]. Beijing: The Geological Survey of China, Ministry of Industry.

Hsia, R. 1961. "The development of mainland China's steel industry since 1958." *The China Quarterly* 7: 112–120.

Huang, Q. 1989. *Shisi -shiqi shiji Zhongguo gangtie shengchan shi* [The production history of iron and steel in China, from the 14th to the 17th century]. Zhengzhou: Zhongzhou guji chubanshe.

International Iron and Steel Institute, ed. 1978. *A handbook of world steel statistics 1978*. Brussels: International Iron and Steel Institute.

International Trade Bureau, Ministry of Industry, ed. 1933. *Zhongguo shiye zhi· Zhejiang sheng* [The industrial gazetteer of China, Zhejiang Province]. Shanghai: International Trade Bureau, Ministry of Industry.

International Trade Bureau, Ministry of Industry, ed. 1935. *Zhongguo shiye zhi· Hunan sheng* [The industrial gazetteer of China, Hunan Province]. Shanghai: International Trade Bureau, Ministry of Industry.

Jefferson, G. H. 1990. "China's iron and steel industry: sources of enterprise efficiency and the impact of reform." *Journal of Development Economics* 33(2): 329–355.

Liu, S. 1993. "*Songdai de tieqian yu tie chanliang* [Iron cash and iron production in the Song dynasty]." *Zhongguo jingjishi yanjiu* (02): 86–90.

Ma, Q. 2011. "*Kuangye jianguan yu zhengfu tiaokong: Qingdai kuangchang zouxiao zhidu shulun* [Supervision on the mining industry and government regulation: a review of the Zouxiao system of mining factories in the Qing dynasty]." *Zhongguo jingjishi yanjiu* (03): 28–37.

Ma, Q. 2013. *Guojia ziyuan Qingdai Dian tong Qian qian kaifa yanjiu* [National resources: a study of the development of Yunnan copper and Guizhou lead in the Qing dynasty]. Beijing: Renmin chubanshe.

Ma, Q. 2017. "*Qingdai Dian tong chanliang yanjiu yi zouxiao shuju wei zhongxin* [A study on the output of Yunnan copper in Qing dynasty: based on the reimbursement data in the memorial to the throne]." *Zhongguo jingjishi yanjiu* (03): 71–81.

Ma, Q. 2018. *Duowei shiye xia de Qingdai Qian qian kaifa* [Multidimensional view: the development of Guizhou lead in the Qing dynasty]. Beijing: Shehui kexue wenxian chubanshe.

McNeill, W. H. 1982. *The pursuit of power: technology, armed force and society since A.D. 1000*. Chicago: The University of Chicago Press.

Minnesota Population Center. 2019. *Integrated public use microdata series, international: version 7.2* [dataset]. Minneapolis, MN: IPUMS. https://doi.org/10.18128/D020.V7.2.

National Bureau of Statistics of China, ed. 1985. *Zhongguo gongye jingji tongji ziliao 1949–1984* [Economic statistics of China's industry, 1949–1984]. Beijing: Zhongguo tongji chubanshe.

National Bureau of Statistics of China, ed. 2012. *Zhongguo tongji nianjian 2012* [China statistical yearbook 2012]. Beijing: Zhongguo tongji chubanshe.

National Economic and Trade Commission. 2001. "Yejin gongye Shiwu guihua [The 'Tenth Five-Year Plan' of metallurgical industry]." *Zhonghua gongshang shibao*, 26 June.

Ni, Yuping. 2017. *Cong guojia caizheng dao caizheng guojia: Qingchao Xian Tong nianjian de caizheng yu shehui* [From state finance to fiscal state]. Beijing: Kexue chubanshe.

Ou, P.-S., ed. 1947. *Zhongguo guomin suode 1933 nian·xia* [National income of China, 1933, Part 2]. Shanghai: Zhonghua shuju.

Peng, Z. 1985. "*Ming Qing liangdai tong qian xin kuang caiye de laodong shengchan lu shuiping* [The labor productivity of mining and smelting in the copper, lead and zinc mines of the Ming and Qing dynasties]." In *Ping zhun xue kan Zhongguo shehui jingji shi yanjiu lunji di 1 ji* [Pingzhun Xuekan, Issue 1], edited by Sun Yutang, 372–382. Beijing: Zhongguo shangye chubanshe.

Peng, Z. 1990. "*Qingdai caizheng guanli tizhi yu shou zhi jiegou* [Financial management system and income and expenditure structure in the Qing dynasty]." *Zhongguo shehui kexue yuan yanjiusheng yuan xuebao* (02): 48–59.

Perkins, D. H. 1969. *Agricultural development in China 1368–1968.* Chicago: Aldine Publishing Company.

Pomeranz, K. 2000. *The great divergence: China, Europe, and the making of the modern world economy.* Princeton: Princeton University Press.

Qu, D. 1687. *Guangdong xin yu* [New voice of Guangdong].

The Second Historical Archives of China, ed. 1994. *Zhonghua Minguo shi dang'an ziliao huibian·di 5 ji·di 1 bian·caizheng jingji (wu): Gong kuangye*, Vol. 5 [Republican China, a collection of archival documents, Book 1, Part 5: Industry and mining]. Nanjing: Jiangsu guji chubanshe.

Shi, Z., and Y. Xu. 2008. *Wan Qing caizheng:1851~1894* [Late Qing finance: 1851~1894]. Shanghai: Shanghai caijing daxue chubanshe.

Spence, J. D. 1991. *The search for modern China.* New York: Norton.

State Statistics Bureau, People's Republic of China, ed. 1991. *Zhongguo tongji nianjian 1991* [Statistical yearbook of China 1991]. Beijing: Zhongguo tongji chubanshe.

Tong, X., C. Luo, and Z. Hu. 2019. "*Gangtie gongye jishu zhuanxing yu quwei bianqian* [The locational evolution of steel industry in China: a perspective from technological transition]." *Jingji dili* 39(02): 146–151.

Van Leeuwen, B., J. van Leeuwen-Li, and P. Foldvari. 2017. "Human capital in Republican and New China: regional and long-term trends." *Economic History of Developing Regions* 32(1): 1–36.

Wagner, D. B. 2008. *Science and civilisation in China. Chemistry and chemical technology. Ferrous metallurgy*, Part 11, Vol. V. Cambridge: Cambridge University Press.

Wang, J., ed. 1934. *Henan kuangye baogao: di yi ci (Minguo ershi'er nian)* [Henan mining report, Issue 1: 1933]. Kaifeng: Henan Provincial Geological Survey.

Wang, J. 1948. "*Zhongguo gongye shengchan zhishu (1931–1946) shi bian* [A preliminary result of China's Industrial Production Index, 1931–1946]." *Zhongyang yinhang yuebao* (4): 23–29.

Wang, J. 2004. "*Zhongguo gongye shengchanli biandong chutan (1933–1946)* [A preliminary exploration on the change of China's industrial productivity, 1933–1946]." *Zhongguo jingjishi yanjiu* (01): 3–17.
Wang, L. 2005. *Songdai kuangye ye yanjiu* [A study on the mining and metallurgy industry in the Song dynasty]. Baoding: Hebei daxue chubanshe.
Wang, Z., ed. 2015. *Zhongyang qiye caiwu xiaolv fazhan baogao 2014* [Report on financial efficiency of central state-owned enterprises]. Beijing: Zhongguo jingji chubanshe.
Wen, C. 2007. "*Qing qianqi Guizhou Dading fu qian de chanliang yu yunxiao* [The output, distribution and sale of lead in Dading prefecture in Guizhou during early Qing]." *Qingshi yanjiu* (02): 65–74.
The World Steel Association, ed. 2017. *Steel statistical yearbook 2017*. Brussels: The World Steel Association.
Wright, T. 2007. "An economic cycle in imperial China? Revisiting Robert Hartwell on iron and coal." *Journal of the Economic and Social History of the Orient* 50(4): 398–423.
Xia, D. 1992. *Yangwu yundong shi* [The history of the Self-Strengthening Movement]. Shanghai: Huadong shifan daxue chubanshe.
Xu, C. 1944. *Xinjiang zhi lüe* [Brief gazetteer of Xinjiang]. Nanjing: Zhengzhong shuju.
Xu, K., and J. Han. 2006. "*Zhongguo gangtie chanye de jizhongdu buju yu jiegou youhua yanjiu jianping 2005 nian gangtie chanye fazhan zhengce* [A study on the degree of concentration, layout and structure optimization of the iron and steel industry in China]." *Zhongguo gongye jingji* (02): 37–44.
Xu, Y., Z. Shi, B. van Leeuwen, Y. Ni, Z. Zhang, and Y. Ma. 2017. "Chinese national income, ca. 1661–1933." *Australian Economic History Review* 57(3): 368–393.
Xu, Y., and Z. Zhang. 2015. "*19 shiji zhongye Zhongguo kuangye shengchan de guzhi yanjiu* [A valuation study on China's mining industry in the middle of the 19th century]." In *Qingshi luncong di 29 ji* [Qing history forum], Vol. 29, edited by 'Qing History Research Group, Institute of History, Chinese Academy of Social Sciences', 165–210. Beijing: Shehui kexue wenxian chubanshe.
Yan, Z. 1948. *Qingdai Yunnan tongzheng kao* [A study of the copper administration of Yunnan in the Qing Dynasty]. Shanghai: Zhonghua shuju.
Yang, D., and H. Hou, eds. 1931. *Liushiwu nian lai Zhongguo guoji maoyi tongji* [Statistics of China's foreign trade during the last sixty-five years]. Nanjing: National Research Institute of Social Sciences Academia Sinica.
Yu, T., and M. Chu. 1982. "*Guanyu woguo gangtie gongye buju de jige wenti* [Several issues about locations of China's steel industry]." *Jingji dili* (04): 289–291.
Yuan, W. 2007. *Juji yu kuosan Zhongguo jindai gongye buju* [Convergence and diffusion: location of China's modern industry]. Shanghai: Shanghai caijing daxue chubanshe.
Zhang, J., G. Wu, and J. Zhang. 2004. "*Zhongguo shengji wuzi ziben cunliang gusuan 1952–2000* [The estimation of China's provincial capital stock: 1952–2000]." *Jingji yanjiu* (10): 35–44.
Zhang, Z. 2014. *Jindai kuangye shengchan de dingliang yanjiu 1850–1933 yi mei tie wei li* [A quantitative study of the mining industry in Modern China, 1850~1933: an example of coal and iron]. Master's thesis, Guangxi Normal University.

Appendix 6.1

Glossary

Table A6.1.1 Glossary

Chinese characters	*Chinese Pinyin*	*Current translation*
大行政区	Da xingzheng qu	Greater Administrative Region
大跃进	Da yuejin	Great Leap Forward
广西矿务局	Guangxi kuangwuju	Guangxi Mining Bureau
广西省统计局	Guangxi sheng tongjiju	Guangxi Provincial Bureau of Statistics
国家统计局	Guojia tongjiju	National Bureau of Statistics of China
户部	Hubu	Ministry of Revenue
三线建设	Sanxian jianshe	The Third Front Movement
实业部	Shiyebu	Ministry of Industry
奏销	Zouxiao	Regulations on the Submission of Expense Accounts to the Imperial Court

Appendix 6.2

Sources and data of the 1933 benchmark

Output of mercury, silver, and the mechanical production of pig iron is taken from the *General statement on the mining industry of China* edited by Hou Defeng (1935). Most native handicraft production of pig iron is estimated based on the same source. The exception is Zhejiang, which is estimated based on the data from both the International Trade Bureau, Ministry of Industry (1933) and Hou (1935). Copper and steel are estimated based on Hou (1935). For antimony, Guangxi is estimated based on Guangxi Mining Bureau (1935), and Hunan is taken from Hou (1935). For tin, Guangxi is estimated based on Guangxi Provincial Bureau of Statistics (1999[1936]); Hunan, Jiangxi, and Yunnan are taken from Hou (1935); and Guangdong is estimated based on Hou (1935) as well. For lead and zinc, Yunnan is estimated with Hou (1935), Hunan is taken from a contemporary survey *1934 Yield table of Shuikoushan* (1934), and Sichuan is estimated based on government archives (The Second Historical Archives of China 1994). For gold, Gansu and Qinghai are estimated based on a survey *1935 gold in Gansu* (1935); Guangxi is proxied with 1932 data from Guangxi Provincial Bureau of Statistics (1934); Guangdong, Hebei, and Rehe are estimated with Hou (1932, 1935); Henan is taken from a survey (Wang 1934); Shandong, Sichuan, Heilongjiang, Jilin, and Liaoning are estimated based on Hou (1935); Hunan is taken from the International Trade Bureau, Ministry of Industry (1935); and Xinjiang is estimated based on Xu (1944). To get total numbers of workers, we used output and output per worker. The output per labourer, used to estimate the number of labourers, of pig iron (both handicraft production and modern mechanical production), copper, gold, lead, steel, tin, antimony, zinc, and mercury, are taken from Ou (1947), and silver is proxied by gold.

Appendix 6.3

Sources and data of the 1850 benchmark

One relevant component of the Qing-Dynasty fiscal system was literally named "*Zouxiao*", also referred to as "Regulations on the Submission of Expense Accounts to the Imperial Court" in existing literature (Chen 2000). In brief, with the *Zouxiao* system, local officials had to regularly report the numbers of "old balance", "new income", "expenditure", and "new balance", as well as the source of "new income" and the destination of "expenditure", to the upper levels of administration and eventually the emperor. Once these reports arrived in Beijing, the Ministry of Revenue executed a verification procedure, including checking these newly reported numbers with the regulation and the performance in the recent years, to find if these reports were trustworthy or if any fraud of the local officials had taken place. Finally, the ministry delivered their opinion, the validation result, and a copy of the original report from local government to the emperor, who would decide whether to approve the report or not.

For the reports which referred to metallurgical factories, ordinarily this whole process started from the officials who were stationed at a factory as supervisor. First, the daily production of a factory was registered per day, and these records were kept by both the businessman who operated the factory and the official who supervised the operation. Further, these records were checked once every ten days by specific higher-ranked officials. Every month, the documents were submitted to the provincial government and were organized as a "monthly report". If these reports passed the check of the provincial government, the governor would then send them to Beijing annually. All these procedures, especially the contemporary verification at each administrative level, endowed these government archives and the resulting data solid credibility (Ma 2011). However, the *Zouxiao* system gradually failed after the mid-nineteenth century. As noticed by various scholars (Ni 2017; Peng 1990; Shi and Xu 2008), the chaos in the second half of the nineteenth century, especially the Taiping Rebellion, significantly damaged the central government's authority and governance capacity. Local officials either were physically unable to send their reports to Beijing due to warfare or neglected the Ministry of Revenue and reported to the emperor directly. All these stories reduced the quantity of this type of archival records for the post-1850 period in general.

Based on these sources, we create an overview of observations of metal smelting, as shown in Appendix 6.4. Unfortunately, it is necessary to notice the relatively low share of ferrous metals. As pointed out previously, iron was not considered as important as nonferrous metals by the Qing government, especially before the Self-Strengthening Movement. As a result, the state control and intervention in the iron industry was limited. For instance, enterprises of nonferrous metals were supervised by local officials who were essentially stationed on site, while most ironworks (apart from those major modern mechanical ironworks built during the Self-Strengthening Movement) were fully operated by private merchants. Also, a difference of tax system can be witnessed. A kind of flat tax was levied to the iron industry, while the investors in the mining and smelting business of nonferrous metal had to pay proportional tax. Therefore, the iron industry was less covered in the *Zouxiao* system. This fact made the observations of iron output much more indirect.

In addition to these *Zouxiao* archives of the central government, we thus also have to use local sources, e.g., local gazetteers, to complement missing data, especially for ferrous products. It is a historical tradition for the local authorities in China, even today, to regularly issue local gazetteers. As explained by Perkins (1969: 9), "each county, prefecture and province in China kept a record of events and data that where considered significant", and the later-published local gazetteers can be viewed as "primary sources for data originally published centuries before", as information of the earlier gazetteers were ordinarily quoted or copied in the later ones. For this reason, not just the contemporary writings of the Qing Dynasty but some local gazetteers that were published in the post-Qing era are also used to trace historical information of the Qing period.

In order to arrive at the number of smelters, we need to divide output by output/labourer. Productivity per worker in 1850 is difficult. For copper, it is calculated using Peng's (1985) estimate of copper for the Qing dynasty. The result for copper is used as the proxy for cupronickel. For mercury, it is proxied by the calculated 1933 productivity. Tin is proxied by Ou's (1947) estimate of Yunnan (without modern produce) for 1934. Lead and zinc are proxied by Ou's (1947) estimate for 1933. Gold is proxied by Ou's (1947) estimate for 1933 and converted from modern tael (500g) to Qing tael (596.8g). Then we use the result of gold to estimate silver. For steel, it is calculated based on Xu and Zhang (2015) and An Chaojun (1941). The productivity of pig iron in 1850 is even more complex than that of the other products, as regional differences were so significant that we had to apply specific rates for each province. For Sichuan, Shaanxi, and Fujian, the productivities are taken from Xu and Zhang (2015). Guizhou and Hunan are also calculated based on Xu and Zhang (2015). For Shanxi, labour productivity is calculated based on Xu and Zhang (2015) and Fan (1985). Guangdong and Guangxi are calculated based on Xu and Zhang (2015) and Qu (1687). The productivity of Jiangxi is proxied by Zhejiang, which is calculated based on Cao and Jiang (2010). Yunnan and Anhui are proxied by Ou's (1947) estimation for 1933.

Appendix 6.4

Physical output observations by province and sector for the benchmark 1850

In Table A6.4.1, an overview is given for the regional and sectoral distribution of output observations, i.e., both the directly recorded output figures in Chinese weight units (e.g. *jin*) and those indirectly converted or computed results of output for 1850.

Table A6.4.1 Physical output observations by province and sector for the benchmark 1850

province	*Ferrous metal*		*Nonferrous metals*								*Sum*
			Precious metal		*Other nonferrous metals*						
	Iron	*Steel*	*Gold*	*Silver*	*Copper*	*Cupro-nickel*	*Lead*	*Zinc*	*Tin*	*Mercury*	
Anhui	1	1	0	0	0	0	0	0	0	0	2
Fujian	8	0	0	0	0	0	0	0	0	0	8
Gansu	0	0	2	0	0	0	0	0	0	0	2
Guangdong	45	0	0	3	0	0	3	0	0	0	51
Guangxi	11	0	0	2	0	0	0	1	1	0	15
Guizhou	14	0	0	3	1	0	4	5	0	5	32
Hunan	26	4	0	0	3	0	3	3	6	0	45
Jiangxi	7	0	0	0	0	0	0	0	0	0	7
Shaanxi	4	0	0	0	0	0	0	0	0	0	4
Shanxi	8	0	0	0	0	0	0	0	0	0	8
Sichuan	20	0	0	4	11	1	4	1	0	1	42
Tibet	0	0	1	0	0	0	0	0	0	0	1
Xinjiang	0	0	5	0	9	0	1	0	0	0	15
Yunnan	14	0	4	25	64	0	2	3	1	0	113
others	0	0	0	0	0	0	0	0	0	1	1
sum	158	5	12	37	88	1	17	13	8	7	346

Source: See text.

Appendix 6.5

Metal smelters in metal smelting industry, 1850–2000 (in 2000 constant prefectural boundaries)

Table A6.5.1 Metal smelters in metal smelting industry, 1850–2000 (in 2000 constant prefectural boundaries)

Province	*Prefecture/region*	*1850*	*1933*	*1982*	*1990*	*2000*
Anhui	Bengbu city, Suzhou city	0	0	200	0	0
Anhui	Chuzhou city	0	0	0	0	0
Anhui	Fuyang city, Bozhou city	0	0	0	0	0
Anhui	Hefei city, Liu'an city, Chaohu city	123	0	2,800	1,100	5,539
Anhui	Huaibei city	0	0	0	300	1,100
Anhui	Huainan city	0	0	400	500	231
Anhui	Tongling city	0	0	1,500	5,200	3,100
Anhui	Wuhu city, Ma'anshan city, Anqing city, Huangshan city, Xuancheng city, Guichi city	0	0	7,900	15,800	10,718
Beijing	Beijing municipality	85	0	9,200	5,300	10,037
Fujian	Fuzhou city, Putian city, Ningde city	22	0	1,700	800	7,933
Fujian	Longyan city	22	0	600	14,200	4,766
Fujian	Nanping city	33	0	1,200	200	3,300
Fujian	Quanzhou city	0	0	400	400	8,600
Fujian	Sanming city	0	0	1,700	15,500	1,495
Fujian	Xiamen city	0	0	100	400	2,050
Fujian	Zhangzhou city	0	0	100	500	5,700
Gansu	Baiyin city, Tianshui city, Wuwei prefecture, Dingxi prefecture, Wudu prefecture	0	0	1,500	1,700	7,337
Gansu	Gannan Tibetan autonomous prefecture	0	0	0	0	0

Province	*Prefecture/region*	*1850*	*1933*	*1982*	*1990*	*2000*
Gansu	Jiayuguan city	0	0	1,400	500	2,000
Gansu	Jinchang city	0	0	1,900	9,300	5,801
Gansu	Jiuquan prefecture	17	0	0	0	0
Gansu	Lanzhou city	0	0	8,300	1,500	6,981
Gansu	Linxia Hui prefecture	0	0	200	0	0
Gansu	Pingliang prefecture	0	0	0	0	0
Gansu	Qingyang prefecture	0	0	0	0	0
Gansu	Zhangye prefecture	0	0	0	200	900
Guangdong, Hainan	Foshan city, Jiangmen city	0	0	600	2,000	19,771
Guangdong, Hainan	Guangzhou city, Shaoguan city, Huizhou city, Heyuan city, Qingyuan city, Dongguan city	354	0	9,000	3,900	25,350
Guangdong, Hainan	Haikou city, Sanya city, Hainan Province direct administrative area	0	0	500	600	464
Guangdong, Hainan	Meizhou city	346	0	300	500	2,000
Guangdong, Hainan	Shanwei city, Jieyang city, Shantou city, Chaozhou city	345	0	200	0	0
Guangdong, Hainan	Shenzhen city	0	0	0	100	253
Guangdong, Hainan	Zhanjiang city, Maoming city, Yangjiang city	345	0	800	200	1,229
Guangdong, Hainan	Zhaoqing city, Yunfu city	0	0	300	100	2,300
Guangdong, Hainan	Zhuhai city, Zhongshan city	0	0	0	100	4,600
Guangxi	Baise prefecture	5	0	600	100	2,150
Guangxi	Beihai city, Qinzhou city, Fangchenggang city	0	0	0	200	150
Guangxi	Guilin city	0	0	1,600	200	2,867
Guangxi	Hechi prefecture	184	0	1,200	0	0
Guangxi	Liuzhou city, Liuzhou prefecture	129	0	2,600	2,200	10,648
Guangxi	Nanning prefecture, Nanning city	66	0	1,200	5,500	2,542
Guangxi	Wuzhou city, Hezhou prefecture	2,248	0	900	500	792
Guangxi	Yulin city, Guigang city	0	0	1,000	200	1,800
Guizhou	Bijie prefecture	0	0	1,200	0	0

(*Continued*)

Table A6.5.1 (Continued)

Province	*Prefecture/region*	*1850*	*1933*	*1982*	*1990*	*2000*
Guizhou	Guiyang city, Anshun city	2	0	4,400	1,500	15,094
Guizhou	Liupanshui city	0	0	700	200	5,700
Guizhou	Qiandongnan Miao-Dong autonomous prefecture	20	0	400	400	0
Guizhou	Qiannan Buyei-Miao autonomous prefecture	2	0	100	0	0
Guizhou	Qianxinan Buyei-Miao autonomous prefecture	0	0	100	0	0
Guizhou	Tongren prefecture	0	0	100	0	0
Guizhou	Zunyi city	2	0	2,500	1,300	6,779
Hebei	Baoding city	0	0	900	500	8,778
Hebei	Cangzhou city	0	0	300	0	0
Hebei	Handan city	0	0	4,300	6,100	22,999
Hebei	Hengshui city	0	0	100	300	21,150
Hebei	Langfang city	0	0	700	100	7,100
Hebei	Shijiazhuang city	0	0	1,100	2,700	11,475
Hebei	Tangshan city, Qinhuangdao city, Chengde city	137	0	8,400	14,100	44,326
Hebei	Xingtai city	0	0	1,200	600	12,900
Hebei	Zhangjiakou city	0	0	2,400	9,300	5,979
Heilongjiang	Daxing'anling prefecture	8	0	0	0	0
Heilongjiang	Hegang city, Jiamusi city, Qitaihe city, Shuangyashan city, Harbin city	59	0	4,600	6,000	6,909
Heilongjiang	Heihe city	542	0	100	200	300
Heilongjiang	Jixi city, Mudanjiang city	0	0	1,000	400	3,943
Heilongjiang	Qiqihar city, Suihua city, Daqing city	0	0	2,300	1,700	5,313
Heilongjiang	Yichun city	0	0	500	500	1,083
Henan	Anyang city, Hebi city, Xinxiang city, Jiaozuo city, Puyang city	0	0	7,500	5,700	25,456
Henan	Luoyang city, Pingdingshan city, Xuchang city, Luohe city, Sanmenxia city	4	0	4,100	5,700	21,421
Henan	Nanyang city	5	0	500	0	0
Henan	Shangqiu city	0	0	0	0	0
Henan	Xinyang city	615	0	700	0	0

Province	*Prefecture/region*	*1850*	*1933*	*1982*	*1990*	*2000*
Henan	Zhengzhou city, Kaifeng city	0	0	3,700	1,600	13,046
Henan	Zhoukou city	0	0	100	17,900	1,800
Henan	Zhumadian city	0	0	0	0	0
Hubei	Exi Tujia-Miao autonomous prefecture	0	0	0	100	600
Hubei	Huangshi city, Xianning city	0	0	4,700	2,800	8,256
Hubei	Shiyan city, Jingzhou city, Jingmen city, Hubei Province direct administrative area	0	0	1,700	700	8,167
Hubei	Wuhan city, Xiangfan city, Ezhou city, Huanggang city, Xiaogan city, Suizhou city	438	0	11,600	13,900	25,089
Hubei	Yichang city	0	0	200	800	2,114
Hunan	Changde city, Zhangjiajie city, Xiangxi Tujia-Miao autonomous prefecture	2	0	400	600	4,267
Hunan	Changsha city, Zhuzhou city, Yiyang city	6,083	0	7,200	1,300	13,260
Hunan	Hengyang city, Shaoyang city, Loudi city, Chenzhou city, Yongzhou city	9,173	0	7,700	3,700	31,282
Hunan	Huaihua city	598	0	300	200	3,000
Hunan	Xiangtan city	0	0	5,500	2,500	7,857
Hunan	Yueyang city	0	0	500	400	800
Inner Mongolia	Alxa prefecture	0	0	0	0	0
Inner Mongolia	Bayannur league	0	0	100	0	0
Inner Mongolia	Chifeng city	1	0	0	300	495
Inner Mongolia	Hohhot city, Baotou city, Ulaan Chab league	0	0	8,800	10,700	18,707
Inner Mongolia	Hulunbuir league	27	0	100	600	750
Inner Mongolia	Tongliao city	0	0	0	100	1,200
Inner Mongolia	Wuhai city	0	0	200	8,500	850
Inner Mongolia	Xilin Gol league	0	0	0	0	0
Inner Mongolia	Xing'an league	0	0	800	0	0
Inner Mongolia	Yikezhao league	0	0	0	700	800
Jiangsu	Nanjing city, Wuxi city, Changzhou city, Suzhou city, Zhenjiang city	0	0	14,600	17,200	27,950

(*Continued*)

Table A6.5.1 (Continued)

Province	*Prefecture/region*	*1850*	*1933*	*1982*	*1990*	*2000*
Jiangsu	Nantong city	0	0	300	1,600	13,360
Jiangsu	Xuzhou city, Lianyungang city, Huaiyin city, Suqian city	0	0	2,900	3,800	10,600
Jiangsu	Yancheng city	0	0	100	200	1,850
Jiangsu	Yangzhou city, Taizhou city	0	0	2,300	1,400	7,160
Jiangxi	Jingdezhen city, Yingtan city, Shangrao city	0	0	1,500	100	1,725
Jiangxi	Jiujiang city	0	0	200	100	1,167
Jiangxi	Nanchang city, Xinyu city, Ganzhou city, Yichun city, Fuzhou city	1,800	0	6,500	1,900	13,606
Jiangxi	Pingxiang city, Ji'an city	0	0	2,000	2,600	1,972
Jilin	Baicheng city, Songyuan city	0	0	100	300	600
Jilin	Changchun city	0	0	1,400	2,000	2,176
Jilin	Jilin city	0	0	4,100	1,700	4,344
Jilin	Siping city, Liaoyuan city	0	0	600	400	1,106
Jilin	Tonghua city, Baishan city	0	0	2,700	3,100	4,650
Jilin	Yanbian Korean autonomous prefecture	35	0	300	3,100	2,188
Liaoning	Anshan city, Dandong city	4,740	0	11,500	10,800	10,383
Liaoning	Benxi city	1,731	0	5,200	6,300	6,623
Liaoning	Dalian city	0	0	2,800	2,100	3,354
Liaoning	Fushun city	21	0	5,800	2,300	7,808
Liaoning	Fuxin city	1	0	500	500	318
Liaoning	Jinzhou city, Chaoyang city, Huludao city	4	0	4,900	10,000	18,583
Liaoning	Liaoyang city	0	0	800	700	2,070
Liaoning	Shenyang city, Tieling city	0	0	7,000	8,600	7,644
Liaoning	Yingkou city, Panjin city	0	0	600	400	1,026
Ningxia	Shizuishan city	0	0	200	1,100	7,869
Ningxia	Yinchuan city, Wuzhong city, Guyuan prefecture	0	0	600	400	4,800
Qinghai	Golog Tibetan autonomous prefecture	0	0	0	0	0

Province	*Prefecture/region*	*1850*	*1933*	*1982*	*1990*	*2000*
Qinghai	Haibei Tibetan autonomous prefecture	67	0	0	0	0
Qinghai	Haidong prefecture, Xining city	133	0	1,700	2,100	7,275
Qinghai	Hainan Tibetan autonomous prefecture	0	0	0	0	0
Qinghai	Huangnan Tibetan autonomous prefecture	0	0	0	0	0
Qinghai	Yushu Tibetan autonomous prefecture, Haixi Mongol-Tibetan autonomous prefecture	0	0	0	0	0
Shaanxi	Ankang city	0	0	100	0	0
Shaanxi	Hanzhong city	2	0	1,700	0	0
Shaanxi	Shangluo prefecture	0	0	0	0	0
Shaanxi	Xi'an city, Tongchuan city, Baoji city, Xianyang city, Weinan city, Yan'an city	2	0	6,500	7,400	16,145
Shaanxi	Yulin city	0	0	0	0	0
Shandong	Jinan city, Tai'an prefecture, Dezhou city, Laiwu city	0	0	7,900	5,600	29,952
Shandong	Liaocheng city	0	0	0	0	0
Shandong	Qingdao city, Zibo city, Dongying city, Yantai city, Weifang city, Weihai city, Rizhao city, Binzhou city, Linyi city	5	0	8,500	61,400	61,584
Shandong	Zaozhuang city, Jining city, Heze city	0	0	800	100	3,467
Shanghai	Shanghai municipality	1,080	0	21,000	27,900	29,381
Shanxi	Changzhi city, Jincheng city	3,692	0	3,700	10,500	31,995
Shanxi	Datong city, Shuozhou city	0	0	900	2,300	7,858
Shanxi	Linfen city	0	0	1,500	2,400	19,950
Shanxi	Luliang prefecture	0	0	700	2,500	15,800
Shanxi	Taiyuan city	720	0	5,100	6,900	14,858
Shanxi	Xinzhou city	0	0	500	2,900	5,300
Shanxi	Yangquan city, Jinzhong city	1,001	0	4,400	13,800	11,275

(*Continued*)

Table A6.5.1 (Continued)

Province	*Prefecture/region*	*1850*	*1933*	*1982*	*1990*	*2000*
Shanxi	Yuncheng city	0	0	600	3,400	15,543
Sichuan, Chongqing	Chengdu city, Deyang city, Mianyang city, Guangyuan city, Suining city, Nanchong city, Dazhou city, Ngawa Tibetan-Qiang autonomous prefecture, Bazhong city, Guang'an city	217	0	11,800	17,600	21,354
Sichuan, Chongqing	Chongqing municipality	308	0	9,500	4,900	16,072
Sichuan, Chongqing	Garze Tibetan autonomous prefecture	0	0	0	0	0
Sichuan, Chongqing	Leshan city, Meishan city	0	0	2,300	1,300	3,952
Sichuan, Chongqing	Liangshan Yi prefecture	411	0	500	0	0
Sichuan, Chongqing	Panzhihua city	0	0	2,300	2,400	6,538
Sichuan, Chongqing	Ya'an city	615	0	300	1,500	1,313
Sichuan, Chongqing	Zigong city, Luzhou city, Yibin city	0	0	1,900	700	6,650
Sichuan, Chongqing	Ziyang city, Neijiang city	308	0	1,400	2,100	3,478
Tianjin	Tianjin municipality	0	0	8,000	15,200	18,694
Tibet	Lhasa city, Chamdo prefecture, Shannan prefecture, Nyingchi prefecture	0	0	0	0	0
Tibet	Nagchu prefecture	0	0	0	0	0
Tibet	Ngari prefecture	0	0			0
Tibet	Shigatse prefecture	0	0	0	100	400
Xinjiang	Aksu prefecture	0	0	200	0	0
Xinjiang	Altay prefecture	1,083	0	0	0	0
Xinjiang	Bayin'gholin Mongol autonomous prefecture	60	0	500	0	0
Xinjiang	Bortala Mongol autonomous prefecture	0	0	0	0	0
Xinjiang	Changji Hui prefecture	0	0	200	0	0

Province	*Prefecture/region*	*1850*	*1933*	*1982*	*1990*	*2000*
Xinjiang	Hami prefecture	0	0	300	0	0
Xinjiang	Karamay city	0	0	100	100	200
Xinjiang	Kashgar prefecture	0	0	0	200	400
Xinjiang	Khotan prefecture	47	0	100	0	0
Xinjiang	Kizilsu Kirghiz autonomous prefecture	0	0	0	0	0
Xinjiang	Shihezi city	0	0	500	0	0
Xinjiang	Tacheng prefecture	0	0	0	0	0
Xinjiang	Turfan prefecture	0	0	300	0	0
Xinjiang	Urumuqi city	0	0	2,100	1,300	2,094
Xinjiang	Yili Kazak autonomous prefecture, Yili prefecture	0	0	400	0	0
Yunnan	Baoshan prefecture	10	0	100	0	0
Yunnan	Dali Bai autonomous prefecture	19	0	200	100	3,400
Yunnan	Dehong Dai-Jingpo autonomous prefecture	0	0	0	0	0
Yunnan	Diqing Tibetan autonomous prefecture	0	0	0	0	0
Yunnan	Honghe Hani-Yi autonomous prefecture	37,155	0	3,300	1,200	10,800
Yunnan	Kunming city, Qujing city, Chuxiong Yi autonomous autonomous prefecture	2,457	0	8,700	3,400	12,737
Yunnan	Lijiang prefecture	0	0	0	0	0
Yunnan	Lincang prefecture	10	0	100	200	500
Yunnan	Nujiang Lisu autonomous prefecture	8	0	300	0	0
Yunnan	Simao prefecture	0	0	400	0	0
Yunnan	Wenshan Zhuang-Miao autonomous prefecture	0	0	100	0	0
Yunnan	Xishuangpanna Dai autonomous prefecture	0	0	0	0	0
Yunnan	Yuxi city	0	0	300	100	4,400
Yunnan	Zhaotong prefecture	0	0	200	0	0
Zhejiang	Hangzhou city	0	0	3,800	1,100	4,562
Zhejiang	Jiaxing city, Huzhou city	0	0	0	1,000	2,926
Zhejiang	Jinhua city, Quzhou city	0	0	1,000	700	7,910

(*Continued*)

Table A6.5.1 (Continued)

Province	*Prefecture/region*	*1850*	*1933*	*1982*	*1990*	*2000*
Zhejiang	Lishui city	8	0	0	500	4,600
Zhejiang	Ningbo city	0	0	1,900	1,500	4,029
Zhejiang	Shaoxing city	0	0	700	1,100	3,922
Zhejiang	Taizhou city	0	0	0	0	0
Zhejiang	Wenzhou city	0	0	200	600	19,800
Zhejiang	Zhoushan city	0	0	0	0	0
Zhejiang	Hangzhou city	0	0	3,800	1,100	4,562
Zhejiang	Jiaxing city, Huzhou city	0	0	0	1,000	2,926
Zhejiang	Jinhua city, Quzhou city	0	0	1,000	700	7,910
Zhejiang	Lishui city	8	0	0	500	4,600
Zhejiang	Ningbo city	0	0	1,900	1,500	4,029
Zhejiang	Shaoxing city	0	0	700	1,100	3,922
Zhejiang	Taizhou city	0	0	0	0	0
Zhejiang	Wenzhou city	0	0	200	600	19,800
Zhejiang	Zhoushan city	0	0	0	0	0

7 Regional industrialization in China

The Yangtze and Zhujiang regions[1]

Yi Xu, Bas van Leeuwen, and Zicheng Zhuang

7.1 Introduction

Industrialization has been a hotly debated topic in the field of economic history, ever since the first Industrial Revolution occurred in Britain in the eighteenth century. Although initially focused on national development, regional industrialization patterns have received increasing attention (e.g. Pollard 1994). This literature, of which the Cambridge school is a prominent example, points out that techniques, industrial production, and income were differently allocated over England, with the textile industry being located in Lancashire as a prime example (Shaw-Taylor forthcoming). Many subsequent publications have aimed to explain regional industrialization (e.g. Crafts and Mulatu 2006; Wolf 2007). This large rise in the number of regional studies, combined with the fast rise in industrial output in China over the past decades, makes it remarkable that Chinese regional industrialization has not attracted a comparable amount of attention (e.g. Pomeranz 2000).

An important reason for this lack of regional studies is the absence of comprehensive data. Even though regional data are not widely available in many countries, the Chinese data are even more erratic. It was only in 1933 that China witnessed the most complete and comprehensive pre-New China industrial census, which was conducted and published by D. K. Lieu, Director of the China Institute of Economic and Statistical Research of Shanghai (Lieu 1937). Yet, even this census contains many gaps, omissions, and inaccuracies. Ou Pao-San (1947) conducted the first attempt to aggregate a modified version of these data up into national estimates of employment for industrial sectors. His pioneering study had three lasting effects on scholarship regarding industrial production. First, it offered subsequent scholars a classification scheme for China's industry. Second, it provided for the first time a perspective on industrialization in China as a whole. And third, by providing estimates for the Republican period, it allowed subsequent scholars to take a long-term view on industry covering both the Republican and New China periods.

For early New China, as Liu and Yeh (1965) have pointed out, the industrial statistics for the years 1952–1954 are the most reliable. They arrived at estimates of industrialization for 1933–1957. Combining Liu and Yeh (1965) with subsequent national statistics, Maddison (1998) and Wu (2011) constructed value added estimates for New China industrialization. Recently, Xu and van Leeuwen (2016) reconstructed a new estimate of Chinese long-term industrialization between 1850 and 2012.

Notwithstanding the academic value of previously mentioned studies, these studies captured a regional perspective on industrialization only to a limited extent. With this chapter, we aim to make a first attempt to fill this hole by analyzing six provinces along the Yangtze (Jiangsu, Shanghai, and Anhui) and Zhujiang (Guangdong, Hainan, and Guangxi) rivers, respectively. There are two reasons for more closely studying these six provinces. First, Guangdong, Shanghai, and Jiangsu were the earliest industrializers in China, where modern factories and technologies had been introduced from the West to China in the 1860s. Industrialization spread along the Yangtze and Zhujiang rivers respectively, which made both Anhui and Guangxi industrial followers. Second, much more detailed statistics and surveys on regional industrialization have remained for these six provinces compared to the rest of China.

Consequently, in this chapter, we will construct industrial employment by prefecture in these six provinces for three benchmark years (1933, 1982, and 2000). We will do this by discussing the industrial classification in Section 7.2. Sources are then discussed in Section 7.3. Sections 7.4 and 7.5 contain a preliminary analysis on the patterns and drivers of regional industries, in which we combine our empirical data with existing historiography to obtain a more complete picture. We end with a brief conclusion.

7.2 Classification of the manufacturing industry

It was in the mid-nineteenth century that the defeat in both Opium Wars caused the Qing bureaucrats to launch the so-called Self-Strengthening Movement (1860–1894), in an attempt to modernize the Chinese military. This was planned through a series of government-financed and/or government-controlled Western-style industrial enterprises. Yet, the attitude of the Self-Strengthening Movement towards private enterprises in the modern sector ranged from indifference to hostility, and there was little interest in supplying modern public goods to the population. Nevertheless, this movement is usually considered the start of the modernization of Chinese industry, a development that continued during the entire Republican period (1911–1949) and was completed with socialist industrialization during the first decades of New China.

This trend of industrialization in China may be argued to have affected the collection of industrial statistics (see Section 7.3), as well as the industrial classification. The classifications around the late-nineteenth and early- twentieth centuries, which varied from region to region, were mainly based on modern industry, with handicraft either being ignored or forming a separate category in the classification. Indeed, this classification remained, in some cases, true all the way into the first years of New China. These were reported in investigations, reports, and local gazetteers.

China's first modern economic survey was conducted only in the final decade of Qing rule and was continued in 1911 by its successor, the Beijing Government in Republican China. The Beijing Government repeated this admittedly incomplete survey nine times between 1911 and 1921, the results of which were published as the *Statistical Tables of Agriculture and Commerce.* Within these statistical surveys, a special chapter devoted to "Manufacturing" reported both the classification of manufacturing and the coverage of products by manufacture sectors on both countrywide and provincial levels. In general, the *Statistical Tables of Agriculture and Commerce* roughly classified manufacturing industry as thirty-two sectors covering 175 products.

After the new government, the so-called Nanjing government, was founded in 1927, D. K. Lieu (1937) published the most complete and comprehensive industrial census in prewar China for 1933, which classified industry in sixteen sectors, eighty-seven sub-sectors, and 161 sub-sub-sectors. By separating mining from these sixteen industry sectors offered by Lieu, Ou (1947) provided subsequent scholars with a classification of the manufacturing industry including fifteen sectors.

When the Chinese Communist Party took over enterprises during 1949 and 1950, they made stringent efforts to collect and improve upon their statistics. Surveys of government and joint government–private enterprises were conducted and published as early as 1950, but the data published during these early years are of particularly questionable reliability until the State Statistical Bureau was established in 1952. Since then, New China's government introduced an industrial classification from the Soviet Union to conduct and compile countrywide industrial comprehensive surveys. In this classification, industry was enumerated as twenty-one sectors, 112 sub-sectors, and 264 sub-sub-sectors. Since the reform and opening up in 1978, New China's government replaced the Soviet classification with a classification which breaks down industry in fourteen sectors, 201 sub-sectors, and 581 sub-sub-sectors.

As linking these sectors over time in detail is almost impossible, in this chapter we follow Brandt et al. (2017) and use major manufacturing groups that are consistent over time. Yet, contrary to Brandt et al. (2017), who used the classification of the planned economy period, we focus on the 1933 period classification (Table 7.1). Two points are worth noting. First, contrary to the present-day Chinese classification, the manufacturing of water, electricity, and gas belonged to manufacturing in 1933. Hence also for today, we define manufacturing as including water, electricity, and gas.

Second, we cannot calculate industrial employment for all sectors, so we focus on four representative sub-sectors, i.e., the manufacturing of machinery, cotton textiles, printing, and electric power (Table 7.2). As pointed out, whereas the first three groups fall at present in manufacturing, the latter is today classified as "electricity, gas and water supply". These manufacturing sectors are chosen as they cover major groups, i.e., "Manufacture of textiles", "Printing and reproduction of recorded media", and "Manufacture of machinery and equipment".

Table 7.1 Classification of manufacturing sectors in 1933

1	Manufacture of Lumber and Wood Products
2	Manufacture of Machinery
3	Manufacture of Metal Products
4	Manufacture of Electrical Equipment, Electrical Supplies, and Electronic Communication
5	Manufacture of Transport Equipment
6	Manufacture of Soil and Stone
7	Manufacture of Water, Electricity, and Gas
8	Manufacture of Chemical Products
9	Manufacture of Textile
10	Manufacture of Clothing
11	Manufacture of Rubber and Leather
12	Manufacture of Beverages and Foods
13	Manufacture of Paper and Printing
14	Manufacture of Accessories & Instruments
15	Miscellaneous

Source: Ou (1947), this text.

Table 7.2 Concordance of the manufacturing of machinery, cotton textiles, printing, and electric power over time

1933		*1982*		*2000*		*Note*
2.2	Manufacture of machinery and repair	42	General machinery (excluding electrical machinery)	35	Common equipment and machinery	
				36	Special equipment	
7.2	Production of electric power	141	Production and supply of electric power	44	Electricity, steam and hot water production and supply	For 2000, we removed hot water by subtracting its share in electricity in 1990
9.2	Manufacture of cotton textile	232	Cotton spinning and weaving	17	Textiles	For 2000, we arrived at cotton textiles spinning and weaving by applying its share from 1990 on textiles in 2000
		233	Cotton spinning and weaving (2)			
13.3	Manufacture of printing	294	Printing industry	23	Printing and replication of recording media	

Source: This text, census 1982 and 2000 (Minnesota Population Center 2019).

7.3 Data and sources for employment in Chinese regional manufacturing

As pointed out, we will construct prefectural data for 1933, 1982, and 2000 using our integrated classification. Due to data limitations, we construct the employment for four manufacture sectors: machinery, electric power, cotton textiles, and printing. We do this by starting from the major available source(s) for each respective benchmark year, and then correct any errors and fill missing data using additional sources.

The data for 1982 and 2000 are obtained from the respective population censuses (see Minnesota Population Center 2019). Because for 2000, we had to filter out "hot water" from electricity, and "other textiles" from cotton textiles, we took those shares from the 1990 census, and then subtracted them from "Electricity, steam and hot water production and supply" and "Textiles" of 2000.

The 1933 benchmark is more complicated. After the establishment of the new government – the so-called Nanjing government, founded in 1927 – it conducted and published two types of surveys on industrialization. One set of surveys specifically reported information on manufacturing sectors. For example, D. K. Lieu (1937), who published the most complete and comprehensive manufacture sectors census in prewar China for 1933, reported detailed information for sixteen sectors of manufacturing industry. Yet, at a spatially disaggregated level, the second volume of this survey only reported statistics on Chinese-owned modern factories, defined as establishments with thirty or more employees and using mechanical power, on the provincial level. The third volume of this survey, for the prefectural level, reported statistics on Chinese-owned modern factories and a part of the handicraft factories. In sum, Lieu's survey lacked complete data for the number of labourers on the prefectural level as, first, it did not report information on the electrical power sector. Second, it excluded information on foreign-funded factories; and third, it lacked most handicraft production.

We can, however, supplement Lieu's survey with other surveys, which either focus on certain manufacturing sectors and/or certain regions (see Appendix 7.1). This second set of surveys focused on employment information by aggregated occupational classifications, differentiating between agriculture, industry, and service. Provincial governments across China in the 1930s usually published the total number of persons employed for all manufacture sectors as a whole by subprovincial level. This allows us to calculate total employment in industry by subprovincial level for six provinces (Appendix 7.1). All surveys combined resulted in our estimates (Appendix 7.3).

Our resulting dataset (see Appendix 7.3) is thus significantly more complete than earlier surveys. As can be seen in Figure 7.1, our employment estimates are higher than those of Lieu in all sectors. Yet this difference is particularly evident in sectors with a large share of handicraft employment, such as cotton textiles.

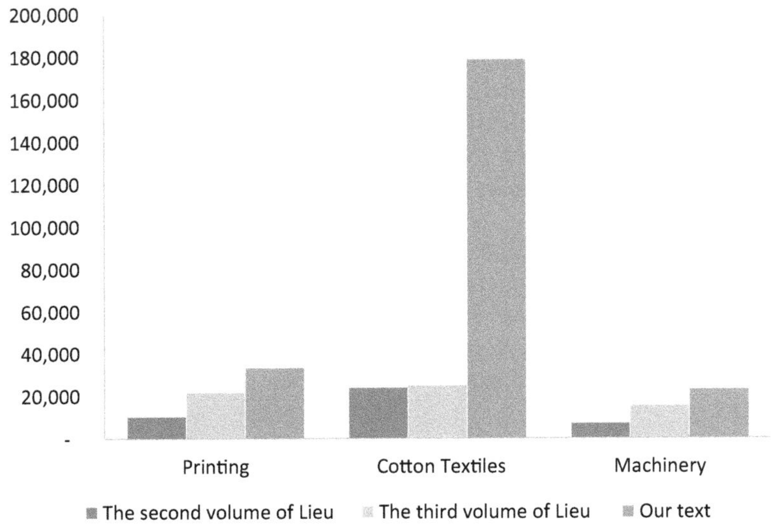

Figure 7.1 A comparison of industrial employment in 1933 in Jiangsu, Shanghai, Anhui, Guangdong, Hainan, and Guangxi from Lieu (1937) and this text compared

Source: Lieu (1937); this text.

7.4 Patterns of regional industrialization

As pointed out, so far our knowledge about regional industrialization is limited. Yet, some studies do exist. For example, Fong (2015) was the first scholar who performed a quantitative study on Chinese regional industrialization based on the 1928 survey focusing on two mining products and four manufacturing products for six provinces. In this study, Fong (2015) argued that industry in the 1920s was mainly concentrated in treaty port cities. This did not apply to all products: Zhongping (2011) pointed to a move of cotton textile production from coastal areas to inland areas between 1894 and 1936. Recently, the Lower Yangtze Delta became a popular region for the study of Chinese industrialization as well. For example, Ma (2008) offered estimates of the annual growth rate of industry covering both modern and handcraft sectors in 1914/1918 and 1931/1936. Li and Van Zanden (2012) also provided an estimate of value added for industry as a whole in Hua-Lou counties, both leading counties in the Lower Yangtze Delta in what is currently known as Shanghai. It is further noteworthy that Brandt et al. (2017) made the first quantitative overview of Chinese regional industrialization over time by providing the share of industrial output by macro region from 1933 to 2008, claiming that industrialization went through two periods (i.e., 1937–1949 and the post-1978 reform era), during which industries moved from coastal areas to the central and western areas.[2] However, they did not offer a more disaggregated regional study on such structural change over time.

In order for us to study prefectural industrialization over time, we have to aggregate the prefectures (1982 and 2000) as well as the counties (1933) of the six provinces under study into thirty-one areas that remain broadly constant for the period covered in this chapter (see Appendix 7.2). This allows showing regional industrial development at a sub-provincial level. Doing so shows that these regional changes were indeed substantial (Appendix 7.3) and may contribute to the debate on the nature of Chinese long-term industrialization.

As shown in Figure 7.2, although Jiangsu and Guangdong were the earliest industrializers in China (starting already in the 1860s), there had formed a substantial gap between them in the 1930s. This was partly because in the "Golden Age of Chinese Capitalism" from 1915 to 1933, industrialization tended to cluster in Jiangsu, even if the other five provinces also went through some industrial development. Although Jiangsu remains important in the later period as well, since the reforms and opening up in the 1980s its position was taken over by Guangdong, making Guangdong the province with the most industrialization across China in the twenty-first century.

The findings that the Yangtze area initially made up the largest share of manufacturing employment in the first half of the twentieth century, and that the Zhujiang area started dominating in the last thirty years, contribute to a debate on the nature of Chinese industrialization. The common view on industrialization was that it was characterized by long-term stagnation until circa 1980. This was described by Wen (2016) as China undergoing four "industrial revolutions", i.e., after the Opium Wars (1861–1911), after the Xinhai Revolution (1911–1949),

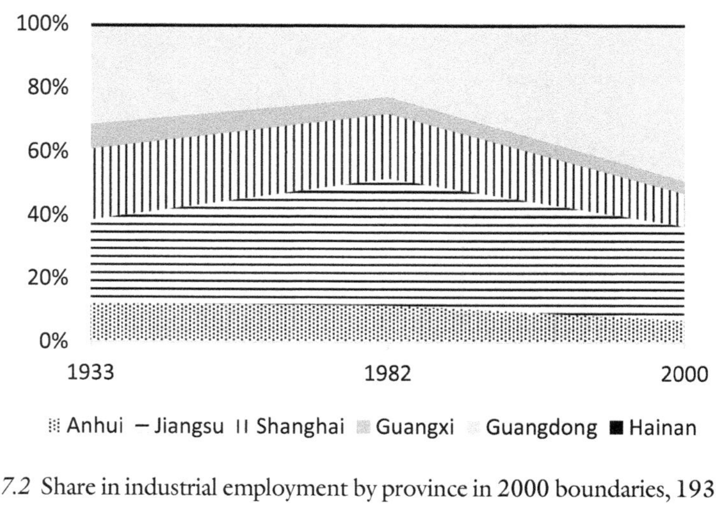

Figure 7.2 Share in industrial employment by province in 2000 boundaries, 1933–2000

Source: Appendix 7.3.

after New China (1949–1978), and the period of reform (1978-present). Yet, as claimed by Wen (2016), whereas the first three "revolutions" were essentially unsuccessful, the reform period boosted China in the ranks of industrial producers. However, this classic consensus is disputed by recent scholars. So have Chang (1969), Rawski (1989), Kubo (2005), and Brandt et al. (2017) argued that there were also periods of rapid industrialization between 1912 and 1949. Likewise, Wu (2002) and Brandt et al. (2017) found rapid growth in the first decades of New China. In this chapter, we find the same rapid growth, with a per compound annual growth rate of employment in industry in our six provinces of 2.5% between 1933 and 1982 and 3.4% between 1982 and 2000.

The traditional view is not only one of slow growth but also claims that industry was mainly concentrated in treaty port cities. Largely based on descriptive sources, this is disputed by the revisionists, who argued that industrialization not only quickly developed in both the Jiangsu and Manchuria areas, but also diffused to the vast inland and border regions. According to our study, for example in Figure 7.3a–b, this can be seen for the electricity industry, which moved increasingly inland between 1933 and 2000. Yet, it is important to note that a sector such as electricity alone does not confirm this revisionist view.

The difference in industrial spread may be attributed to the type of industry. Initially, China's advantage was in labour-intensive industries such as textiles. Slowly, they became increasingly capital- and skill-intensive. As pointed out by Chen et al.

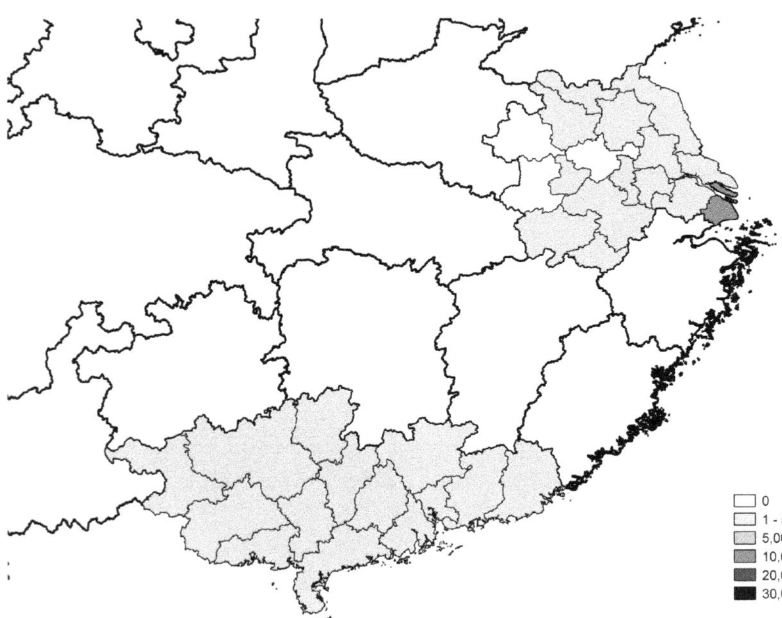

Figure 7.3a Labourers in the electricity industry by prefecture, 1933

Source: Appendix 7.3.

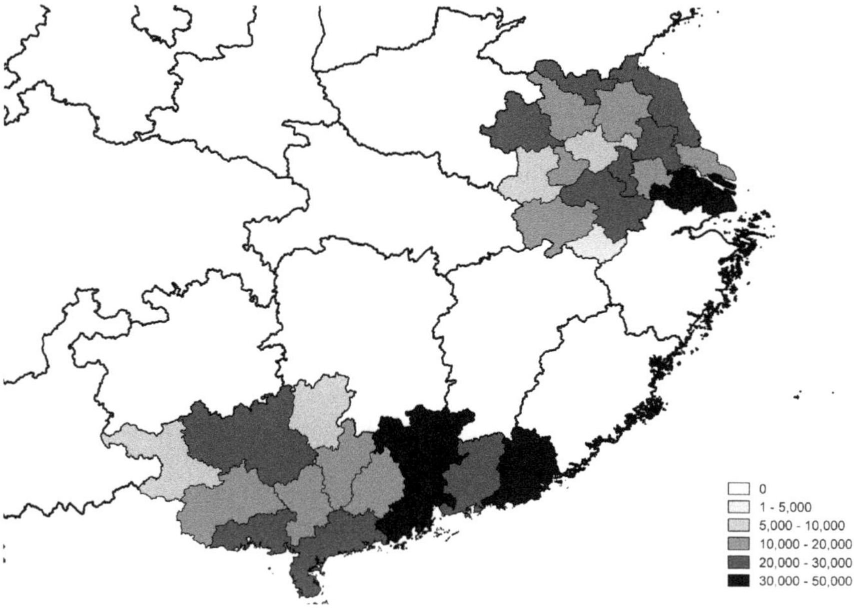

Figure 7.3b Labourers in the electricity industry by prefecture, 2000

Source: Appendix 7.3.

(2008), labour-intensive industries are converging in labour productivity, while skill-intensive industries show regional divergence. Hence, with the continuing development towards capital- and skill-intensive industries, we expect a regional divergence. This seems to be confirmed, on a province level, by Brandt et al. (2017: Table 9.4) who find increasing industrial dispersion up to 1995.

7.5 Drivers of regional industries

As the previous example on skill intensity of industry shows, regional industrialization may be driven by various factors, most notably the presence of factor endowments (capital, labour, raw materials), market potential (consumer markets), and institutions. Yet, each of these factors differs over time and across sectors because of a reduction in transportation cost.

Indeed, a first driver is factor endowments where, due to economies of scale, there is often a clustering in industries. Obviously, this may vary by industrial sector. If we again look at skills (i.e., the share of employees with secondary or higher education in China), at the end of the twentieth century we witness especially high skill levels in electricity (60.2%), followed by machinery and printing (40.7% and 36.6% respectively), and finally textiles (22.8%). Indeed, as shown in the previous section, looking at our data, it is those sectors with high skill intensity, such as electricity, where dispersion is lowest, followed by machinery, printing, and cotton textiles respectively. Likewise, other industries, such as iron smelting, were heavily dependent on other factor endowments such as raw materials or physical capital. For example, Pomeranz (2000) highlights the importance of coal for the development of the Yangtze region, while Lieu (1937) and Ou (1947) attributed the long-term stagnation of China's industry to insufficient capital accumulation.

Second, distance from consumer markets is important for firms (e.g. Ge 2006), but it faces several issues. The most important issue is that, if returns to scale are large, factories are less likely to be located close to their consumer markets. But other issues play a role as well. As pointed out by Wen (2007), besides having rich markets, East China also profits from direct access to export markets. Cui and Lui (2000) add to this that culture, as well as different consumption habits, limit the possibility of firms to move to inland areas. This makes our six provinces attractive to locate factories from a market potential point of view.

Yet, these scale effects and market potential are not the only factors influencing regional industrialization. After all, being located far away from your consumers is not a problem if cheap and fast transport is available. For that reason, there is literature that looks at transportation costs and distance to consumer markets as a third factor: the lower transportation costs are, the more important are scale effects, and the least important becomes distance to consumer markets. In such a situation, concentration occurs (Vanhove 2018). Yet, if transport costs become negligible, factories may locate in regions with low wages, as labour is less mobile than, for example, coal – thus leading to dispersion.

This explains why a sector like machinery was mostly located close to ports in 1933; transport of heavy machinery needed to occur over water. Indeed, Figure 7.4a–b clearly shows industry moving inland via major transportation lines. For other sectors, though, scale effects were more important. To this we may add, as found in Chapter 10 of this volume, that even though transport in China improved massively over time, indirect transportation costs still provide a major obstacle, thus limiting the effect of improvements in transportation.

A fourth factor driving industrialization concerns institutions and politics. Obviously, we cannot ignore the role of the Japanese in the occupation of Manchuria and the Sino-Japanese Wars for the Republican period. But notwithstanding this, authors have pointed to a variety of other institutional and political causes. Perkins (1967) argued that the Late Qing government was hostile to commerce and industry and that this hostility was a major element in the country's failure to achieve industrialization, even though the Late Qing government launched the military industrialization in early 1860s. Likewise, Acemoglu and Robinson (2012) claimed that being an exclusive society, in which a large share of the population did not share in either economic or political power, put a break on Chinese growth. In addition, heavily influenced by the Marxist stages of social evolution and class revolution, the studies from mainland China (Xu and Wu 2003) insisted on the double oppression of foreign imperialism and domestic feudalism as the reason for industrial stagnation between 1840 and 1949.

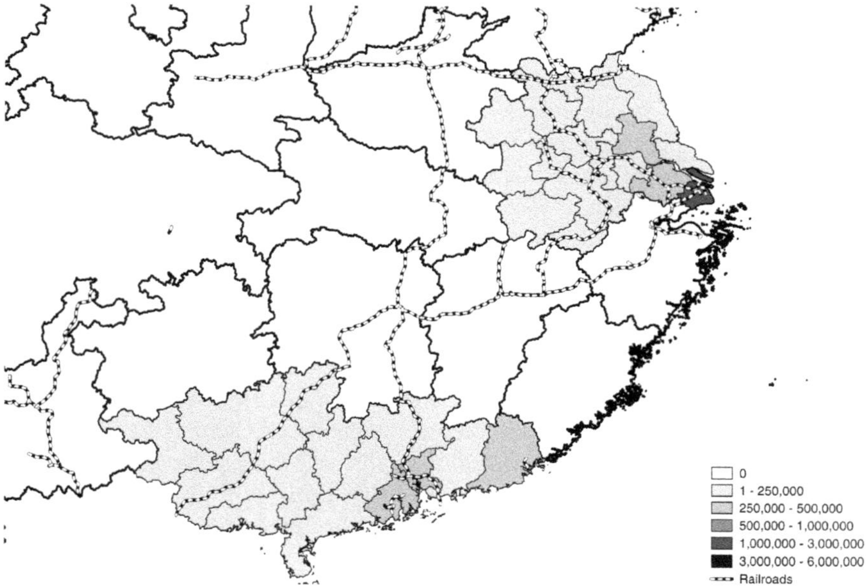

Figure 7.4a Labourers in industry and rail by prefecture, 1933

Source: Appendix 7.3.

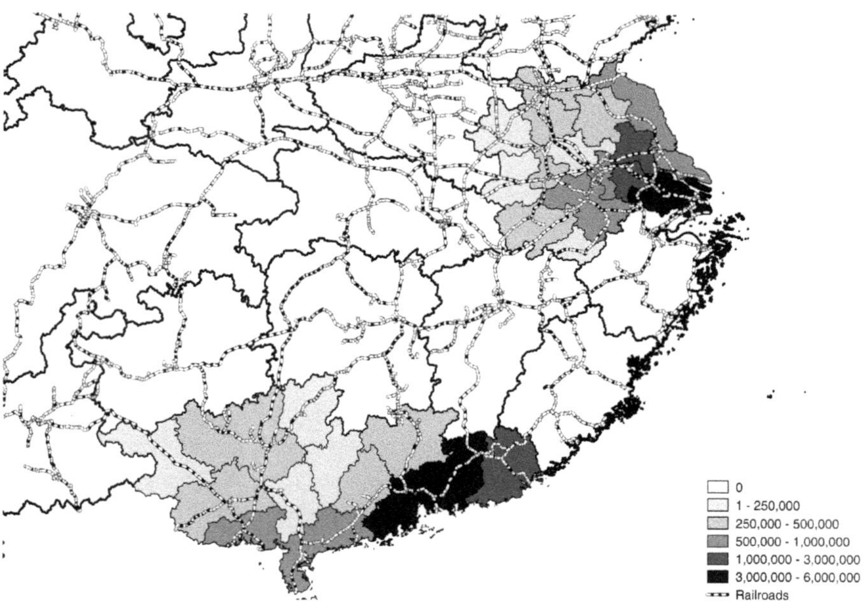

Figure 7.4b Labourers in industry and rail by prefecture, 2000

Source: Appendix 7.3.

Some have argued that the situation improved during the Republican Period. Rawski (1989) questioned this array of economic and political explanations by arguing that China's economy was from the 1880s dominated by domestic, private, and competitive forces rather than monopoly of imperialism and feudal warlords. He then attributed relatively fast industrialization to a freewheeling market by which penetration of international trade and domestic traditional economic pattern cross-pollenized during the Republican China period (see also van Leeuwen and van Zanden 2019). This view is partly shared by Ma (2008), who attributed the takeoff of industrialization in the Yangtze to the treaty port institution, a unique political institution focusing on its rule of law, and secure property rights laying the foundation for industrialization in the Lower Yangtze. Indeed, as pointed out earlier, part of the growth rate we find in our data is explained by institutional, political, and cultural advantages of the Eastern provinces.

This all changed with the advent of New China in 1949. When the Chinese Communist Party established the People's Republic of China (PRC) in 1949, they started with forced industrialization in the following steps. First, the People's Republic of China government nationalized private firms and established public ownership across China. Second, through an enlarged and integrated version of separate planning bureaucracies inherited from the former *Guomindang* and *Manshūkoku* governments, the People's Republic of China government moved to fully replace market behaviour with administrative resource allocation. Between 1953 and 1980, the People's Republic of China government produced in total 5 five-year plans to force industrialization. Beginning in 1978, a succession of reform and opening by the People's Republic of China government gradually led to a hybrid system that combines important elements of planning, state ownership, and official direction with a revival of the open, private, market-based system of the 1920s and 1930s. This arrangement has enhanced the rapid growth attained under the former plan system.

7.6 Conclusion

In this chapter, we made a first attempt to analyze regional industrialization for six provinces and their sub-regions, four of which were considered early industrializers and two of which were considered economic followers. Based on available data, we choose 1933, 1982, and 2000 as benchmarks. After discussing classification and other data issues, we found that there was a clear move in industry from port cities in 1915–1933 to the inland regions in the recent decades. Even though more research is necessary, by combining our data with historiography, we found that four factors played a role. The first factor is the presence of factor endowments that cause a clustering of industries, most notably of cotton textiles and printing. Second is the distance to consumer markets, which has an opposite effect, i.e., dispersion. The answer to the question of which determinant is stronger (scale effect or market potential) varies by sector and leads to either clustering or dispersion. Over time, a third factor, the railroad network, shifted the balance to returns to scale (i.e., clustering). Yet in the 1990s, we witness that further improvements in transport led to a rise in the effect of market potential and, hence, dispersion. A fourth factor concerns politics and institutions. Although they evidently played a role in China, they did not overturn the effects of the other three factors.

Notes

1 This research received funding from the European Research Council under the European Union's Horizon 2020 Programme / ERC-StG 637695 - HinDI, as part of the project "The historical dynamics of industrialization in Northwestern Europe and China ca. 1800–2010: a regional interpretation".

2 In their study, a macro region usually consists of several provinces.

References

Primary sources

Agricultural Journal. 1942. 1(2).

Anhui Statistical Bureau, ed. 1934. *Anhui statistical yearbook*. unpublished.

Attached Journal of Urban Area in Wu County. 1983. Taipei: Chengwen Press.

Bank of Guangdong Provincial Quarterly. 1943. 3(4).

Chongshan Xian Zhi. 1975. Taiwan: Chengwen Press.

Collection of economic surveys and reports along with railways in Republican China. 2009. Vol. 9. Beijing: National Library Press.

Construction Committee, ed. 1932. *China's power plant statistics*. unpublished.

Construction Committee, ed. 1934. *China's electrical industry statistics*, 4th ed. unpublished.

Fengyang Xian Zhi Lue. 1975. Taiwan: Chengwen Press.

Guangdong branch of the National Economic Construction Campaign Committee, ed. 1937. "Report on the investigation in basic industries, special industries and rural side-industry in Guangdong Province. unpublished. Guangxi Statistical Bureau. ed. 1933–1944." In *Guangxi provincial yearbook*, Vol. 1–3. unpublished.

Guangxi Statistical Bureau, ed. 1933. *Survey of counties in Guangxi*. unpublished.

Guangzhou Municipal Government, ed. 1933. *Municipal bulletin of Guangzhou municipal government*, Vol. 419.

Gui Xian Zhi. 1966. Taiwan: Chengwen Press.

International Trade Bureau of the Ministry of Industry of the National Government, ed. 1933. *China's industrial chronicles: Jiangsu province*. unpublished.

Kaiping Xian Zhi. 1965. Taiwan: Chengwen Press.

Lieu, D. K. 1937. *Industrial Survey in China*. Shanghai: Economic and Statistic Research Institute.

Lingchuan Xian Zhi. 1975. Taiwan: Chengwen Press.

Pingle Xian Zhi. 1967. Taiwan: Chengwen Press.

Pingnan Xian Zhi. 1974. Taiwan: Chengwen Press.

Provincial gazetteer of Jiangsu, Anhui, Guangdong and Guangxi province. 2004. Obtained in 2019 from http://jssdfz.jiangsu.gov.cn, http://lafz.ishang.net/web/Channel.aspx?chn=545, www.gd-info.gov.cn/shtml/guangdong//sqsjk/zsk/gdsz/

Qianjiang Xian Zhi. 1967. Taiwan: Chengwen Press.
Sanjiang Xian Zhi. 1975. Taiwan: Chengwen Press.
Shanglin Xian Zhi. 1968. Taiwan: Chengwen Press.
Shantou Municipal Government, ed. 1933. *Municipal bulletin of Shantou municipal government*, Vol. 1, 19–121.
Shoudu Zhi. 1983. Taiwan: Chengwen Press.
Sien Xian Zhi. 1975. Taiwan: Chengwen Press.
Statistical Yearbook of Guangzhou Municipal Government. 1929. Vol. 1.
Xindu Xian Zhi. 1966. Taiwan: Chengwen Press.

Secondary publications

Acemoğlu, D., and J. A. Robinson. 2012. *Why Nations Fail.* London: Profile Books.
Brandt, L., D. Ma, and Th. Rawski. 2017. “Industrialization in China.” In *The spread of modern industry to the periphery since 1871*, edited by K. O’Rourke and J. Williamson, 197–228. Oxford: Oxford University Press.
Chang, J. K. 1969. *Industrial development in pre- communist China: a quantitative analysis.* Chicago: Aldine Publishing Co.
Chen, V., H. X. Wu, and B. van Ark. 2008. *Measuring changes in competitiveness in Chinese manufacturing industries across regions in 1995–2004: an unit labor cost approach.* Economics Program Working Papers 08–03, The Conference Board, Economics Program.
Civil Affairs Department. 1986. *Evolution of administrative divisions above county level in people’s republic of China from 1949 to 1983.* Beijing: Surveying and Mapping Publishing House.
Crafts, N., and A. Mulatu. 2006. “How did the location of industry respond to falling transport costs in Britain before World War I?” *Journal of Economic History* 66(3): 575–607.
Cui, G., and Q. Liu. 2000. ”Regional market segments of China: opportunities and barriers in a big emerging market.” *Journal of Consumer Marketing* 17(1): 55–72.
Fong, H. D. 2015. *The statistical analysis of Chinese industrialization: collected works of H. D. Fong*, Vol. 4. Beijing: Commercial Press.
Ge, Y. 2006. *Regional inequality, industry agglomeration and foreign trade: the case of China.* WIDER Research Paper, No. 2006/105, ISBN 9291908894, The United Nations University World Institute for Development Economics Research (UNU-WIDER), Helsinki.
Kubo, T. 2005. “Minguo Shiqi Zhongguo de Gongye Fazhan: Xin Xiuding Zhishu, 1912–1948 [Industrial development during the period of Republican China: Newly Revised Index, 1912–1948].” [in Chinese] In *Shijie Jingji Tizhi xia de Minguo Shiqi Jingji* [China’s economy during the republican period under the world economy system], edited by D. Zhang. Beijing: Zhongguo Caizheng Jingji Chubanshe.
Li, B., and J. L. van Zanden. 2012. “Before the great divergence? Comparing the Yangzi Delta and the Netherlands at the beginning of the nineteenth century.” *Journal of Economic History* 72(4): 956–989.
Liu, T.-C., and K.-C. Yeh. 1965. *The economy of the Chinese Mainland: national income and economic development, 1933–1959.* Princeton: Princeton University Press.
Ma, D. 2008. “Economic growth in the lower Yangzi Region of China in 1911–1937: a quantitative and historical analysis.” *Journal of Economic History* 68(2): 355–392.

Maddison, A. 1998. *Chinese economic performance in the long-run.* Paris: OECD Development Centre.

Minnesota Population Center. 2019. *Integrated public use microdata series, international: version 7.2* [dataset]. Minneapolis: IPUMS. https://doi.org/10.18128/D020.V7.2.

Ou, P. S. 1947. *National income of China, 1933.* Shanghai: Zhonghua Book Company.

Perkins, D. 1967. "Economic growth in China and the cultural revolution (1960–April 1967)." *The China Quarterly* 30: 33–48.

Pollard, S. 1994. "Regional and inter-regional economic development in Europe in the eighteenth and nineteenth centuries." In *Debates and controversies in economic history*, 57–94. Eleventh International Economic History Congress, Milan.

Pomeranz, K. 2000. *The great divergence. China, Europe, and the making of the modern world economy.* Princeton and Oxford: Princeton University Press.

Rawski, T. G. 1989. *Economic growth in prewar China.* Berkeley: University of California Press.

Shaw-Taylor, L. forthcoming. "Occupational structure and the escape from Malthusian constraints in England and Wales, 1381–1911." In *Population histories in context*, edited by R. M. Smith and E. A. Wrigley.

Vanhove, N. 2018. *Regional policy: a European approach*, 3rd ed. London and New York: Routledge.

Van Leeuwen, B., and J. L. van Zanden. 2019. "China as a nation." In *China in the local and global economy – history, geography, politics and sustainability*, edited by S. Brakman, Ch. van Marrewijk, P. Morgan, and N. Salike, 3–19. London and New York: Routledge.

Wen, M. 2007. "Foreign direct investment, regional market conditions and regional development: a panel study on China." *Economics of Transition* 15(1): 125–151.

Wen, Y. 2016. "China's rapid rise: from backward agrarian society to industrial powerhouse in just 35 years." *The Regional Economist* April: 8–14.

Wolf, N. 2007. "Endowments vs. market potential: what explains the relocation of industry after the polish reunification in 1918?" *Explorations in Economic History* 44(1): 22–42.

Wu, H. X. 2002. "How fast has Chinese industry grown? – Measuring the real output of Chinese industry, 1949–97." *Review of Income and Wealth* 48(2): 179–204.

Wu, H. X. 2011. "The real growth of Chinese industry debate revisited – Reconstructing China's industrial GDP in 1949–2008." *Economic Review* 62(3): 209–224.

Xu, D., and C. Wu, eds. 2003. *Development history of Chinese capitalism*, Vol. 2. Beijing: The People Press.

Xu, Y., and B. van Leeuwen. 2016. "China in world industrialization." *China Economist* 11(6): 98–109.

Zhang, Z., and Z. Zhang. 1934. *Yearbook of Shun Pao.* Shanghai: Department of Special Issue of Shun Pao.

Zhongping, Y. 2011. *A history of Chinese cotton textiles.* Beijing: Commercial Press.

Appendix 7.1

Regional industrialization data, 1933

As mentioned in this chapter, since the Nanjing government was founded in 1927, there are two types of sources that provide us with direct, though limited, quantitative information on employment in the manufacturing industry for our six provinces. Based on surveys specially reporting on manufacturing sectors, we can construct the employment for the four manufacture sectors – i.e., machinery, electric power, cotton textiles, and printing – using the following steps.

1) Employment in modern factories for six provinces is constructed by combining Lieu's census (1937) with other surveys, such as *China's industrial Chronicles (Jiangsu Province)* (*International Trade Bureau of the Ministry of Industry of the National Government 1933), Investigation Report on Basic Industries, Special Industries and Rural Side-industry in Guangdong Province* (Guangdong branch of the National Economic Construction Campaign Committee 1937), *Guangxi Provincial Yearbook* (Guangxi Statistical Bureau 1933–1944), and *Anhui Statistical Yearbook* (Anhui Statistical Bureau 1934), which provide employment in Chinese-funded factories for three sectors (machinery, cotton textiles, and printing). The *China's electrical industry statistics*, and *China's power plant statistics* (Construction Committee 1932; Construction Committee 1934) provide us with quantitative information for the electric power sector. All foreign-funded factories are derived from Ou's study (1947).
2) Employment in handicraft for the six provinces is estimated by taking the output value in the machinery, electric power, cotton textiles, and printing sectors by sub-provincial level for six provinces from the previously mentioned sources. Dividing output by labor productivity for each of the four sectors allows us to estimate employment in handicraft.

The year 1933 witnessed the second type of surveys focusing on the quantitative employment information by broad occupational classification, i.e., agriculture, industry, and service. Provincial governments across China in the 1930s usually published the total number of persons employed for all manufacture sectors as a whole by sub-provincial level. We obtained fifty-six samples in total from such sources as journals (*Agricultural Journal 1942*; *Attached Journal of Urban*

Areas in Wu County 1983; and *Bank of Guangdong Provincial Quarterly 1943*), regional statistics (*Collection of economic surveys and reports along with railways in Republican China 2009*; *Survey of Counties in Guangxi 1933*; *Municipal Bulletin of Guangzhou Municipal Government 1933*; *Municipal bulletin of Shantou Municipal Government 1933*; *Statistical Yearbook of Guangzhou Municipal Government 1929*), and local gazetteers (*Chongshan Xian Zhi 1975*; *Fengyang Xian Zhi Lue 1975*; *Gui Xian Zhi 1966*; *Kaiping Xian Zhi 1965*; *Lingchuan Xian Zhi 1975*; *Pingle Xian Zhi 1967*; *Pingnan Xian Zhi 1974*; *Qianjiang Xian Zhi 1967*; *Sanjiang Xian Zhi 1975*; *Shanglin Xian Zhi 1968*; *Shoudu Zhi 1983*; *Sien Xian Zhi 1975*; *Xindu Xian Zhi 1966*; Shoudu Zhi 1983). By taking these fifty-six samples by county level, which accounts for 20% of a total of 274 counties in the six provinces in 1933, it is possible to estimate total employment in industry sector for each of the thirty-one areas for six provinces.

Appendix 7.2

Concordance table of political units for the year 2000

Table A7.2.1 Concordance table of political units for the year 2000

Provinces	*Name of political prefectures*	*2000 Prefectures*
Jiangsu	Nanjing	Nanjing city
	Xuzhou	Xuzhou city
	Zhenjiang	Changzhou city
		Zhenjiang city
	Huai'an	Huaiyin city
		Suqian city
	Lianyungang	Lianyungang city
		Yancheng city
	Yangzhou	Yangzhou city
		Taizhou city
	Nantong	Nantong city
	Suzhou	Wuxi city
		Suzhou city
Shanghai	Shanghai	Shanghai municipality
	Hefei	Hefei city
	Wuhu	Wuhu city
		Chaohu city
		Xuancheng city
		Ma'anshan city
	Fuyang	Fuyang city
		Huainan city
		Bozhou city
Anhui	Bengbu	Bengbu city
		Suzhou city
		Huaibei city
	Chuzhou	Chuzhou city
	Liu·an	Liu'an city
	Anqing	Anqing city
		Guichi city
		Tongling city
	Huangshan	Huangshan city
	Guangzhou	Guangzhou city
		Dongguan city
Guangdong	Shantou	Shantou city
		Shanwei city
		Jieyang city

Provinces	*Name of political prefectures*	*2000 Prefectures*
		Meizhou city
		Chaozhou city
	Foshan	Foshan city
		Zhuhai city
		Jiangmen city
		Zhongshan city
	Shaoguan	Shaoguan city
		Qingyuan city
	Zhaoqing	Zhaoqing city
		Yunfu city
	Zhanjiang	Zhanjiang city
		Yangjiang city
		Maoming city
		Beihai city
		Fangchenggang city
		Qinzhou city
	Huiyang	Shenzhen city
		Huizhou city
		Heyuan city
Hainan	Hainan	Haikou city
		Hainan Province direct administrative area
		Sanya city
Guangxi	Nanning	Nanning city
		Nanning prefecture
	Liuzhou	Hechi prefecture
		Liuzhou city
		Liuzhou prefecture
	Guilin	Guilin city
	Wuzhou	Hezhou prefecture
		Wuzhou city
	Yulin	Yulin city
		Guigang city
	Baise	Baise prefecture

Appendix 7.3

Employees in industry by region, sector, and year

Table A7.3.1 Employees in industry by region, sector, and year

Province	2000 Region	Electricity			Machinery			Cotton textiles			Printing			Other		
		1933	1982	2000	1933	1982	2000	1933	1982	2000	1933	1982	2000	1933	1982	2000
Anhui	Anqing	60	7,600	17,000	73	19,200	25,300	3,024	16,400	28,141	414	4,100	4,700	106,442	291,000	338,159
	Bengbu	25	4,000	17,400	190	33,200	23,000	596	23,800	25,403	0	3,900	3,100	82,620	176,700	218,997
	Fuyang	0	6,500	23,700	0	27,000	22,800	34	14,500	16,729	0	4,300	4,500	119,357	158,700	134,671
	Wuhu	140	9,600	25,100	223	61,400	48,600	10,283	30,500	30,462	323	7,300	5,600	107,611	484,800	525,738
	Chuzhou	0	1,200	5,300	0	9,800	17,700	403	5,100	6,494	0	1,600	2,700	27,325	91,400	141,906
	Hefei	3	2,100	10,300	0	33,200	29,700	800	16,300	13,786	0	4,800	8,800	35,905	161,100	221,214
	Liu'an	1	4,100	8,900	0	23,000	7,300	2,067	5,300	3,524	0	2,100	2,500	84,856	144,500	144,776
	Huangshan	7	2,200	3,200	0	15,600	3,900	44	2,500	2,000	14	1,800	800	21,581	87,200	56,600
Guangdong	Guangzhou	1,210	11,100	37,500	2,157	115,100	118,100	10,334	46,200	54,421	5,337	17,600	90,800	419,331	719,400	5,099,179
	Shantou	114	21,300	38,100	443	43,000	25,700	26,943	20,100	15,160	503	7,100	18,500	315,636	1,009,200	1,492,940
	Foshan	318	11,700	33,300	609	58,300	101,800	344	26,700	91,508	1,077	10,000	57,700	276,983	622,000	2,948,192
	Shaoguan	11	14,600	30,200	0	34,000	19,400	10	10,500	14,395	0	2,100	4,000	55,745	142,700	219,305
	Zhaoqing	14	7,700	14,600	0	18,200	11,400	0	1,700	7,800	0	2,200	3,700	114,981	131,100	230,100
	Zhanjiang	3	13,100	28,100	0	28,100	23,300	3,124	6,200	8,332	0	6,900	10,500	216,779	326,400	451,068
	Huiyang	20	5,900	27,200	0	15,900	50,000	1,157	1,900	4,097	20	1,700	82,600	70,746	213,600	3,722,003
Guangxi	Nanning	42	6,500	14,700	134	24,600	18,000	17,713	7,700	1,080	414	5,700	6,700	84,656	159,700	248,820
	Liuzhou	6	8,800	22,800	0	41,800	44,000	2,823	15,600	9,833	129	4,400	4,700	35,596	207,200	310,067
	Guilin	11	4,700	9,000	0	28,000	19,900	7,393	8,500	3,701	87	3,600	4,000	29,317	117,100	138,499
	Wuzhou	67	5,200	11,200	117	8,500	8,800	7,209	3,200	2,350	101	1,900	2,000	71,993	89,100	104,150
	Yulin	32	3,400	10,800	0	16,000	14,600	12,377	3,000	3,341	29	2,600	2,900	100,629	95,900	166,059
	Baise	4	2,600	8,100	0	4,200	3,200	5,457	1,100	1,050	33	300	700	11,937	30,700	59,750

Shanghai	Shanghai	17,025	26,000	43,100	15,341	518,800	340,000	27,271	350,100	172,226	18,516	43,200	63,600	1,033,243	2,561,900	2,581,074
Jiangsu	Nanjing	719	7,000	20,300	999	95,300	88,300	1,757	19,500	9,948	3,929	9,100	13,900	83,874	600,700	672,452
	Xuzhou	56	7,400	23,252	0	57,500	42,600	1,736	26,200	26,166	127	3,800	5,200	104,001	305,300	318,634
	Zhenjiang	270	8,400	18,600	1,311	107,100	211,900	5,300	81,100	86,342	636	11,100	18,000	221,927	847,500	1,015,558
	Huai'an	5	5,300	19,200	0	32,300	28,500	499	28,000	25,211	126	5,900	11,200	99,987	272,600	398,489
	Lianyungang	7	5,500	25,000	0	48,600	83,200	0	39,000	42,927	0	6,400	9,000	80,704	420,000	549,473
	Yangzhou	94	6,300	22,900	0	123,700	168,700	253	49,100	61,725	107	6,300	11,400	359,525	914,600	1,011,475
	Nantong	307	4,200	16,800	259	70,800	79,100	18,375	99,800	106,079	62	6,000	6,700	74,090	739,000	720,221
	Suzhou	1,937	10,900	43,100	1,270	209,300	375,400	18,376	179,700	344,773	1,410	19,000	52,700	247,868	1,353,000	2,584,027
Hainan	Hainan	5	9,800	17,500	0	15,900	6,100	0	1,200	3,699	0	2,700	4,400	45,038	115,600	186,801

Source: This text.

8 Regional industrialization in Japan

Jean-Pascal Bassino, Kyoji Fukao, and Tokihiko Settsu

8.1 Introduction

A regional divide appeared during the process of industrialization in most European countries and in the United States, but not in Japan, where there was no equivalent of the *Mezzogiorno* of Italy or the Deep South of the United States. Initial conditions in early nineteenth century Japan were characterized, as in European countries, by the presence of manufacturing activities in all regions, albeit with some degree of specialization. A spatial polarization took place around the turn of the twentieth century, when Japan was becoming the first non-Western industrial nation, with a concentration of high-productivity activities in the main urban areas – in particular Tokyo, Osaka, Nagoya, and Fukuoka. But various high-productivity activities eventually spread to all regions during the period of high-speed growth when Japan had become a major industrial power, with an extraordinary diversified manufacturing sector whose companies were catching up with the global technology frontier in a number of high-tech industrial sectors.

The country did not experience a spatial concentration of negative social externalities induced by deindustrialization during the phase of decline of the manufacturing activities at the end of the twentieth century. There is no Japanese equivalent to the Rust Belt of the midwestern and northeastern United States or in the north of England. There was not even the equivalent to the reversal of fortune experienced in Germany in the second half of the twentieth century, where formerly lagging southern regions became the most dynamic manufacturing areas while the northern regions declined in relative terms. In Japan, the regions that were most famous for their cottage industry production during the early modern period were still the most industrialized in the early twentieth century, although the range of manufacturing activities changed entirely.

As in other developed economies, the intertemporal movement of the share of the manufacturing sector in Japan's total economy follows the Petty-Clark law with an inverse U-shaped curve. From around 14% of the labour force before World War I, and around 16% in the period 1917–1934, the share of the manufacturing sector increased sharply to 20% in 1940, fell temporarily to 18% in 1950, and then increased steadily to 22% in 1955, to 25% in 1960, and reached a historical peak close to 27% in 1970. It went down to 24% in 1980 but then remained at the same level until 1990. It is only from the 1990s, after the burst of the real estate and stock market bubble of the second half of the 1980s, and the entrance into a long stagnation usually described as "the lost decades", that the percentage of workers in the manufacturing sector in the total economy declined rapidly, to around 19% in 2000 and 12% in 2010.

From 1885 to 2015, labour productivity (GDP per working hour) increased 46 times, from 87 yen per hour (in 2015 prices) to 4,000 yen per hour. In order to identify the determinants of growth in the prewar and postwar periods, Fukao et al. (2020) conducts growth accounting analysis on Japan for 1885–2015 using a multi-sector model accounting for labour quality improvement through labour allocation across industries (Kendrick 1961) and labour quality improvement through increase of schooling years (Denison 1962). Capital deepening, labour quality improvement, and Total Factor Productivity (TFP) explain 39%, 25%, and 36% of labour productivity growth, respectively. Yet, the importance of each factor varies over time; from 1885 to 1939, labour productivity increased 3.3 times and the contribution of each factor was 32%, 37%, and 32%, respectively (the total is higher than 100% due to rounding). Therefore, human capital accumulation was more important as a determinant of growth in the prewar period than in the postwar period.

This chapter proposes a spatial analysis of long-term regional trends by relying as much as possible on quantitative information at the level of the forty-seven present-day Japanese prefectures to account for the regional dimension of structural change in Japan. However, as prefecture-level estimates are unavailable for the period 1800–1868, for this period we rely mostly on qualitative information at the level of the sixty-eight ancient provinces and, for some quantitative estimates, on fourteen macro-regions. For the period of gradual shift to modern economic growth starting with the Meiji era (1868–1912), we can use prefecture-level estimates of shares of value added and employment, as well as levels of productivity in manufacturing as a whole at the prefecture level for the benchmark years that are available for 1874, 1890, and 1909. For the period starting in the twentieth century, we can also rely on estimates by sub-sector for the benchmark years 1909, 1925, 1935, and 1940 (Fukao et al. 2015), and yearly series are available from 1955 (Statistics Bureau of Japan). The following sections present regional patterns in Japanese industrialization for five sub-periods corresponding, respectively, to the final phase of development of the cottage industry (1800–1858), the gradual shift to manufacturing (1858–1914), the emergence of Japan as an industrial power (1914–1950), the high-speed growth and then sustained growth (1950–1990), and the "lost decades" of stagnation (since 1990).

8.2 The geography of cottage industry during its final phase of development (1800–1858)

Regional specialization in cottage industry during the Tokugawa shogunate (1603–1868) can be easily identified at the provincial level using qualitative information. Lists of items are, for example, reported in *Kefukigusa*, a handbook for haiku poets published in 1637 (Takenouchi 1943). This source reports not only processed foods and high-quality *sake* and tea but also cotton and silk yarn, fabrics, and clothes; horse gears and other leather goods; paper (*washi*); furniture made of precious wood; metal products such as cutlery, mirrors, swords, and armours; finely decorated ceramics; candles; pharmaceutical products; as well as cultural goods, such as musical instruments, ink and brushes for calligraphy, books, and ritual items used in Buddhist ceremonies; and various other items.

The list of manufacturing goods is particularly impressive in Osaka and in the most urbanized parts of present-day Kyoto, Hyogo, and Nara prefectures (see Figure 8.1 for a map of prefectures). The importance of the Kinai region, Osaka, Kyoto, Nara, and the surrounding areas, is confirmed by a study commissioned by the Tokugawa shogunate and published in 1714 that indicates the total value of various goods originating from the Izumi and Kawachi provinces (corresponding to present-day Osaka), exported to other provinces. The list includes books, swords, spears, bows and arrows, horse gears, clothes, dolls, doors, wooden Buddha statues, tatami mats, *shogi* (Japanese chess) and go boards, pans, knives and other iron tools, ceramic wares, *sake*, vinegar, soy sauce, candles, paper, oil, umbrellas, and ropes (Oishi 1975: 143–153). Edo was also a major region of production due to the enormous demand for handicraft items resulting from the presence in the shogunal capital of the domanial lords (*daimyo*) and their entourage under the mandatory alternate residence systems (*sankin kotai*). Edo's manufactures were also exported to the main cities of eastern Japan, and to a much lower extent to western Japan.

Cottage industry was not restricted to the major urban areas. The political fragmentation of Tokugawa Japan in more than 200 large and small feudal domains created conditions conducive to the gradual development throughout the country of new ventures in a wide range of industries, particularly from the mid-eighteenth century (Saito 2018). With a limited territory and almost no perspective of expansion of their fiscal revenues from land tax that focused on paddy-fields, most administrators of the domains were keen to promote cash crops and their processing, as well as other types of cottage industry using as much as possible local resources such as kaolin clay, metal ores, and relatively cheap sources of energy. Due to the high transportation costs, a large part of the production was consumed locally. But each of the sixty-eight provinces became known for various products, some of which were extensively traded throughout the country.

Even the most rural provinces became famous for at least a few items traded in the three biggest early modern Japanese cities of Edo (present-day Tokyo, the shogunal capital), Kyoto (the imperial capital), and Osaka (the major national commercial hub), and their products were also consumed by high- and medium-rank samurai, wealthy merchants, peasants, and artisans in different parts of the country. These semi-luxury items produced outside the major urban areas included *Kiso* lacquerware from present-day Nagano prefecture; *washi* paper from present-day Fukui, Kochi, Shimane, and many other prefectures; ceramics from present-day Saga, Okayama, Yamaguchi, Aichi, and Gifu prefectures, respectively;

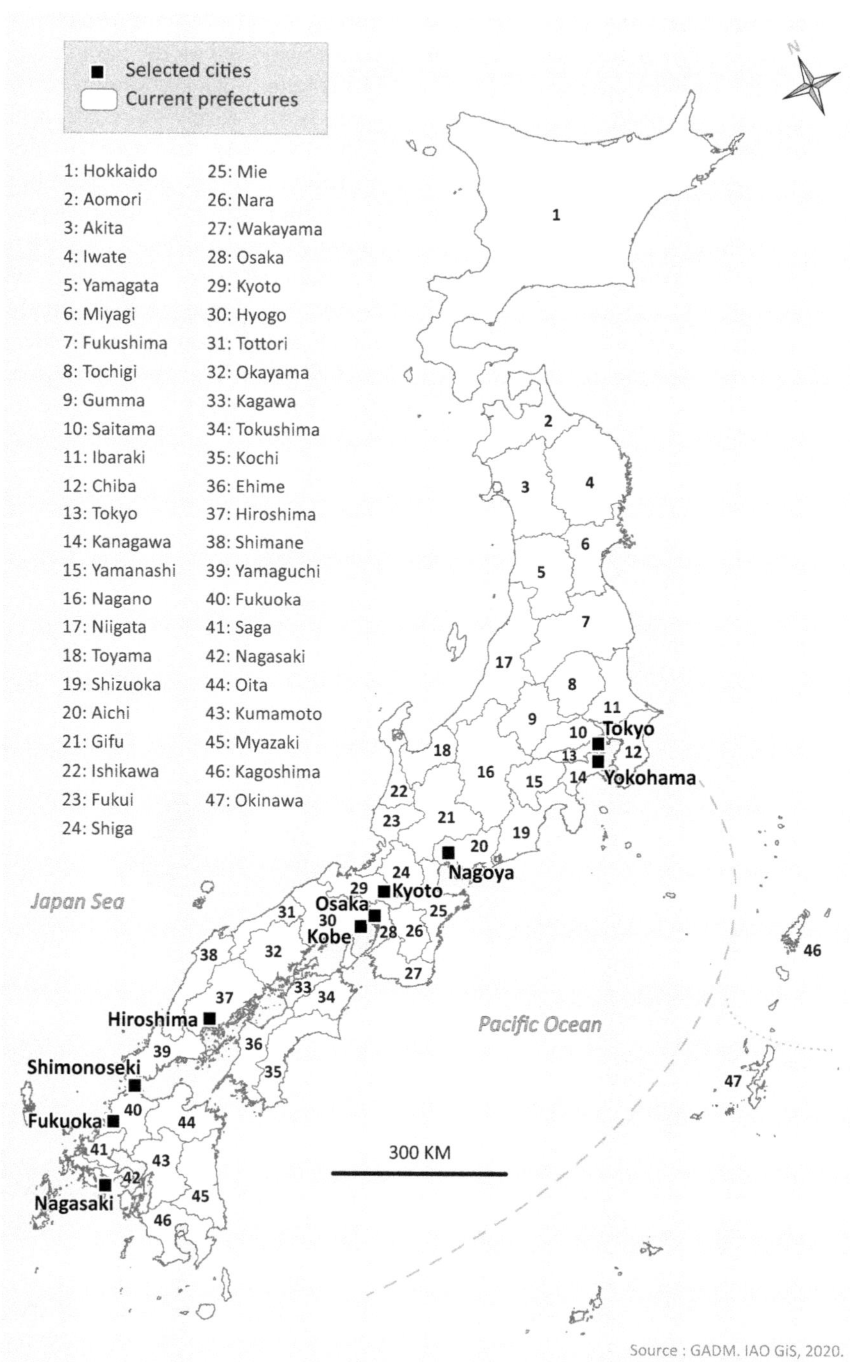

Figure 8.1 Map of present-day Japanese prefectures and regions

Satsuma kiriko glassware from present day Kagoshima prefecture; and *nanbu* iron teapots from present-day Iwate and Yamagata prefectures (Watanabe 1964).

Further evidence of regional specialization can be identified on the basis of estimated shares of manufacturing in GDP in 1846 (Figure 8.2). Although cottage industry was present in all regions, western Japan was relatively more advanced than eastern Japan. This east–west divide was due to a large extent to the high transportation cost from the northeast region (Tohoku) to the commercial hub of Osaka, in comparison with regions at relatively short distance. Another possible explanation is that the lower population density of the northeast resulted in a comparative advantage in the production of raw material, particularly foodstuffs for export to Edo and western Japan. The Edo and Osaka areas were clearly the most specialized regions. The comparison of cottage industry output per resident in 1804 and 1846 (Figure 8.3), converted into rice terms in a crude attempt to adjust for inflation (the income of each daimyo was measured in rice and fixed for

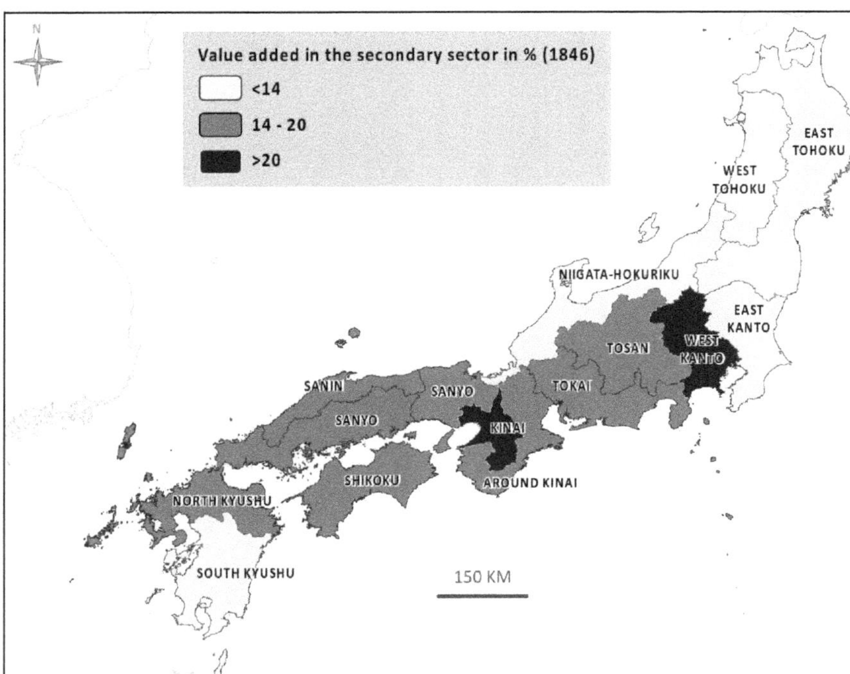

Figure 8.2 Value added in the secondary sector in % of GDP in 1846

Source: Authors' calculation using estimates by Takashima (2017).

Note: The term Kinai was used in the early modern period to designate the central part of the Kansai region; Tosan corresponds to present-day Nagano and Yamanashi prefectures; Tokai corresponds to present day Aichi, Gifu, and Shizuoka prefetures; Kinai corresponds aproximately to Kyoto, Nara, and Osaka prefectures; and around Kinai to Hyogo, Mie, Shiga, and Wakayama prefectures.

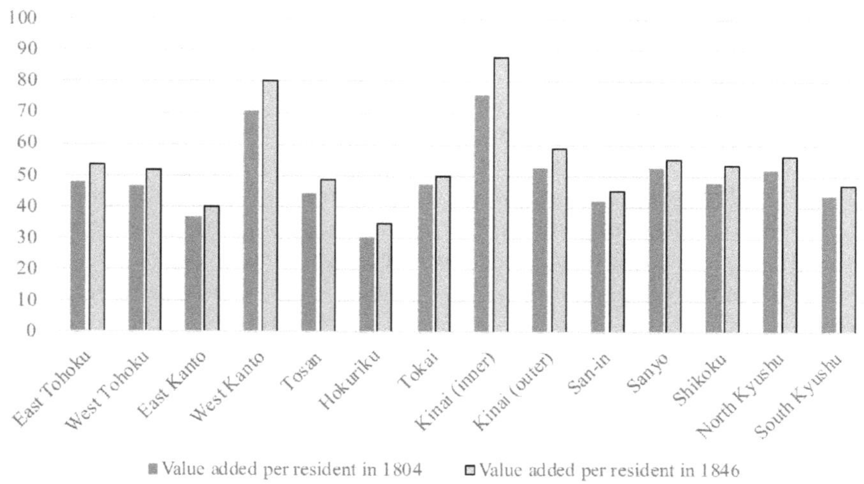

Figure 8.3 Value added per resident in the secondary sector in rice equivalent (kg) in 1804 and 1846

Source: Calculated using estimates by Takashima (2017); figures in yen for 1874 converted in rice terms using the national average of rice price.

Note: No data for Gunma, Toyama, Fukui, Tokushima, Kagawa, and Kumamoto.

each domain), suggests that there was a modest growth rate of output throughout the country.

In a major part of the cottage industry, early nineteenth century technology was not essentially different from that of the late medieval period, but several techniques imported from China, Korea, and Western Europe in the sixteenth century had been gradually adopted in various Japanese regions. The most important of these were Chinese silk reeling, Korean ceramics production, and metal smelting. The major source of technological change in the seventeenth and eighteenth centuries was not related to radical innovations but to a slow process of incremental innovation upgrading local production. In most feudal domains, particularly in western Japan, the local administration of each daimyo endeavoured to disseminate the best practices identified in other regions by inviting craftsmen to undertake production in the castle-towns. Some important technological changes occurred nevertheless in the nineteenth century, in particular in the textile and metal sectors (Odaka 1996). A steady increase in cotton processing took place between circa 1800 and 1850, mostly in the Kinai region, and there was also an increase of iron production due to the shift between circa 1800 and 1830 from the sixteenth-century *nanban* (literally, "southern barbarians", i.e., Europeans) technology to the eighteenth-century European technology transmitted through manuals procured from the Dutch trading post of Nagasaki.

8.3 Regional patterns during the gradual shift to manufacturing (1858–1913)

The forced opening of a number of Japanese ports to foreign trade in 1858, under the pressure of the US Navy, followed by free trade treaties with the main Western powers, resulted in asymmetric shocks that drastically affected regional specialization in cottage industry during the last decade of Tokugawa rule (1858–1868). The 1858 treaties, signed in the Asian context of the Second Opium War (1856–1860), obliged in particular the Japanese authorities to entirely open the country to international trade with low import and export duties. The major winners were the silk processing areas of eastern Japan, located in particular in present-day Gunma, Nagano, and Yamanashi prefectures, that benefitted from the strong European and US demand for silk yarn and silk fabric produced using local techniques. The main losers were the rural cotton processing areas of western Japan, in particular around Osaka, that suffered from the competition from cheaper imported British cotton yarns.

A few factories using imported technologies, for instance in wheat milling and printing, were set up in the 1860s by Westerners in the international settlements of the new port cities of Yokohama and Kobe – opened in 1859 and 1868, respectively – but the scale of production remained modest. Public investments by the Shogun and local lords resulted in the creation of arsenals and factories using Western technologies, but these new enterprises had only a limited impact and were hardly profitable. It is only from the 1870s that imported technologies started to play a significant role, although in a small number of manufacturing activities and with a rather small output volume until the 1880s. During the initial phase of expansion of manufacturing activities, the cottage industry remained dominant and relied extensively on labour available during the agricultural slack periods, with a pattern of by-employment that also included the tertiary sector (Nishikawa 1978; Saito and Settsu 2010).

The estimates for 1874 indicate that the manufacturing sector, which consisted at that time exclusively in traditional urban handicraft and rural cottage industry, accounted for only 8.5% of Japanese GDP and less than 13% of the total labour force, even after adjustment for by-employment (including mining and construction, for which separate estimates can be generated only from 1890). Regional estimates of per capita GDP and industrial structure for 1874 confirm that, although manufacturing activities were present in all prefectures, large differences existed in terms of overall size of the sector (Figure 8.4). Manufacturing accounted for a much smaller share of GDP than the Japanese average in most prefectures of Kyushu Island and the Tohoku region. Only a few prefectures had a much higher share of manufacturing in their GDP than the national average – the areas corresponding to the major cities of Tokyo, Kyoto, Osaka, and Nagoya, as well as Wakayama prefecture that included an extension of the industrial district of Osaka, and Gunma prefecture (in the Kanto region) that was a major silk reeling district.

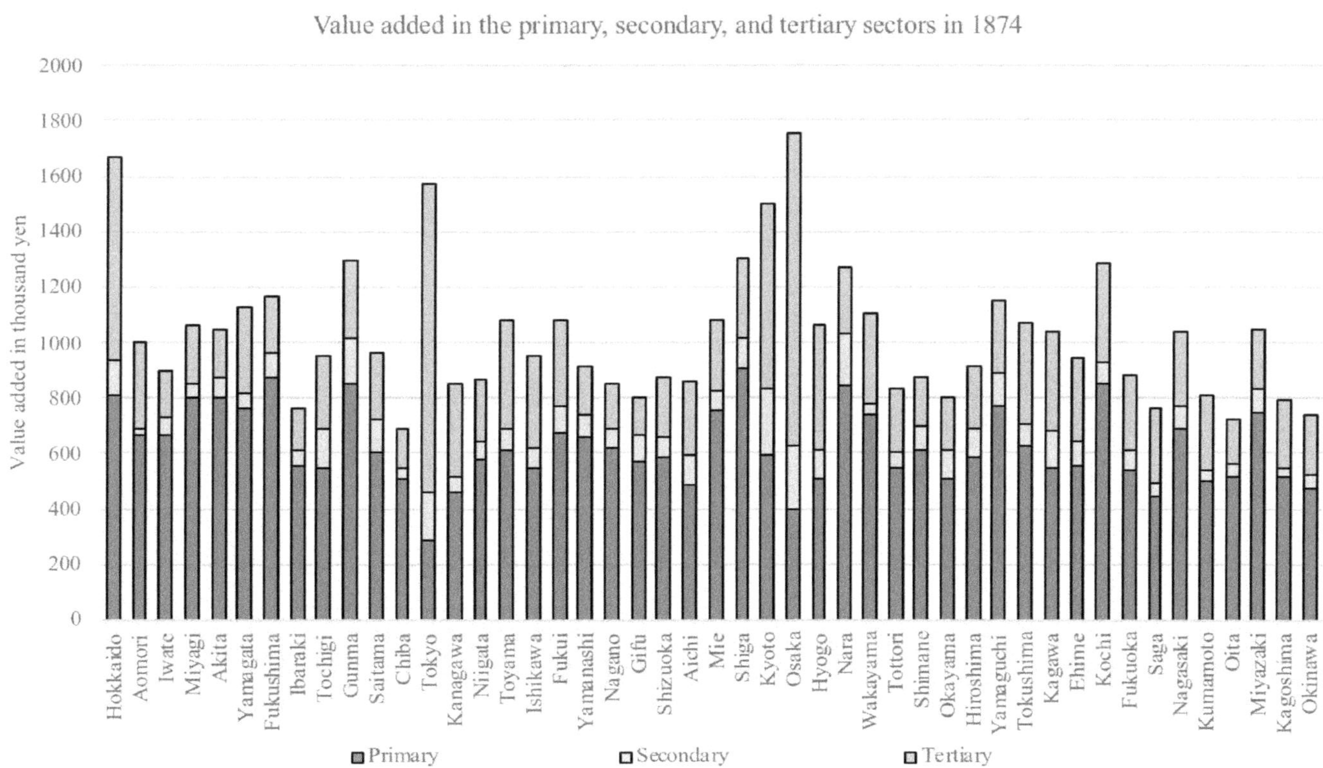

Figure 8.4 Per capita GDP and industrial structure in 1874

Source: Fukao et al. (2015).

Note: Prefectures ranked from the northeast to the southwest.

In spite of the decline of the cotton spinning industry, the Kinai remained a major industrial region due to the diversification of activities. Figure 8.5 presents regional-level information on sectoral specialization in the manufacturing sector in 1874, the first year for which such a breakdown is possible, which reflects the impact of the opening to international trade after 1858. Although food processing was unsurprisingly the most important activity, accounting in a majority of regions with low specialization in manufacturing for around 40% of total output value, a diversity of production existed. The low share of textile in the Kinai is the consequence of the decline of the production of cotton yarn, while the high share in east Kanto provides evidence of the important role of silk processing in this region.

Manufacturing activities expanded rapidly throughout the Japanese archipelago during the Meiji era (1868–1912). On the basis of prefecture-level estimates for the benchmark years 1874, 1890, and 1909, we can observe that labour input shares were increasing much faster in the secondary sector than in the tertiary sector in most prefectures in 1874–1890, a period of labour-intensive industrialization that we can label as Meiji I. It was characterized by the development of cottage industry activities using technologies already available in the late Tokugawa period that were now spreading from the most advanced regions to the rest of the country as a consequence of initiative by local entrepreneurs (Tanimoto 1998; Nakabayashi 2003; Tanimoto 2006; Nakamura 2010).

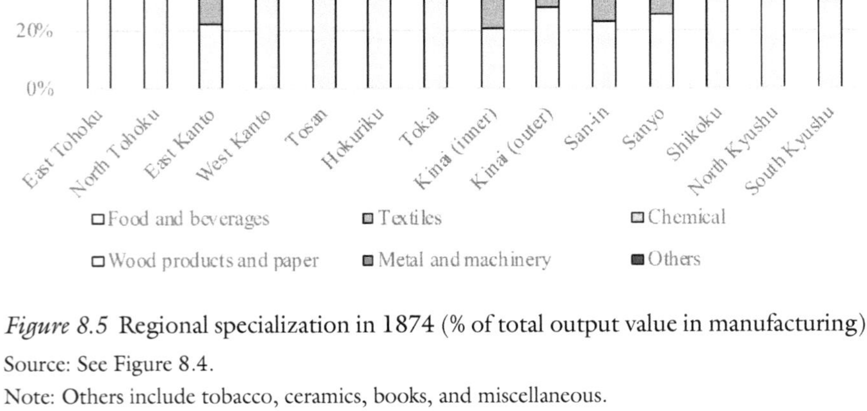

Figure 8.5 Regional specialization in 1874 (% of total output value in manufacturing)

Source: See Figure 8.4.

Note: Others include tobacco, ceramics, books, and miscellaneous.

Between 1890 and 1909, labour input shares increased more slowly in the secondary sector than in the tertiary sector. This was a period of gradual shift toward a more physical and human capital-intensive industrialization, which we can label as Meiji II. Spatial concentration increased steadily, with the share of manufacturing rising rapidly in Osaka and Tokyo and in a number of new industrial districts (e.g., mechanical industry and shipbuilding in Aichi and Fukuoka), as well as in silk reeling districts of eastern Japan, in particular in Nagano and Yamanashi prefectures. Although regional labour productivity gaps in the secondary sector were small circa 1874, they were increasing in Meiji I. This is due to the fact that modern manufacturing techniques with high labour productivity were deployed only in a few prefectures. The gaps remained rather stable in Meiji II owing to the diffusion of best practices (e.g., silk reeling) and imported technologies (e.g., British cotton spinning technology).

Restrictions on regional migrations imposed by the lords of the feudal domains ended in 1868, but the cost of travel remained an hinderance in Meiji I as the railway network was limited to strategic east–west lines along the Pacific coast. Only relatively skilled workers were able to take advantage of new opportunities. Cross-prefectural migration flows increased in Meiji II, in particular by unskilled female workers employed in cotton spinning factories. These new migration flows were enhanced by the development of the local and regional railway networks (Saito 2018). This marks the beginning of a process of spatial agglomeration of manufacturing and high value added service activites in the most important urbanized areas, in line with the positive externalities described by Krugman (1993), Fujita and Thisse (1996), and Fujita et al. (1999). In the Japanese case, however, local industrial districts also expanded in comparatively rural prefectures, in particular in the silk reeling district of eastern Japan (Arimoto et al. 2014).

The location of the major industrial center on the coast of the Pacific Ocean and the formation of silk reeling rural industrial districts suggest that nature was the main driver of spatial concentration in manufacturing activities. The development of an extensive railway network, by far the highest density in Asia, had only limited effect, which is understandable in an archpelago where most urban areas are located either on the coast or on estuaries at short distance from the coast. For most items traded, shipping was more economical and convenient than rail transportation. This impression is confirmed when taking coal mines into account. Japan benefitted from an geological anomaly of location; most of the major mines were close to the coast, in northern Kyushu, in the Joban area at the northeast of Tokyo, and in the east of Hokkaido. The second nature determinants are present in two ways: first, two main Japanese urban areas at the turn of the twentieth century, Tokyo and Osaka, were already the major cities in the early eighteenth century; and second, the colonization of Taiwan and Korea (1896 and 1910, respectively) had a strong spatial effect on industrial activities in the most western prefectures of Japan, in particular Fukuoka and Yamaguchi (Nakajima and Okazaki 2018).

8.4 Regional convergence in productivity during the emergence of Japan as an industrial power (1914–1955)

The Russo-Japanese war (1904–1905) provided a boost in demand for a number of Japanese manufacturing producers, but it was insufficient to put the country on a trajectory of rapid industrial growth and diversification. This shift took place later as a consequence of World War I during which, as belligerent allies to Britain, France, and Russia, Japan was essentially expected to dedicate its Navy to protecting allied maritime convoys against German submarines on the routes from Yokohama, Shanghai, or Singapore to Suez. Due to the embargo on German exports, high freight costs, and militarization of the British and the French industries, the Japanese market became cut off from European supplies in 1914–1918 for a wide range of capital and intermediate goods. Japanese business groups immediately initiated import-substitution in metal processing, shipbuilding, chemical products, optical and telecommunication equipment, and various other relatively high-tech sectors.

The industrial boom resulted in a rapid increase of real wages in urban areas. Cheap labour costs ceased to be a comparative advantage of Japanese producers in East Asia. Chinese wages were now significantly lower and, from the late 1910s, Japanese textile producers started expanding their production activities in China, particularly in Shanghai. These new conditions created incentives for Japanese producers operating in the most urban areas to adopt capital-intensive technologies. This shift was facilited by the rise of enrolment rates in primary education for both males and females, and to the rise of a tiny but extremely well-trained elite of engineers trained in the Imperial universities explicitly modelled after research-intensive German universities. In-house on-the-job training, however, remained the dominant form of accumulation of upper tail technical knowledge in Japanese manufacturing firms until the late 1930s.

Factor substitution strategies resulted in a increase of the regional concentration of high-productivity manufacturing activities. However, opportunities to take advantage of lower labour costs in the most rural prefectures favoured the spatial technology diffusion throughout Japan. A number of manufacturing producers became increasingly involved in high-tech sectors and in some cases managed to reduce drastically the gap with foreign competitors, particularly in military industries (explosives, railways, shipbuilding, aeronautics, precision machinery, optical, and telecommunication equipment). The interwar period is therefore one that can be characterized as the first phase of Japanese productivity catch-up with the global technology frontier. Although these issues are well documented using firm-level data, the process of regional diffusion of advanced technology has not been extensively studied.

In 1899, Japan recovered its tariff autonomy and from 1911, started to protect its industry by substantially raising its tariff rates (Yamazawa 1973). Also in 1899, a revision of commercial code and abolishment of the Foreigners' Treaty Boundary rule and foreign settlements located at major ports opened in the early

Meiji period substantially relaxed inward foreign direct investment (FDI). Foreign firms increased their investment in Japan partly in order to keep access to Japanese markets, which was becoming more protected. Inward FDI became a major route for the introduction in Japan of the new technologies of the Second Industrial Revolution (Paprzycki and Fukao 2007). Japanese major electrical machinery firms, such as Toshiba and NEC, started from 1899 to the 1990s as joint ventures of Japanese and US firms, such as General Electric and Western Electric. Ford and General Motors started knockdown production of automobiles in Japan in the 1920s. These activities were mainly concentrated in metropolitan areas, such as the Tokyo and Kanagawa prefectures.

A quantitative investigation of regional gaps in labour productivity in Japanese manufacturing is possible using estimates of value added and labour force (adjusted for by-employment) at the prefecture level presented in Fukao et al. (2015), with a breakdown of manufacturing in nine subsectors for the benchmark years 1909, 1925, 1935, and 1940. The evolution during the period 1940–1955 is omitted as industrial production was under command economy until 1945, and under strict control by the US military occupation authorities until the outbreak of the Korean War in 1950. The Japanese manufacturing sector experienced a rapid recovery during the first half of the 1950s, but the lack of detailed information before 1955 does not enable investigating the regional implications.

The analysis is therefore centred on the period 1909–1940 and is based on indicators of changes in prefectural ranking and on the calculation of regional gaps in productivity between the technology frontier and the rest of the country. The technology frontier is measured as the level of labour productivity in the top five prefectures. Table 8.1 presents changes in ranking for the five prefectures with the highest labour productivity.

The ranking in 1909 and 1925 is rather similar to the situation in early Meiji – with the notable exception of Hokkaido, which started to industrialize in the last decade of the nineteenth century, mostly for the processing of natural resources, and had until then very little production in cottage industry. It can be noted

Table 8.1 Top 5 prefectures for labour productivity in manufacturing

	Rank 1	*Rank 2*	*Rank3*	*Rank 4*	*Rank 5*
1909	Tokyo	Osaka	Hyogo (Kobe)	Hokkaido (Sapporo)	Aichi (Nagoya)
1925	Osaka	Tokyo	Hyogo (Kobe)	Kanagawa (Yokohama)	Hokkaido (Sapporo)
1935	Kanagawa (Yokohama)	Fukuoka	Osaka	Tokyo	Yamaguchi (Shimonoseki)
1940	Fukuoka	Yamaguchi (Shimonoseki)	Kanagawa (Yokohama)	Hyogo (Kobe)	Tokyo

Source: Fukao et al. (2015)

Note: Name of the prefectural capital city in parentheses (omitted if same as prefecture name).

that the Great Kanto Earthquake of 1923, which destroyed a large part of the residential and nonresidential buildings of the Tokyo-Yokohama area, had limited effect on the ranking of Tokyo. It was even associated by the rise of Kanagawa prefecture in the top five in 1925 after a swift renaissance of manufacturing activities, the most modern large-scale factories having been more resilient than the small-scale labour-intensive workshops (Okazaki et al. 2019).

The most remarkable change in comparison from the early nineteenth century is the decline of Kyoto prefecture, which was part of the core Kinai area of Japanese proto-industry and was specialized in producing high-quality tea, traditional handicraft, and textile products. From rank seven in 1909, Kyoto declined to rank nine in 1925, rank sixteen in 1935, and rank eighteen in 1940. The ranking became more instable in the 1930s with the rise of Fukuoka and Yamaguchi, two new industrial districts emblematic of the development of heavy industry driven by the Navy arsenals and more broadly the demand for military equipments during the militarization of the economy in the 1930s.

These changes resulted in a relative decline of Osaka, the most diversified industrial district of early twentieth century Japan, whose strength was to a large extent based on relatively small-scale and labour-intensive workshops, comparable to Tokyo in that regard. Osaka exited from the top five from 1935 but remained in the top ten. The relative instability of the ranking was not limited to the top five.

With these changes in the top five ranking in mind, we can new assess how other prefectures performed in terms of labour productivity in comparison with that of the frontier (i.e., the top five prefectures). Figure 8.6 presents the trends in labour productivity in the frontier (*yf*) and in other more backward regions (*yb*), and the ratio *yf/yb* for the manufacturing sector as a whole (frontier defined as top five prefectures; *yf* and *yb* as indices, 1 for *yb* in 1909). A steady increase in

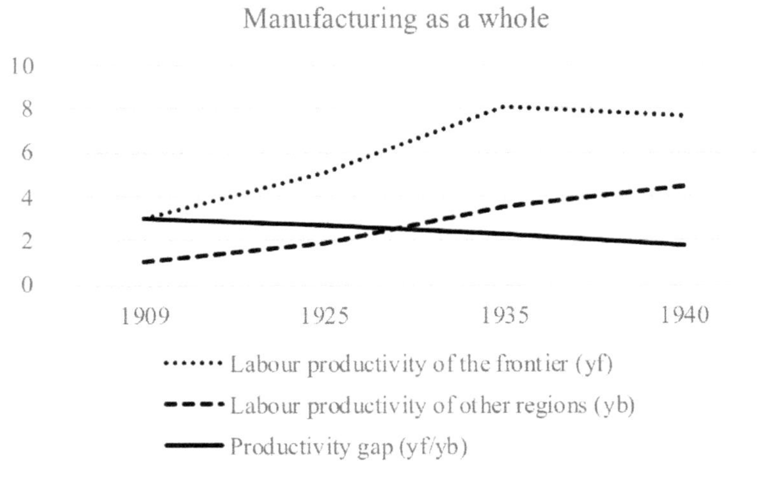

Figure 8.6 Changes in regional labour productivity gaps for manufacturing as a whole

Source: See Figure 8.4.

labour productivity took place in both the frontier and the non-frontier during the period studied. It came to a halt in 1935 in the frontier prefectures but continued to rise in the rest of the country. More importantly, the compound growth rate was lower in the frontier, which can be interpreted as evidence of technology diffusion from the high- to low-productivity prefectures. Manufacturing producers in the non-frontier prefectures were therefore involved in the Japanese productivity catch-up of the first decades of the twentieth century.

Did this pattern of regional convergence in productivity occur in the same manner in all manufacturing subsectors? Figure 8.7 presents the evolution of productivity gaps with a breakdown in nine subsectors: food, textile, wood, printing, chemicals, ceramics, metals, machinery, and miscellaneous manufacturing. A sharp decline of regional gaps (ratio *yf/yb*) is observed in all subsectors. The convergence was particularly rapid between 1909 and 1925, which can be interpreted as the consequence of the strong demand for manufactured goods during World War I amid rising labour costs. In the food, textile, wood, printing, and chemicals subsectors, most of the convergence took place during 1909–1925; the gap declined further between 1925 and 1940 but only marginally. The contraction of the gap was particularly impressive in the metal and machinery subsectors, corresponding to the major part of the heavy industry. It was reduced by almost half between 1909 and 1925, and again by close to half between 1925 and 1935. By then, the gap was only around two, which was the same magnitude as in other sectors that were mostly part of the light industry.

The evolution of the regional gap during the period 1940–1955 is for the time being a matter of conjecture due to the lack of dependable information at the prefecture level. The overall impression is that manufacturing producers in

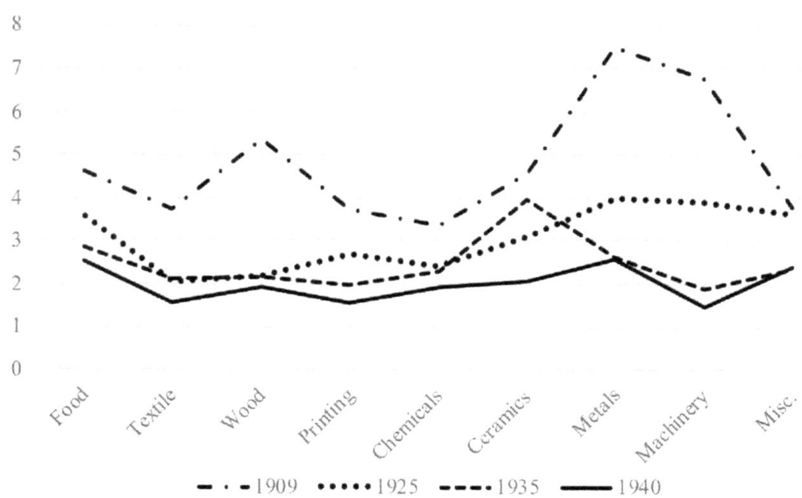

Figure 8.7 Regional gaps in productivity level (ratio yF/yB) by subsector

Source: See Figure 8.4.

non-frontier prefectures have been rather resilient, and therefore did not experience an increase of the productivity gap. The situation in 1955 was therefore rather similar to that of 1940, but it likely does not capture the effects of the temporary decline of production in the non-military sector in 1940–1945, in particular the collapse of textile output due to the lack of imported raw cotton and the loss of access to the US market for silk fabrics. The Japanese economy experienced a recovery during the period 1945–1950 but with restrictions on imports due to the lack of foreign currency, and limited domestic transportation capacities due to the destruction of a large part of the merchant fleet and railways rolling stock during the last month of the war.

Did the war result in transient or permanent effects? The evidence is mixed. Permanent effects can be observed in the westernmost prefectures of Japan that had benefitted from access to the Korean market after 1910. The changes in external borders resulting from the independence of Korea in 1945 clearly had an adverse impact on these prefectures (Nakajima 2008). However, the massive bombing by the US Air Force resulting in the destruction of Japanese cities in 1945, particularly residential areas where a large part of the small-scale light industry was concentrated, had only transient effects. With the exceptions of the merchant fleet and the railway rolling stock, the major part of the physical capital was only marginally affected, in particular in the most capital-intensive branches of manufacturing (United States Strategic Bombing Survey 1946).

The degree of disorganization resulting from the command economy, both at the end of the year and during the first postwar year, is the major explanation for the slow recovery that occurred only in the late 1940s. When it took place, the regional patterns reemerged almost unaffected. This is in particular the case for Tokyo, which had suffered comparatively more than Osaka, while Kyoto was almost entirely spared (due to a deliberate decision of the US military command). The primacy of Tokyo reappeared even stronger than in the prewar period from in the late 1940s. It took much more time, however, for Hiroshima and Nagasaki to recover and retrun to the level corresponding to the 1925–1940 population growth trend, until circa 1960 and 1970, respectively (Davis and Weinstein 2002).

8.5 Expansion of manufacturing and decline in regional inequality (1955–1990)

Japan experienced a period of acceleration of economic growth rate from the mid-1950s that, although amplified by a demographic dividend in a context of sudden decline of fertility rate in the late 1940s combined with a rapid increase of enrolment rates in secondary and higher education, was essentially driven by the development of the manufacturing sector. After almost two decades of isolation from the main sources of advanced technology (1937–1955), Japanese producers became able to acquire foreign patents and know-how in a wide range of manufacturing branches. In-house incremental innovations resulted in rapid technical changes that were facilitated by the rapid rise of education levels of young men and women entering the labour market. Technical change was also made indispensable by the steady increase of real wages in a context of a close to zero unemployment rate, in spite of massive migration from rural to urban areas.

During the two decades of high growth (1955–1973), the economic expansion was almost uninterrupted at a compound rate of around 7%, by far the best performance among OECD countries. During this short period, Japan morphed from a middle-income country whose manufacturing sector was relatively low-tech into the world's third biggest economy. Japanese enterprises appeared from the late 1960s as unexpected challengers of their US and German competitors in a wide range of high-tech industries, transforming the country into an industrial superpower from the early 1970s. After the sudden but short-lived halt of the 1973 Oil Shock, the country enjoyed a decade and a half of sustained growth (1974–1990) at a compound rate of around 4%, much higher than the performances of any other developed country.

Regional inequality declined in Japan during the high-growth era and remained at a low level during the sustained growth era. We can assess the role played by the manufacturing sector in reduction of regional gaps by relying on prefecture-level data of sectoral labour productivity and employment shares, enabling measurement of the differences between the wealthiest and poorest prefectures. The indicator used, for both sectoral labour productivity and employment shares, is the ratio of the top 50% prefectures versus the bottom 50% prefectures for the benchmark years 1955, 1970, 1990, and 2010.

Table 8.2 provides a comparison of sectoral labour productivity. Looking at the secondary (mining, manufacturing, and construction) and tertiary sectors in the top and bottom 50% of prefectures in terms of gross prefectural product (GPP) per capita, prefectural inequality in labour productivity in both sectors diminished throughout the period, but fell particularly rapidly between 1955 and 1970, in the high-speed growth era (by 7 percentage points in the secondary sector and 11 percentage points in the tertiary sector).[1] The largest decline in differences in the secondary sector occurred in the period from 1970 to 1990

Table 8.2 Prefectural differences in nominal labour productivity, postwar period: Top 50% versus bottom 50% of prefectures

	1955	*1970*	*1990*	*2010*
	Top 50% average/bottom 50% average	*Top 50% average/bottom 50% average*	*Top 50% average/bottom 50% average*	*Top 50% average/bottom 50% average*
Primary sector	1.30	1.07	0.91	0.89
Secondary sector	1.37	1.30	1.19	1.14
Tertiary sector	1.35	1.24	1.21	1.16
Total	1.77	1.51	1.29	1.17

Source: See Table 8.1.

Note: Primary sector in Table 8.1 consists of agriculture, forestry, and fisheries.

(11 percentage points), meaning that productivity differences declined for longer and substantially more than in the tertiary sector.

Table 8.3, which compares sectoral employment shares in the top and bottom 50% of prefectures, shows that the employment share of the secondary sector in poorer prefectures roughly doubled from 1955 to 1990. The decline in prefectural inequality from 1955 to 1990 was therefore the result of the combination of two factors: (1) the decline in labour productivity differences in the secondary sector, and (2) structural change in poorer prefectures toward a larger secondary sector share. The most dramatic changes in employment shares took place not in the secondary but in the tertiary sector – the employment share of the tertiary sector in poorer prefectures in 1955 was around 26–27%, but by 2010, this had nearly tripled. As a result, the employment share of the tertiary sector in 2010 both in the top and bottom prefectures stood at around 70–75%, so that tertiary sector employment shares in wealthier and poorer prefectures were almost identical. Given that, as seen in Table 8.2, prefectural differences in labour productivity in the tertiary sector have not shrunk as much as in the secondary sector, the fact that the tertiary sector labour share in poorer prefectures has increased rapidly is one of the reasons why the decline in prefectural inequality has decelerated since 1990.

Using prefecture-level data, let us now examine how the manufacturing share in total prefectural output and labour productivity have changed. Figures 8.8, 8.9, and 8.10 show the evolution of prefecture-level shares of manufacturing industry in gross prefectural product (GPP) from 1955, 1970, and 1990 – the period when the secondary sector greatly contributed to the reduction in prefectural differences in labour productivity. In these figures, prefectures are ordered in terms of their GPP per capita at the beginning of the year. Information on labour shares is also provided.

The figures indicate that in 1955, manufacturing was still concentrated in relatively wealthy prefectures. However, by 1970, the share of manufacturing in prefectural output had increased sharply in prefectures such as Okayama, Chiba, and

Table 8.3 Employment share by sector, postwar period: Comparison of top and bottom 50% of prefectures

	1955		*1970*		*1990*		*2010*	
	Top 50% average	*Bottom 50% average*	*Top 50% average*	*Bottom 50% average*	*Top 50% average*	*Bottom 50% average*	*Top 50% average*	*Bottom 50% average*
Primary sector	26	56	10	30	5	14	4	6
Secondary sector	32	17	40	28	35	31	25	22
Tertiary sector	42	27	50	42	60	56	71	71

Source: See Table 8.1.

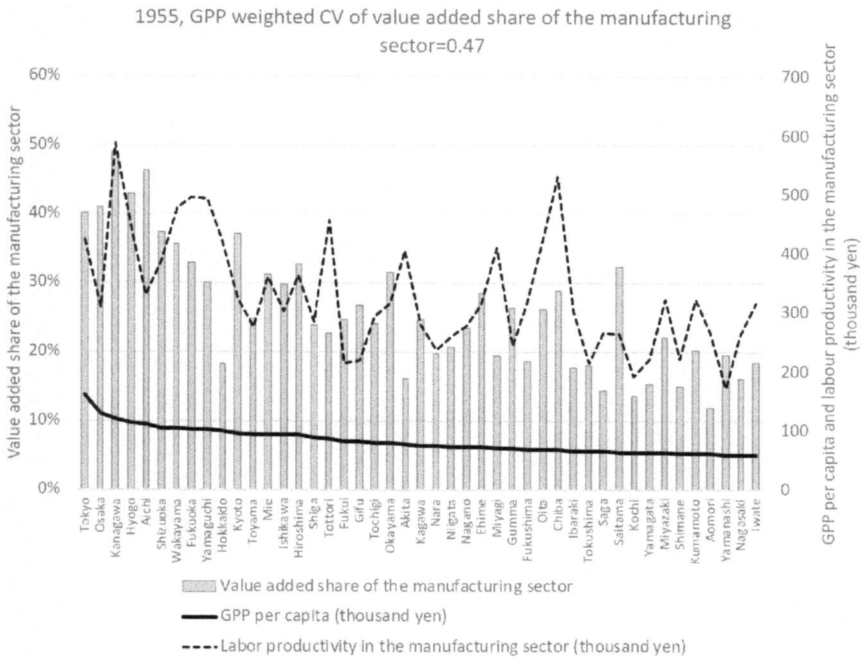

Figure 8.8 Value added share and labour productivity in the manufacturing sector by prefecture in 1955

Source: See Figure 8.4.

Note: Prefecture ranked by average per capita GDP in current yen.

Niigata, which were ranked below tenth place in terms of GPP per capita. In these prefectures, port facilities were developed during the high-speed growth era, and coastal industrial zones were formed. Following World War II, Japan enjoyed rapid growth of processing trade thanks to the expansion of free trade under the Pax Americana, technological innovations in ship engines, and the spread of container ships, and the industrialization of these prefectures likely reflects these postwar changes (Yasuba 1980, Yasuba and Inoki 1989). As a result, the coefficient of variation for the share of manufacturing in GPP fell sharply.

By 1990, the manufacturing share in wealthy prefectures had declined further, and the correlation between the share of manufacturing in GPP and GPP per capita further weakened. This is likely due to a range of factors, including the shift to an increasingly service-based economy as well as congestion effects in metropolitan areas such as rising land prices and longer commuting times reflecting the concentration of services such as finance, real estate, business services, and headquarters functions, especially in the Greater Tokyo area. In addition, metropolitan areas lost their locational advantage in manufacturing

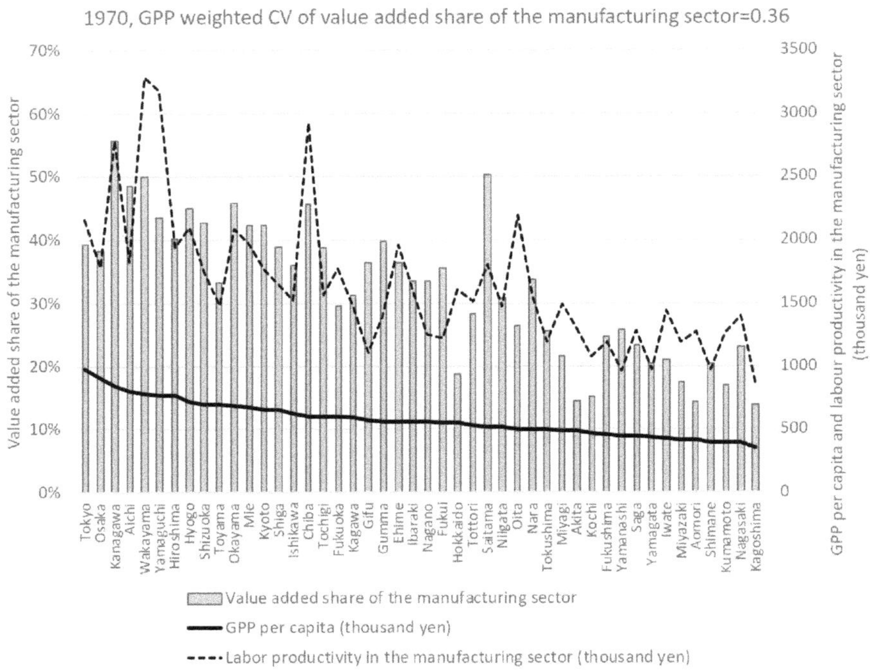

Figure 8.9 Value added share and labour productivity in the manufacturing sector by prefecture in 1970

Source and note: See Figure 8.4.

(the output of which is highly tradable) as the government began to impose restrictions on the establishment of factories in urban areas due to growing pollution, the entry of the Baby Boomer generation into the labour market and their move to metropolitan areas such as Greater Tokyo came to an end, and firms started to increasingly look for cheaper labour and decided to move production to regional areas.

Let us now consider the changes in prefectural labour productivity differences in manufacturing over time. The coefficient of variation increased slightly from 1955 to 1970 but then fell sharply from 1970 to 1990. Moreover, by 1990, the correlation between labour productivity in manufacturing and GPP per capita had weakened further. It seems that prefectures that had developed coastal industrial areas such as Chiba, Okayama, Yamaguchi, and Oita also played a major role in reducing prefectural differences in labour productivity.

Using level accounting, let us examine what factors gave rise to the observed differences in prefectural labour productivity. The (log) difference of each prefecture's labour productivity from the national average can be decomposed into

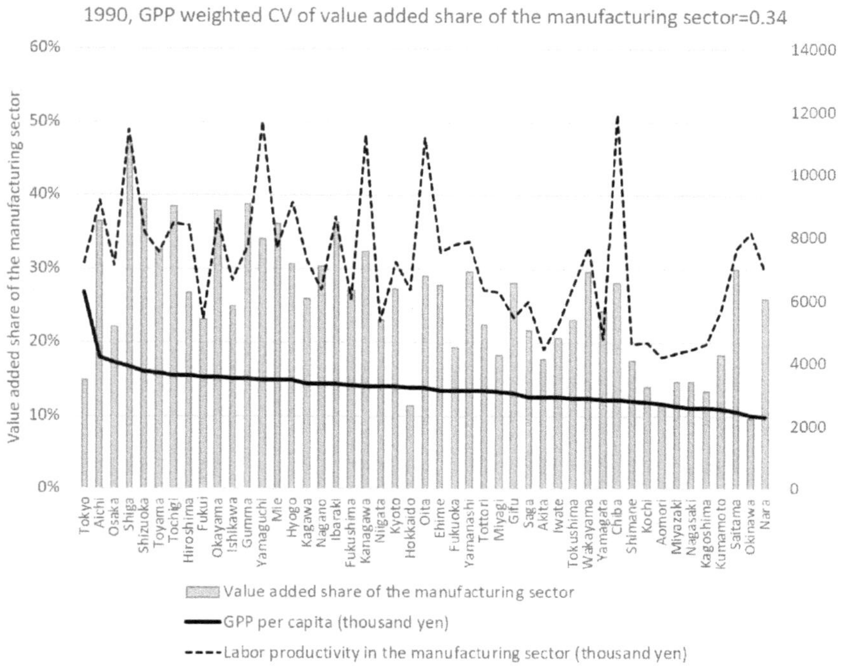

Figure 8.10 Value added share and labour productivity in the manufacturing sector by prefecture in 1990

Source and note: See Figure 8.4.

(1) the contribution of differences in the capital–labour ratio, (2) the contribution of differences in labour quality, and (3) the contribution of differences in TFP, which is calculated as the residual. By calculating the covariance of these three terms and the (log) difference of each prefecture's labour productivity from the national average, the dispersion in the log of prefectural relative labour productivity can be decomposed into these three covariances.

Table 8.4 shows the results of the factor decomposition of this dispersion in fifteen- to twenty-year intervals. It appears that the largest source of prefectural differences in labour productivity in 1955 were differences in TFP and capital–labour ratios. However, whereas the contribution of differences in capital–labour ratios rapidly decreased, the contribution of TFP differences declined only moderately. For this reason, TFP differences in 1990 accounted for about three-fourths of regional economic inequality as measured by the coefficient of variation. Meanwhile, prefectural differences in labour quality, both at the beginning and end of the period 1955–1990, only accounted for a relatively small part of regional inequality.

Table 8.4 Factor decomposition of the dispersion in the log of prefectural relative labour productivity

	Dispersion of labor productivity differences	*Contribution of differences in capital–labor ratio*	*Contribution of differences in labor quality*	*Contribution of TFP differences*
1955	0.070	0.019	0.008	0.042
1970	0.050	0.018	0.007	0.025
1990	0.025	0.006	0.004	0.014
2008	0.017	0.003	0.003	0.011

Source: See Table 8.1.

8.6 Manufacturing decline and regional inequality during the low-growth era (since the 1990s)

The contraction of the manufacturing employment share in the 1970s took place in a context in which total labour force was still rising, and therefore the number of workers in manufacturing barely declined in absolute terms. This indicates that Japan experienced a rather mild deindustrialization until the end of the 1980 in spite of the second oil crisis of 1979–1980 and the sudden appreciation of the yen against the US dollar in 1985, both of which resulted in rather massive investment in manufacturing activities overseas, with a first wave in energy-intensive activities and a second wave in labour-intensive activities.

The first one corresponded to genuine delocalization and left a number of Japanese heavy industry districts severely affected, but it led to relatively few job destructions. The second mostly resulted in additional capacities, particularly in Association of Southeast Asian Nations (ASEAN) countries, and led to an international division of labour internal to Japanese business groups that was not essentially different from the process of creation of additional production capacities in Japanese rural areas, where labour costs were lower, that had occurred until the 1970s. When massive Japanese FDI resulted in an international fragmentation of the production process in the 1990s and 2000s, negative externalities resulting from the deindustrialization appeared but remained localized and mitigated by internal migrations. In comparison with most other OECD countries, the spatial effects were therefore limited.

Several factors mitigated Japan's rust belt problem. First, after World War II, Japan's heavy and chemical industries almost completely depended on imported materials. Therefore, they were located around large seaports. Several of these brownfields, particularly former industrial polders, became immediately reused for the expansion of logistic facilities in these transportation hubs. Second, from the 1970s, Japan's machinery sectors, such as electrical machinery and automobile, succeeded in improving international competitiveness and increased their exports. Before the 1990s, these sectors created jobs mainly in rural parts of Japan because of relatively cheap labour. From the 1990s, these sectors relocated their factories abroad but by that time, the declining working-age population – which was especially serious in rural Japan – and the expansion of service-sector activities, such as elder care, mitigated job losses caused by factory closures.

The third explanation, which appears as the most important, is that the Japanese government took active industrial policies to slow down the shrinkage of the declining sectors and promote labor and reallocaton to the service sector. A similar remark applied to the former industrial land that was often located along the coast at short distance from major urban areas, and sometimes within the core area of the city, for instance in Yokohama. Brownfield land had a high market value and became easily reconverted into shopping malls or residential and office buildings. The major exceptions were in areas of heavy industry located close to coal mines at some distance from important urban areas, in particular in northern Kyushu and Hokkaido. Most of the labour force was encouraged to migrate to urban areas, resulting in a decline of population in the case of Hokkaido.

As shown by Beason and Weinstein (1996), most of the budget for industrial policies and trade protection measures was used for this type of backward-looking purpose. After the first and second oil crises and the yen appreciation caused by the end of the adjustable-peg exchange rate system, energy-intensive sectors and labour-intensive sectors – such as metal processing, petroleum processing, shipbuilding, and textile – had lost international competitiveness. As in Italy or Germany, Japan experienced a gradual decline in the share if manufacturing in GDP. The country therefore avoided the effects of the American or British type of deindustrialization that resulted in massive rust belts and poverty traps for their inhabitants, a phenomenon also observed in northern France and southern Belgium.

In the post-1990 context of a decline of employment in manufacturing, what role did the manufacturing industry play in the reduction of TFP and capital–labour ratio differences? In order to answer, we should distinguish between two effects: the share effect and the within-industry effect. The share effect refers to the fact that if, for example, the share of industries with an above-average capital–labour ratio increases in a prefecture, the capital–labour ratio for the prefecture as a whole and, as a result, labour productivity, will increase. On the other hand, the within-industry effect refers to the fact that if, in a given prefecture, the capital–labour ratio in a particular industry rises relative to the capital–labour ratio in other prefectures, this will also result in an increase in the capital–labour ratio, and hence labour productivity. Using this distinction, we examine the contribution of the two effects in each of the sectors to prefectural differences in capital–labour ratios, and hence prefectural differences in labour productivity.

The decomposition was conducted for each industry and the results were then aggregated for the three sectors (primary, manufcturing, and services). Due to data constraints, the analysis is possible only for the period from 1970 onward. The results are presented in Table 8.5. The second and third columns show the results for the capital–labour ratio for 1970, 1990, and 2008. In addition, the table shows the results for the same type of decomposition of differences in labour quality in the fourth and fifth columns and of TFP differences in the sixth column. It should be noted that because TFP levels cannot

Table 8.5 Factor decomposition of the dispersion in the log of prefectural relative labour productivity by sector

	Capital–labor ratio		*Labor quality*		*TFP*
	Share effect	*Within effect*	*Share effect*	*Within effect*	*Within effect*
1970					
Primary sector subtotal	−0.89	6.51	20.08	30.18	6.63
Manufacturing subtotal	10.12	20.30	50.72	39.16	76.61
Services subtotal	2.54	61.42	−92.57	52.42	16.76
Total	11.77	88.23	−21.76	121.76	100.00
1990					
Primary sector subtotal	−8.42	21.40	11.72	8.86	−15.52
Manufacturing subtotal	8.56	21.05	31.29	44.00	63.14
Services subtotal	29.41	28.01	−47.95	52.08	52.39
Total	29.55	70.45	−4.94	104.94	100.00
2008					
Primary sector subtotal	−31.51	14.48	6.80	5.65	−7.25
Manufacturing subtotal	14.23	30.99	27.40	44.43	38.95
Services subtotal	44.70	27.13	−66.65	82.37	68.29
Total	27.41	72.59	−32.45	132.45	100.00

Source: See Table 8.1.

be compared across industries, the decomposition of TFP differences is only possible for the within effect.[2]

As seen in Section 8.4, prefectural TFP differences were the main source of prefectural differences in labour productivity throughout in the second half of the twentieth century but declined in the recent decades. Table 8.4 indicates that TFP differences in 2008 accounted for about two-thirds of regional economic inequality as measured by the coefficient of variation (against three-fourths in 1990). Table 8.5 suggests that the major reason why prefectural TFP differences declined over time is the decline in TFP differences in manufacturing-sector industries (the within effect). In contrast, prefectural TFP differences in service-sector industries declined only relatively slowly.

Looking at prefectural differences in capital–labour ratio and labour quality, Table 8.5 indicates that the share effect and the within effect in the manufacturing sector remained largely unchanged between 1970 and 1990 and increased between 1990 and 2008, so that they remained comparatively large in relation to the total for all sectors. However, as we see in Table 8.4, the impact of prefectural differences in capital–labour ratios and labour quality fell sharply during the period from 1970 to 2008, so it could be said that the manufacturing sector also contributed to the decline in prefectural differences in capital–labour ratios and labour quality.

The results may therefore be summarized as follows. Prefectural differences in labour productivity declined in recent decades as a result of a decline in prefectural differences in capital–labour ratios, labour quality, and TFP. The manufacturing sector made a large contribution to the decline in prefectural labour productivity differences through a decline in prefectural TFP differences within individual manufacturing industries. The manufacturing sector also contributed to some extent to the reduction of prefectural differences in capital–labour ratios and labour quality.

8.7 Conclusion

The Japanese manufacturing sector consisted exclusively of urban handicraft and rural cottage industry until the mid-nineteenth century. It experienced only a slow expansion between circa 1800 and 1858, with a very limited impact of imported technologies or foreign competition. Although all regions had some kind of specialization, the Osaka-Kyoto area and the Edo area were the most important centres of production. The opening to international trade in 1858 resulted in regional asymmetric shocks in the following decade. In the period 1868–1913, a gradual shift to modern economic growth occurred across most Japanese prefectures during a phase lasting until around 1890, followed by a phase of spatial concentration in urban areas from 1890 to 1912. The period 1914–1965 was a phase of diversification and amplification of the geographical concentration in heavy industry, but labour-intensive manufacturing activities spread throughout the country. There was no equivalent of the *Mezzogiorno* of Italy or the Deep South of the United States.

In the period of high-speed growth in 1955–1970, driven by the expansion of the manufacturing sector, the spatial dominance of the major urban areas slightly increased, but new manufacturing activities spread to middle-income regions. During the period of sustained growth in 1970–1990, within-manufacturing-sector differences in labour productivity across prefectures declined. Labour productivity differences across prefectures declined in the second half of the twentieth century because manufacturing activities spread to middle-income regions during the period of 1955–1970. Within-manufacturing-sector differences in labour productivity across prefectures also declined during the period of 1970–1990. In spite of the rapid decline of the share of manufacturing in total employment and economic stagnation in the post-1990 period, the negative externalities of deindustrialization, identified in most OECD countries as the apparition of rust belt areas, had only a limited and very localized manifestation.

Notes

1 The employment share of the primary sector has consistently fallen both in the top and bottom prefectures, so that the impact of the decline in productivity differences

in the primary sector on prefectural economic inequality was small, and therefore is not considered here.

2 For details of the methodology underlying the analysis here, see Chapter 6 of Fukao et al. (2015).

References

Arimoto, Y., K. Nakajima, and T. Okazaki. 2014. "Sources of productivity improvement in industrial clusters: the case of the prewar Japanese silk-reeling industry." *Regional Science and Urban Economics* 46: 27–41.

Beason, R., and D. Weinstein. 1996. "Growth, economies of scale, and targeting in Japan (1955–1990)." *The Review of Economics and Statistics* 78(2): 286–295.

Davis, D. R., and D. E. Weinstein. 2002. "Bones, bombs, and break points: the geography of economic activity." *American Economic Review* 92(5): 1269–1289.

Denison, E. F. 1962. "Education, economic growth, and gaps in information." *Journal of Political Economy* 70(5): 124–128.

Fujita, M., P. R. Krugman, and A. Venables. 1999. *The spatial economy: cities, regions, and international trade.* Cambridge: MIT Press.

Fujita, M., and J.-F. Thisse. 1996. "Economics of agglomeration." *Journal of the Japanese and International Economies* 10(4): 339–378.

Fukao, K., J.-P. Bassino, T. Makino, R. Paprzycki, T. Settsu, M. Takashima, and J. Tokui. 2015. *Regional inequality and industrial structure in Japan: 1874–2008.* Tokyo: Maruzen.

Fukao, K., T. Settsu, and T. Makino. 2020. "Nihon ni okeru jinteki shihon to keizai seicho:1885–2015 [Human capital and economic growth in Japan: 1885–2015]." *Keizai Kenkyu (Economic Research).*

Kendrick, J. W. 1961. *Productivity trends in the United States.* Cambridge: NBER Books.

Krugman, P. R. 1993. "First nature, second nature, and metropolitan location." *Journal of Regional Science* 33: 129–144.

Nakabayashi, M. 2003. *Kindai Shihonshugi no Soshiki: Seishigyo no Hatten niokeru Torikiki no Tochi to Seisan no Kozo* [Institutional origin of modern capitalism in Japan: governance of trade and structure of production in the silk reeling industry]. Tokyo: Tokyo University Press.

Nakajima, K. 2008. "Economic division and spatial relocation: the case of postwar Japan." *Journal of the Japanese and International Economies* 22(3): 383–400.

Nakajima, K., and T. Okazaki. 2018. "The expanding Empire and spatial distribution of economic activity: the case of Japan's colonization of Korea during the prewar period." *The Economic History Review* 71(2): 593–616.

Nakamura, N. 2010. *Chiho Kara no Sangyo Kakumei: Nihon ni okeru Kigyo Bokko no Gendoryoku* [Industrial revolution from the countryside: the driving force of the rise of enterprises in Japan]. Nagoya: Nagoya University Press.

Nishikawa, S. 1978. "Productivity, subsistence, and by-employment in the mid-nineteenth century Choshu." *Explorations in Economic History* 15(1): 69–83.

Odaka, K. 1996. "Hinoseisan Shihon keisei [Capital formation in non-primary sectors]." In *Nihon keizai 200 nen* [The Japanese economy since 200 years], edited by K. Odaka, O. Saito, and S. Nishikawa, 371–398. Tokyo: Nihon Hyoronsha.

Oishi, S. 1975. *Nihon kinsei shakai no shijo kozo* [Market structure in Japanese early modern society]. Tokyo: Iwanami Shoten.

Okazaki, T., T. Okubo, and E. Strobl. 2019. "Creative destruction of industries: Yokohama City in the Great Kanto Earthquake, 1923." *The Journal of Economic History* 79(1): 1–31.

Paprzycki, R., and K. Fukao. 2007. *Foreign direct investment in Japan: multinationals' role in growth and globalization*. Cambridge: Cambridge University Press.

Saito, O. 2018. "Placing early modern Japan in world history: growth, inequality and the state in a longer-term perspective." *Transactions of the Japan Academy* 72: 89–108.

Saito, O., and T. Settsu. 2010. *Unveiling historical occupational structures and its implications for sectoral labour productivity analysis in Japan's economic growth*. Global COE Hi-Stat Discussion Paper Series 143, Hitotsubashi University.

Takashima, M. 2017. *Keizai seichō no Nihon shi: kodai kara kinsei no chōchōki GDP suikei 730–1874* [Economic growth in the Japanese past: estimating GDP, 730–1874]. Nagoya: Nagoya University Press.

Takenouchi, W. 1943. *Kefukigusa*. Tokyo: Iwanami Bunko, Yellow 200–201.

Tanimoto, M. 1998. "Nihon ni okeru 'Chiiki Kogyoka' to Toshi Katsudo ['Regional industrialization' and investment behavior in Japan]." *Shakai Keizai Shigaku* [Socio-Economic History] 64(1): 88–114.

Tanimoto, M., ed. 2006. *The role of tradition in Japan's industrialization: another path to industrialization*. New York: Oxford University Press.

United States Strategic Bombing Survey. 1946. *Summary report (Pacific War)*. Washington, DC: United States Government Printing Office. www.anesi.com/ussbs01.htm

Watanabe, I. 1964. "Kinsei shokōgyō no hatten [The development of early modern industries]." In *Sangyōshi* [Industrial history], Vol. II, edited by K. Kodama, Chapter 8. Tokyo: Yamakawa Shuppansha.

Yamazawa, I. 1973. "Nihon no Kogyo-ka to Hogo Boeki Seisaku [Industrialization and protection trade policies in Japan]." *Keizai Kenkyu* [Economic Review] 24(1): 22–34.

Yasuba, Y. 1980. *Keizai Seicho-ron* [Economic growth theory]. Tokyo: Chikuma Shobo (Dai Nihan; Keizai-gaku Zenshu 12 [Economics collection, 2nd ed., Vol. 12].

Yasuba, Y., and T. Inoki. 1989. "Gaisetsu 1955–80-nen [Outline 1955–1980]." In *Kodo Seicho (Nihon Keizai-shi 8)* [High-speed growth (economic history of Japan)], Vol. 8, edited by Y. Yasuba and T. Inoki, 1–55. Tokyo: Iwanami Shoten.

Part III

Theories on regional industrialization

9 Regional industrialization

Determinants of industrial location

Glenn Rayp and Stijn Ronsse

9.1 Introduction

The diffusion of industrialization is a subject of common interest to both historians and economists. Scarcity of data and benign neglect in theory building by economists explain why historical study in this field has taken, during a long time, the exclusive form of more qualitative regional analysis or business and entrepreneurial history. Since the 1990s, the field has been changing, and attention has increasingly shifted from analyzing case studies towards quantification and testing of theories.

Two developments seem to have been important in this respect. First is the renewed interest in location theory following the rethinking of international trade highlighting economies of scale and production differentiation as the main determinants of specialization and trade, which resulted in the so-called new economic geography. Although economists already showed interest in location theories in the nineteenth and twentieth centuries (Johann Von Thünen in the first place), they rather soon settled with the classical Heckscher-Ohlin idea of the importance of natural endowments in explaining industrial locations. Throughout the rest of the twentieth century, location questions were basically regarded as minor issues mainly because, beyond differences in endowments, they were difficult to understand. New economic geography had to merit to put forward a framework in which location patterns emerged from endogenous economic decisions rather than ex-ante differences that allowed the viewing of location at different geographical levels (cities, regions, or countries) from a new perspective.

Second, the adoption of the Midelfart-Knarvik et al. (2000) model has become the reference for empirical analysis, in particular in the quantitative analysis of historical industrial location. This model's main advantage is that it provides an encompassing framework for the different theoretical hypotheses on the location of economic activity and therefore allows assessment of their relative importance. It became increasingly popular among (economic) historians and is used in an expanding set of country studies of industrial location. The use of a common framework improves the cumulative character and allows for a better comparability of the evidence that is collected. As such, beyond understanding historical industrial location, it may provide interesting evidence for the test of the validity of location theories.

In this chapter, after a brief introduction of the theory of economic location and a review of the methodology used in the empirical analysis, we discuss more in depth the main characteristics of the present applications of the Midelfart-Knarvik et al. (2000) model in the study of historical location of industrial activity. We review their findings and assess the more general conclusions that can be drawn from this set of methodologically quite comparable, i.e., almost replication studies, taking into account what in our view are the main limitations and challenges. In a final section, we give some suggestions about data and methodological issues for consideration in future applications.

9.2 The economics of industrial location: Theoretical background

Despite some early nineteenth century contributions, the relation of economic thinking with respect to space was essentially one of neglect (Combes et al. 2008). In traditional economic theory, the only relevant distance was that *between* nation-states, i.e., the border that demarcates countries, and then mostly in terms of differences of internationally immobile labour and capital or of technological knowledge. *Within* nation-states, production factors were traditionally assumed to be fully mobile, as if distance had vanished with the abolition of local tolls and the improvement of the transportation network.

The explanation why might be theoretical. Including space in a modelling framework implies that the assumptions of perfect competition and constant returns to scale may have to be abandoned – something economists were reluctant to do, as they were the cornerstone of the major formal theoretical achievements in economic science.

The incompatibility of space with perfect competition and constant return to scale is the essence of the Starret Impossibility Theorem (Starrett 1978). Space implies indivisibilities (a finite number of locations) and transportation costs (between locations). Starrett showed that a perfectly competitive equilibrium with trade between locations (transportation of goods) is then impossible. Suppose there is one consumer and one firm, each occupying a (homogeneous) space of one unit, too small to accommodate both. Suppose in addition that moving people and goods from the one unit location to the other is costly. The firm produces one unit of a good, using labour supplied by the consumer. The wage earned by the consumer is used to buy the good, the revenue of which allows the firm to earn a profit. Consumer and firm are respectively utility and profit maximizing agents. Then, they will always have an incentive to move closer to each other (i.e., to share the same location) in order to avoid the transportation costs – which is, however, impossible as firm and consumer cannot use less than one unit of space. Hence, there is no equilibrium: the agents have a permanent incentive to move wherever they are located.

Given the Starrett Impossibility Theorem, how can the location of economic activity then be explained? Three alternatives have been suggested. The first way is to assume *exogeneous differences* in space such that all geographical locations are not equivalent anymore. With geographical heterogeneity, perfect competition on good markets and constant returns to scale in production can be maintained, which is why this was for a very long time the economists' preferred solution. The Heckscher-Ohlin model that links economic specialization and international trade by exogenously given differences in factor endowments, does precisely this. Under perfect competition, non-increasing returns to scale, and the absence of trading costs, differences in natural endowments and resources will entirely determine the industrial geographical pattern (Brühlhart 2003).

The second alternative is the assumption of *Marshallian externalities*, allowing for spatial indivisibilities (increasing returns to scale) in a way still consistent with perfect competition, from which endogenous differences in space emerge. The central idea is that the industrial concentration in one region generates scale effects that are beneficial for the whole industrial agglomeration. Examples of this process are labour pooling, knowledge spillovers, and close proximity to other industrial actors, allowing forward and backward linkages, external to all individual economic agents. All of these may explain why industrial agglomeration becomes self-enforcing. The main shortcoming of Marshallian externalities as determinant of industrial location is the lack of an explicit explanatory mechanism. The reason for the occurrence of agglomeration and location can a priori be manifold, and therefore remains unspecified until ex post observed.

The third option is to abandon the idea of a competitive equilibrium and to allow for some form of imperfect competition (predominantly monopolistic competition) and spatial indivisibilities. The latter is the new economic geography approach that takes as point of departure that location and agglomeration are the result of intentional decisions (of utility and profit maximization) by consumers and firms. New economic geography explains geographical patterns of economic activity from the interaction between increasing returns (actually pecuniary externalities) and transportation costs, summarized in what Krugman (1991) defined as the *home market effect*: conditional upon the transportation costs, firms (economic activity) will concentrate more than proportionately in the largest market, which is (*ceteris paribus*) the most profitable location (as it allows to sell a higher share of output without paying transportation costs, and hence is the most attractive location for export as well). In this concept, location of economic activity is determined by centripetal and centrifugal forces. The centrifugal (or dispersion) forces refer to the higher competition that agglomeration of firms and economic activity imply (and therefore induce firms to move to avoid competition and earn higher margins). The centripetal forces, allowed in agglomerations, refer to the higher sales exempt of transportation costs to consumers and firms in downward activities (forward spillovers), as well as the cheaper intermediate goods (by avoiding transport costs) that a firm can buy (backward spillover effects). At very (e.g., prohibitively) high transportation costs, the centrifugal forces prevail and an equilibrium with dispersion is expected. If transportation costs are reduced to insignificance, then location becomes irrelevant (therefore no bias against dispersion). Typically for *intermediate levels* of the transportation costs, agglomeration of economic activity (e.g., core-periphery patterns) will dominate. Hence, in the new economic geography perspective, location of economic activity is determined by transportation costs: with constant decreasing of transportation costs, a bell-shaped agglomeration pattern will emerge. For (intermediate) transportation costs, industries have an incentive to locate near strong markets, close to customers and other industries. Hence, regions with a strong market potential attract industries and economic activity.

From the perspective of research on the historical location of industry and the diffusion of industrialization, there is obviously neither a reason to discard a priori one of the three hypotheses as a way out of the Starrett Impossibility Theorem, nor to assume a priori that this remains constant over time. One can easily understand that both natural endowments and agglomeration matter for location, even in a time-specific manner. Traditional industrial regions may have had an initial start determined by endowments (e.g., of raw materials or energy resources such as coal), leading to a concentration of industry and hence allowing for agglomeration effects. However, when locational patterns of the last two centuries are studied, the impact of transportation costs also needs to be considered. The industrial revolution and spatial diffusion of industrialization were characterized by a spectacular fall in transportation costs (due to innovations in shipping and the introduction of the railway). This evolution continued throughout the twentieth century. Infrastructure all over Europe and in the United States multiplied and technological progress intensified, resulting in a further decrease in transportation costs and changing dramatically the pattern and location of economic activity.

Therefore, in empirical research the question is not that much *whether* endowments or transportation costs and local scale matter for the spatial distribution of economic activity, but rather *to what extent* and, moreover, *in which period*. This calls for a comprehensive analytical framework that includes both categories of determinants of location, allowing us to determine their respective weight.

9.3 From the verification of the home market effect to the empirical analysis of industrial location

As stated earlier, the home market effect was the crucial element put forward in the new economic geography framework to *understand* the occurrence of agglomeration, and therefore to improve on the externality hypothesis that takes agglomeration for granted. The first to empirically examine this effect, and hence the relevance of the new economic geography, was Krugman (1991). From his theoretical model, it follows that a regression of the share of producers on the share of demand identifies the home market effect, assuming the validity of some restrictions, factor price equalization between regions and identical fixed costs in particular.

Yet, as the existence of a home market effect *per se* was not put into doubt, the question of its impact on location relative to regional resource abundance (the Heckscher-Ohlin determinants) was considered more relevant. A pioneering study in this respect is Kim (1995). He analyzed the impact of resource abundance and increasing returns on regional specialization in the United States at the level of nine US Census divisions, based on an empirical model including average industry plant size and raw material intensity, as well as industry and time fixed effects. He concluded that both mattered for the explanation of location, in contrast with economic externalities that he found not significant. Kim's study was frequently subject to criticism, the most detailed by Combes et al. (2008), who pointed in particular to a striking problem of omitted variables in either category of determinants that cannot just be captured by including fixed effects (which implies that omitted variables must be time invariant). In addition, they note that there was no theoretical model linking the spatial concentration index (that Kim took as regressand) to the explanatory variables, which questions the identification of the effects.

Davis and Weinstein (2003) argued that the home market effect could be identified from a regression of the production of a good *k* in a country *r*. They proposed a sparse model with two explanatory variables included – first, the country's production of the good, assuming that the share in production of good *k* in country *r* would be the same as in the rest of the world, and second, the deviation of good *k* in the expenditures of country *r* with respect to the share of expenditures in the rest of the world (*ideodem*). The coefficient of the latter variable is considered to be informative about the home market effect. As external control variables, Davis and Weinstein added the country's endowments of labour, capital, and land. Hence, the model allowed users to empirically estimate the impact of both new economic geography and Heckscher-Ohlin factors. Yet the test on the coefficient of *ideodem* is exclusive: either is concluded to the validity of the new economic geography model from a significant home market effect (i.e., a parameter estimate, significantly higher than 1) or, to a constant returns to scale Heckscher-Ohlin model when the estimated parameter of *ideodem* does not significantly exceed 1. This is illustrated, for example, by the study of the industrialization pattern in Spain of Rosès (2003), who follows the Davis and Weinstein approach and controls for regional endowments (the Heckscher-Ohlin determinants) when identifying an "economic-geography" effect of industrialization (from the significance of *ideodem*). While finding a significant effect of both categories of determinants, their relative weight remains unconsidered.

Midelfart-Knarvik et al. (2000) proposed a model that integrated the two main mechanisms of location: exogenous differences in space (endowments, the Heckscher-Ohlin determinants) and the size of economic activity, as well as upstream and downstream linkages between industries (the new economic geography determinants) in such a way that the underlying structure of the home market effect can be identified and the relative impact of both categories of determinants could be estimated. Since its publication, the Midelfart-Kvarnik framework has been repeatedly used by economic historians in country-specific studies of location and distribution of industrial activity and has a more or less paradigmatic position. The use of a common framework would not only allow evaluation of the relative impact of two categories of determinants of industrial location, but also comparison of this impact across countries and over time.

The Midelfart-Kvarnik model explicitly derives empirical specification from a theoretical model, in which they assume perfect competition and constant returns to scale production. Preferences are characterized by love-of-variety, represented by a Constant Elasticity of Substitution utility function, and each industry produces an exogenously fixed number of varieties.[1] Goods are mobile between regions but subject to an industry- and region-specific iceberg type transportation cost.

From these assumptions, it follows that the value of production in each industry and region is determined by factor supply prices, intermediate goods prices, and transportation costs. The number of varieties a region can produce in an industry is assumed to be proportional to size of the region and the industry, more specifically the region's and industry's share in total production. In the empirical model, the value of production in region and industry (as the industry-region production share) is twice normalized by the region's and industry's share in total production. This normalization implies that the dependent variable in the empirical model is the location quotient, i.e., a sector's share in regional output relative to the region's share in total output (see Kim 1995: 883).

As the input factor prices are assumed to depend on local resource endowments, the model captures the Heckscher-Ohlin determinants of location. The presence of transportation costs implies that geography and location of demand are included as determinants of regional industrial activity as well. The *market potential* of each region will therefore matter for the spatial distribution of economic activity. The market potential of a region consists of two components: final goods demand and intermediate goods demand by other producers. The latter constitute the *backward linkages* (downstream demand of the goods a firm produces) between industries. Finally, intermediate goods are used as inputs and constitute an argument of the unit cost function, therefore *forward linkages* between industries are included as a determinant of location as well. In regions of larger size, firms are able to buy more intermediate goods exempt from transportation costs.

Linearizing around a reference level in unit costs and market potential results in the following empirical model, for industry *k* in region *i*:

$$ln(r_i^k) = \sum_j \beta[j](x_i[j] - \bar{x}[j])(y^k[j] - \bar{y}[j]) + \varepsilon_i^k,$$

where r_i^k represents the twice normalized output share of industry *k* in region *I*,[2] $x_i[j]$ and $y^k[j]$ denote respectively the jth characteristic of region *i*, and industry *k* and $\bar{x}[j]$ ($\bar{y}[j]$) the region (industry) reference level (of the jth characteristic). Working out the right-hand side gives:

$$ln\left(r_i^k\right) = \xi + \sum_j \left\{\beta[j]x_i[j]y^k[j] - \beta[j]\bar{x}[j]y^k[j] - \beta[j]\bar{y}[j]x_i[j]\right\} + \varepsilon_i^k,$$

The Midelfart-Kvarnik model explains the region-specific size of an industry by the correlation of region and industry characteristics, the extent to which in a region is available (compared to a reference level) what profit-maximizing firms in the industry demand. Hence, the main focus in estimating the model is the parameter estimations ($\hat{\beta}[j]$) of the interaction term between industrial and regional characteristics ($x_i[j]y^k[j]$). The industry characteristics ($y^k[j]$) and region characteristics ($x_i[j]$) must be included to estimate the level of the interaction effects.[3] $\xi = \sum_j \beta[j]\bar{x}[j]\bar{y}[j]$ does not vary with *i* or *k* and therefore represents the constant of the model.

9.4 Analyzing the historical pattern and diffusion of industrialization using the Midelfart-Knarvik framework

Over the past two decades, the Midelfart-Knarvik (MK) model was used by several researchers to test the relative importance of Heckscher-Ohlin and new economic geography determinants in explaining the historical pattern of industrial locations. In particular (though not exclusively), we refer to Crafts and Mulatu (2005), who studied the location of industry in Great Britain between 1871–1931; to Wolf (2007), who analyzed how the unification of the internal market, combined with investments in infrastructure and changing endowment (relocation of human capital), affected the location of industry in post-World War I reunified Poland (1926–1934); to Klein and Crafts (2012), who studied the persistence of the manufacturing belt in the United States between 1880–1920; to Martinez-Galarraga (2012), who considered the determinants of industrial location in Spain between 1860 and 1930; to Nikolic (2018), who analyzed industrial location in Yugoslavia in the 1930s, characterized by market unification (abolition of all administrative barriers and reduction of transportation costs) similar to Poland in the same period; and to Missiaia (2019), who studied industrial location in the early stages of the Italian state, between 1871 and 1911.

In addition to the use of the same empirical framework, including Heckscher-Ohlin and new economic geography determinants of industrial location, these studies strikingly focus on a comparable period, i.e., the end of the nineteenth century to the beginning of the twentieth century, characterized by the first wave of globalization and substantial economic transformation, though for countries of different levels of initial economic development. One of the few studies considering the very long term, including the second wave of globalization after World War II, is Ronsse and Rayp (2016), who analyzed industrial location in Belgium.

The MK model considers location of industry as function of the correlation between region and industry characteristics, for which data are required at the region level, the industry level, and the region-industry level. Hence, the model is quite demanding in the amount of quantitative data needed. As regards the determinants included, there is a clear common denominator between the different studies in terms of the regional and industry characteristics. Table 9.1 gives a summary.

Data availability implied that proxies for industrial location are constructed in terms of employment rather than output, and proxies for endowments

Table 9.1 Industrial and regional characteristics included in the studies of industrial location using the Midelfart-Knarvik framework

Regional characteristics	*Industrial characteristics*	*Interaction effects*
Heckscher-Ohlin factors		
Land endowment		
• Agricultural farm land (Klein and Crafts 2012; Ronsse and Rayp 2016)/ share agricultural employment (Crafts and Mulatu 2005; Missiaia 2019)/ agricultural production (Martinez-Galarraga 2012)	• Agricultural input (% total costs or output)	• Agricultural endowment x agricultural input
Energy endowment		
• Coal abundance (Crafts and Mulatu 2005; Klein and Crafts 2012)/mines (Ronsse and Rayp 2016)/ mineral output (Wolf 2007)/ coal price (Missiaia 2019)\ hydroelectric power production (Missiaia 2019)/waterpower production (Missiaia 2019)	• Coal input (Nikolic 2018; Ronsse and Rayp 2016)/fuel intensity (Wolf 2007)/ steam power use (Crafts and Mulatu 2005; Klein and Crafts 2012)/ horsepower use (Missiaia 2019)	• Energy endowment x energy input
• Wood availability (Nikolic 2018)	• Wood intensity (Nikolic 2018)	• Wood availability x wood intensity
Labour endowment		
• Share in total population (Wolf 2007) /active population (Martinez-Gallaraga 2012; Ronsse and Rayp 2016) /labour wages (Nikolic 2018) force	• Labour intensity (Wolf 2007; Martinez-Galarraga 2012; Nikolic 2018; Ronsse and Rayp 2016)	• Labour endowment x labour intensity
Human capital endowment		
• Educated proportion labour force (Crafts and Mulatu 2005; Klein and Crafts 2012)/ literate population (Wolf 2007; Martinez-Galarraga 2012; Nikolic 2018; Ronsse and Rayp 2016; Missiaia 2019)/school achievement (Ronsse and Rayp 2016)	• White-collar worker intensity (Crafts and Mulatu 2005; Klein and Crafts 2012; Wolf 2007; Martinez-Galarraga 2012; Ronsse and Rayp 2016; Missiaia 2019)/ skilled worker intensity (Nikolic 2018)	• Educated population x skilled worker intensity
Physical capital endowment		
• Regional credit allowance (Nikolic 2018)/ deposits per capita (Missiaia 2019)	• Capital stock (Nikolic 2018)/ horsepower use (Missiaia 2019)	• Physical capital endowment x capital intensity
Innovation		
• Innovation (Wolf 2007; Nikolic 2018)	• Patent intensity (Wolf 2007)	• Innovation x patent intensity

Regional characteristics	*Industrial characteristics*	*Interaction effects*
Heckscher-Ohlin factors		
New economic geography factors		
Market potential (Crafts and Mulatu 2005; Klein and Crafts 2012; Wolf 2007; Martinez-Galarraga 2012; Nikolic 2018; Ronsse and Rayp 2016; Missiaia 2019)	• Use of intermediate goods in % of output (Crafts and Mulatu 2005; Klein and Crafts 2012; Wolf 2007; Martinez-Galarraga 2012; Nikolic 2018; Ronsse and Rayp 2016; Missiaia 2019)	• Market potential x Intermediate goods
	• Sales to industry in % of output (Crafts and Mulatu 2005; Klein and Crafts 2012; Martinez-Galarraga 2012; Nikolic 2018; Ronsse and Rayp 2016; Missiaia 2019)	• Market potential x Sales to industry
	• Size (Crafts and Mulatu 2005; Klein and Crafts 2012; Martinez-Galarraga 2012; Nikolic 2018; Ronsse and Rayp 2016; Missiaia 2019)	• Market potential x Size

in terms of factor quantities rather than prices. Whereas the specification of the new economic geography determinants is quite uniform between the studies – the only exceptions being that Wolf (2007) only includes the interaction effect between market potential and intermediate use, and that Nikolic (2018) explicitly distinguishes the domestic from the foreign component of market potential but excludes the interaction effect of market size and economies of scale – the Heckscher-Ohlin part shows much more case specificity. In general, interaction effects in terms of land, energy, and (skilled or unskilled) labour endowment and use are included, though in Wolf (2007) and Nikolic (2018) land interaction effects are lacking, despite that these are found significant in Crafts and Mulatu (2005), Martinez-Galarraga (2012), and Klein and Crafts (2012). Klein and Crafts (2012), Crafts and Mulatu (2006), and Missiaia (2019) did not take (unskilled) labour interaction effects into account that Martinez-Galarraga (2012) and Ronsse and Rayp (2016) found significant. They find a significant impact of human capital interaction effects, just like Wolf (2007) and Nikolic (2018), who however take both categories of labour (skilled and unskilled) into account. More case-specific endowments (physical capital, innovation, hydroelectric, and water power) are all insignificant, except for innovation in Wolf (2007).

Region and industry characteristics are included in the model in interaction form, as well as separately as control variables. Rather than to try to determine a priori the relevant region and industry characteristics and to control for an omitted variables bias, Wolf (2007), Klein and Crafts (2012), Nikolic (2018), and Missiaia (2019) include region and industry fixed effects. Its main drawback is that the determinants of industrial location remain unidentified but, given that the interaction effects are the main variables of interest, this can be considered to be less of a problem. The main model assumption remains, however, that *only* the interaction effects included are potentially significant, i.e., missing (or error in) variable issues at this level are not solved by a fixed effect estimation.

Market potential is mostly calculated according to the approach first proposed by Harris (1954) as the sum of the size (M) of the home and neighbouring regions, weighted by the distance (D) to the home region *i*: $MP_i = \sum_j \left({M_j}/{D_{ij}} \right)$. As indicator of size, most studies use Gross Domestic Product (GDP), though in general, historical GDP data at the regional level are not available. Following Crafts and Mulatu (2005) and provided that the data are available, the Geary and Stark (2002) approximation of regional GDP is used, which assumes that regional to national average output per worker in industry *k* is proportional with regional to the nationwide wage in industry *k*. From this, the output per worker by region and industry is derived. Multiplied by regional employment by sector and summed over all sectors gives then the GDP of region *i*.[4] Market potential has a foreign component as well (the region's export potential and proximity to foreign suppliers of intermediates), which is similarly determined as the distance-weighted sum of the GDP of the country's main trading partners. In the distance discounting of regional GDP, Crafts and Mulatu (2005), Martinez-Gallarraga (2012), and Missiaia (2019) correct for transportation modes by converting sea shipping in miles to a land-based equivalent based on data of transportation costs.

A theoretically more accurate proxy of market potential would use an estimate of the bilateral good flows between regions that can be obtained from a gravity estimation of bilateral trade. For two regions (countries) *r* and *s*, the exports from *r* to *s* are modelled as (e.g. Combes et al. 2008):

$$\ln X_{rs} = FX_r + \ln \phi_{rs} + FM_s + \varepsilon_{rs}$$

where ϕ_{rs} represents the distance between regions (countries) *r* and *s*. FX_r and FM_s are respectively exporter and importer fixed effects, of which the latter is an estimate of the market potential of region *s*. Summing FM_s over all regions *s* then gives the market potential of region *r*. The obvious obstacle to this approach is data availability of bilateral regional flows of goods. Intraregional trade flow data are probably even more demanding than regional GDP data. Therefore,

Wolf (2007), who considered Polish regions that belonged to different countries before World War I, is the only example where a gravity equation is used to estimate market potential (although a "naïve" gravity model, using GDP rather than exporter and importer fixed effects). Also, Klein and Crafts (2012) adopted the Harris (1954) approach of market potential for their study of the industry location at the US state level. Martinez-Galarraga (2012) combines the Harris approach for the domestic component of market potential with gravity estimates of bilateral trade for its foreign component.

The dependent variable in the MK model is the location coefficient of region *i* in industry *k* (see page 214), though only Wolf (2007) estimates the model as such. All other studies use the regional share in the output (or employment) in industry *k* as regressand, but either add the regional share in total manufacturing output (employment) as control variable (such that denominator of the location coefficient is included in the model, though not with an identical coefficient as the numerator) or regional fixed effects (which controls for the regional output share in manufacturing). Table 9.2 gives an overview of the model estimation results, in terms of the mechanisms of industrial location found significant and their respective weights.

In general, all present studies conclude to the significance of both endowments and market potential in the regional location of industry. Table 9.2, however, makes clear that the variability in the estimates is substantial both *between* the two categories of determinants (i.e., the relative weight) and *within* each category (the specific mechanisms that were found significant). Whereas for the United States, market potential is the dominant if not the sole determinant of location, in the United Kingdom (at least in the twentieth century) and Italy, the opposite was found. Other studies conclude to a more or less equal weight of both categories, except Ronsse and Rayp (2016), who see an evolution from location determined by endowments and market potential at the end of the nineteenth century to a dominating impact of the latter determinant in the twentieth century.

As regards the new economic geography determinants of location, indications are found for scale as well as linkage effects, though only for the United States both simultaneously. For the European countries, linkage effects of location seem to be found in the early stages of industrial development, which is theoretically not so straightforward. Nikolic (2018) refers in this respect to the export-led industrialization (as well as the need to import intermediate goods) that would be relevant for countries lagging in economic development.

Concerning the endowments that determine location, we notice a fairly high volatility of determinants within the period of study. Few endowments are found to be persistently significant. The most robust determinant seems to be human capital, which in view of the remark of Klein and Crafts (2012), mentioned in Martinez-Galarraga (2012: 272), "that in the 'factory-production' phase of manufacturing, physical capital was a substitute for skill and technological advance was downgrading the role of skilled labour", may seem somewhat puzzling. In addition, while energy (coal availability) is significant in at least one estimation in

Table 9.2 Summary of the model estimation results

Country	*Source*	*Heckscher-Ohlin determinants*	*New economic geography determinants*	*Weight of Heckscher-Ohlin and new economic geography determinants*
United Kingdom	Crafts and Mulatu (2005)	Human capital (1871–1931) Energy (1871–1931) Agriculture (1871–1911)	Scale (1871–1911)	(0, 100)
Poland	Wolf (2007)	Human capital (1926–1934) Innovation (1926–1934)	Linkages (1926–1934)	(60,40)
Spain	Martinez-Galarraga (2012)	Agriculture (1856, 1929) Energy (1913) Labour (1893,1913)	Scale (1893–1929)	(50,50)
United States	Klein and Crafts (2012)		Scale (1880–1920) Linkages (1880–1920)	(100, 0)
Belgium	Ronsse and Rayp (2016)	Energy (1896)	Scale (1937, 1961)	(66,33) (1896); (100,0) (1937, 1961)
Yugoslavia	Nikolic (2018)	Human capital (1932–1939)	Linkages (1932–1939)	(60,25)
Italy	Missiaia (2019)	Human capital (1871–1911) Energy (1871)	Linkages (1871–1881) Scale (1911)	(75, 25) (1871,1881) (90,10) (1891–1911)

several studies, labour availability is almost never significant (though not included in several studies). However, just like market potential, human capital endowment could be endogenous with industrial location (e.g., if there is an impact of industrial concentration on public goods provision – like schooling, or because of people moving to areas of industrial location). In the present literature, this doesn't seem to be examined thoroughly.

It is not straightforward at first sight to find a pattern in the variability of the results. For example, the estimations for the United Kingdom and Italy are very similar, despite their difference in industrial development at the turn of the twentieth century; whereas emerging economies at that time, like Poland, Yugoslavia, and Spain, with a similar level of development, have a quite distinct pattern of location. Perhaps the clearest conclusion that can be drawn from these studies is the strength of the new economic geography factors in the largest economy with a unified market and the lowest trade costs, namely the United States, of which Klein and Crafts (2012) claim – in contrast with Kim (1995) – that industrial location is exclusively determined by scale and linkage effects. On the other hand, for the fragmented, national economies in Europe (with lower factor mobility and higher trade costs), endowments are systematically found to be as important, if not more so, than market potential. This would suggest that in terms of Heckscher-Ohlin and new economic geography determinants, that European market unification after World War II may have had an impact on industrial location, perhaps exceeding that of national market integration at the turn of the century. Therefore, it might be interesting to extend the analysis to the second half of the twentieth century – for which, in addition, data availability is less of a concern.

Finally, only one study ventures a more detailed economic interpretation of the estimation results, namely Klein and Crafts (2012), who verify the impact on industrial location of a 10% increase (decrease) in the four states with the lowest (highest) market potential. With a range of 13 to 27% (29 to 44%), this is quite substantial but intuitively not implausible. Other studies just give an indication of the relative weight of Heckscher-Ohlin and new economic geography determinants (by calculating standardized coefficients) but remain silent about the level of the expected effects, in particular whether these are within a reasonable and economic significant range. This more general and less quantitative interpretation makes it harder to evaluate their contribution and assess their methodological choices.[5]

9.5 Methodological challenges?

The variability of the estimation results beyond the fairly unsurprising conclusion that overall, both endowments and market potential matter for industrial location, may reflect country-specificity of industrial location, e.g., as a consequence of idiosyncratic geographical characteristics. However, the lack of robustness of the results could as well be the consequence of a number of methodological challenges that need consideration. In the first place, we think of the following three issues.

First, we examine the level of aggregation in the analysis. Kim (1995: 884) already pointed to the need for defining "an appropriate regional unit of analysis and the proper level of industry aggregation". In this perspective, the theoretical framework one adopts is relevant:

> If one uses a model of regional specialization based on external economies, the regional unit should be defined such that the external economies are potentially strong within a region but less so across regions. If one employs the Heckscher-Ohlin framework, factors should be mobile within the region but less so across regions.
>
> (Kim 1995: ibid.)

Similarly, the industry aggregation level should be defined such that external economies are strong within but much less between industries, and that factor intensities within the industry are sufficiently similar and distinct from other industries. Rosenthal and Strange (2001) estimated the determinants of agglomeration for the United States at three different geographical scales and showed that the determinants of concentration depend on the spatial scale considered. One may conjecture that the impact of transportation costs (hence market potential) will appear more clearly in an analysis at a spatially more detailed level that captures better the impact of proximity, and that an analysis at a spatially higher aggregated level could be biased in favour of endowments as determinants.

Probably because of data availability constraints, in none of the studies considered here is the appropriate spatial level of analysis explicitly dealt with. Crafts and Mulatu (2005) and Missiaia (2019), who found the weakest new economic geography effects, define fairly aggregate spatial units (respectively ten and sixteen regions), whereas Martinez-Galarraga (2012) and Ronsse and Rayp (2016), who conclude to much stronger new economic geography effects, analyze spatial concentration at the NUTS-3 level. Admittedly, Wolf (2007) and Klein and Crafts (2012) find a strong new economic geography impact of location at a spatial aggregation level similar to Crafts and Mulatu (2005) and Missiaia (2019).

Second, the industry characteristics included in the model are taken from available input-output tables that register the use of intermediate goods, sales to other industries, and the use of factor inputs, from which indicators of input intensity can be constructed. As input-output tables are a tool developed in the twentieth century, the first editions in most cases go back at the earliest to the 1930s. Crafts and Mulatu (2005), Klein and Crafts (2012), and Missiaia (2019) were able to use some input-output estimates for the nineteenth century. Other studies extrapolate input-output data from the 1930s–1950s.

Obviously, this causes error in variables. Whatever the direction of the error (either an underestimation or overestimation of the factor and intermediate good intensities), this results in an OLS estimate of $\beta[j]$ biased towards zero (the *attenuation bias*).[6] Even if the measurement error is uncorrelated with the stochastic error term of the empirical model, this implies an underestimation of the true significance of the variables in the model. In addition, the attenuation bias of measurement can be exacerbated for the interaction terms (the product of the industry characteristics derived from the input-output tables and those of the region), which are the variables of interest in the model. Available input-output tables may also have an impact on the relevant scale of analysis, given that for a number of countries they could only be constructed for a fairly small number of rather aggregated industries that are less well distinguished in terms of externalities or factor intensities. Martinez-Galarraga (2012) and Ronsse and Rayp (2016) have data for only seven industries; Wolf (2007) and Nikolic (2018) have data for ten industries.

Scholars should therefore be encouraged to build detailed input-output tables that go further back in time. Alternatively, provided that (relative) factor and intermediate good prices do not differ too much from the British in the second half of the nineteenth century such that technology can be assumed to be comparable, one could consider estimating the model using the Crafts and Mulatu (2005) factor and intermediate good intensities for the United Kingdom. Wolf (2007) proceeded already in this sense, by taking the input-output table of Germany for 1936 to proxy the use of intermediates in the Polish industry.[7]

Third, there is a clear case of simultaneity bias when regional market potential is included as an explanatory variable of the location of economic activity (the larger the region's share in industrial activity, the higher the region's market potential). This is the methodological problem to which attention is paid in most studies, and which is coped with by instrumental variable estimation. Wolf (2007) and Martinez-Galarraga (2012) use lagged market potential as instrument, whereas Klein and Crafts (2012), Ronsse and Rayp (2016), and Nikolic (2018) use an indicator of centrality. Therein, the first two do not impose an explicit centre, while the latter considers the distance to the main economic centre abroad (Berlin) or the distance to the three main regional centres. Only in Wolf (2007) does instrumenting seem to have a substantial impact on the coefficient estimations as well as their significance.

Might this disagreement about the instrument used qualify their adequacy? An adequate instrument should meet the conditions of exogeneity, i.e., orthogonality with respect to the error term, as well as relevance, i.e., a strong correlation with the endogenous determinant(s). Exogeneity implies the *exclusion* restriction, i.e., instrument(s) that do not affect the dependent variable directly or through unmeasured variables, and the absence of reverse causation between the dependent variable and the instrument(s). Almost all the studies considered report that the instruments used are relevant, yet do not deal with the exogeneity condition explicitly. If more instruments are available than endogenous regressors, then indications about the exogeneity of the instruments can be obtained from a test on overidentified restrictions. Given that this test necessarily assumes the exogeneity of at least as many instruments as endogenous regressors, it is however never sufficient. The case of none of the instruments meeting the exclusion restriction cannot be tested.

Only Klein and Crafts (2012) test for exogeneity by overidentifying restrictions. In the presence of path dependency (i.e., persistency in economic centres) of which significant indications are found in Nikolic (2018), "centre-neutral" indicators of centrality, like the ones used by Klein and Crafts (2012) and Ronsse and Rayp (2016),[8] are more convincing in terms of exogeneity than lagged market potential or distance to economic centre(s). Because of persistence in industrial location, lagged market potential may affect present concentration in employment through other channels as well. Yet, Martinez-Galarraga (2012) and Nikolic (2018) report the irrelevance (weakness) of these instruments for the cases they study.

There are few alternatives for instrumental variables (IV) estimation to deal with endogeneity, though. Even in the case of a large exogeneous shock, which disrupts the feedback effects from employment concentration on market potential, Wolf (2007) or for that matter, Nikolic (2018), use IV to estimate their model (even with the most substantial impact on the results in the case of Wolf 2007). Therefore, it seems unlikely that a natural experiment setting solves the endogeneity issue. However, one might explore the method Lewbel (2012) proposes to cope with mismeasurement of variables or a simultaneity bias. He shows that in the presence of heteroscedasticity in the error terms (which in the case of industrial location is more than likely) and, provided that restrictions can be imposed on the structure of this heteroscedasticity, then the correlation of (a subset of) the exogenous variables in the model with the second moment of the error terms provides valid instruments for the potentially endogenous or mismeasured variables. Besides of its ease of application, the main advantage of this approach is the redundancy of external variables as instruments, which can be important when data are not abundantly available, like in a historical framework.

9.6 Conclusion

Together with the increasing availability of (digitalized) historical data, the new economic geography approach to economic location and spatial equilibrium that emerged in the 1990s led to a surge in the quantitative historical analysis of industrial location. From Crafts and Mulatu (2005) onwards, an enlarging set of country studies used a common model based on Midelfart-Knarvik et al. (2000). In this model, industrial location is considered as a function of the correlation between region and industry characteristics and takes two categories of determinants into account: endowments (or Heckscher-Ohlin determinants) and scale effects, and backward and forward linkages (the new economic geography determinants). The attractiveness of the model is the integration of the main determinants of different location theories into one framework, allowing estimation of their respective weight and evaluation of the validity of the different hypotheses about industrial location in the past.

The convergence of different studies in methodology and even in the variables included (and definition of the data) enable comparing the results more easily, to identify common findings and country specificities. There is seemingly a consensus that overall, both classes of location determinants matter. However, the quite strong impact of Heckscher-Ohlin determinants for a number of European countries may come as a surprise, just like the theoretically less expected significant endowment categories and the volatility of the determinants between countries as well as over time. The contrast with the United States regarding the impact of endowments on industrial location may suggest that market fragmentation and trade costs (more comprehensive than mere transportation costs) have weakened the effect of market potential on location in Europe. In this respect, it may be interesting to verify the impact of market integration on industrial location after World War II.

High volatility of the results could of course be the consequence of methodological complications as well. In particular, we distinguish three that scholars in future research may want to address: the relevant level of aggregation when analyzing industrial location, measurement error in the industrial characteristics, and the adequacy of the instruments to control for endogeneity in the model estimation.

Notes

1 In view of the Starrett Impossibility Theorem, the assumption of perfect competition and constant returns to scale in a framework highlighting the location choice may be surprising. One may ask how, with these assumptions, regional autarky is avoided. Assuming constant returns to scale implies that there is no scale penalty and the goods can be equally efficiently produced at any arbitrary scale. Perfect divisibility then allows production of all varieties locally, thus avoiding transportation costs and resulting in autarkic regional equilibria. However, this is excluded in the Midelfart-Knarvik model by assuming an exogenously limited number of varieties that can be produced in each region and industry. Love of variety then implies that there will be trade between regions (there will always be a positive demand for a variety, whatever the price) and, therefore, that location matters.

2 i.e., the output share of industry *k* in region *i* (z_i^k) divided by the share of region *i* in total production $\left(\sum_k z_i^k\right)$ and the share of industry *k* in total production $\left(\sum_i z_i^k\right)$, i.e. the location coefficient: $\dfrac{z_i^k \Big/ \sum_i z_i^k}{\sum_k z_i^k}$.

3 They give together with the parameter estimate of the interaction effect, an estimate of the region and industry reference level, $\bar{x}[j]$ and $\bar{y}[j]$.

4 The factor of proportion is such that the GDP of industry k at the country level (Y_k) equals the sum of the regional estimations, i.e., $\beta_k = \dfrac{Y_k}{\sum_i y_k \frac{w_{ik}}{w_k} L_{ik}}$. Inserting this in the expression for regional GDP $\left(Y_i = \sum_k y_{ik} L_{ik} = \sum_k y_k \beta_k \frac{w_{ik}}{w_k} L_{ik}\right)$ gives $Y_i = \sum_k Y_k \dfrac{w_{ik} L_{ik}}{\sum_i w_{ik} L_{ik}}$, i.e., regional GDP as the sum of national GDP by industry, weighted by the regional share in the total wage sum.

5 An economic interpretation of the results, i.e., the impact of endowment or market potential variation on industrial location, requires that the variables are included in the model as interaction effects as well as separately, in order to have the total effect on location. This precludes the estimation of the Midelfart-Knarvik model with fixed region and industry fixed effects.

6 See, e.g., Johnston and Di Nardo (1997)

7 Measurement error is, of course, a more general concern than the sales and use linkages between sectors. Regarding the *region characteristics*, the sources most often used are population, agricultural, and socioeconomic censuses – to the most available every ten years. Some variables can readily be found. For others, proxies must be taken or extrapolations have to be made. Usually, indicators of natural endowments like the number of mines and agricultural surface are readily available, just like the location of industry if proxied with regional employment by industry, rather than output or turnover. Indicators for skill endowments tend to differ (and evolve) over time and are therefore period specific. Data on the nineteenth century usually include the literacy rate, whereas for the twentieth century, indicators of

specific employment categories (e.g., white-collar workers) or the number of years of education are more common (and relevant).

8 Following the suggestion of Head and Mayer (2006).

References

Brühlhart, M. 2003. "Economic geography, industrial location and trade: the evidence." *World Economy* 21(6): 775–801.

Combes, P., T. Mayer, and J. Thisse. 2008. *Economic geography: the integration of regions and nations.* Cambridge: MIT Press.

Crafts, N. F. R., and A. Mulatu. 2005. "What explains the location of industry in Britain, 1871–1931?" *Journal of Economic Geography* 5(4): 499–518.

Crafts, N. F. R., and A. Mulatu. 2006. "How did the location of industry respond to falling transport costs in Britain before World War I?" *The Journal of Economic History* 66(3): 575–607.

Davis, D., and D. Weinstein. 2003. "Market access, economic geography and comparative advantage: an empirical test." *Journal of International Economics* 59(1): 1–23.

Geary, F., and T. Stark. 2002. "Examining Ireland's post-famine economic growth performance." *The Economic Journal* 112(482): 919–935.

Harris, C. D. 1954. "The market as a factor in the localization of industry in the United States." *Annals of the Association of American Geographers* 44(4): 315–348.

Head, K., and T. Mayer. 2006. "Regional wage and employment responses to market potential in the EU." *Regional Science and Urban Economics* 36(5): 573–594.

Johnston, J., and J. Di Nardo. 1997. *Econometric methods.* New York: McGraw Hill.

Kim, S. 1995. "Expansion of markets and the geographic distribution of economic activities: the trends in U.S. regional manufacturing structure, 1860–1987." *The Quarterly Journal of Economics* 110(4): 881–908.

Klein, A., and N. Crafts. 2012. "Making sense of the manufacturing belt: determinants of U.S. industrial location, 1880–1920." *Journal of Economic Geography* 12: 775–807.

Krugman, P. 1991. "Increasing returns and economic geography." *Journal of Political Economy* 99(3): 483–499.

Lewbel, A. 2012. "Using heteroscedasticity to identify and estimate mismeasured and endogenous regressor models." *Journal of Business and Economic Statistics* 30(1): 67–80.

Martinez-Galarraga, J. 2012. "The determinants of industrial location in Spain, 1856–1929." *Explorations in Economic History* 49(2): 255–275.

Midelfart-Knarvik, K. H., H. G. Overman, S. J. Redding, and A. J. Venables. 2000. *Comparative advantage and economic geography: estimating the location of production in the EU.* CEPR Discussion Paper, 2618, London, CEPR.

Missiaia, A. 2019. "Market versus endowment: explaining early industrial location in Italy (1871–1911)." *Cliometrica* 13(1): 127–161.

Nikolic, S. 2018. "Determinants of industrial location: Kingdom of Yugoslavia in the interwar period." *European Review of Economic History* 22(1): 101–133.

Ronsse, S., and G. Rayp. 2016. "What determined the location of industry in Belgium, 1896–1961?" *Journal of Interdisciplinary History* 46(3): 393–419.

Rosenthal, S., and W. Strange. 2001. "The determinants of agglomeration." *Journal of Urban Economics* 50(2): 191–229.

Rosés, J. 2003. "Why isn't the whole of Spain industrialized? New economic geography and early industrialization, 1797–1910." *Journal of Economic History* 63(4): 995–1022.

Starrett, D. 1978. "Market allocations of location choice in a model with free mobility." *Journal of Economic Theory* 17(1): 21–37.

Wolf, N. 2007. "Endowments vs. market potential: what explains the relocation of industry after the polish reunification in 1918?" *Explorations in Economic History* 44(1): 22–42.

10 Regional industrialization

Evidence on industry agglomeration[1]

Bas van Leeuwen, Péter Földvári, Robin C. M. Philips, and Meimei Wang

10.1 Introduction

The tendency of industries to cluster in some areas is well known since the publication of Alfred Marshall's (1890) *Principles of Economics*. As Marshall (1890) pointed out, benefits of agglomeration were crucial in the localization of industries. Whereas initially firms located based on factors such as the presence of raw materials, in the course of time these primitive locational pull-factors could develop additional advantages such as the development of local skills and subsidiary trades, which make them develop in what Marshall coined "industrial districts" (e.g. Belussi and Caldari 2009). By co-location or locating near firms of the same sector, firms could benefit from scale effects by sharing nearby people, goods, and ideas and potential agglomeration spillover effects, in turn developing in such districts. For instance, Marshall pointed at the end of the nineteenth century in England to the clustering of knitted/worsted textile manufacture and cutlery manufacturing as examples of such industrial districts.

Studies testing agglomeration and co-location are plentiful but suffer from two drawbacks. First, these publications predominantly feature case studies in Europe and the United States (e.g. Combes and Overman 2004). Only recently have studies on other parts of the world emerged – such as on India (e.g. Shukla 1996), Japan (e.g. Mori and Smith 2011), and China (e.g. Guo and Cai 2000; Brakman et al. 2016) – which have contributed to our understanding of different patterns of agglomeration due to, for example, differences in institutions or government policy. Yet, the continuing lack of comparative studies between Western and non-Western regions places a barrier on our knowledge of such differences. Second, most studies draw upon data for the recent period, with the exception of Meyer (1998) and Crafts and Wolf (2014), thereby limiting our understanding of the evolution of co-location over time. Nonetheless, these studies have proven the relevance of looking at the past to understand present-day patterns of agglomeration. Indeed, Meyer (1998) showed that although for New England during the period of 1790–1820, initial conditions mattered at first, different factors such as subsidiary economic sectors increased in importance over time, thus creating industrial districts. Likewise, Crafts and Wolf (2014) showed that initial conditions such as access to waterpower were crucial for the clustering of cotton textiles in the United Kingdom in 1838.

Therefore, to gain a clearer view on co-location patterns, one needs to include comparative samples, using both a long timeframe and global coverage. In this chapter, we use two recent and two historical samples: two Dutch manufacturing firms in 1896 and 2010, and two manufacturing firms in the Chinese province of Hunan in 1954 and 2004 (Section 10.2). The choice of the historical data (1896 for the Netherlands and 1954 for Hunan) is based on data availability, as both draw upon recently developed datasets that provide us with unique micro-geographic data for historical periods (Hunan Provincial Archives 1954; Philips 2019). We argue that both datasets, combined with twenty-first-century data, allow us to gain insight to some extent into time-varying drivers of co-location.

Of course, the regions differ greatly. Whereas the Netherlands has a long coastline in addition to the multitude of rivers and canals in its regions, Hunan is a landlocked region with few accessible waterways. In addition, whereas the Netherlands is geographically very low relative to sea level, Hunan is a mountainous region, with the Wuling, Xuefeng, Luoxiao, and Nanling mountains running through its territory. Nonetheless, although we should bear in mind the limitations of this comparison, we argue that both regions present an ideal case study to compare a region that is representative for a West European, open market economy and a region that is representative for an Asian region in which planned government policy played a larger role. Our comparison of these two different regions therefore aims to see whether, notwithstanding the differences between the regions, we can find commonalities and differences in the patterns of co-location in both benchmark years between these regions.

By using the Duranton and Overman (2005) method, we measure co-location for both regions for four selected industry sectors (see Sections 10.3 and 10.4). For both the Netherlands (1896–2010) and Hunan (1954–2004), we find an increase in the inter-firm distances, with most sampled industry sectors in both countries becoming less co-located over the course of the twentieth century. However, we find large differences across both sectors and countries. In Section 10.5, we focus on explaining these patterns of co-location by one of the most stressed factors in explaining the decline of co-location over time: the decline in transport costs. In line with the new economic geography literature, which emphasizes the role of the fall of transport costs as a major factor in de-clustering, we measure the distance from establishments to different hubs of transport infrastructure: the distance to nearest roads, railroads, and navigable and non-navigable waterways; and the distance to centres of consumers. Based on these results, we can attribute the decrease in co-location in most sectors to a shift away from rail and river transport to road transport, an evolution which removed many benefits from a shared proximity of goods and labour in the former clusters, in both the Netherlands and China. Even though government policy was important in China, our findings confirm that the co-location patterns there mostly followed the theoretical assessments in the new economic geography literature, similar to the Netherlands, confirming the dominance of initial conditions and Marshallian externalities even within regions under a strong influence of public policy. In Section 10.6, we conclude.

10.2 Data and method

Measuring industrial agglomeration is heavily influenced by the choice of methodology. In recent years, two main methodologies of measuring co-location among industrial firms have gained importance. First is the dartboard approach developed by Ellison and Glaeser (1997), which became a widely used application among spatial economists (e.g. Devereux et al. 1999; Maurel and Sédillot 1999). Essentially, this method measures the agglomeration of an industry sector in specific spatial units (e.g., county, province, country) as darts thrown randomly on a map. Second, there is the distance-based method (Duranton and Overman 2005, 2008), which has become widely used by economic geographers (e.g. Puga 2010; Delgado et al. 2014), and which uses distances between establishments to study agglomeration of industries. Essentially, this method uses latitudes and longitudes to calculate inter-firm distances.

In practice, both methods have their advantages but also their disadvantages. The disadvantages of the Duranton and Overman method are twofold. Not only is it computationally intensive but it also calculates a general level of clustering without making clear in which region, city, or other spatial unit the clustering is highest (e.g. Kosfeld et al. 2011). The approach of Ellison and Glaeser (1997), on the other hand, uses aggregated data, as it allocates manufacturing companies to aggregated spatial units. However, this in turn leads to a possible modifiable areal unit problem, as the aggregate value can vary greatly over the size of the spatial units for which the variables are collected (Yule and Kendall 1950; Cressie 1993).

As it is easier to obtain aggregated data across spatial units than to obtain data with micro-geographic coordinates, it is no surprise that the few publications in economic history on this topic have opted for the dartboard method (e.g. Meyer 1998; Crafts and Wolf 2014). Yet, the modifiable areal unit problem is especially important when studying agglomeration over time, as the construction and change of boundaries often reflect a historical evolution grounded in an economic and political, and therefore non-random, process that potentially biases the results. For instance, politically motivated boundaries changed strongly over the nineteenth and twentieth centuries in many countries, in particular in China (Li 2001; Lin 2004; Fu and Zheng 2007). Therefore, we argue that the Duranton and Overman (2005) method provides a more efficient method for economic history studies, for which reason we opt for this method in this chapter.

For the Duranton and Overman (2005) method, we first have to assess the concentration of establishments with respect to their industry by calculating the Euclidian distance between every pair of establishments. For an industry with n establishments, there are $n\ (n - 1)$ unique bilateral distances between establishments. Second, because these Euclidian distances are only a proxy for true physical distances, we kernel-smooth to estimate the distribution of bilateral distances;

more specifically, we denote by $d_{i,j}$ the Euclidian distance between establishments i and j. With n establishments, the estimator of the density of bilateral distances (henceforth k-density) at any distance d is:

$$K(d) = \frac{1}{n(n-1)h} \sum_{i=1}^{n-1} \sum_{j=i+1}^{n} f\left(\frac{d - d_{i,j}}{h}\right) \tag{1}$$

where h is the bandwidth and f is the kernel function. All densities are calculated using a Gaussian kernel with optimal bandwidth (Silverman 1986).

Besides the choice of model, we face the decision of which industrial sectors to select. Following the seminal work by Duranton and Overman (2005, 2008), we have selected four sectors for analysis. Duranton and Overman (2005: 5) chose their four sectors based on "illustrative purposes". More specifically, they used the manufacture of dairy, the manufacture of ceramic products, the manufacture of hinges and locks, and the manufacture of electric domestic products. With this selection, Duranton and Overman (2005) followed the examples of clustering identified by Marshall (1890: 155): cutlery in Sheffield, furniture in Wycombe, and pottery in Staffordshire. In their 2008 study, Duranton and Overman (2008) used pharmaceuticals, derived pharmaceuticals, agricultural machinery, and textile machinery products.

Given the complexity of historical data collection, we decided to follow a pragmatic approach in our selection of four sectors. Based on the International Standard Industrial Classification (ISIC) Revision 4 classification system, we selected four industries for which our datasets on historical and present-day China and historical and present-day Netherlands provide a sufficiently large number of observations: manufacture of bakery products (ISIC 1071), manufacture of carpets and rugs (ISIC 1393), manufacture of casting of iron and steel (ISIC 2431), and manufacture of cutlery, hand tools, and general hardware (ISIC 2593).

For each of our samples, we focus on large establishments, which are defined as above ten employees in China and above twenty employees in the Netherlands. This choice is based on two practical issues. First, micro-geographic data on firms below these thresholds proved unobtainable for both historical samples, as sources documenting the addresses for small firms in nineteenth century Netherlands and early twentieth century China are nonexistent. Second, one may argue that handicraft or family labour follows different co-location patterns compared with large firms, patterns that cannot be compared to modern factories, rendering a comparison between historical and contemporary co-location for all firms potentially irrelevant.

For our sample on 2004 Hunan, we use the 2004 Chinese economic census, which covers all enterprises, excluding those of the self-employed. Unfortunately, calculating the share of large enterprises in the total industry share in Hunan of 1954 is complicated by the lack of complete sectoral data, in addition to the fact that the sectors do not completely match international sectoral classifications such as the ISIC classification. Therefore, we matched each individual factory for

1954 with ISIC classification sectors by taking the sector that most resembled the description of the factory's activities as described in the Hunan Provincial Archives. For instance, we took the rice and wheat grinding sector (碾米磨粉) for ISIC sector 1071, the daily cotton textile industry (日用棉纺) for ISIC sector 1393, the iron and steel smelting industry (钢铁冶炼) for ISIC sector 2431, and the metal products for daily life industry (日用金属制品) for ISIC sector 2593. For our sample of 2004, we matched each China 2000 classification sector with the best-fitting ISIC classification sector, as reported in Table 10.1.

For the Netherlands, we composed samples for two benchmark years: 1896 and 2010. For 1896, we relied on a recently reconstructed census of industry (Philips 2019), which documented larger factories. Large factories in these reports were defined as establishments which employed at least twenty employees; these were then linked to our four selected sectors within the fourth revision of the ISIC classification. Based on the company names, we were able to retrieve the addresses and coordinates of these companies by matching them with a multitude of historical sources, such as address books, private company archives, and advertisements in local newspapers. For 2010, we relied on the extensive LISA dataset of 2010 (Stichting LISA 2015), a privately composed dataset that provided data on the establishment level. Although this survey did not cover all businesses in the Netherlands, it did succeed in capturing the majority of the larger establishments, especially for the manufacturing sector, including their location.[2] To make a comparison with the sample of 1896 possible, we excluded all establishments with fewer than twenty employees. For classifying these companies into sectors, the LISA dataset used the *Standaard Bedrijfsindeling* (SBI), a specific Dutch classification system that did not diverge much from the ISIC classification system. Therefore, we could attribute the best-fitting SBI sectors to ISIC sectors with a correspondence table, the result of which is shown in Table 10.2.

Given the focus on large establishments in our four selected sectors, it is important to first provide an estimate of the share of large establishments in the total industry, to assess the representativeness of our selected samples (see Table 10.3). All in all, the

Table 10.1 Concordance of Chinese manufacturing sectors in 2004 with ISIC Rev 4

ISIC Revision 4 sector	*China 2002 classification*
1071, Manufacture of Bakery Products	1411, Manufacture of Pastry and Bread
	1419, Manufacture of Biscuit and Other Baked Foods
1393, Manufacture of Carpets and Rugs	1759, Other Textile Made-Ups Manufacturing
2431, Casting of Iron and Steel	3210, Iron Making
	3220, Steelmaking
	3230, Rolling Steel Processing
	3240, Ferroalloy Smelting
2593, Manufacture of Cutlery, Hand Tools, and General Hardware	3422, Hand Tools Manufacturing
	3429, Other Metal Tools Manufacturing

Table 10.2 Attribution of Dutch manufacturing sectors in 2010 to ISIC Rev 4

ISIC Revision 4 sector	*Dutch SBI 2008 classification*
1071, Manufacture of Bakery Products	1061, Manufacture of Grain Mill Products 1062, Manufacture of Starches and Starch Products
1393, Manufacture of Carpets and Rugs	1393, Manufacture of Carpets and Rugs
2431, Casting of Iron and Steel	2451, Casting of Iron 2452, Casting of Steel
2593, Manufacture of Cutlery, Hand Tools, and General Hardware	2571, Manufacture of Cutlery 2572, Manufacture of Locks and Hinges 2573, Manufacture of Tools

Table 10.3 Share of modern factories and labourers in total number of factories and labourers by sector in Hunan (China) and the Netherlands

	Hunan				*The Netherlands*			
	1954		*2004*		*1896*		*2010*	
	Labourers	*Factories*	*Labourers*	*Factories*	*Labourers*	*Factories*	*Labourers*	*Factories*
1071, Manufacture of Bakery Products	45.8%	12.5%	91.5%	53.1%	3.7%	0.5%	55.5%	12.5%
1393, Manufacture of Carpets and Rugs	23.1%	0.5%	99.6%	78.3%	20.2%	11.1%	89.5%	82.4%
2431, Casting of Iron and Steel	9.5%	0.5%	99.1%	47.1%	32.6%	27.2%	93.9%	19.7%
2593, Manufacture of Cutlery, Hand Tools, and General Hardware	28.0%	0.6%	99.4%	49.0%	23.0%	7.5%	66.0%	14.9%

Source: For China in 1954, we drew upon Hunan Provincial Archives, File No. 187-1-108. For 2004, we used the Economic Census (China Statistical Office 2004). For the Netherlands in 1896, we used the reconstructed industry census of 1896 (Philips 2019), whereas 2010 was drawn from the LISA dataset (Stichting LISA 2015).

Notes: For Hunan 1954, we selected the following sectors: 1071 or bakery products (碾米磨粉), 1393 or daily cotton textile industry (日用棉纺), 2431 or iron and steel smelting (钢铁冶炼), and 2593 or the manufacture of metal products for daily life (日用金属制品). In addition, the sample of 2004 excludes self-employment.

2004 Hunan and 2010 Netherlands samples represent at least 90% of all employment in their industries, and the 1954 Hunan and 1896 Netherlands samples represent 20–40% of all employment in their industries, though with two notable exceptions. First, the bakery sector in the 1896 Netherlands sample and the iron casting sector in the 1954 Hunan sample represent a small coverage of all employment, due to the dominance of many smaller firms in these sectors at the time. Second, the bakery products and manufacturing of cutlery in the 2010 Netherlands sample represent respectively 55 and 66% of the total industry's share of employment.

10.3 Measuring co-location in the Netherlands (1896–2010)

As a first step, we calculated the average distance between firms in our four sampled sectors in 1896 and 2010 (see Table 10.4). At first sight, it is noticeable that the inter-firm distances increased in the Netherlands over the twentieth century in all four selected sectors. Hence, co-location, proxied by the average inter-firm distances, seems to have decreased. Yet, this dispersion pattern is different across sectors. In 1896, the highest co-located sectors were the manufacture of carpets and rugs (ISIC 1393) and the manufacture of cutlery, hand tools, and general hardware (ISIC 2593), whereas the manufacture of bakery products (ISIC 1071) and the casting of iron and steel (ISIC 2431) appear on average more dispersed. We find that by 2010, both the manufacture of carpets and rugs (ISIC 1393) and the manufacture of cutlery, hand tools, and general hardware (ISIC 2593) remain more dispersed, although they seem to have experienced the largest increase in inter-firm distances during the 1896–2010 period.

Figures 10.1 and 10.2 show the location of all instances for our four selected industries in 1896 and 2010 respectively, where each dot represents a single

Table 10.4 Average distance (km) to nearest establishment across four selected sectors in the Netherlands

	1896		*2010*		*Difference*	
	Mean	*St. Dev.*	*Mean*	*St. Dev.*	*Mean*	*St. Dev.*
Manufacture of Bakery Products (ISIC 1071)	81.32	58.47	100.08	52.83	+23%	−10%
Manufacture of Carpets and Rugs (ISIC 1393)	40.58	39.54	57.50	48.97	+42%	+24%
Casting of Iron and Steel (ISIC 2431)	84.07	50.11	100.33	62.48	+19%	+25%
Manufacture of Cutlery, Hand Tools, and General Hardware (ISIC 2593)	63.43	44.43	89.75	49.28	+41%	+11%

Source: See Table 10.3.

Notes: All distances are expressed in km.

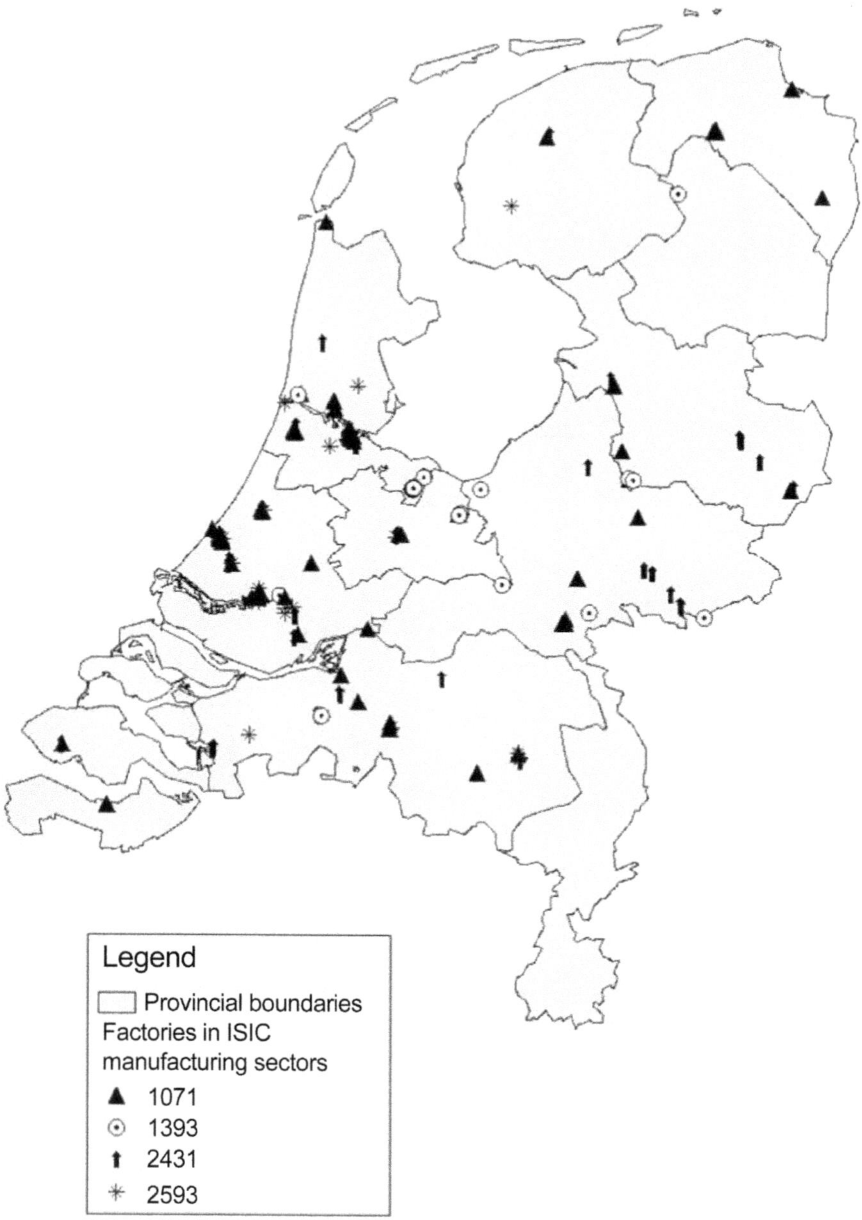

Figure 10.1 Location of large establishments in the Netherlands (1896)

Source: See Table 10.3.

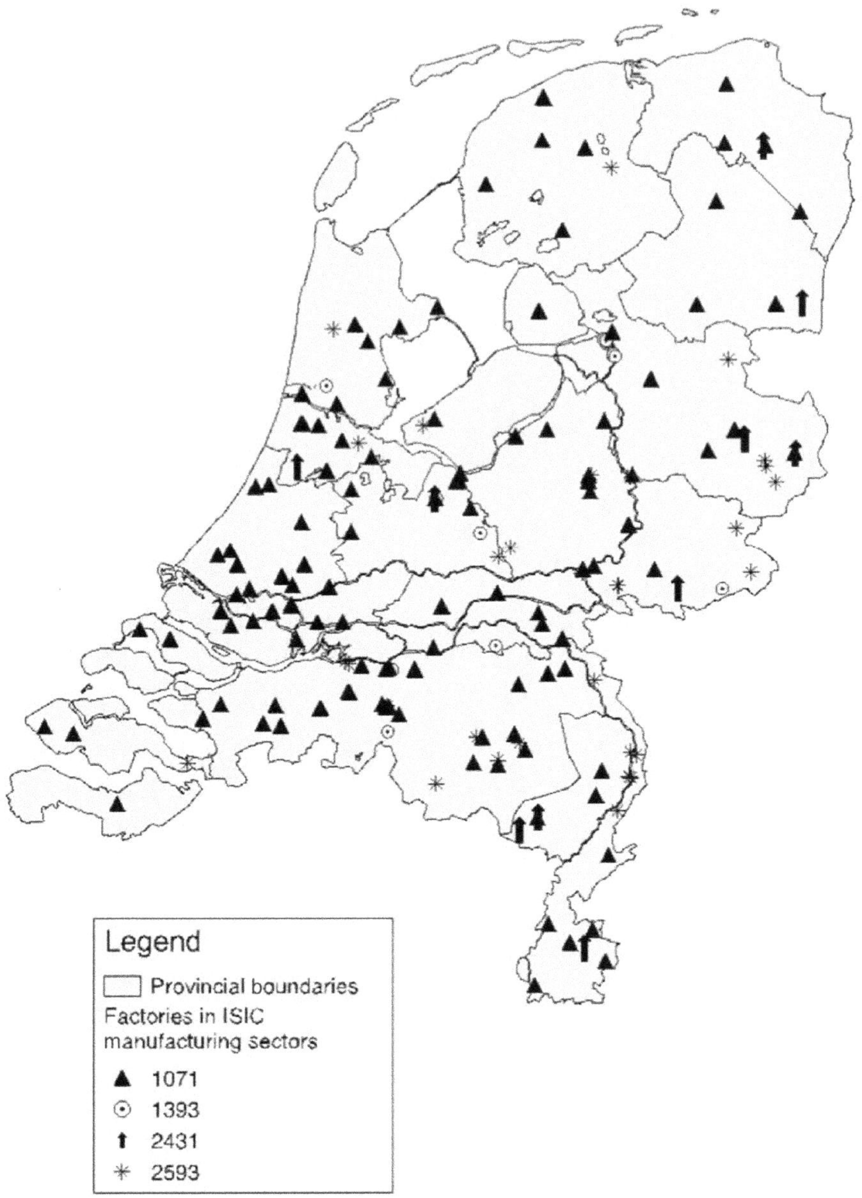

Figure 10.2 Location of large establishments in the Netherlands (2010)

Source: See Table 10.3.

establishment. The first observation we can make when comparing Figures 10.1 and 10.2 is how the establishments are more spatially dispersed in 2010 compared with 1896. Thus, at first sight, co-location and agglomeration seem to have played a larger role in 1896 compared with 2010. In 1896, the manufacturing of carpets and rugs (ISIC 1393), the casting of iron and steel (ISIC 2431), and the manufacturing of cutlery (ISIC 2593) were more concentrated, while the manufacturing of bakery products (ISIC 1071) was highly dispersed over the Dutch territory. The casting of iron and steel (ISIC 2431) and the manufacturing of cutlery (ISIC 2593) are more concentrated in clusters, mainly around the IJssel River in the east and the Maas River in the west; the sector of carpets and rugs manufacturing (ISIC 1393) was clustered near the North Holland and Utrecht border, whereas bakery manufacturing concentrated near larger Dutch cities. Yet, by 2010, we find that all four selected sectors appear more dispersed over the Dutch territory, removing many of these clusters.

Next, we calculated the k-densities for each of our four selected sectors, in order to compare the results of 1896 and 2010. In Figure 10.3, we start with the k-densities of bakery products (ISIC 1071), which reveal a pyramidal structure in both 1896 and 2010. In other words, most firms co-located at a medium distance from each other, with no real clusters, as is evident from the fairly limited share in the lowest percentiles. In 1896, this was due to the lack of large establishments (see Table 10.3), limiting potential benefits for agglomeration. Similarly, De Jonge (1968: 218–219) and Van Zanden (1996: 82) described how in the nineteenth century Netherlands, the market for bread – the most purchased bakery product at that time – was highly fragmented over regional markets. The sector was less open to economics of scale, as retail trade was dominated by small local producers, and multiple regional markets for bread existed due to the high transportation costs of flour. The few larger factories primarily operated in the urbanized, populous, western part of the country within a small selection of large cities, such as Rotterdam, Amsterdam, Haarlem, and The Hague. One of the few larger factories of our dataset compromised a bakery within a military barracks, as the Dutch navy and army were among the few bulk purchasers of bread.

Although the production of bakery products saw an increase in the number of large establishments, the market for bread remained a combination of both larger and smaller firms in 2010. For instance, the market share of larger establishments increased (Table 10.3), with large establishments making up 0.5% of all establishments in 1896 and 12.5% of all establishments in 2010. As the bread market became more specialized over the twentieth century, a less homogenous market was created in which small players could sustain competition. In the 1896–2010 period, a lower share of closely located enterprises – understood here as companies located within less than 50 kilometres from each other – was a result.

Another pattern unfolds for the manufacture of carpets and rugs (ISIC 1393). For this sector, we find a downward-sloping co-location pattern in 1896 and 2010 in Figure 10.4, with a high share of establishments in the lowest percentiles and a low share in the highest percentiles, indicating a clear pattern

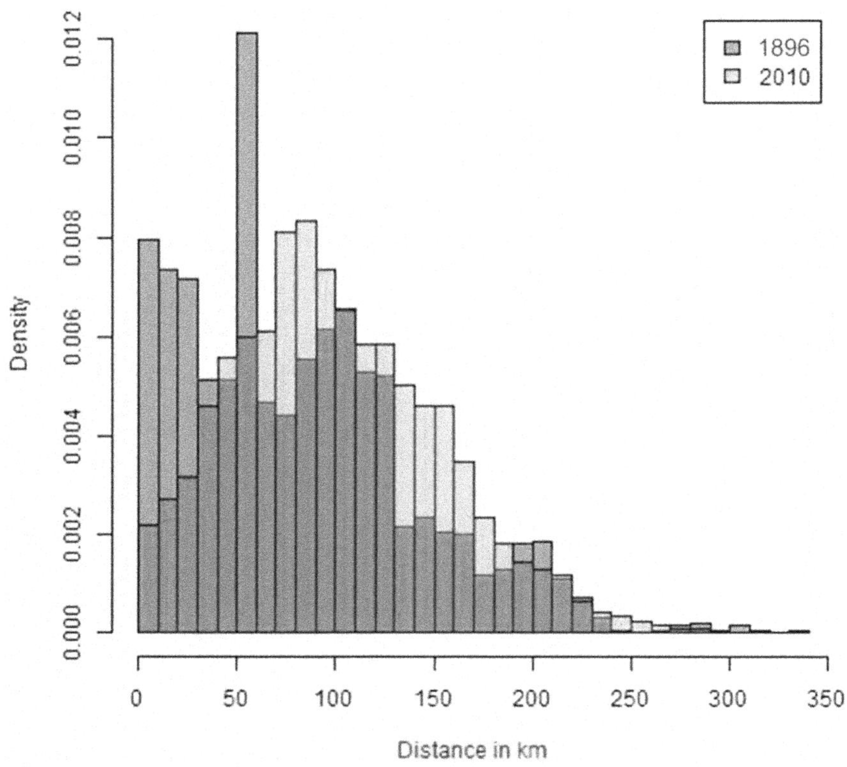

Figure 10.3 Agglomeration in the Manufacture of Bakery Products (ISIC 1071) in the Netherlands

Source: See Table 10.3.

of agglomeration compared with the results for the manufacturing of bakery products. Indeed, in 1896, although the manufacturing of carpets and rugs was still performed by smaller handicraft companies or even by domestic producers, larger factories increasingly took over their market share. Most notably, one cluster emerged in Hilversum, a minor city in the vicinity of Amsterdam, where thirteen of the twenty-nine establishments in this sector were located. As is demonstrated in local historical journals at the end of the nineteenth century, this small city even became known as the Dutch "carpet city" (Van Mensch 1979; Pelgrim 1997). In addition, four factories operated in the direct neighbourhood of Hilversum, in the smaller, nearby villages of Naarden and Laren. Smaller nearby clusters were the cities of Amersfoort and Deventer in the eastern

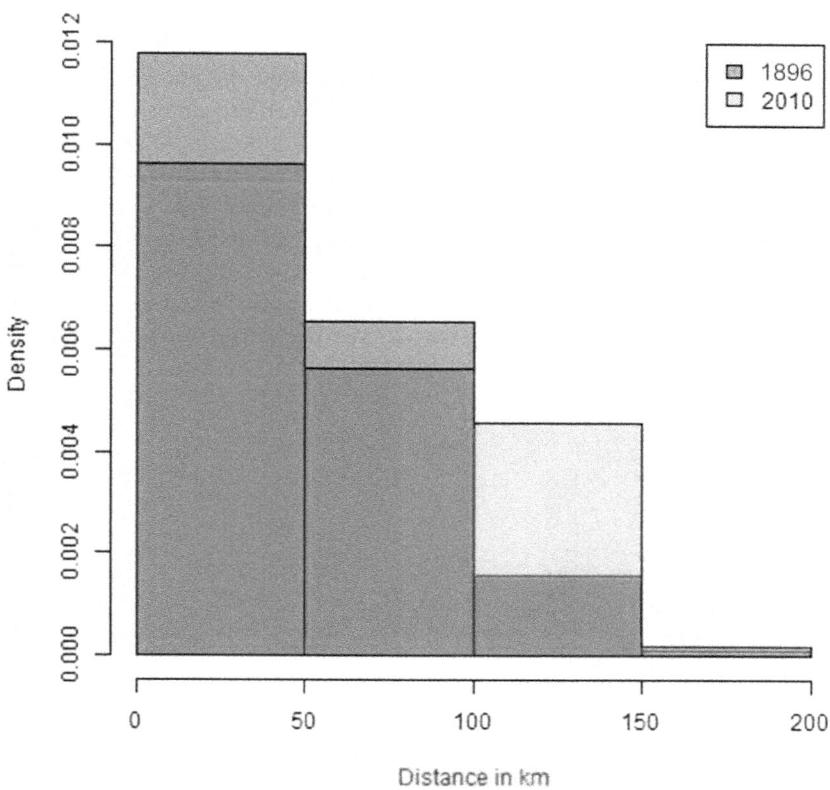

Figure 10.4 Agglomeration in the Manufacture of Carpets and Rugs (ISIC 1393) in the Netherlands

Source: See Table 10.3.

Netherlands, where the textiles sector was of great importance to the regional economy (e.g. Hendrickx 1993).

By 2010, although the Hilversum cluster had completely disappeared from the map, with not a single carpet factory being active within its boundaries in 2010, the sector retained its downward-sloping trend of co-location. Its cause was the emergence of a new cluster – in particular, in Genemuiden, where five out of a total of fifteen factories were located in 2010. Yet, a decline in the lowest percentiles in Figure 10.4 indicates that the Genemuiden cluster failed to reach the relative height of co-location that Hilversum once occupied, indicating an increased level of dispersion in this sector during the 1896–2010 period.

Lastly, we turn to the casting of iron and steel (ISIC 2431) and the manufacture of cutlery, hand tools, and general hardware (ISIC 2593). We find for both sectors an evolution from a downward-sloping co-location pattern in 1896 to a pyramid-like co-location pattern in 2010, indicating a pattern of clustering in 1896 but higher dispersion in 2010 (see Figures 10.5 and 10.6). In the casting of iron and steel, two clusters emerged around the middle of the nineteenth century: one near the IJssel River in the east of the country, and one on the outskirts of the city of Amsterdam (Smit and Van Straalen 2007). Similarly, in cutlery, a cluster emerged around Rotterdam and its nearby regions of Ridderkerk and Nieuw-Lekkerland. While eight of the twenty-eight factories in cutlery were located in the Rotterdam cluster, eight of the forty-six factories of the iron and steel casting sector were located in the IJssel cluster. The historiography stresses two particular factors for the emergence of both clusters in both sectors: the access to water, a necessary input product in the production process of both

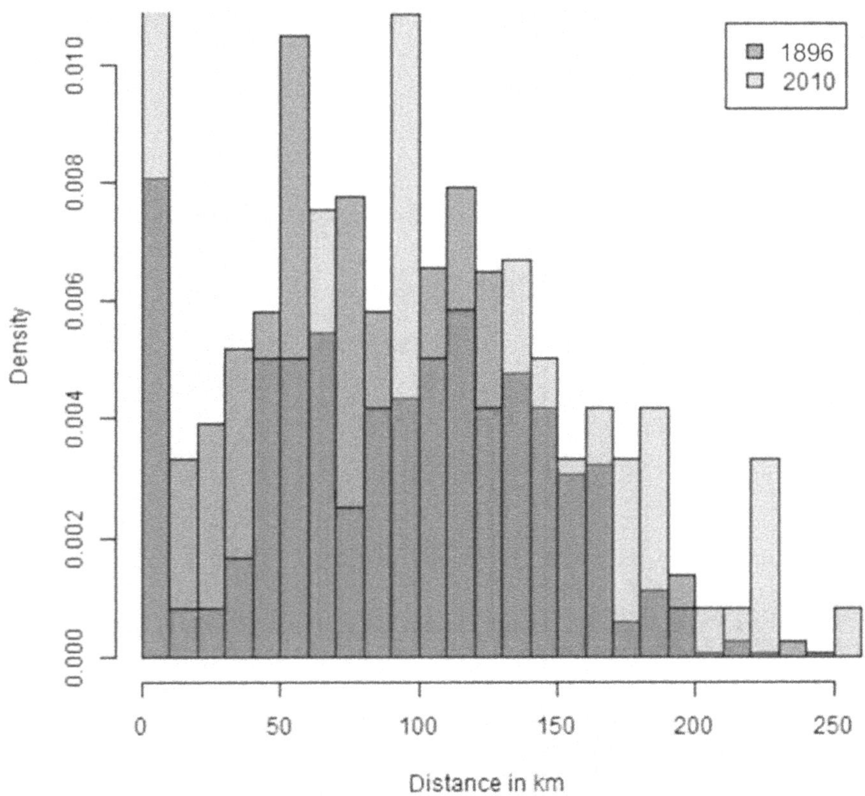

Figure 10.5 Agglomeration in the Casting of Iron and Steel (ISIC 2431) in the Netherlands

Source: See Table 10.3.

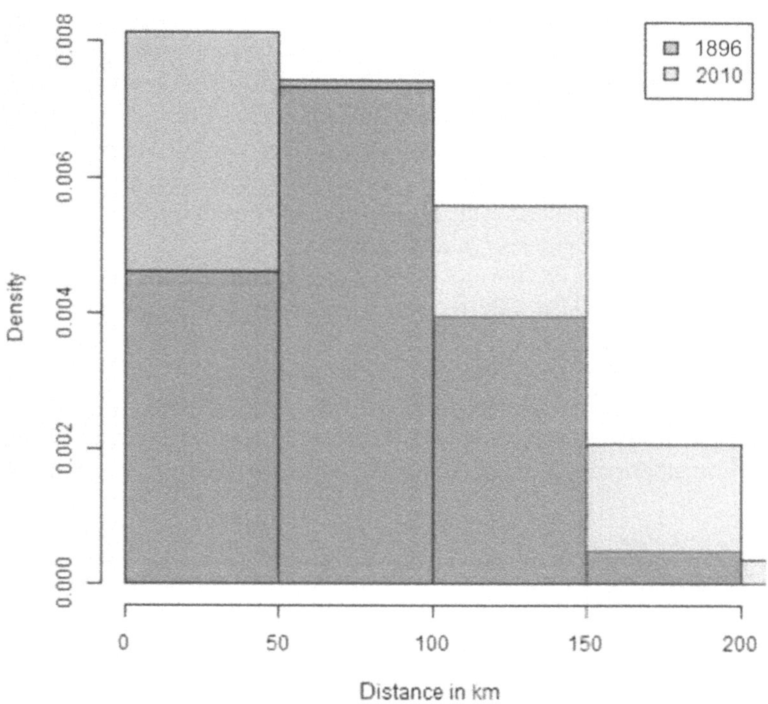

Figure 10.6 Agglomeration in the Manufacture of Cutlery, Hand Tools, and General Hardware (ISIC 2593) in the Netherlands

Source: See Table 10.3.

sectors; and a transport facility of either a navigable waterway or a railway, ensuring access for the import of inputs and export of the finished products.

Yet, by 2010, the co-location within the sectors had decreased, due to the disappearance of the clusters. Rotterdam and Amsterdam do not seem to house a single large-scale iron casting or hardware manufacturing company today, whereas only one iron casting company remains in the IJssel cluster: Lovink Technocast B.V. in Terborg. In addition, in contrast to the manufacturing of carpets and rugs, no recent cluster has emerged in either iron and steel casting or cutlery.

10.4 Measuring co-location in Hunan (1954–2004)

Much like the Netherlands at the beginning of the twentieth century, Hunan was, in the middle of the twentieth century, at the start of its industrialization process, increasingly attracting labour from the agricultural sector into industry. Being a physically bounded area, surrounded on three sides by mountains and facing a large lake to the north, its economy was based primarily on agricultural cultivation and on the utilization of its wide distribution of small iron ore deposits (Chang 1983). This led to the indigenous rise of handicraft industries, mainly in food processing, cotton and ramie textiles, and metal utensils. During the Westernization Movement in the nineteenth century, rich nonferrous metal deposits were discovered and mined in Hunan, and metallurgy became the earliest developed modern industry (Guo 2013).

After the beginning of the war of resistance against Japan in 1937, due to the already existing metal industry and its sheltered location, some sectors of strategic importance, such as that of machinery, were moved to Hunan by the central government. During this period the urban region, with cities such as Changsha and Xiangtan (birthplace of Mao Zedong), developed local industry and commerce, while Hengyang and Zhuzhou became manufacturing centres of the most important strategic goods. In particular, Hengyang experienced a

Table 10.5 Average distance (km) to nearest establishment across four selected sectors in Hunan

	1954		*2004*		*Difference*	
	Mean	*St. dev.*	*Mean*	*St. dev.*	*Mean*	*St. dev.*
Average distance to nearest establishment in Manufacture of Bakery Products (ISIC 1071)	155.86	107.08	125.40	95.13	–20%	–11%
Average distance to nearest establishment in Manufacture of Carpets and Rugs (ISIC 1393)	40.11	68.85	111.61	83.61	+178%	+21%
Average distance to nearest establishment in Casting of Iron and Steel (ISIC 2431)	167.07	109.75	216.84	113.12	+30%	+3%
Average distance to nearest establishment in Manufacture of Cutlery, Hand Tools, and General Hardware (ISIC 2593)	123.64	109.19	99.66	91.36	–19%	–16%

Source: See Table 10.3.

Notes: All distances are expressed in km.

rapid development in manufacturing caused by the westward shift of the political, economic, and cultural centre of the central government due to the war. In 1943, Hengyang had even developed into the second large industrial city in China, with a population of around one million (Local Gazetteers Compilation Committee of Hengyang 1998).

After a decline during the Chinese civil war (1945–1949), and with Mao having been born in this province, the industrial development in Hunan obtained further political significance. For instance, in the first five-year plan, Zhuzhou was listed as one of the eight most important industrial cities in China, with four key projects built by the Soviet Union and more than twenty enterprises directly under the central ministries (or provincial enterprises) planned to be built there (The National Planning Commission 1955). Being a focus in the five-year plans, in addition to its significant promotion by the central government, Hunan experienced a rapid recovery from the depression of the war years and laid the foundation for a subsequent period of growth. Indeed, the first four five-year plans (The National Planning Commission 1955, 1956, 1965, 1970) focused on the past strengths of Hunan – that is, self-sufficiency and supplying the possible future front lines with civil and military products. This was advanced by restarting factories that had stopped production owing to the wars, establishing a number of new factories, and moving factories from other provinces to Hunan. This resulting complete industrial system, which covered thirty-nine out of forty industrial sectors recorded by the national statistics, has been maintained by and large until today.

Figure 10.7 shows the location of factories in 1954, at a point in time when we find the industries in the second year of the first five-year plan and, consequently, as a product of the inheritance of the Westernization movement and the Nanjing government. Yet, looking at Figures 10.7 and 10.8, we can see a strong persistence during the period 1954–2004. One way of looking at this is to examine the ownership type, which was close to 65% solely private modern industry factories in 1954, compared with approximately 40% in 2004 (Hunan Provincial Archives 1954; China Statistical Office 2004). Second, the Changsha–Zhuzhou–Xiangtan Economic Zone and the Hengyang–Loudi–Shaoyang triangle had the highest densities of industrial factories in both years. This also becomes clear when looking at the individual sectors where the main producing areas did not change that much either.

Indeed, Hunan's modern industrial foundation and framework were built in the early stage of New China, and the majority of enterprises started and operated under strong support from the government. The only thing that individual businesses could make decisions about was production. The sale, cost, price, raw materials, and use of technology or human capital were decisions made by the government planners. However, after government planning regarding economic output had been reduced, economic rationality became once more a prime concern for meeting the planned output quota. Therefore, the explanation for the path dependence should be that, to some extent, economic rules about industrial distribution were taken into account when the government made a decision

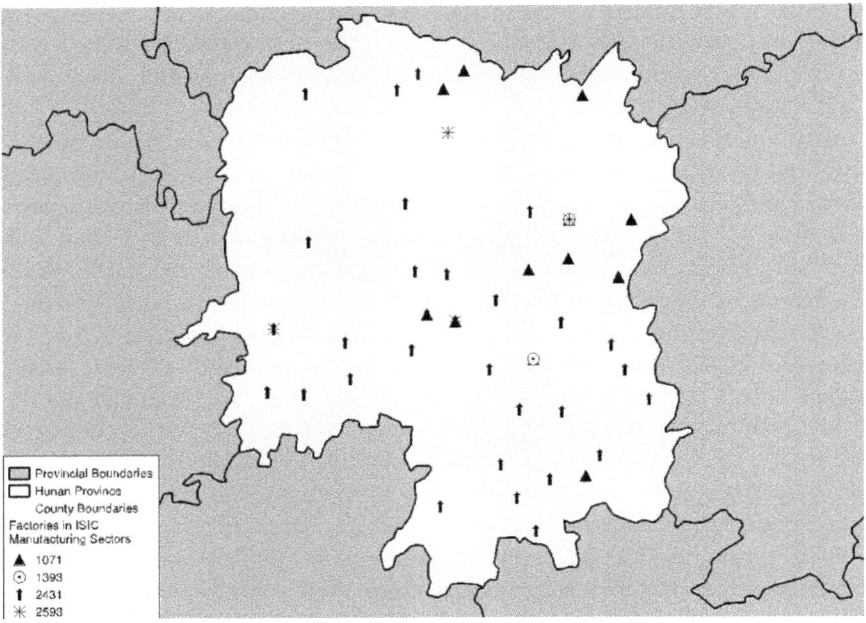

Figure 10.7 Location of factories in the selected sectors in Hunan, China (1954)
Source: See Table 10.3.

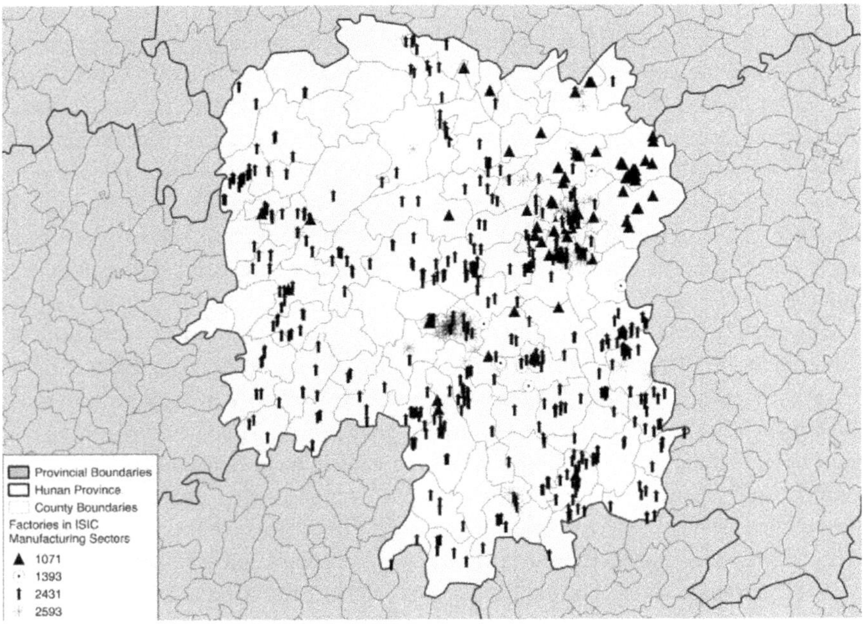

Figure 10.8 Location of factories in the selected sectors in Hunan, China (2004)
Source: See Table 10.3.

about the establishment of a company. How well the government's decisions about location matched economic rules created potential for the companies' survival after the reforms.

Perhaps the clearest example is provided by the iron smelting industry, where the government motivation to build new factories was undeniably strategic. For example, the establishment of the Henyang Steel Company in Henyang – besides serving for the supply of steel to other key industries such as machinery, auto parts, and electric equipment – also belonged to twelve state-owned nuclear industry factories that were moved there. Another example is the Xiangtan Iron and Steel Company, which was planned under the national strategy to improve the industrial production in the hinterlands and to shift the economic centre of the country from the coast to the hinterland (Planning Commission of Hunan Province 1958).

As noted earlier, Hunan had a history in basic metals, especially nonferrous ones (i.e., other than iron and steel). Iron and steel smelting factories were scattered all over the province, but modern industry was mainly concentrated in the Changsha–Zhuzhou–Xiangtan Economic Zone and the Hengyang area to supply materials for other industries (such as machinery, auto, and auto parts), and the Loudi area due to the abundant coal, iron ore, and limestone, which were important raw materials for iron and steel melting. Furthermore, these regions had convenient access to railways as well as access to skilled workers, something that had accumulated during their long history with the iron smelting industry. In the twelfth five--year plan (2011–2015), the high-quality steel processing industry cluster was still located in Xiangtan, Loudi, and Hengyang (Development and Reform Commission of Hunan Province 2011). Using the supply of the iron and steel smelting industry, the main producing area of metal products for general purposes overlapped with the core production base of basic iron and steel smelting (see Figures 10.10 and 10.11). As noted earlier, these patterns have hardly changed up to the present. Indeed, current leading enterprises in this industrial sector can all be dated back to the early stages of New China.

As for the bakery sector, it was located mainly in two clusters, with one being alongside the Dongting Lake Area including Changde, Yiyang, and Yueyang, which was (and still is) a producing area of grains. The other cluster is the Changsha–Zhuzhou–Xiangtan Economic Zone, which was the most prosperous urban area of Hunan. In these cities, a large and relatively prosperous population constituted a large market for bakery products. In addition, many surplus rural labourers who migrated to large cities to earn a living functioned as labour resources. This dual pattern can to some extent be observed in Figure 10.9, which shows for 1954 a dual peak around 0–50 km and around 200 km.

This pattern with two producing areas has remained in existence until today, but the relative importance of each area has changed. Over time, factories were increasingly built close to the Changsha–Zhuzhou–Xiangtan Economic Zone, while growth around the Dongting Lake Area stagnated, thus removing the dual peak structure (around 200–250 km). An explanation may be that today the benefit of proximity to raw materials is increasingly eroded by other advantages

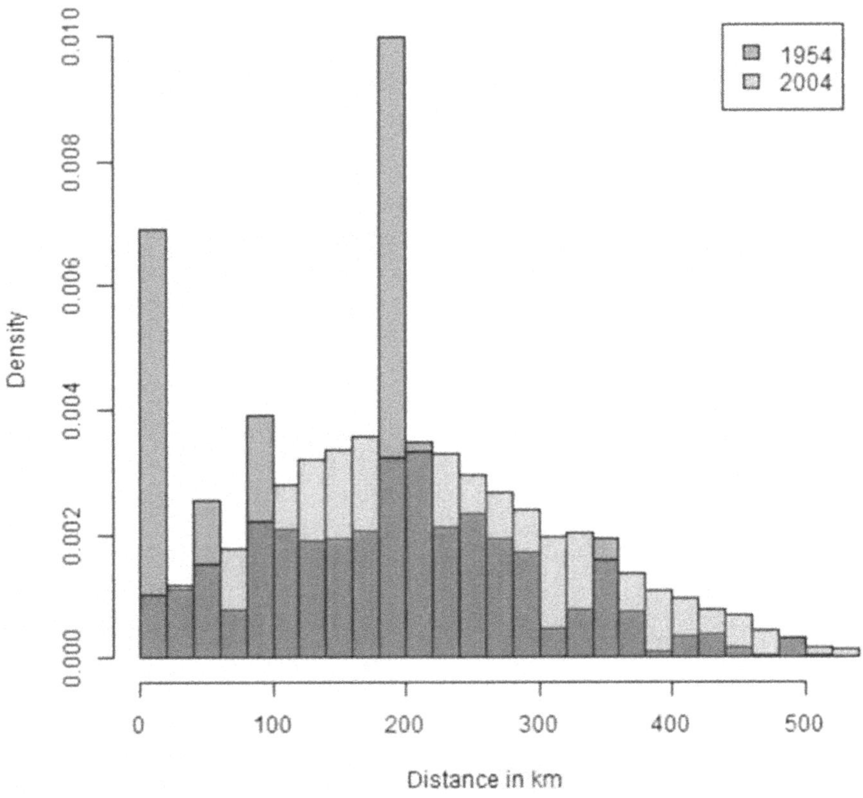

Figure 10.9 Agglomeration in the Casting of Iron and Steel (ISIC 2431) in Hunan

Source: See Table 10.3.

such as investments, demand markets, management, and technology. These processes were enhanced by two additional factors. The first factor was lowering transport costs; the second was that with the relatively rapid improvement in urban living standards, large cities with a larger market and abundant labourers attracted more investment in a wide range of industrial sectors, including the bakery industry.

The most dispersed sector in the 1950s was textiles, with many small companies and only a handful of modern ones located mainly in the Changsha–Zhuzhou–Xiangtan Economic Zone. Yet, over time, some home cotton textile companies and garment companies went on to grow into core enterprises, such as Mengjie, Duohia, Wan'an, Yixintai, and Caizi. Part of this process of increasing textile production may be explained by the modernization of industrial structure in the

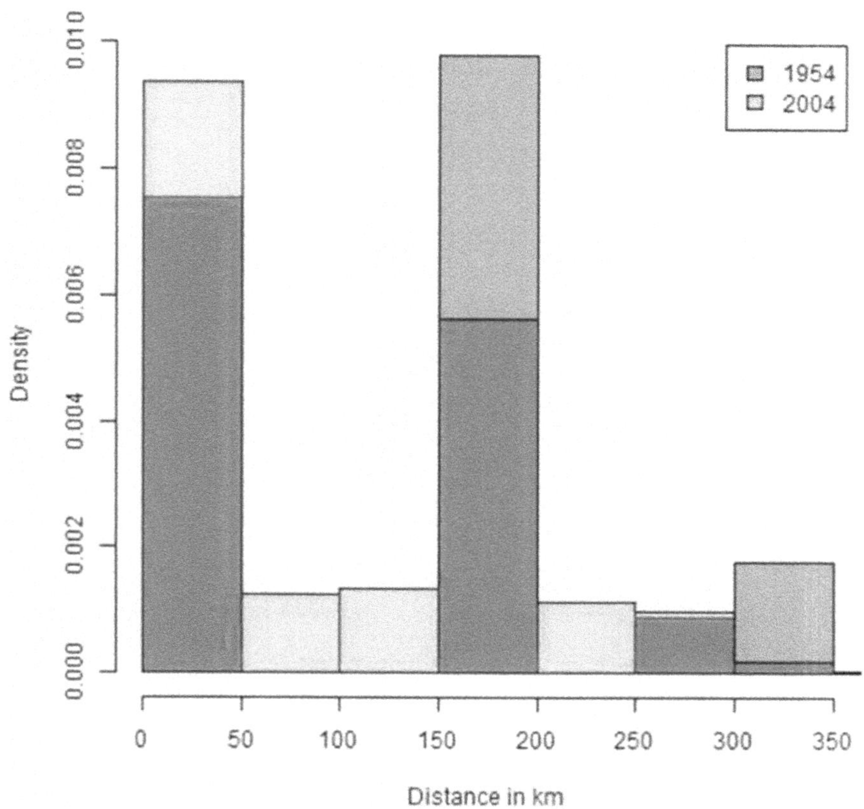

Figure 10.10 Agglomeration in the Manufacture of Cutlery, Hand Tools, and General Hardware (ISIC 2593) in Hunan

Source: See Table 10.3.

nearby province of Guangdong, thus pushing textile production into Hunan's more rural hinterland (i.e., into the southeast counties). Advanced modern technology introduced from advanced regions, combined with abundant natural sources of ramie and cotton (Xiong 2017), supported the stable development of the textile industry in Hunan. This trend is clearly reflected in Figure 10.12, with distances among factories increasing substantially since the 1950s.

10.5 The role of transport

The observed decline in co-location in both the Netherlands and China over time can obviously be linked to a great many factors, such as accruing benefits by sharing – as argued by Marshall (1890) – a proximity to similar labourers, goods,

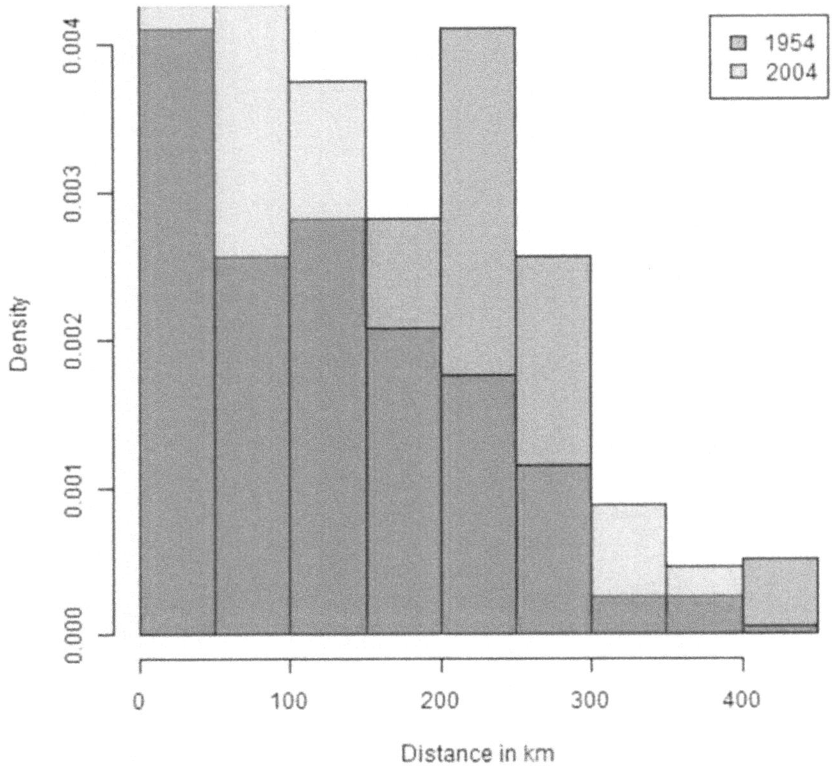

Figure 10.11 Agglomeration in the Manufacture of Bakery Products (ISIC 1071) in Hunan

Source: See Table 10.3.

and ideas, and possible agglomeration spillover effects. Yet, in this chapter we look at an indicator that has become prominent in the field of new economic geography in explaining patterns of agglomeration: transportation costs. Indeed, transportation costs have played a central role in location theory since its inception by Von Thünen (1826) and Weber (1929). Both models are based on the assumption of a static situation with given transport costs, transport technology, and transport networks. Dynamics in the interaction between location and transport costs were introduced by Krugman (1991), who modelled the interaction between forces of agglomeration and dispersion – often referred to as a core–periphery model. Within this model, agglomeration is strengthened by different sources of increasing returns to scale caused by the effects of high fixed costs, technology spillovers, and pools of skilled labour, while dispersion is motivated by lower wages and

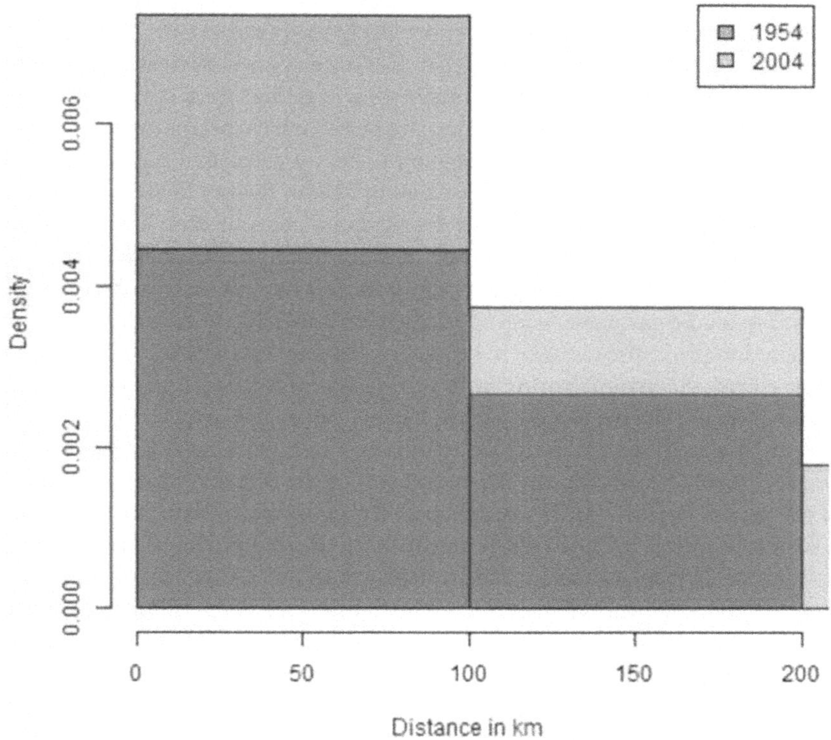

Figure 10.12 Agglomeration in the Manufacture of Carpets and Rugs (ISIC 1393) in Hunan

Source: See Table 10.3.

different proximities to markets. Krugman (1991) argued that at low transport costs, firms that enjoy economies of scale will be concentrated in one place, as no dispersion factors are in action. In the opposite situation, high transport costs may counterbalance the effects of economies of scale and lead to a more even dispersion of industries.

The core–periphery model of Krugman (1991) is especially applicable to the problem discussed in this chapter, for two reasons. First, we compare different periods in both geographical regions; hence, transport costs cannot be assumed to be constant. Second, we compare industries with different degrees of economies of scale. ISIC sectors 2431 (casting of iron and steel) and 2593 (manufacture of cutlery, hand tools, and general hardware) have higher fixed costs, compared with sectors 1071 (manufacture of bakery products) and 1393 (manufacture of carpets and rugs). As the first-mentioned sectors (2431 and 2593) have higher returns to scale, they are more likely to cluster, whereas sectors 1071 and 1393, being more subject to closeness of markets, are more likely to spread evenly over a region. The core–periphery model suggests that as transport costs decrease, agglomeration effects will initially become stronger, thus creating more clustering. When transportation costs lower even further, dispersion effects become stronger.

In order to test these theoretical assumptions, we calculated the averages and standard deviations of distances of factories in all four sectors to the nearest hubs of transport networks. Based on the topographic maps of both China and the Netherlands, we calculated the average distance from each establishment to the nearest hub of the following types of transport facilities: railroads, primary roads, secondary roads, navigable waterways, and non-navigable waterways. Lastly, we attempted to proxy the distance to centres of economic activity by calculating the distance from the manufacturing firms to the nearest municipal city centre in the Netherlands and the nearest county capital city centre in China.

As discussed in Section 10.3, we found divergent patterns in co-location for our four sampled sectors in the Netherlands. For the sector of manufacturing of bakery products (ISIC 1071), a pyramid-like co-location pattern in 1896 and 2010 was revealed, with no clustering in both years. For the sector of manufacturing of carpets and rugs (ISIC 1393), we found a downward-sloping co-location pattern in both 1896 and 2010, with high clustering in both benchmark years. For the sector of casting of iron and steel (ISIC 2431) and the sector of manufacturing of cutlery, hand tools, and general hardware (ISIC 2593), we found an evolution of a downward-sloping pattern to a pyramid-like pattern of co-location, with high clustering in 1896 but a high level of dispersion in 2010.

Based on Table 10.6, we can relate these changes in clustering and dispersion to the distance to transport network hubs. Overall, it appears that the average distances to almost all transport network hubs increased. The distance to waterways, both navigable and non-navigable, and the distance to railways increased most spectacularly. In contrast, the distance to primary roads did not increase as markedly as to railroads and waterways, whereas the distance to secondary roads in almost all sectors even decreased. As such, we empirically affirm the well-documented hypothesis in new economic geography studies (e.g. Krugman 1991) that the fall of transport costs occurred simultaneously with a shift from predominantly railway and waterway transportation to road transportation. In addition, we find that the distance from industry establishments to municipality city centres also increased: whereas enterprises preferred to locate near city centres, for proximity to consumer and labour markets and easy access for shipping inputs and finished products from these city centres, the fall of transport costs decreased these benefits during the period 1890–2010, causing a relocation further away from city centres.

However, differences in distances to transport networks also seem to explain part of the differences found in co-location and dispersion across sectors. For the manufacturing of carpets and rugs (ISIC 1393), we find that the distance to primary and secondary roads increased during the period 1890–2010, whereas it decreased substantially for the other sectors during the same period, indicating that this sector benefitted less from the proximity of roads than did the other

Table 10.6 Average distance to nearest transport facilities of factories in the Netherlands

	Manufacture of Bakery Products (ISIC 1071)	*Manufacture of Carpets and Rugs (ISIC 1393)*	*Casting of Iron and Steel (ISIC 2431)*	*Manufacture of Cutlery, Hand Tools, and General Hardware (ISIC 2593)*
Average distance to nearest railroad (in km)				
1896	2.23	2.14	2.18	2.06
2010	4.04	6.14	2.30	2.67
Difference	+81%	+187%	+5%	+29%
Average distance to nearest primary road (in km)				
1896	1.32	0.96	0.94	2.02
2010	1.25	1.31	0.94	1.01
Difference	–5%	+37%	0%	–50%
Average distance to nearest secondary road (in km)				
1896	0.86	0.40	0.68	0.73
2010	0.36	0.45	0.57	0.56
Difference	–58%	+14%	–16%	–23%
Average distance to nearest navigable waterway (in km)				
1896	0.97	2.27	1.40	0.90
2010	2.40	2.60	4.23	2.81
Difference	+147%	+14%	+203%	+214%
Average distance to nearest non-navigable waterway (in km)				
1896	1.09	2.12	1.50	1.53
2010	1.70	1.25	2.34	2.61
Difference	+56%	–41%	+57%	+71%
Average distance to nearest municipality city centre (in km)				
1896	0.889	0.686	1.356	1.239
2010	2.029	1.527	3.470	2.526
Difference	+128%	+123%	+156%	+104%

Source: See Table 10.3.

sectors. In addition, the enterprises for the manufacturing of carpets and rugs were found to be located substantially closer to the city centres, both in 1890 and 2010. As such, the high clustering in this sector in both 1890 and 2010 can be explained by a combination of two factors: a lack of dispersion, due to the limited role of road transportation in the sector, and high benefits related to locating close to city centres.

In contrast, for the sectors of casting of iron and steel (ISIC 2431) and manufacturing of cutlery, hand tools, and general hardware (ISIC 2593), we find higher values of relocation from navigable waterways and railroads compared with the other sectors during the period 1890–2010. Here, we can argue that the agglomeration benefits of these sectors diminished more compared with those of the sectors of bakery production and carpet and rugs production. We can relate the high clustering in 1890 in the casting of iron and steel and manufacturing of cutlery to the high benefits from proximity to a railroad and river, as metallurgic sectors are documented to have been using waterways and railroads to transport the bulk of their inputs and finished products via these transportation networks. For instance, Smit and Van Straalen (2007) documented the iron casting cluster near the IJssel River, where they argued that all factories depended heavily on the connection to the ports of Rotterdam and Amsterdam and the German market via railroads and the IJssel River. Yet, with the shift from railroad and water transportation to road transportation, these benefits disappeared, explaining the large decrease found in co-location and agglomeration in both sectors during the period 1890–2010.

Unlike the case of the Netherlands, as indicated before, government policy played an additional role for co-location patterns in Hunan, for which we can hypothesize regarding three indirect effects. First, the indirect costs of tolls, added to the congestion in traffic arteries, may explain why in Hunan the distance from a factory to roads declined little over time in absolute terms compared to the Netherlands, while railroads and waterways retained their importance. Even in present-day China, there is a tendency for companies to remain closer to non-road transportation lines. For instance, based on an observation about the influence of traffic facilities such as railway and highway on the economy after the reform and opening of the Chinese economy in recent decades, Banerjee et al. (2012) found that there was a higher density of industrial factories and a higher average benefit rate in those areas closer to the traditional traffic network in China.

Second, the active intervention of the government in transport infrastructure investment influenced patterns of co-location. The government often took a more economic-pragmatic approach to the choice of the location of an industrial plant. For example, the Xiangtan Iron and Steel Company was located in Xiangtan due to its favourable access to the water and electric power necessary for iron and steel smelting, as well as its geographical advantage for the transport of raw materials and final products, as one of the most important railway lines connecting Beijing and Guangzhou had a stop there. Moreover, given the company's location in the Changsha–Zhuzhou–Xiangtan Economic Zone, human capital was relatively abundant. From the perspective of the demand side, there was a large demand for steel caused by a nearby industrial cluster of auto and auto parts in Changsha and the cluster of rail and electric locomotive equipment in Zhuzhou (Xiangtan Iron and Steel Company Archives 1983). Likewise, the location of the establishment of Lianyuan Iron and Steel Company was aimed to cater to local demand. Its exact location was decided by the provincial government, based on a comparison of natural resources with five alternative locations: Lianyuan, Youxian, Shaoshan, Laodaohe (Changsha), and Dajiangkou (Xupu). According to the investigation, the latter four options were rejected because of the lack of coal, iron, water, or convenient transportation. However, economic pragmatism did not always determine decisions about location (Zhao 2014). The Henyang Steel Company, for example, was built to supply iron and steel to nearby industry, despite the lack of related resources. A large quantity of raw materials was transported to Hengyang via railways (e.g., coal from Shanxi, billet from Tangshan, Anshan, and Xiangtan), while large steel enterprises in Anshan and Shanghai offered training services for its workers (Shan 2014).

Third, it has also been argued that Hunan's industry has featured predominantly small-scale and scattered companies (Liu 2000), with the result that government policy to stimulate public or private funds for investment was of only limited effect. These small and scattered companies had no option but to follow government policy. Whether this scattered nature is the cause or consequence of being small in scale is uncertain, but it is clear that the government policy, implemented since the sixth five-year plan (1981–1985), of focusing on productivity rather than scale met with limited success in Hunan. Hence, government-initiated companies largely remained of low productivity. Compared with other provinces that had fewer government-initiated companies, the industrial development in Hunan was more difficult, with the consequence that many enterprises maintained a small scale. As a result, during the reform of state-owned enterprises, some of these enterprises were purchased by private investors. This development led Liu (2000) to argue that the dispersed allocation of resources of Hunan since the 1950s was responsible for the current industrial dispersion.

Yet, notwithstanding the larger impact of policy in China, our results in Table 10.7 seem to indicate more similarities than one might expect. Just as in the Netherlands, Hunan witnessed, for the manufacture of carpets and rugs (ISIC 1393) and the casting of iron and steel (ISIC 2431), decreasing levels of co-location between 1954 and 2004. Given the increase in public infrastructure, we find that, with a few minor exceptions, the distance of factories to transport facilities has similarly declined (see Table 10.7), though we find large differences across sectors. All in all, the decrease in the distance to transport facilities in China remains lower compared with the Netherlands. This offers supporting evidence for the studies which argued that, even today, high transport costs reduce the possibility for undeveloped areas to attract enterprises.[3]

Overall, given that policy played a more important role in making decisions about industrial location in China, investment in transportation infrastructure is considered a priority in China. For large companies, new railways and roads were built to solve the transportation problems of cities. Alternatively, industrial factories would be located in cities that already had quick access to transportation facilities, explaining the overall reduction in distance to transport facilities (Table 10.7). Nevertheless, the caveat remains that many small factories or manual workshops, which could not influence the government's planning of transport infrastructure, had to make their own decisions and had to follow transport infrastructure investment. Some of these enterprises made their locational decisions based on the availability of natural resources and the distance to markets, while others tended to choose those areas with convenient traffic that offered good connections to markets or factor endowments. As a result, there was a relatively high density of factories along major traffic arteries, regardless of whether these were developed naturally or were the result of direct government action. With the rapid economic development in China in recent decades, the clustering of factories has increased rapidly along these traffic lines.

In particular, investment in roads has spiked in China in recent decades. Indeed, in China the adage "Want to be rich? Build roads first!" is widely accepted. As a strategy to help undeveloped areas out of poverty and to promote economic growth through investment, country roads and expressways were paved at a rapid

Table 10.7 Average distance to nearest transport facilities of factories in Hunan (China)

	Manufacture of Bakery Products (ISIC 1071)	*Manufacture of Carpets and Rugs (ISIC 1393)*	*Casting of Iron and Steel (ISIC 2431)*	*Manufacture of Cutlery, Hand Tools, and General Hardware (ISIC 2593)*
Average distance to nearest railroad (in km)				
1954	105.91	58.57	118.32	113.17
2004	30.97	9.78	23.59	11.62
Difference	–71%	–83%	–80%	–90%
Average distance to nearest primary road (in km)				
1954	65.37	48.92	98.84	71.06
2004	8.97	7.96	13.96	11.86
Difference	–86%	–84%	–86%	–83%
Average distance to nearest secondary road (in km)				
1954	28.32	27.71	40.92	37.97
2004	17.83	18.85	20.04	20.07
Difference	–37%	–32%	–51%	–47%
Average distance to nearest navigable waterway (in km)				
1954	122.61	59.3	83.78	90.02
2004	159.25	91.22	123.24	61.12
Difference	+30%	+54%	+47%	–32%
Average distance to nearest non-navigable waterway (in km)				
1954	52.76	46.33	57.12	65.65
2004	34.17	37.05	34.17	24.07
Difference	–35%	–20%	–40%	–63%
Average distance to nearest municipality city centre (in km)				
1954	10.38	1.17	20.03	6.62
2004	14.54	15.86	14.51	11.52
Difference	+40%	+1,251%	–28%	+74%

Source: See Table 10.3.

speed and became the most important channel of transportation. In 2016, road transport accounted for more than 78% of the total freight volume (Wei 2017). In hinterlands like Hunan, road transport carried a much higher proportion of freight traffic than this average level. In 2006, the proportion was around 85% (Bureau of Statistics of Hunan Province 2007), a figure that rose to 86.6% in 2009 (Bureau of Statistics of Hunan Province 2010). Today, expressways have connected 115 counties, and it is expected that every county will be connected by expressway in 2020 (Liang 2016). Given the overall improvement in traffic conditions, the relative importance of the closeness to transport networks for factories decreases, as pointed out by Krugman (1991). Yet, despite the vast majority of areas having convenient access to road transport, the transport costs are still high in China. Here, most notably institutional and organizational factors, such as expensive tolls and underdeveloped logistics, played a role. Even though the ratio of the total logistics cost to GDP showed a downward tendency from 17.8%

Table 10.8 Turnover of freight traffic by means of transport (in 100 million ton/km)

Year	*Hunan*		*China*	
	1950	*2010*	*1954*	*2010*
By railroad	7.93	1,068.12	932.48	27,644.10
By road	0.10	1,539.36	39.88	43,005.40
By waterway	5.50	350.93	269.73	64,305.30

Source: Annual Government Work Report 1955; National Bureau of Statistics 2000; National Bureau of Statistics 2011; Bureau of Statistics of Hunan Province 2011; Bureau of Statistics of Hunan Province 2009.

in 2010 to 14.6% in 2016, this is still over twice that of developed countries such as the United States, Japan, and Germany. For industrial enterprises, the average proportion of the logistics expenses as a share of business revenue was more than 8%, a share much higher than most countries in the world (Cai 2016).

10.6 Conclusion

Agglomeration and clustering of industries are important for both factory management and government policy. Various studies have analyzed this topic in detail, even though most have focused on recent decades and on the developed world. In this chapter, we have attempted to broaden the temporal and geographic scope of the studies on co-location. The temporal aspect is introduced by comparing the early and late twentieth century, allowing us to test whether co-location did indeed decrease over time and what the role of transportation costs was in this process, as proposed by notable studies in economic geography (e.g. Krugman 1991). We examined four specific manufacturing sectors: manufacture of bakery products (ISIC 1071), manufacture of carpets and rugs (ISIC 1393), manufacture of casting of iron and steel (ISIC 2431), and manufacture of cutlery, hand tools, and general hardware (ISIC 2593), in four samples: the Netherlands in 1896 and 2010 and Hunan province in China in 1954 and 2004.

In the Netherlands, we indeed find evidence for an overall process of dispersion. Nonetheless, our evidence indicates large differences over sectors. For the sectors of the manufacture of bakery products, we found that co-location was high neither in 1896 nor in 2010. In contrast, co-location in the manufacturing of carpets and rugs was high in 1896 and in 2010, with notable clusters in place in both time periods, though at different locations. The firms in the sectors of casting of iron and steel and the manufacturing of cutlery, hand tools, and general hardware were found to have been highly co-located in 1896. Yet, both sectors appear to have experienced a substantial dispersion process during the twentieth century, with no co-location at present. When looking at the distance from factories to transport hubs, we can relate these co-location patterns to notable shifts in transportation costs. Here, we find that the shift from rail and water transport to road transport – being fundamental for the bulk transport of iron and steel and the manufacturing of cutlery, hand tools, and general hardware – involved the removal of many incentives for those firms to co-locate. As such, we affirm that the change of transportation costs is to a large degree responsible for the removal of clusters for sectors with high economics of scale.

In China, we find that co-location of the manufacture of bakery products remained at a high level in both benchmark years. The sectors of casting of iron and steel and the manufacturing of cutlery, hand tools, and general hardware became dispersed, but to a large extent this occurred thanks to the development of many small factories. Leading companies in these sectors still show a strong tendency towards agglomeration. For the manufacturing of carpets and rugs, co-location was high neither in 1954 nor in 2010. Also, in China, transport and the distance from transport facilities played a role in these changes and continuities. However, the increasing importance of car transport in Hunan did not alter the co-location patterns as much as it did in the Netherlands, due to high indirect transport costs and undeveloped logistics.

All in all, the comparison between the Netherlands and Hunan reveals that, even though the regions differ considerably, the long-term trends of declining co-location have been fairly similar in both regions. While the change in Hunan to a state-led system in the 1950s and another transition back to a market economy in the 1980s has proven that government policy substantially altered the co-location patterns in the region, we find that these changes often involved the same outcome as in the Netherlands under a free market economy.

Notes

1 The research leading to these results received funding from the European Research Council under the European Union's Horizon 2020 Programme / ERC-StG 637695 – HinDI, as part of the project "The historical dynamics of industrialization in Northwestern Europe and China ca. 1800–2010: a regional interpretation".

2 For more information regarding the LISA dataset, we refer to Stichting LISA (2015).

3 Obviously, this also depends on other factors. Indeed, Tang (2017) showed that both developed areas and undeveloped areas benefitted from the improvement of transport facilities, but enterprises still tended to gather in developed areas and an increasing gap between regions appeared.

References

Annual Government Work Report. 1955. (年国务院政府工作报告). [in Chinese]. www.gov.cn/test/2006-02/23/content_208705.htm, Accessed 2019.

Banerjee, A., E. Duflo, and N. Qian. 2012. *On the road: access to transportation infrastructure and economic growth in China*. NBER Working Papers, no. 17897.

Belussi, F., and K. Caldari. 2009. "At the origin of the industrial district: Alfred Marshall and the Cambridge school." *Cambridge Journal of Economics* 33(2): 335–355.

Brakman, S., H. Garretsen, and Z. Zhao. 2016. "Spatial concentration of manufacturing firms in China." *Papers in Regional Science* 96(1): 179–205.

Bureau of Statistics of Hunan Province. 2007. *Statistical communique of Hunan Province on the 2006 economic and social development.* [in Chinese]. www.hunan.gov.cn/zfsj/sjfb/201212/t20121210_4845962.html

Bureau of Statistics of Hunan Province. 2009. *60 Years of economic and social development in hunan 1949–2009* (*1949–2009* 湖南经济社会发展60年). Changsha: Hunan People's Publishing House. [in Chinese].

Bureau of Statistics of Hunan Province. 2010. *Statistical communique of Hunan Province on the 2009 economic and social development.* [in Chinese]. www.hunan.gov.cn/zfsj/tjgb/201507/t20150701_4832872.html

Bureau of Statistics of Hunan Province. 2011. *Statistical communique of Hunan Province on the 2010 economic and social development.* (湖南省2010年国民经济和社会发展统计公报). [in Chinese]. www.hunan.gov.cn/zfsj/tjgb/201507/t20150701_4832879.html

Cai, J. 2016. "Lower logistics cost of enterprises and promote economic transition and upgrading." *Chine Enterprise News*, September 3. [in Chinese].

Chang, P. 1983. *Modernization in China, 1860–1916: a regional study of social, political and economic change in Hunan Province.* Taipei: Institute of Modern History, Academia Sinica. [in Chinese].

China Statistical Office. 2004. *Economic census.* Beijing: China Statistical Office.

Combes, P. P., and H. G. Overman. 2004. "The spatial distribution of economic activities in the European Union." In *Handbook of regional and Urban economics*, edited by J. V. Henderson and J. F. Thisse, 2845–2909. Amsterdam: Elsevier.

Crafts, N., and N. Wolf. 2014. "The location of the UK cotton textiles industry in 1838: a quantitative analysis." *The Journal of Economic History* 74(4): 1103–1139.

Cressie, N. A. C. 1993. *Statistics for spatial data.* New York: John Wiley.

De Jonge, J. A. 1968. *De industrialisatie in Nederland tussen 1850 en 1914.* Amsterdam: Scheltema & Holkema NV.

Delgado, M., M. E. Porter, and S. Stern. 2014. "Clusters, convergence, and economic performance." *Research policy* 43(10): 1785–1799.

Development and Reform Commission of Hunan Province. 2011. *The 12th five-year plan of Hunan.* [in Chinese]. www.czs.gov.cn/html/zwgk/hgjj/fzgh/content_211039.html

Devereux, M., R. Griffith, and H. Simpson. 1999. *The geographical distribution of production activity in the UK.* Working Paper No. 26/99, IFS, London.

Duranton, G., and H. G. Overman. 2005. "Testing for localization using micro-geographic data." *Review of Economic Studies* 72(4): 1077–1106.

Duranton, G., and H. G. Overman. 2008. "Exploring the detailed location patterns of U.K. manufacturing industries using microgeographic data." *Journal of Regional Science* 48(1): 213–243.

Ellison, G., and E. Glaeser. 1997. "Geographical concentration in U.S. manufacturing industries: a dartboard approach." *Journal of Political Economy* 105(5): 889–927.

Fu, L., and B. Zheng. 2007. *History of Chinese administrative division: Republican China.* Shanghai: Fudan University Press. [in Chinese].

Guo, H., and C. Cai. 2000. "Network structure: the organizational model of the sock-making industry in Datang." *Zhejiang Economy/Zhejiang Jingji* 9: 16–17. [in Chinese].

Guo, Q. 2013. *Modern industrial history of Hunan.* Changsha: Hunan Publishing House. [in Chinese].

Hendrickx, F. M. M. 1993. “From weavers to workers: demographic implications of an economic transformation in Twente (the Netherlands) in the nineteenth century.” *Continuity and Change* 8(2): 321–355.

Hunan Provincial Archives. 1954. *The statistics of state-owned, local government-owned, joint public – private and private industrial enterprise of Hunan in 1954.* File No. 187-1-108. [in Chinese].

Kosfeld, R., H. F. Eckey, and J. Lauridsen. 2011. “Spatial point pattern analysis and industry concentration.” *The Annals of Regional Science* 47(2): 311–328.

Krugman, P. 1991. “Increasing returns and economic geography.” *Journal of Political Economy* 99(3): 483–499.

Li, G. 2001. “Administration boundary changes in New China.” *Journal of Literature and History* 1: 10–11. [in Chinese].

Liang, X. 2016. “Every county in Hunan will be connected by expressway in 2020.” *Sanxiang City Express*, February 2. [in Chinese].

Lin, J. 2004. *Study on the administrative regionalization reform of the Qing Dynasty.* Completed Ph.D. manuscript at Fudan University. [in Chinese].

Liu, M. 2000. “The economic location of Hunan and the reconfiguration of leading industries in Hunan.” *Hunan Social Sciences* 2: 41–45. [in Chinese].

Local Gazetteers Compilation Committee of Hengyang. 1998. *Hengyang gazetteer.* Changsha: Hunan People’s Publishing House. [in Chinese].

Marshall, A. 1890. *Principles of economics.* London: Macmillan.

Maurel, F., and B. Sédillot. 1999. “A measure of the geographical concentration in French manufacturing industries.” *Regional Science and Urban Economics* 29: 575–604.

Meyer, D. 1998. “Formation of advanced technological districts: new England textile machinery and firearms, 1790–1820.” *Economic Geography* 74: 31–45.

Mori, T., and T. E. Smith. 2011. *Analysis of industrial agglomeration patterns: an application to manufacturing industries in Japan.* KIER Working Papers, 794.

National Bureau of Statistics. 2000. *Compilation of 50-year statistical data of China’s industry, transportation and energy.* 中国工业交通能源50年统计资料汇编. Beijing: China Statistics Press. [in Chinese].

National Bureau of Statistics. 2011. *Statistical communique of The People’s Republic of China on the 2010 national economic and social development.* 中华人民共和国2010年国民经济和社会发展统计公报. [in Chinese]. www.stats.gov.cn/statsinfo/auto2074/201310/t20131031_450703.html

The National Planning Commission. 1955. *The 1st five-year plan of China.* Beijing: People’s Publishing House. [in Chinese].

The National Planning Commission. 1956. *The 2nd five-year plan of China.* Beijing: People’s Publishing House. [in Chinese].

The National Planning Commission. 1965. *The 3rd five-year plan of China.* Beijing: People’s Publishing House. [in Chinese].

The National Planning Commission. 1970. *The 4th five-year plan of China.* Beijing: People’s Publishing House. [in Chinese].

Pelgrim, E. 1997. “Hilversum als tapijtstad.” *Textielhistorische Bijdragen* 37: 114–139.

Philips, R. C. M. 2019. “Construction of a census of companies for the Netherlands in 1896.” *TSEG/Low Countries Journal of Social and Economic History* 16(1): 87–108.

Planning Commission of Hunan Province. 1958. *The second five-year plan of Hunan.* Changsha: Hunan People’s Publishing House.

Puga, D. 2010. "The magnitude and causes of agglomeration economies." *Journal of Regional Science* 50(1): 203–219.

Shan, R. 2014. "Hengyang steel company: once was guarded by an anti-aircraft troop." *Hengyang Evening News*, July 30. [in Chinese].

Shukla, V. 1996. *Urbanization and economic growth*. Delhi: Oxford University Press.

Silverman, B. W. 1986. *Density estimation for statistics and data analysis*. London: Chapman & Hall.

Smit, J., and B. Van Straalen. 2007. *Ijzergieterijen langs de Oude Ijssel (1689 - heden)*. Utrecht: Stichting Gelders Erfgoed.

Stichting LISA. 2015. *LISA: het werkgelegenheidsregister van Nederland*. Enschede: Stichting LISA.

Tang, X. 2017. "Regional difference of the influence of investment on transport facilities to economic growth." *Finance and Accounting Monthly* 8: 124–128. [in Chinese].

Van Mensch, E. 1979. "De tapijtindustrie in Hilversum." *Textielhistorische Bijdragen* 21: 35–51.

Van Zanden, J. L. 1996. "Industrialization in the Netherlands." In *The industrial revolution in national context: Europe and the USA*, edited by M. Teich and R. Porter, 78–94. Cambridge: Cambridge University Press.

Von Thünen, J. H. 1826. *Der isolierte Staat in Beziehung auf Landwirtschaft und Nationalökonomie*. Hamburg: Perthes.

Weber, A. 1929. *Theory of the location of industries. Translation from Carl J. Friedrich*. Chicago: The University of Chicago Press.

Wei, J. 2017. "What is the reason for China's high logistics cost?" *Economic Daily*. [in Chinese].

Xiangtan Iron and Steel Company Archives. 1983. "The history of the establishment of the Xiangtan Iron and Steel Company." *Gazetteer of the Xiangtan Iron and Steel Company 1958–1980*, 123–142. [in Chinese].

Xiong, Y. 2017. "The development and influence of modern cotton textile industry in Hunan." *Seeking* 6: 33–41. [in Chinese].

Yule, G. U., and M. G. Kendall. 1950. *An introduction to the theory of statistics*, 3rd ed. New York: Harper Publishing Company.

Zhao, X. 2014. "A memoir about the planning stage of Liangyuan Iron and steel company." *Xiangchao* 3. [in Chinese].

11 Regional industrialization

Role of industrial policy

Patrizio Bianchi and Sandrine Labory

11.1 Introduction

Industrial policies, defined as sets of instruments implemented in order to promote structural changes, have been implemented in most countries since the Industrial Revolution, although to varying degrees of consciousness, planning, and monitoring. Industrial revolutions represent deep transformations in the socioeconomic structure, where the very root of industries change, namely the organization of production, with a view to produce new products and new production processes (Bianchi and Labory 2011, 2018). Industrial revolutions are thus essentially transitions in manufacturing regimes (Bianchi and Labory 2019a) that have impact not only on industrial sectors and therefore the economic system but also on society via the division of labour, hence jobs and social status, as well as skills requirements and on culture.

In this chapter, we consider four transitions in manufacturing regime: the first Industrial Revolution represents the introduction of division of labour in the factory system, between the end of the eighteenth century and the beginning of the nineteenth century; the second Industrial Revolution or the shift to mass production, between the end of the nineteenth century and the first half of the twentieth century; the third Industrial Revolution in the second half of the twentieth century, which introduced flexible production systems; while in the current fourth Industrial Revolution, scientific and technological innovations are deeply changing the organization of production, making mass customization possible in smart manufacturing or digital factories (Bianchi and Labory 2018, 2019a).

Industry is the capacity to organize production, mobilizing both tangible and intangible assets. Industrial policy originates from the affirmation of the modern state and the first Industrial Revolution, which imply that the capacity to organize production, rather than the availability of natural resources, becomes the main determinant of the wealth of nations (Smith 1776). The factory system transforms the organization of production from craftsmanship to the division of labour. Its diffusion requires new resources and skills, and a new social structure. A bourgeois class develops with entrepreneurs creating and managing factories. The rural workforce previously hired in agriculture massively moves to cities to work in factories, leading to a growth of urban areas, which have to reorganize and offer new services, from transport to housing and progressively schooling. Countries unify their internal markets, eliminating tariffs, thereby creating large domestic markets that the new production systems are able to supply.

The states thus define their institutional structure, necessary rules such as contract law and protection of intellectual property rights but also financial systems able to provide the resources for industrialization. State action tends to be *dirigiste*, namely strong in the sense of making large investments, particularly in infrastructure, and imposing new regulations and standards – often directly intervening in the economy by being producers with state-owned enterprises. Regarding international trade, all countries – be they early industrializers or followers – tend to protect their national industry.

This strong action culminates after World War II, during the third Industrial Revolution, and is followed by a "laissez-faire" phase where industrial policy is abandoned because it is considered inefficient and ineffective. The new century starts with a return of industrial policy (Bianchi and Labory 2011, 2018), whereby the challenges induced by globalization and technological changes make structural changes necessary in a growing number of industries, which ask for supportive measures. As a consequence, many countries reconsider industrial policy in order to favour the adaptation of their industrial systems.

Industrial policy throughout history thus appears as experimental: periods of strong government intervention are often followed by relative withdrawal of the state from the markets, because both approaches have side effects that have to be attenuated. Strong intervention and protection of industry favours the development of monopolies which tend to reduce consumers' benefits. Periods of strong protection are followed by more "laissez-faire" phases, where competition is favoured to increase consumers' surplus; however, competition may increase so much that national industry is weakened, especially relative to foreign enterprises, so that some protective measures or support may be reintroduced.

This chapter examines industrial policies defined in major Western countries, as well as in some Asian countries, from the first Industrial Revolution to today, in order to outline their main characteristics. We do not pretend to carry out an exhaustive historical analysis, but we use the results of our numerous studies on industrial policy (Bianchi and Labory 2006, 2011, 2018, 2019a, 2019b) in order to read the historical evolution of this policy. A detailed analysis of all the different measures of industrial policy would be impossible in such a short chapter, therefore we focus on outlining the main broad lines of policies. We find that industrial policy has been implemented along similar broad lines in all countries in the different phases of development: industrialization and reconstruction after deep crises such as World War II appear to require strong intervention, the states often becoming producers through state-owned enterprises. At later stages, innovation policy becomes a higher focus of industrial policy, in order to favour the upgrading of existing sectors and the emergence of new ones. Examples are scientific and technological programmes carried out in the United States after World War II, and in other countries after their reconstruction – for instance, France, the United Kingdom, and Japan. Research and industrial application are also the focus nowadays, in the current era of numerous scientific discoveries and technological innovations that has been defined as a new Industrial Revolution – the fourth one (Bianchi and Labory 2018; Bailey and de Propris 2019). In addition, a regional focus of industrial policy as a systematic and long-term orientation of industrial development started to emerge in the second half of the twentieth century, especially after the crises of the 1970s and, for Europe at least, the start of the regional policy at supranational – European Union – level.

11.2 Industrial policy as complex sets of actions supporting productive processes

Industrial policy tends to be a fuzzy concept with a variety of conceptualizations (Vanden Bosch 2014; Cherif and Hasanov 2019; Labory 2006); hence, the importance of starting this research by clarifying its definition.

While many conceptualizations consider industrial policy as a support to specific firms or industries (McFetridge 1985; Brander 1987), implying doubts as to its effectiveness as many such selective industrial policies have failed in the past (Bianchi and Labory 2006, 2011), we define industrial policy as a set of measures aiming at favouring productive transformation, hence industrial development (Bianchi and Labory 2018). The latter can take different forms, depending on the characteristics of the territory under consideration. On the one hand, industrial development can mean industrialization when the economy is predominantly based on agriculture, as in Western European countries in the eighteenth century or Asian countries after World War II. On the other hand, it may primarily mean industrial upgrading (adaptation of existing industries to changes in the competitive environment) or development of new sectors, generally using new technologies and innovations, as the competitive context – the extent of the market, in Smith's (1776) words – changes.

Many policy actions affect industries: fiscal, monetary, environmental, trade, innovation, and labour policy instruments have an impact on industries, in a direct or indirect manner. One could therefore argue that all countries and territories implement industrial policies in one way or another. However, what is important to stress is that industrial policy is a deliberate attempt by the government (at the local, regional, or national level) to orientate industrial development towards specific paths. Such orientation can take various forms, from reducing specialization in declining industries to favouring high-tech industries. It can be interventionist, in the sense of choosing specific industries that are developed from scratch – with, for instance, high investments, creation of appropriate infrastructure, and training human capital. It can be more inclined to letting market forces play – by, for instance, providing the conditions for industrial development and letting entrepreneurs make choices and implement strategies, from which new industries can emerge.

Given this definition, a taxonomy of industrial policy actions can be made (Labory 2006). Briefly, these actions can be gathered in two groups: measures not aimed at industry but which have an impact on it, and measures aimed at industry. The first group includes macroeconomic stabilization policies (monetary policies influence the inflation and interest rates, with impact on both consumers' purchasing power and business investment opportunities), or social and labour policies. Education policies aim at the social development of the territory but also influence the availability of human capital for business.

The second group includes all measures directly aimed at industry, which can be divided into three subgroups: first, measures defining the competitive conditions, such as antitrust policy and product regulation; second, measures aimed at enhancing business capabilities, which can be horizontal (second group), namely regarding all firms and industries, such as support to research and development (R&D), development of human capital, access to financing, and so on; or vertical measures (the third group), namely specific to particular industries, such as public procurement of specific products, investment in specific technologies, or specific skills (e.g., creation of engineering schools).

Bianchi and Labory (2011) defined four main pillars that policy action should follow in order to promote industrial development: entitlements, innovation, provisions, and territory. **Entitlements** are socially defined means of access, namely the capability of buying goods and finding a job, and also civil rights. They are necessary for industrial development, especially in times of important structural changes; individuals must have access to education and training in order to have the skills required by the new production structures, or to participate in the innovation process.

Entitlements are therefore a key factor of innovation and upgrading, in addition to an appropriate knowledge base and knowledge absorption capacity. The latter aspect is what we call the **innovation** dimension. Policy actions aimed at increasing or updating the knowledge base, such as the promotion of university–industry relationships or other R&D programmes, are part of this dimension. The dimension of "provisions", however, is more straightforward and concerns the resources for development, from access to raw materials and low-cost energy sources, to infrastructure more generally. Finally, the territory is also a key dimension, in the sense of institutions and their governance, at different levels of government, namely local, regional, and national, and also supranational.

All the dimensions are important and comprise different determinants and factors that should be assessed and combined in an appropriate manner with respect to the socioeconomic and political conditions of the given territory. The issue for policy is to identify possible development paths on the basis of the current situation of the economic system and its historical evolution and orientate it towards the chosen path using the different instruments of industrial policy.

These four dimensions are enabling conditions for both industries and the whole socioeconomic system to adapt to changes in the competitive context (Bianchi and Labory 2019b). They can be compared to the four main measures outlined by Allen (2011), who identified the necessary ingredients for countries to catch up with the industrialization process. Allen indeed argues that all countries that have caught up after the first Industrial Revolution – namely the Low Countries, France, and Germany in the nineteenth century, Italy by the end of the nineteenth century, as well as Asian countries after World War II (Japan, Taiwan and Korea) – implemented the following four policies: (1) unification of the internal market by both the elimination of internal tariffs and the development of transport infrastructure; (2) the setting of an external tariff that protects the domestic industry from foreign competition; (3) the chartering of banks to stabilize the currency and finance industrial development; and (4) mass education to upgrade the labour force. These measures are both direct (enlarging the market and trade protection) and indirect (financial policy serves industry; education policy affects the society but also the human capital available to industry).

Mass education regards entitlements, hence the ability of individuals to take part in the development process. Inventors in Britain in the seventeenth century had access to basic education, acquiring both literacy skills and craft skills learned in apprenticeship. This is the case of British inventors of the eighteenth century such as Thomas Newcomen and James Watt, who invented and improved the steam engine, as well as Charles Tennant, who invented bleaching powder and founded an industrial dynasty.

Besides entitlements, market unification, transport infrastructure, external tariffs, and banking systems regard provisions and territory. They require a governance system at a national level, which is what was set up when national states started to strengthen in the eighteenth century, especially in Western countries. These were the basis for inventions that could be applied in the internal market, developing industries, which required in turn new entitlements (human capital); primary school became universal, and secondary and tertiary education progressively developed in the twentieth century. As a consequence, new territorial institutions and new provisions allow the development of innovations which in turn imply the need to further develop entitlements and adjust territorial institutions for this, so that a sort of development spiral develops between the four dimensions we have outlined.

In a historical perspective, one can argue that industrialization has always required industrial policy. This is especially true for countries which have caught up relative to pioneers, as they had to develop industries in a competitive context where their new industries were immediately challenged by industries in first industrializers. Strong industrial policy has more direct measures such as market unification, trade protection, and creation of factories, and is implemented when industry is underdeveloped and industrialization not yet complete, or when it is affected by particular circumstances like destructions after World War II. The evolution of industrial policy described in the next sections shows that industrial policy remains strong (with more direct measures) up to the 1980s, at least in Western countries. After that, measures aimed at providing the conditions for business competitiveness, with more indirect actions, are preferred especially in Europe. In recent decades the rise of Asian countries, and particularly China, challenged the position of industries in Western countries, which have considered again more direct industrial policy measures, and implemented them in the United States but not in the EU, where this type of action tends to distort competition on the single market (for instance, the rules on state aids are stringent).

The first Industrial Revolution started in the United Kingdom (UK). As shown in the next sections, all countries that have followed Britain have implemented strong industrial policies. Whether the UK itself has implemented industrial policy is debated, as shown in the next section.

11.3 Pioneer in the first Industrial Revolution: Unconscious industrial policy?

Whether the pioneer of the first Industrial Revolution, Britain, used industrial policy to promote industrial development is debated in the literature. Some scholars argue in favour of the existence of a strong active state. Thus, Bairoch (1993) claims that the British government implemented industrial policy to support the woollen industry well before the industrial revolution, from the fourteenth century. Tariff protection and subsidies were included in this policy, while export taxes, and occasionally export bans, guaranteed the availability of raw materials to British producers. According to Bairoch (1993), these actions were aimed at making Britain a manufacturing centre of woollen textile. By the eighteenth century, woollen textile accounted for about half of Britain's export revenue, which was used during the Industrial Revolution to import raw materials such as cotton, as well as food, which the growing cities required. Under prime minister Walpole (serving from 1721–1742), this support was extended to all industrial sectors. In addition, massive investment in infrastructure and development of the financial sector to support these investments were complementary measures for industrialization. New roads were built (turnpike roads) and new water canals enabled an increase in the communication network via rivers.

As a consequence, it appears that industrial policy in Britain started much earlier than the late seventeenth century. Elizabeth I (1553–1603) initiated it with trade restrictions, and later it was continued by James I (1603–1625) and Charles I (1625–1649). As a result, substantial industrial activities existed in Great Britain before the first Industrial Revolution. In 1700, this sector accounted for 32.3% of the labour force and 32% of GDP (Broadberry et al. 2013: Tables 11.3 and 11.7). Protection of industry continued well into the Industrial Revolution and until the 1860s. The agricultural sector was also protected, with the Corn Bounty Act (1614–1689) and later by the Corn Law of 1815. Technical improvements in agricultural production were made as a result, leading to increased productivity, which was useful to provide food to the growing cities. Farmers' income therefore increased, allowing them to buy industrial products, thus providing a more secure domestic demand for these products.

According to Allen (2011), this situation implied rising wages in the country, in turn favouring the mechanization of production by providing incentives to entrepreneurs to innovate and use machines instead of human capital. This author argues that the reason the first Industrial Revolution started in Britain probably lies in these incentives, which did not exist in other countries where wages were extremely low.

The British government also supported the development of the cotton textile industry. The Calico Act of 1721, backed by the British woollen and silk industry lobby, indeed protected British industry from the import of cotton textiles from India, having the result of spurring the development of the cotton industry in the country. This sector pioneered industrialization thanks to technological innovations, such as the inventions of the jenny to the water-frame and the mule, which had impact on other industries. The share of cotton in total value added of industry grew from 2.6% in 1770 to 17% in 1801 (De Simoni 2016).

Regarding the financial sector, the Bank of England, established in 1694, eased public borrowing. The stock exchange was also instituted to allow entrepreneurs to increase the dimension of their firms, especially during the second Industrial Revolution. Private banks were created in 1716 and slowly developed up to the beginning of the first Industrial Revolution (1760s), and experienced rapid growth thereafter. In addition, savings banks were created in 1798 to mobilize the savings of small savers and the working class. The law of partnership was adopted to promote a sense of corporation, and the insurance sector also rapidly developed to reduce investment risks. Overall, the government provided the legal framework for institutional development, enforcing contracts and preserving property rights, which contributed to the development of infrastructure and markets, and provided public services (O'Brien 1995; Goldsmith 1995; Streeten 1993).

Despite numerous actions taken by the government in favour of industrial development, the issue as to whether this constituted a true industrial policy is debated among economic historians. Many scholars indeed argue that these different measures were essentially adopted to follow the interests of some particular lobbies, but did not constitute an intentional industrialization programme, in the sense of a long-term vision of development (Mokyr 1999; Allen 2011). It seems that the different elements which favoured the industrial revolution in Britain, highlighted previously, all combined to create an environment favourable to industrialization but were not intentionally designed for this purpose by the British government. For example, the Calico Act aimed at protecting specific lobbies and not intentionally at developing the cotton industry (Mokyr 1999). Similarly, the central government raised a large amount of taxes, but these were almost entirely spent for military purposes, not on industrial development. However, even this spending on military equipment was favourable to industrial development, as it allowed the Royal Navy to become the "Master of the Oceans", which favoured trade. Public expenditures on education, transport, and the development of science and technology, that could have represented elements of an intentional industrial policy, were left to private initiative (Van Neuss 2015). Thus, training specific to the needs of the new expanding industries was left to the responsibility of the private sector. For instance, the Mechanics' Institutes that opened in Scotland and England to provide instruction to adults and training to engineers were financed by industrialists.

It appears that industrial policy was not implemented at the local or regional levels either. According to Van Neuss (2015), local authorities in Britain managed many public functions in that period, except international and colonial trade, which was dealt with by the central government. However, they did not implement economic policies, unlike many continental countries where local authorities did implement such policies, mainly in a protectionist manner. According to Mokyr (1999), Britain thus had the characteristics of a decentralized "laissez-faire" economy.

11.4 Industrial policy in followers or late industrializers

Other countries followed industrialization in the nineteenth century, given the political power provided by industrial development (both wealth and military equipment). The United States, Belgium, Germany, France, Japan, and Italy also implemented industrial policies in order to – perhaps primarily – increase their military strength. The need for stronger industrial policy in followers is due to several factors. First, technology already exists and later industrializers have to adopt it quickly, absorbing all the knowledge and developing productive and innovative capacity. Second, economies of scale resulting from the division of labour continuously improved during the first and second Industrial Revolutions, implying the need to create larger firms or more strongly support firm growth for later industrializers. Third, the competition from first industrializers made it necessary for them to rapidly improve competitiveness.

The United States became the pioneer of the second Industrial Revolution thanks to a large unifying domestic market, as well as strong industrial policy. This policy consisted of investment in infrastructure, namely roads and railways, as well as ports, development of the education and financial systems, and infant industry protection. On the last point, Bairoch called the United States "the mother country and bastion of modern protectionism" (Bairoch 1993: 30). The country thus had one of the highest average tariff rates on manufacturing imports in the world between 1816 and the end of World War II. The United States also strongly regulated FDI. Between 1817 and 1914, coastal shipping was completely closed to FDI, while only American citizens could become directors in national banks, and foreign shareholders were not allowed to vote in annual general meetings. Mining rights were only conceived to US citizens and companies incorporated in the country (federal laws of 1866, 1870, and 1872). In addition, the 1885 labour contract law prohibited the import of foreign workers.

The US model differed from the European one in many aspects. First and foremost, the internal market was extremely large after the unification induced by the American Revolution. Hence, US industry had to develop in order to serve the integrated and large market. Entrepreneurs created factories and financial institutions that grew in size while the state provided infrastructure. The US first imported technology from the UK and were soon able to surpass it, and became the leader in industrialization and technological change in the second Industrial Revolution. Human capital also developed to provide an appropriately skilled labour force to the industries and financial institutions. Over 70% of adult white males were literate at the end of the eighteenth century, and close to 100% were by 1859 (Allen 2011: 81). While in Europe, countries supported the growth and competitiveness of their national champions, the United States had a different focus because the large unified market made it possible for firms to reach a very large size, hence market power and also political power, possibly threatening democracy. Hence, senator John Sherman proposed in 1890 the first "antitrust" law, initiating competition policy aimed at avoiding excessive monopoly power by prohibiting both collusion between firms and anticompetitive strategies such as predatory pricing or the creation of strategic barriers to entry.

Continental European countries that followed Britain in industrialization in the nineteenth and twentieth centuries also implemented strong industrial policy. Belgium was the second European country to industrialize. During the 1815–1830 period, Willem I implemented an industrial policy for the United Kingdom of the Low Countries, composing of both Belgium and the Netherlands. Some of the measures taken by Willem I included the promotion of economic integration through the building of infrastructure such as roads and canals, as well as exports, and the creation of a central national investment bank and of new universities. However, these policies tended to favour the already developed south of Belgium (see Philips and Buyst, Chapter 3 in this volume). After the Belgian Revolution in 1830, the Netherlands and Belgium were separated again. Regional differences were maintained for some time, dividing the industrialized Belgium from the lagging Netherlands. According to Mokyr (2000), the latter country really industrialized after 1860.

Prussia was also active in this forced industrialization. The King, Frederick the Great (1740–86), implemented until the unification of the Reich an active policy of promotion for new industries, and for schools and universities to develop the capabilities to both absorb the new knowledge and create new knowledge in turn. Examples are the Gewerbeschulen or the Gewerbe Institüt of Berlin and the massive obligatory schooling that resulted in a schooling rate of 97% (Landes 1969). At the beginning of the nineteenth century, Willhelm von Humbold, a Prussian administrator, proposed the creation of new universities that would teach the "pure idea of science" rather than specific training. Teaching at universities became intimately linked to research, in that university teachers would not only transmit knowledge but also primarily develop knowledge together with the students. As a result, academic research substantially developed in Germany. From the second half of the nineteenth century, research at German universities was increasingly oriented towards the needs of both the state (military developments) and business (for instance, chemistry).

The industrialization process was initiated by creating "model factories" in the steel and linen industries. Nascent industries were protected, following Friedrich List, who lived in the United States from 1825 to 1832 and recommended the implementation of this measure in his book *The National System of Political Economy* (1841). The German government also heavily invested in infrastructure, building roads and railways, especially in the Ruhr, the centre of German manufacturing. Market unification had already happened in Germany in 1818 with the Zollverein. Railways were developed, especially after the 1850s. Investment banks were set up; the first bank was the Bank of Darmstadt, a joint-stock investment bank established in 1853. By 1872, all large German banks were created (Commerzbank, Dresdner, Deutsche, etc.). Education was almost universal in the country by the 1850s.

Despite political upheavals and numerous wars, economic growth also significantly rose in France over the nineteenth century, thanks to the creation of factories by entrepreneurs, state investment in public goods such as railways and other infrastructure, and the development of a financial system based on banks and shareholders' associations (the so-called "caisses"). The state intervened to unify the market, with the abolition of "octroi", sorts of tariff barriers between municipalities and subsequently the development of transport infrastructure over the whole territory, building roads and canals, and also railways from the 1840s. The French territory represented a large market, from both a geographical and demographic point of view, which was protected up to the mid-1850s. Corporations were abolished and freedom of industry and commerce was established during the Revolution, in 1791. This enabled industrialization to proceed in the country, following a different model than the British one, with lower territorial concentration of industry and more diffuse specialization. The French government also developed education, with the famous Grandes Écoles created between the end of the eighteenth century and the beginning of the nineteenth century which trained technicians and engineers (from *Ponts et Chaussées* in 1747, specialized in civil engineering, *École Polytechnique* in 1794 and the *École Centrale des Arts et Manufactures* – central school for arts and manufactures – in 1828). The financial system also developed throughout the nineteenth century, with an increasing centralization on Paris and the strong role of the Paris stock exchange in the financing of industry.

Italy started industrialization much later than France and Germany, about forty years after the unification of the country in 1871 (see Missiaia, Chapter 5 in this volume). Unification implied the need to develop a heavy industry that could consolidate the power of the new state. Economic growth was supported by public orders of armaments and infrastructure, while foreign capital was attracted, first from France and then from Germany, in order to invest in business banks and to develop large firms in the steel and chemical sectors. This system, based on public demand for military goods and on inflation without limits, generated growth but was based on weak fundamentals. The system collapsed after World War I and the financial crisis, so that the state became the owner of many industrial and financial enterprises by taking shares in them through the state holding IRI (Istituto per la Ricostruzione Industriale). IRI existed until the end of the twentieth century, so that Italian industry has remained characterized by a peculiar dual system, with many state-owned enterprises in strategic sectors (steel, energy, transport, and communications) and private businesses mainly in consumption goods sectors such as automobile, food, textile, and clothing.

In Asia, Japan industrialized thanks to important government support to industry creation and development, starting from the Meiji Revolution of 1868, which initiated deep institutional reforms in the country. Like in the UK, a political change towards more democracy, implying increasing entitlements in the sense of wider participation of the Japanese population, entrepreneurs in particular, in the industrial development process opened the possibility for the profound structural changes of the first and second Industrial Revolutions to take place.

Institutional reforms launched during the Meiji Revolution included the end of feudalism in 1869, the equality of all social classes before the law, taxation centralization, and the creation of a modern bureaucratic state. In addition, the domestic market was unified and individual property rights on land as well as freedom of enterprises were introduced. The national state was active in building infrastructure (particularly railways and steamships) and developing a manufacturing industry. Japan became a constitutional monarchy in 1890, with an elected Parliament, the Diet, as well as an independent judiciary. The government also supported the creation of large firms with the support to zaibatsus, namely industrial and financial groups made of a number of firms gathered around a (typically) family-owned holding, such as Mitsui, Mitsubishi, Sumitomo, and Yasuda. These groups received tax breaks and subsidies, diversified at the beginning of the twentieth century, and helped in channelling financial resources from old to new industries.

In Japan, industrialization was associated with the development of military industry in order to reduce military vulnerability. The Meiji revolution, however, benefitted from earlier developments during Tokugawa Japan, from the seventeenth century to the Meiji Revolution (Mosk 2001). Thus, cities and road networks were developed and river water flow was channelled with embankments, allowing improvements in communication and transport. Agricultural productivity rose thanks to new irrigation methods, as well as improvements in seed varieties and the use of fertilizers. Proto-industrial (craft) production by merchant houses in the major cities like Osaka and Edo (now called Tokyo) grew and diffused to rural areas. Capabilities also developed thanks to education and population control among both the military elite (the samurai) and the well-to-do peasantry.

The leaders of the Meiji government unified the country by centralizing political power in the capital, Tokyo. The Ministry of Education promoted compulsory primary schooling for the masses and elite university education aimed at deepening engineering and scientific knowledge. The Ministry of Finance created the Bank of Japan in 1882, laying the foundations for a private banking system. The government began building railway infrastructure that contributed to the unification of the country.

According to Bassino et al. in Chapter 8 of this volume, industrial development did not produce uneven development at the regional level in Japan. This was different in Europe. Industrial development was stronger in some regions due to various factors such as the availability of raw materials and human capital, and the pre-existence of productive activities (as shown by different chapters in this volume). Despite this, industrial policy was not differentiated according to regional territories. This prevailing national level of industrial policy would remain up to the 1980s.

Overall, the broad lines of industrial policy implemented by governments to support industrialization have consisted of strong public investment in infrastructure, hence in industries involved, as well as sometimes other leading or strategic industries (e.g., coal and steel in Germany); unification of the internal market and protectionism, especially protection of nascent industries; regulation of the financial system so that it develops and provides resources for industrial investment; education of technicians and engineers that could develop the new technologies and apply them to industries; and later, towards the end of the nineteenth century, mass basic education for the population together with the development of tertiary education (e.g., universities in Germany). Countries that realized industrialization after World War II, especially in East Asia, also carried out strong industrial policy including infant industry protection, as shown in the next section.

11.5 Pushing for industrial upgrading: Innovation policy after World War II

After World War II, many countries pushed for scientific developments and industrial application of research, generally in big national programmes; this is the birth of innovation policy. A particular "pioneer" in such an approach was the United States, which pursued industrial policy primarily based on R&D support and public procurement for defence and public health (Mazzucato 2013). According to Mowery and Rosenberg (1993: 41), the federal government financed 47 to 65% of national R&D spending between 1950 and 1980, compared with about 20% in Japan and Korea and less than 40% in Belgium, Finland, Germany, and Sweden. As a result, most industries in which the United States has leadership, such as aircraft, computer, semiconductor, internet, and genetic engineering, are industries that were created and developed by the government thanks to these industrial policy actions.

In Germany, industrial policy has constantly been implemented since the beginning of the twentieth century (Feldenkirchen 1998). It has supported the development of strategic industries, especially those with military applications before World War II; it has favoured exports and innovation in the last few decades. In addition, constant attention has been paid to education and training at all levels.

Besides large R&D programmes, France implemented an interventionist industrial policy after World War II and up to the 1980s. In particular, state-owned enterprises (SOEs) were used to promote industrial upgrading, with the aim of creating large firms able to compete with American ones. The SOE sector was one of the largest among developed countries. Many banks were also owned by the state, allowing the development of credit programmes. Large R&D programmes were also carried out, to develop industries of the future: from the aerospace to the telecommunication industries, and also nuclear energy. Industrial policy has been really a national strategy in France after World War II, defined and implemented by a specific institution, the Commissariat Général au Plan, created in 1946. Many firms have been privatized since the 1990s but most remain controlled by the state, through state holding of shares in these companies. Besides state ownership, the state subsidized many industries and carried out large R&D programmes from the 1960s – especially in sectors with strong military impact such as the nuclear, aerospace, and telecommunication industries – characterized by a strong role of public research and state-owned firms, as well as public procurement. These strategic sectors are still a focus of R&D policy today, although other sectors have been added, such as artificial intelligence, nanotechnologies, and other technologies and scientific fields of the fourth Industrial Revolution.

The role of the state in industrial development was also significant in Italy after World War II (Bianchi 2002). Industrial policy consisted of subsidies, large investments supported by the state holding IRI (Istituto per la Ricostruzione Industriale, Institute for Industrial Reconstruction), and state ownership. The industry substantially developed and contributed to the "economic miracle" of the 1950s and 1960s. Yet, the strong interventionism showed weaknesses from the 1970s onwards, especially with inefficiencies of state-owned firms, and a large privatization programme was implemented in the 1990s, leading to the closing of IRI in 2000. Many authors point to the incompleteness of the Italian industrial policy in the period, lacking support both to the development of an efficient capital market and to innovation and new sectors (Montobbio 2000; Rolfo and Calabrese 2003).

Trade was progressively liberalized in the European integration process from the 1950s onwards, with growth increasingly based on exports. From the 1970s, declining industries were supported, while the role of innovation policy was increasingly stressed. The role of small and medium-sized enterprises (SMEs) in industrial development was progressively recognized, especially those organized in industrial districts. Industrial policy has been decentralized from the end of the 1990s, with the reform of the constitution providing legislative power to regions to implement regional industrial policies (Bianchi and Labory 2019b).

In Japan, the role of the Ministry of Industry and Trade (MITI) in industrial development after World War II is well known (Hirono 2001). From 1948, the government defined national strategies aimed at reaching the US level of industrial development in a first phase and, successively, developing specializations in the new sectors: the first White Paper on technological development in 1948, big projects started in the 1960s, up to the scientific and technological basic plan II of 2000 (see Harayama 2001). Like the German konzerns, zaibatsus were broken up after World War II by the allied forces with the aim of increasing competition in markets. However, the large groups were progressively rebuilt in the shape of new industrial export-oriented groups in the 1950s and 1960s. The success of Japanese industry after World War II in catching up and becoming more competitive than Western industry in many sectors from about the 1980s onwards raised much interest in the Japanese experience of industrial policy.

Similarly, East Asian countries which caught up in that period, such as Korea, Taiwan, and Singapore, used selective industrial policy, protecting infant industry and subsidizing strategic sectors with large sets of measures including state-owned enterprises (Taiwan) to develop strategic sectors; support to investment (Singapore has had the public holding Temasek which had shares in businesses); regulation of FDI (entry and ownership restrictions, local content requirements, and so on); support to firm growth (state-mediated mergers and acquisitions, licensing conditional on production scale); export promotion; and support to technological transfer, as well as development of the education system to make appropriate labour available to the industry.

Korea implemented industrial policy based on heavy and chemical industries over the period from the 1950s to the 1980s, favouring both import substitution and exports (Labory 2006). Labour-intensive industries such as textile, where the country had a comparative advantage, were also promoted from the 1960s. From the crisis of the 1970s and the tendency for many countries to take protectionist measures as a result, Korea started promoting through its industrial policy an increase in the quality and sophistication of its products (for instance in the steel, mechanical engineering, automobile, and electronics industries). Complementary to this industrial policy, Korea invested in human capital by promoting education first at the primary level, and then at secondary and tertiary levels. From the 1980s the national government started caring for SMEs and regional development, leading to the setting up of technological parks where SME investment is favoured.

Taiwan also based economic development on a strong industrial policy. In the 1950s, many firms became state-owned and import substitution was promoted. Industrial policy concentrated on the promotion of exports in the 1960s and 1970s, while some liberalizations were realized in the 1980s (banking sector, opening of the capital market to foreign capital) and technological policy was pushed.

To sum up, we can outline the main measures of industry policy implemented after World War II according to broad lines of intervention. Countries having to reconstruct after the war or to industrialize were interventionist, with strong support to industries and state ownership in many cases, investment in infrastructure, support to the development of supportive financial systems, training and education, and export promotion. In addition, industrialization is generally associated with protection of infant industries. At later stages of development, the research capacity useful for developing new technologies is a particular focus, in order to favour both upgrading of existing sectors and development of new industries. Hence the importance of scientific and technological programmes in many advanced countries.

As the world economy has become more and more integrated throughout the twentieth century, industrial policy has evolved from direct selective support to focus on providing the conditions for the development and competitiveness of national industry in a more indirect way. Competition between nations prevailed in the nineteenth and early twentieth centuries, while after World War II, nations have progressively recognized interdependencies and industrial policy has become partly common or similar; common in trade policy

(General Agreement on Tariffs and Trade [GATT] and World Trade Organization [WTO]), and similar in terms of focus and approach (antitrust, innovation, support to SMEs).

11.6 The late consideration of regional imbalances in industrial development

Industrial policies aimed at promoting the productive system were implemented at the local level in Europe before the first Industrial Revolution (e.g., local guilds and internal tariffs protecting local production). After the first Industrial Revolution, national states strengthened and implemented national industrial policies, primarily because a strong industry makes the national state powerful and able to withstand possible conflicts with other nations. Yet, even national industrial policy tended to create or reinforce regional imbalances; support to industries primarily went to industrialized regions, while other regions would remain unaffected unless specific actions were taken to develop industry. A clear example is the industrial policy of Willem I in the Low Countries in 1815–1830, which benefitted the already industrialized Belgium while the Netherlands was left behind (see Philips and Buyst, Chapter 3 of this volume).

Industrial policy started to have a regional dimension again at the end of the twentieth century, for two major reasons. First, the crisis of old industrial regions, characterized by a strong specialization in what increasingly became declining industries, created large stress because they affected entire regional communities with a high social and political cost. For instance, the crisis of mining regions in the 1970s in France, Belgium, Germany, and the UK induced national governments to adopt specific industrial policy at the regional level to help these regions restructure and convert to other, emerging industries. Second, there was increasing evidence in the 1970s and 1980s that industrial development is rooted in territories and can only take place when favourable conditions are created in the territory. A particular example from this perspective is the literature on industrial districts and clusters, which grew in this period, showing how geographical, social, and cognitive proximity can lead to the development of industrial specialization, with particular industrial organization, at the local level (Brusco 1982; Becattini 1990; Pyke and Sengenberger 1992). The awareness that both industrial development has a strong regional dimension and regional imbalances can be addressed by policy increased thus essentially from the 1980s. Industrial development is indeed rooted in territorial communities that historically develop capabilities. For instance, the Italian industries of textile, leather, and ceramics developed out of strong craft production over many centuries. In this industry, industrial policy measures were taken at the regional level even before the 1980s; so did the Emilia Romagna region in Italy set up technical mechanical engineering schools before World War II in order to increase the regional capabilities in this sector. Similarly, Foray et al. (2011) mention actions taken by the local government that supported the development of the eyewear industry in the Jura region in France.

Nation-states also took regional measures before the 1980s; for instance, policy for the lagging Southern Italy from the 1950s (see Missiaia, Chapter 5 in this volume). However, systematic regional industrial policy really appears in Europe after the 1980s within the framework of the European structural funds. This policy was first focused on lagging and declining regions and subsequently extended to all regions, also helping developed regions adapt to changing competitive conditions so that they could continue leading overall growth in the sense that less developed regions could benefit by getting spillovers.

11.7 Conclusions

This chapter has briefly reviewed industrial policies defined in a number of countries, including the United Kingdom, the United States, France, Germany, Italy, Japan, Korea, and Taiwan, from the first Industrial Revolution to today. It has shown that industrial policy consists in sets of actions with both direct and indirect effects, that have to be implemented coherently in order for industrial development to be spurred. Entitlements have to be extended in order for people to take part in the development process, both as workers and entrepreneurs; provisions and capabilities for innovation must be extended and the institutional framework must be adapted in the territory. In addition, it appears that a regional focus of industrial policy as a systematic and long-term orientation of industrial development has started to emerge in the second half of the twentieth century, especially after the crises of the 1970s and the increasing attention of economists paid to local and regional development.

The historical evidence shows that there is never one factor or one institution that favours economic growth or industrialization; but rather, it is a system of institutions that creates the right conditions. One institution may play a particular role, such as property right protection promoting innovation, but the single institution produces positive effects only when it is part of a particular system of institutions. Historical evidence shows that some institutions may have a large role in one system but may not produce any effect within other systems.

Similarly, industrial policy is made of different types of actions and measures that combine to favour industrial development. One particular action may have noteworthy effects, such as innovation policy spurring new industries, but it is likely to do so only if other measures and actions are coherently implemented. For instance, support to R&D is useless if human capital does not have the necessary skills to actively take part in innovation processes; support to SMEs does not produce large effects if monopolies are also favoured.

Industrial policy was mainly carried out at a national level when nation-states consolidated and aimed at strengthening their power in the competition between nations. It has been strong (with mainly direct measures) in phases of industrialization or reconstruction (for instance, after World War II). The approach becomes more oriented towards providing the conditions for business development, with less direct actions, from the 1980s onwards. However, Western countries' industrial supremacy has been increasingly challenged by

Asian countries in the last decades. As a result, more direct measures have progressively been considered by governments to support their industries; not in the EU, where this type of policy creates distortions in the single market, but rather in the United States. The trade policy adopted by President Donald Trump is an example.

However, the paradox today is that most firms' horizons are much wider than nation-states because they operate in global markets while also basing their competitive advantages on local and regional capabilities, investing in regions which succeed in becoming hubs of knowledge and competencies. The coherence between the different levels of policy action – namely regional, national, and supranational – is therefore key today. How this can best be done is an important issue of further research.

References

Allen, R. C. 2011. *Global economic history. A very short introduction*. Oxford: Oxford University Press.

Bailey, D., and L. de Propris. 2019. "Industry 4.0, regional disparities and transformative industrial policy." In *Revitalising lagging regions: smart specialisation and industry 4.0*, Vol. 1, edited by M. Barzotto, C. Corradini, F. Fai, S. Labory, and P. Tomlinson, 67–78. Regional Studies Policy Impact Books.

Bairoch, P. 1993. *Economic and world history*. Brighton: Wheatsheaf.

Becattini, G. 1990. "The Marshallian industrial district as a socio-economic notion." In *Industrial districts and inter-firm cooperation in Italy*, edited by F. Pyke, G. Becattini, and W. Sengenberger, 37–51. Geneva: International Institute for Labour Studies.

Bianchi, P. 2002. *La rincorsa frenata. L'industria italiana dall'unità nazionale all'unificazione europea*. Bologna: Il Mulino.

Bianchi, P., and S. Labory (eds.). 2006. *International handbook of industrial policy*. Cheltenham: Edward Elgar.

Bianchi, P., and S. Labory. 2011. *Industrial policy after the crisis. Seizing the future*. Cheltenham: Edward Elgar.

Bianchi, P., and S. Labory. 2018. *Industrial policy for the manufacturing revolution. Perspectives on digital globalisation*. Cheltenham: Edward Elgar.

Bianchi, P., and S. Labory. 2019a. "Manufacturing regimes and transitional paths: lessons for industrial policy." *Structural Change and Economic Dynamics* 48: 24–31.

Bianchi, P., and S. Labory. 2019b. "Regional industrial policy for the manufacturing revolution: enabling conditions for complex transformations." *Cambridge Journal of Regions, Economy and Society* 12(2): 233–249.

Brander, J. 1987. "Shaping comparative advantage: trade policy, industrial policy and economic performance." In *Shaping comparative advantages*, edited by R. Lipsey and W. Dobson, 1–55. Toronto: C.D. Howe Institute.

Broadberry, S., B. M. S. Campbell, and B. van Leeuwen. 2013. "When did Britain industrialise? The sectoral distribution of the labour force and labour productivity in Britain, 1381–1851." *Explorations in Economic History* 50(1): 16–27.

Brusco, S. 1982. "The Emilian model: productive decentralization and social integration." *Cambridge Journal of Economics* 6(2): 167–184.

Cherif, R., and F. Hasanov. 2019. *The return of the policy that shall not be named: principles of industrial policy*. IMF Working Paper, WP/19/74, Washington.

Chu, Y-P., T-J. Chen, and B-L. Chen. 2001. "Rethinking the development paradigm: lessons from Taiwan – The optimal degree of state intervention." In *Industrial policy, innovation and economic growth: the experience of Japan and the Asian Nies*, edited by P.-K. Wong and C.-Y. Ng, 197–244. Singapore: Singapore University Press.

De Simoni, E. 2016. *Storia economia. Dalla rivoluzione industrial alla rivoluzione informatica*. Quinta edizione, Milano: Franco Angeli.

Feldenkirchen, W. 1998. "Germany: the intervention of interventionism." In *Industrial policies in Europe*, edited by G. Federico and J. Foreman-Peck, Chapter 4. Oxford: Oxford University Press.

Foray, D., P. A. David, and B. H. Hall. 2011. *Smart specialization. From academic idea to political instrument, the surprising career of a concept and the difficulties involved in its implementation*. MTEI Working Paper no. 1, Ecole Polytechnique, Lausanne.

Goldsmith, A. A. 1995. "The state, the market and economic development: a second look at Adam Smith in theory and practice." *Development and Change* 26(4): 633–650.

Harayama, Y. 2001. *Japanese technology policy: history and new perspective*. RIETI Discussion Paper Series 01-E-001.

Hirono, R. 2001. "Economic growth and restructuring in post-war Japan – contributions of industrial and technology policies." In *Industrial policy, innovation and economic growth: the experience of Japan and the Asian NIEs*, edited by P.-K. Wong and C.-Y. Ng, 85–172. Singapore: Singapore University Press.

Labory, S. 2006. "La politica industriale in un'economia aperta e basta sulla conoscenza." *L'Industria* 2: 255–281.

Landes, D. S. 1969. *The unbound prometheus*. Cambridge: Cambridge University Press.

Mazzucato, M. 2013. *The entrepreneurial state – Debunking public vs. private sector myths*. London: Anthem Press.

McFetridge, D. 1985. "The economics of industrial policy." In *The Canadian economic policy in action*, edited by D. McFetridge (a cura di), 1–49. Toronto: Toronto University Press.

Mokyr, J. 1999. "Editor's introduction: the new economic history and the industrial revolution." In: *The British industrial revolution: an economic perspective*, 2nd ed., edited by J. Mokyr, 1–127. Boulder: Westview Press.

Mokyr, J. 2000. "The industrial revolution and the Netherlands: why did it not happen?" *De Economist* 148(4): 503–520.

Montobbio, F. 2000. "Istituzioni e attività innovativa: i sistemi innovativi." In *Economia dell'innovazione*, edited by F. Malerba, 375–402. Roma: Carocci.

Mosk, C. 2001. *Japanese industrial history: technology, urbanization, and economic growth*. Armonk, New York: M.E. Sharpe.

Mowery, D. C., and N. Rosenberg. 1993. "The US national system of innovation." In *National innovation systems. A comparative analysis*, edited by R. Nelson, 79–106. Oxford University Press.

O'Brien, P. 1995. "Central government and the economy, 1688–1815." In *The economic history of Britain since 1700*, 2nd ed., Vol. II, edited by R. Floud and D. McCloskey, 204–237. Cambridge: Cambridge University Press.

Pyke, F., and W. Sengenberger. 1992. *Industrial districts and local economy regeneration*. Geneva: International Institute for Labour Studies.

Rolf, o. S., and G. Calabrese. 2003. "Traditional SMEs and innovation: the role of industrial policy in Italy." *Entrepreneurship and Regional Development* 15(3): 253–271.

Smith, A. 1776. *An enquiry into the wealth of nations*, 2 Vols. London: reprinted in 1960 by J.M. Dent & Sons Ltd.

Streeten, P. 1993. "Market and state: against minimalism." *World Development* 21(8): 1281–1298.

Vanden Bosch, X. 2014. *Industrial policy in the EU: a guide to an elusive concept*. Egmont Paper 69, The Royal Institute for International Relations, Bruxelles.

Van Neuss, L. 2015. *Why did the industrial revolution started in Britain?* Working Paper, University of Liège.

Index

Note: *Italicized* page numbers indicate a figure on the corresponding page. Page numbers in **bold** indicate a table on the corresponding page.

For Product Safety Concerns and Information please contact our EU
representative GPSR@taylorandfrancis.com
Taylor & Francis Verlag GmbH, Kaufingerstraße 24, 80331 München, Germany

www.ingramcontent.com/pod-product-compliance
Ingram Content Group UK Ltd.
Pitfield, Milton Keynes, MK11 3LW, UK
UKHW020015200926
475702UK00014B/1905
9780367561956